God, Greed, and Genocide

God, Greed, and Genocide
The Holocaust through the Centuries

Arthur Grenke

New Academia Publishing, LLC
Washington, DC

Printed in the United States of America

Library of Congress Control Number: 2005924262
ISBN 0-9767042-0-X paperback (alk. paper)

NAP

NEW ACADEMIA
PUBLISHING

New Academia Publishing, LLC
P.O. Box 27420, Washington, DC 20038-7420
www.newacademia.com - info@newacademia.com

To my daughter, Ingrid. Sometimes we are left only with words and the prayer that they will heal the pain and help us comprehend what in many ways is incomprehensible.

Contents

Preface

I begin work on this project during the 1980s when the Ottawa School Board's Multicultural Advisory Committee was exploring the issue of introducing holocaust studies into public schools in that city. During the discussions, representatives of the Jewish community argued that only their particular experience in Nazi Germany ought to be taught because their case was unique and represented an especially valuable lesson. Yet, at the same time, other communities argued that they had suffered genocides and that their experiences also had something to teach Canadian students. A number of these groups described their experiences as "holocausts." Upon exploring the issue further, I found that many of the scholars studying different genocides had described these as holocausts. In part to clarify for myself the difference between holocaust and genocide, I researched the subject further.

After several years of research, I found that these genocides had enough similarities to warrant a more rigorous study of their similarities and differences. I had specialized in content, systems, and factor analysis while working as a teaching assistant in historiography at university, and I decided to apply some of the things I had learned to this particular problem. As I looked at the different cases, I isolated patterns, and noted similarities and differences.

When I decided to commit my findings to paper, I was confronted by a number of issues. One was the emotionality of the subject, not only for Jewish people but also for others who believed that their group had suffered a holocaust. I wanted to respect their experiences and at the same time clarify issues arising from these experiences. Objectivity was difficult yet indispensable, best achieved, I concluded, by focussing on the views of experts. I therefore have presented each genocide as scholars working in their particular field described it for us.

Of course, selecting the works and analysing them involved a certain degree of subjectivity. Still, I tried to guide my selection on the basis of the arguments made by each expert and to present their point of view as fairly as possible. I hope I have done these scholars justice. My goal was to present a summary of each of the cases and, at the same time, to extrapolate from each situation the major causes that contributed to mass destruction. This involved, among other things, determining motivation, looking at the goals pursued by the genocidal group and their relationship to how it defined itself and the group(s) it decimated.

Having isolated the dynamics in a variety of cases, I compared and contrasted patterns to determine what made a particular genocide unique and what dynamics it shared with other genocides. I looked at arguments presented by scholars to support their claim about the uniqueness of the destruction of European Jewry. I then examined other genocides to determine whether arguments presented for uniqueness of the destruction of European Jewry also applied to them. To determine whether clusters emerged, I compared and contrasted dynamics leading to destruction in the different situations. Following this, I looked at the clusters in the context of the sociological literature to determine where they best fit in terms of existing typologies. After completing the study, I sent my manuscript to scholars working in the different fields. I took cognizance of their arguments and integrated their views into the present work. After all, the best way to strengthen one's argument is to look at it from the perspective of someone who sees a weakness in it. In reasoning together, perhaps we will throw a little more light on the subject and see the past with a little more clarity. That is the only way to draw lessons from the past, lessons that, when applied, may help us make a better future.

Arthur Grenke, Ph.D.
Ottawa, Canada

Introduction

Is there a relationship between our belief in God, our pursuit of salvation, and a holocaust—a destruction aiming at the total eradication of a target group? When does greed become so pervasive that it leads us to destroy not merely another person but entire groups? How does defining a group as demonic and contaminating justify its annihilation? How does defining a group as less than human encourage people to despoil and destroy it? These questions particularly beg for answers when one explores whether the term "holocaust" more properly describes a pattern or one particular historical instance of genocide.

The term "holocaust" became fixed in the language of genocide when it was applied to describe the Nazi destruction of European Jewry, with some scholars maintaining the term is applicable only to this case. Thus, Steven Katz argues that the Nazi destruction of European Jewry is "phenomenologically unique," basing his view on the claim that never prior to this has a state, "as a matter of intent and principle and actualizing policy," undertaken to destroy every member of a specific group.[1] He therefore sees the term "holocaust" properly applying only to this genocide. A similar argument is put forward by Yehuda Bauer, who uses the term "holocaust" to differentiate between Nazi aims for the Jews and their aims for other nationalities, such as the Czechs, Poles, or Gypsies. Of these groups, only the Jews were to be totally destroyed. He sees the main feature of the holocaust as being the focus on the total destruction of the Jews, this being the first time in history that a sentence of death has been pronounced on anyone guilty of having been born of certain parents, who in this case were Jews.[2] Other researchers have broadened the category somewhat and included under the "holocaust" not only the destruction of European Jewry but also the Nazi destruction of European Gypsies and the Nazi policy on eugenics. At the same time, they consider the holocaust to be the ultimate ideological genocide.[3] However, generally researchers who focus on the holocaust as a unique event apply the term strictly to the destruction of European Jewry by the Nazis, with some writers positing that this event is so unique that even comparing it to other genocides constitutes a type of holocaust denial.[4]

This has not, however, dissuaded other scholars from using the term to describe genocides totally unrelated to the Nazi case. They did so essentially because they saw a similarity in the dynamics leading to the annihilation of people in all these cases. This was true in particular in instances where an ideology, or the attempt to transform society according to an ideological system, was seen to lead to genocide. Thus, Hryshko describes the holocaust as essentially an ideological genocide and applies the term to the destruction of Ukrainian peasantry during the man-made famine in 1932 and 1933.[5] Conquest describes not only this famine but also the mass destruction of peoples carried out under Stalin, in particular during the 1930s, as a holocaust.[6] Vahakn Dadrian sees the slaughter of the Armenians by the Turks during the First World War as constituting a holocaust.[7] Schawcross uses the term to describe the killings under the Khmer Rouge in Cambodia during the 1970s.[8]

Other scholars, rather than pointing to the ideological dimension of Nazism, focus on what they see as the racist and the Christian roots of Nazi anti-Semitism as causal factors in the destruction of European Jewry. They see similar dynamics at work in the decimation of Native peoples. Thus, Thornton and Stannard use the term "holocaust" to describe the near annihilation of Aboriginal peoples in the Americas by the European invaders after 1492.[9]

Other researchers, while preferring to confine the term holocaust to the destruction of European Jewry, nevertheless see its dynamics inherent in other genocides. Norman Cohn and H. R. Trevor-Roper, for example, believe that the same dynamics characterized the Nazi war on the Jews and the witch hunts in medieval Europe.[10] Similar dynamics are also evident in the Israelite war against the idolaters, as described in both Deuteronomy and the Book of Joshua of the Old Testament.[11]

Thus, we have essentially two different views regarding uses of the term "holocaust." For some, the term applies only to the slaughter of European Jewry. Other scholars, however, use the term for a category into which a variety of genocides can be placed. Exploring the differences in these perspectives does not simply revolve around the use of a term. It provides insight into how words are used, whether to mark events in time or space or to categorize reality so as to facilitate our comprehension. Words establish identity and create linkages. In a Platonic sense, they establish linkages between the real world and the ideal world or the world of abstract thought. In our everyday experience, by giving a name to an event we give it an identity that serves both to relate it to, and differentiate it from, other events.

For example, by labelling the uprising of the American colonists against British imperial rule as the American Revolution, we give the event an identity; the term indicates where the event occurred and what type of event it was (i.e., an American revolution, the nature of which may be determined by comparing it to other revolutions). The term "holocaust" is not as obviously specific. Indeed, how the term relates to the destruction of people through genocide is little evident in the word itself, in part because that word has had but a brief history in this context and, as we have already seen, disagreements exist regarding its proper usage.

Disagreement over use of a term might be expected in the field of genocide studies. The area has been subject to intense investigation only since the Second World War. Its terminology and the different concepts used to guide explorations in the field are relatively new. To explore the term "holocaust" and its significance in the context of genocide, it is necessary to examine not only the word but also the genocides to which the term has been applied. In this book, I shall do both. To gain insight into what the term means when applied to genocide, it would be useful, first, to look at the word as it was originally used. A combination of two Greek words, *holos* (whole) and *kaustos* (burnt), the term "holocaust" means to bring a burnt offering, or to be offered as a whole burnt offering.[12] Chamoux gives some idea as to the meaning of this word as it was used to describe a particular religious ritual when he writes that in Greek polytheism the gods were divided into two broader categories: the gods of the sky ("uranian") and the gods below or of the underworld ("chthonian"). The gods of the sky were considered to be helpful to man and the gods below dangerous. In religious rituals, worshippers, therefore, participated in partaking of sacrifices offered to gods of the sky, while in the chthonian sacrifice, to placate gods that were considered to be maleficent, the entire sacrifice was given up to the divinity, with the entire sacrifice being totally consumed by fire.[13]

Thus, the term "holocaust" referred originally to a sacrifice that involved the complete consumption by flames of the sacrificial animal being offered to the gods. It was part of a religious ritual intended to placate a deity, and was used by a community to avert danger and achieve harmony with the universal order.

To clarify how the term holocaust is pertinent when describing genocide, we need to examine more closely what is meant by genocide. The word was derived from the Greek *genos,* race, and from the Latin *caedere,* to kill. Literally translated, the word means to kill or annihilate a race. However, in genocide studies, use of the term was not confined to its literal meaning. Raphael Lemkin, who coined the term, defined "genocide"

4   Introduction

as the planned and coordinated annihilation of a national, religious, or racial group.[14] Lemkin also developed a typology to classify actual cases of genocide. He outlined three types of genocide, basing his typology on the intent of the perpetrator. The objective of the first type of genocide is to destroy totally a victim group or nation. According to Lemkin, wars of extermination in antiquity and the Middle Ages were examples of this first type of genocide. The second type is characterized by the destruction of a culture without an attempt to kill its bearers, prevalent in our time in instances where force is used to destroy the cultural identity of a group. The third type, a Nazi-style genocide, targeted some groups for immediate annihilation, while others were selected for ethnocidal assimilation.[15] At Lemkin's urging, the United Nations agreed to consider the issue of preventing and punishing genocide, and the UN Genocide Convention was adopted in 1948. This convention defined genocide as any of the following acts committed with the intent to destroy, in whole or in part, a nation or a national, ethnic, racial, or religious group:

a. Killing members of a group;
b. Causing serious bodily or mental harm to members of a group;
c. Deliberately inflicting on the group conditions of life calculated to bring about its physical destruction in whole or in part;
d. Imposing measures intended to prevent births within the group;
e. Forcibly transferring children of the group to another group.

Generally, the UN definition has been seen as too vague, unworkable, and politically charged to be useful in scholarly analysis. Given these problems, Vahakn Dadrian set aside the UN definition and formulated a definition he considered more suitable for research purposes. He defined genocide as "the successful attempt by a dominant group, vested with formal authority and/or with preponderant access to the overall resources of power, to reduce by coercion or lethal violence the number of a minority group whose ultimate extermination is held desirable and useful and whose respective vulnerability is a major factor contributing to the decision for genocide."[16]

Dadrian also established a five-category typology of genocide: (1) cultural genocide, in which the objective is the assimilation of a target group; (2) latent genocide, or a destruction not intended by the perpetrator, an example being deaths caused by infectious diseases unintentionally spread by invading armies; (3) retributive genocide, intended to punish a group for actions committed by it or group(s) wherewith it is associated; (4) utilitarian genocide, in which mass killings become part of a process of taking possession of economic resources; and (5) optimal genocide, in which the perpetrator has as his main aim the annihilation of a group, goals Dadrian sees expressed in the destruction of European Jewry and the Ottoman Armenians.[17]

Although it has merits, Dadrian's typology also presents problems. An example is the first category of his typology. Most states have sought to assimilate minorities within their boundaries, be these newly arrived or long-established groups. Does Dadrian see endeavours to assimilate these different groups as acts of cultural genocide? If he does, then the term is too broad to be useful as a category for the study of genocide. If he does not, then a problem arises in determining when attempts at assimilation become cultural genocide. To be useful, this category as well as others he developed need further elaboration.

Other scholars have also sought to improve on the UN definition of genocide. In 1983-84 Helen Fein made an effort to replace the UN definition of genocide with a more analytically rigorous concept by defining genocide as the calculated murder of a segment or all of a group regarded to be outside the perpetrator's "sanctioned universe of obligation." She introduced a four-part typology, that characterized genocide as (1) developmental, in which the perpetrator intentionally or unintentionally destroys peoples who stand in the way of the exploitation of resources; (2) despotic, in which a despot eliminates a real or potential opposition, as in a polarized multiethnic state; (3) retributive, involving the perpetrator's attempt to destroy an actual opponent; and (4) ideological, a category in which she places genocides against groups that an ideological system identifies as enemies or as embodying absolute evil. She argues further that ideological genocides and slaughters are primarily an outgrowth of myths that place the victims outside the "sanctioned universe of obligation." She considers murder a "latent implication of all totalitarian ideologies which elevate the concept of the people or class(es) of the people" and consider the concept of the individual as the product of an outdated, decadent social system.[18]

Later, Fein elaborated on her conceptualization, defining genocide as a "series of purposeful actions by a perpetrator(s) to destroy a collectivity through mass or selective murders of group members and suppressing the biological and social reproduction of the collectivity. . . . The perpetrator may represent the state of the victim, another state, or another collectivity."[19] Fein includes both political and social groups as victims, and in her explanation of her revised definition insists that individuals, and not only states and other authorities, can perpetrate genocides.

Leo Kuper, whose concept of genocide is based on the UN definition, divides genocide into two main groups: domestic genocides arising from the internal divisions within a society; and genocides arising in the course of international warfare. He distinguishes four types of domestic genocide: (1) genocides against indigenous peoples; (2) genocides against hostage groups; (3) genocides ensuing from decolonization which involves a two-tier structure of domination, in which the colonial power imposes its rule through a local surrogate; and (4) genocides resulting from the struggle between ethnic, racial, or religious groups, brought on when one group seeks greater power, status, or autonomy.

Under genocides of international warfare, Kuper includes examples such as the Allied bombing of Dresden, the American atomic bombing of Nagasaki and Hiroshima, the Chinese subjugation of Tibet, and the Indonesian invasion and occupation of East Timor. Cases of political mass murder are placed outside his typology of genocide because they do not fall within the UN definition. Kuper places the mass murders carried out by the governments of the Soviet Union, Nazi Germany, Kampuchea, Indonesia, and other states into this last category.[20]

Although Kuper makes a useful contribution to the development of a theoretical framework of genocide, many of his categories are too broad to be useful for the purpose of analysis. Building on earlier models of genocide, Roger W. Smith, in his 1987 essay on the twentieth century as an age of genocide, presents a five-part typology of genocide based on the motives of the perpetrator. His categories are: (1) retributive genocide, based on the desire for revenge; (2) institutional genocide, generally part of military conquest, in particular in ancient and medieval times; (3) utilitarian genocide, arising from the drive for material gain, and especially prevalent during the European conquest of the New World as well as in the decimation of small Aboriginal communities standing in the way of resource exploitation in the twentieth century; (4) monopolistic genocide, resulting from the competition for power, in particular in pluralistic societies; and (5) ideological genocide, driven by the desire to save or purify a society, and common to the twentieth century (examples are the destruction of the enemy of the people in the Soviet Union and the Nazi destruction of European Jewry).[21]

Although Smith narrows Kuper's framework by looking at genocide essentially in terms of intent, this also presents problems, as will be seen later. Furthermore, what is not clear from the typologies discussed is whether genocide involves the total or partial destruction of a group. Analysts appear to agree that genocide involves either the total destruction or the destruction of a large part of a group. Chalk and Jonassohn see genocide as being synonymous with mass killing committed with the intent to destroy physically a real or imaginary category of people, as defined by the perpetrator. Expanding on this definition, they define genocide as a "form of one-sided mass killing in which a state or other authority intends to destroy a group, as that group and membership in it are defined by the perpetrator."[22] In addition, Chalk and Jonassohn classify genocides according to the motive of the perpetrator. These include (1) eliminating a real or potential threat; (2) spreading terror among real or potential enemies; (3) acquiring economic wealth; or (4) implementing a belief, theory, or ideology.[23]

Ward Churchill takes issue with the Chalk and Jonassohn definition, in particular its emphasis on one-sided mass killing, arguing that it is too restrictive.[24] Also, it is unclear how intent in the mass killing is linked to action. What is intent? How is it expressed? There have been examples in the past where groups have expressed the intent to wipe out other groups but have not done so. At what point does expression of intent, linked to action, make mass murder genocide? This emphasis on intent also raises the problem of linking cause with effect. The problem is evident in the example of murder for money. A person may kill someone else to take that person's money. The perpetrator does not necessarily want to kill this person, but does so to expedite the robbery. Our legal system defines this as murder. On a large scale, groups have in fact been wiped out in instances where the intent was not necessarily to destroy them but to deprive them of their possessions. In the process of working out its conceptualization of genocide, the United Nations General Assembly defined genocide as the denial of the right of existence to entire groups, just as homicide is the denial of the right to life for individual human beings.[25] The UN did not differentiate between killings in which a group was directly targeted and those carried out by a perpetrator pursuing some other objective. It focussed on the final result, namely the destruction of the group. This definition is also more in keeping with Webster's Dictionary (1984), which defines genocide as involving the systematic annihilation of a political, racial or cultural group. Here, again, emphasis is on process rather than intent.

The problem with arriving at a workable definition of genocide is partially political: different groups focus on definitions that emphasize their particular experience. In such instances, a definition, as Churchill points out, all too often serves to deny genocide or to support the claim that one group or another has a more valid claim to having suffered genocide.[26] The problem is also functional. How does one arrive at a definition that will describe the crime under the different conditions in which it occurred and, at the same time, not be so broad as to make it near to impossible to measure? This problem at times becomes evident in Churchill's definition of genocide. At the opposite extreme of Chalk and Jonassohn's extremely narrow definition, Churchill's definition is so broad and varied that it raises problems regarding classification, in particular in his categories outlining the types and degree of genocide.[27]

Perhaps the different views regarding targeting as it relates to genocide can best be brought together by looking at genocide not so much in terms of cause and effect but as a process that involves the systematic annihilation of a political, racial, social, or cultural group, or a major segment of such a group. As used here, "systematic" implies the repeated violent destruction of members of a group, which leads to the physical annihilation of the group or a large segment thereof. Such violence may express itself in direct killing. It may also express itself through imposing conditions that lead to the destruction of the group or a large segment thereof. Accordingly, the term "genocide" may be seen to involve the systematic violent destruction of a large segment or all of a group as defined by the perpetrator. The mass murder may result from a particular group being targeted either directly or indirectly. Direct targeting involves killing members of a group whose destruction is deemed desirable because the group is seen as having characteristics justifying such action. Indirect targeting involves the murder of members of a group whose destruction is justified, not in itself, but to achieve some other objective. In most instances, this objective involves robbery, with the killing being carried out to deprive the target group of its possessions. For the purpose of this study, I will not further break down this definition according to type of genocide. Researchers whose works I have mentioned have already presented ample categories. My objective is not to add to them, but rather to determine how genocides described as holocausts fit into the categories I have outlined in my discussion of their work.

How does the term "holocaust," coined to describe a religious ritual, apply to describe genocide or a particular type of genocide? It may be applicable in several respects. It may describe genocide insofar as that genocide is associated with a certain type of hero worship. More significant, it is applicable in situations where genocide has as its goal the total destruction of a group, particularly where the genocidal group links this destruction to the search for salvation. Of the different types of genocide examined, these dynamics are most evident in what researchers have called ideological genocides, that is, where the introduction of an ideological system becomes linked with the destruction of a target group that is seen as thwarting endeavours to create an idealized state of existence for the genocidal group.

Of course, use of the term "holocaust" also has major limitations when applied to genocide. The basic driving force in the holocaust sacrifice as practised by the Greeks was atonement. In making a sacrifice, the Greek felt no hatred toward the sacrificial animal and did not consider it evil. The basic intention behind the ritual was to bring humanity into harmony with the universal order. In contrast, the basic intention motivating one group to destroy another is not atonement but hatred and anger. These emotions have little to do with atonement, but rather derive their motivating force from war psychology. As such, the group isolated for destruction is used to keep the genocidal group continuously aware of the outside threat. This threat is, in large part, moral rather than physical in nature. Killing the agent of this danger involves overcoming a powerful, corrupting evil and destroying its nefarious influences.

Using the term "holocaust" in the context of genocide also presents another problem. This relates to the feasibility of using a term developed in one context in another context. Thus, Novic mentions that certain Jewish scholars object to the term "holocaust," which they see as a Christian concept, being used to describe Jewish suffering. They prefer the Hebrew term for catastrophe, *shoah*— seen as purely Jewish and secular.[28] Of course, the term "holocaust" refers to the pagan Greek rather than to the Christian religious experience. At the same time, in particular Jewish scholars stress the holocaust nature of the destruction of European Jewry. They see this as differentiating Nazi goals regarding the Jews from Nazi goals regarding other groups, with the difference making the Jewish case unique. Therefore, I will use the term "holocaust" to describe the different genocides under discussion here. However, it is to be understood that when I use the term "holocaust" to describe the destruction of European Jewry by the Nazis, I am also speaking of the *shoah*.

The question may be asked whether it really matters if we use the term "holocaust" or any other to describe a particular genocide. In many respects it doesn't. Yet, clearly, once a term or category has been applied to a particular event or type of event, it is important to have some agreement as to its meaning. This is even more necessary when words or terms are used to categorize the behaviour of one group or a number of groups for comparative purposes. Categorization has been used in all areas of study, especially in the sciences. In the biological sciences, terms have been coined to help us describe species and sub-species. In the social sciences, such as psychology, terms such as schizophrenia or paranoia have been coined to describe patterns of dysfunctional behaviour. These terms not only help us understand certain patterns of behaviour but also help us do something about the behaviour in question so as to change it.

If we are to use terms to help us understand and prevent genocide, it is very important that the terms used be as clear as possible. With the study of genocide still in its infancy, we are still searching for suitable concepts to describe these horrendous deeds. It is important that we make real efforts to reach some consensus regarding the descriptive terms used. Only in this way can we be certain that others know what we are talking about. Consensus would not only contribute to a better understanding of genocide but would also help us identify means of doing something to combat such actions.

This is why it is important to clarify terms and concepts that have been developed to date, in particular the term "holocaust," it being the only instance where a name has been applied to identify a specific genocide, with some scholars arguing that the term can apply only to the destruction of European Jewry by the Nazis, and others going so far as to argue that this event is so unique that even comparing it to other genocides constitutes a type of genocide denial. Of course, this has not discouraged others from applying the term to other genocides. Disagreement over usage has been further encouraged by the fact that no one has looked at the term in detail, exploring the various situations in which it has been used to describe genocide and then isolating those features that make the term applicable in one situation and not in another.

For any term to be useful, it must help us to establish limits that differentiate one pattern of behaviour from others. Although some overlap is inevitable, sufficient differentiation is needed to permit us to say that this pattern of behaviour more properly fits into one category than another. For example, in psychology the various categories used to classify different behavioural patterns are generally clear enough to permit an analyst to identify a person with mental illness as being schizophrenic, paranoid, or as having a combination of both conditions. Yet, conclusions were possible only after terms were coined to describe different patterns of mental illness. Before this could be done, different examples of mental illness had to be examined, compared, and contrasted so as to determine to what pattern of mental illness a certain term applied. If the term "holocaust" is not to be used to argue that a genocide is unique and then again applied to different types of genocide, certain characteristics must be isolated to define it. One way of accomplishing this is by examining different genocides in which the term has been used and then extrapolating common features. Such an exercise will help determine whether the term applies more suitably to a single, unique genocide, or a pattern of genocide, and, if the latter, to what pattern.

As most researchers see the holocaust as an ideological genocide, I will first look at ideological genocides that have been described as holocausts to see in what ways they are similar and different. I will look at the destruction of the idolaters as described in the Old Testament, essentially because it is the earliest account I have found where a group undertook to totally destroy another group in order to attain its own salvation. Following this, I will look at the destruction of witches in early modern Europe, of the Armenians, of the enemies of the people in the Soviet Union during the 1930s, of European Jewry, and of the enemies of the people in Cambodia under the Khmer Rouge.

I will then examine genocides committed as Europeans conquered the

New World. When doing so, I will look at the nature of the destruction, the motives behind the killings, as well as at other features evident in these genocides. I will also examine more closely the similarities between ideological genocides that have been identified as holocausts and the genocides in the Americas to determine what may have caused researchers to identify the genocides committed in the New World as holocausts.

Genocides committed as Europeans colonized the Americas tend to be little known, and, where they are known, ignored. It was not until some five hundred years after Columbus's initial voyage to the New World that any significant attention was given to the negative effect of European conquest on Aboriginal societies. Where these genocides have been studied, researchers have tended to place them rather arbitrarily into general categories of genocide with little attempt to analyse how particular instances fit into the framework. Thus, Fein places these genocides collectively into the category of developmental genocides, while Roger W. Smith labels them utilitarian genocides. In neither case is an attempt made to determine how any of the genocides committed against Native peoples fits into these categories.

Increasingly, scholars are recognizing that these genocides must be looked at in detail if we are going to understand contemporary genocides, including the destruction of European Jewry by the Nazis. Commenting on this, Vinay Lal states that, although the destruction of European Jewry may serve as a prime example of exclusion and victimization in European history, from the standpoint of Third World scholars, similar destruction has been visited upon Native peoples by their European conquerors during the last five hundred years. The main difference is that the Nazis inflicted their destruction on white Europeans rather than on peoples of colour.[29] Commenting on Lal's statement, Bartov remarks that, while Europeans exported their perception of society to the rest of the world, they imported into Europe the manner of conduct and views of humanity that evolved in the colonies. He concludes that this complex relationship, which affected not only Europeans but also the rest of the world, has to be further explored if we are to understand the mechanics of modern genocide.[30] Stannard is one of the first scholars to make a major effort to explore the literature in some detail to place genocides committed in the Americas into the context of present-day genocide. For this purpose, he compares the dynamics involved in the destruction of European Jewry with the dynamics leading to the destruction of Natives in the Americas, which he describes as the most massive act of genocide in the history of the world.[31]

A variety of motives fuelled the drive for expansion by the different European powers. Essentially medieval, and still relishing its victories over the Moors, Spain was driven to expand into the New World by the quest for gold, Indian subjects, land, military title, and souls. Under the *encomienda* system, land and people were distributed among the conquerors, who proceeded to enslave and exploit the Native population. Legal protection promised by Spanish legislation did little to protect Native peoples from inhumane treatment. The most glaring example of this may be seen in the annihilation of the Arawak in Hispaniola (comprised today of Haiti and the Dominican Republic).

France and Britain, embarking on a quest for colonies in the seventeenth century, had a somewhat different focus than the Spaniards in their colonial ambitions. France's colonial policy was dictated by its interests in the fur trade, a corollary of which was the necessity for good relations with Native peoples. To forward its interests, France did little to expand settlement in New France, its major colony in the Americas: in 1715, French settlement here stood at only18, 500, compared to a population of 400,000 of European origin in Britain's American colonies. French interest in the fur trade also led it to recognize the sovereignty of the Indians in 1701.[32] Although the record of France in dealing with Native peoples is much better than that of Spain, there is evidence that France did not shy away from genocide when it suited its purpose, as may be seen in the destruction of the Natchez in 1731. Genocides in the British colonies resulted from a desire by the invader to obtain possession of Native lands, as may be seen from the decimation of Native groups in both North America and the Australian subcontinent.

In this book, I shall use a multiple case-study approach to gain insight into ideological genocides and genocides committed as Europeans conquered the New World. In a multiple case-study approach, argues Yin,[33] a major goal is to build a general explanation that fits each of the individual cases, even though the cases will vary in their details. Such an approach was used, for example, in Barrington Moore's *Social Origins of Dictatorship and Democracy* to isolate common features of development in different cultural milieus.[34] My objective is to examine the different genocides identified as holocausts to determine in what respects a particular case of genocide is unique, as well as to isolate the features individual cases share with other genocides.

Thus, after having looked at the different ideological genocides described as holocausts, I will isolate basic features in them so as to be better able to compare and contrast dynamics leading to destruction. Genocides committed as Europeans conquered the New World will then be compared and contrasted with each other to determine whether common patterns emerge and, if so, what these patterns are. Ideological genocides and genocides committed as Europeans took possession of the New World will be compared to determine similarities and differences.

All genocides looked at will be examined with reference to the typology of genocide as it has been developed to date. Therefore, the study will do much more than seek to determine whether the term "holocaust" more accurately describes a particular genocide or a type of genocide. Using the holocaust as its focus, the study will explore the usefulness of applying a typology to understand the holocaust and genocide in general. It will seek to refine some of the typologies used to date. At the same time, by isolating basic dynamics in the holocaust and other genocides under consideration, the study will endeavour to provide insight into the forces leading to genocide under different conditions. Such insight may suggest what might be done to prevent similar cataclysms from recurring in the future.

PART I

IDEOLOGICAL GENOCIDES
AS HOLOCAUSTS

Researchers who identify the holocaust as an ideological genocide see it as part of a process of planting an ideological system in the social environment. An ideology can be defined as a structured body of ideas used in support of an economic, political, or social theory. Essentially, an ideology spells out how the economic, political, and/or social relationship between peoples should be structured. An ideology might have a religious base, in which it is integrally linked to people's belief in the sacred. Alternatively, it might have a secular base, setting out beliefs regarding how people and society relate to each other, without any reference to the sacred. One example of the latter would be Marxism, which offers a non-religious explanation of the relationship between the individual and society as well as the evolution of society.

In the following chapters, I analyse genocides carried out in the name of a particular religion as well as genocides carried out in the name of secular ideologies. Both religious and secular ideologies share common ground in this context. While religious beliefs specify people's relationship to the sacred, they also set out how people should relate to each other in non-religious spheres, including the economic and the social. Secular ideologies under consideration here, such as Nazism or Marxism, while not relating to the sacred, serve essentially the same function. They draw their inspiration from comprehensive social theories about how society has evolved in the past and therefore will evolve in the future. As such, both sacred and secular belief systems draw their inspiration from a higher authority. At the same time, they spell out an order for society based on a particular set of beliefs. The genocides reviewed in this section were carried out as different groups sought to restructure society according to a certain system of beliefs.

1
The Destruction of the Idolaters

The biblical record of the annihilation of the idolaters is included here for several reasons. First, it is the earliest existing detailed account in which an identifiable group is targeted for total destruction, and such targeting is seen, in particular by some scholars, as the main feature of a holocaust. Secondly, when searching for the roots of the slaughter of European Jewry, scholars such as Norman Cohn, Hyam Maccoby, and Yehuda Bauer look to the Christian tradition, which they see as having had a significant influence on Nazi thought and action. Cohn draws a close parallel between Christian witch-hunts and the Nazi excesses. Bauer argues that the Nazis altered Christian symbols to create the Nazi ideological system, with Hitler taking the place of Christ as saviour of the German people and the Jews taking the place of the Devil.[1]

Of course, Christian beliefs and attitudes evolved from the Jewish tradition. While some scholars see a link between Nazi destructiveness and Christianity, others point to the Old Testament as having laid the basis not only for Christian attitudes and actions but also for Stalinism and Nazism. Thus, Moore argues that only the Western world gives evidence of "a discernable line of historical causation that begins with the monotheism of the ancient Hebrews; runs through the heresies of early Christianity, the slaughters of the Crusades, the Inquisition, and the Reformation; turns secular in the French Revolution; and culminates in what the great nineteenth-century Swiss historian Jacob Burckhardt presciently termed 'the terrible simplifiers'-Nazism and Leninism-Stalinism."[2] Discussing the influence of Christian beliefs on the destruction of Native peoples in the Americas, Stannard argues that while the New Testament view of war is ambiguous, there is little such ambiguity in the Old Testament. He points to sections in Deuteronomy in which the Israelite God, Yahweh, commanded that the Israelites utterly destroy the idolaters whose land they sought to reserve for the worship of their deity (Deuteronomy 7:2, 16, and 20:16, 17). Stannard argues that the Christian idea of the just war is based on the Old Testament tradition, which allows the conqueror to use any means to wipe out an enemy or perceived enemy.[3] According to Stannard, this view of war contributed to what he calls the American holocaust, namely the destruction of Native peoples in the Americas. It was this view of war that also led to the destruction of European Jewry. Accordingly, it is important to look at this particular segment of the Old Testament: it not only describes a situation where a group undertakes to totally destroy other groups, but it also had a major influence on shaping thought and belief systems that permitted, and even inspired, genocide.

In the following, I will present the biblical account of the destruction of the idolaters, the establishment of monotheism and the creation of the Holy Land. Of course, there are other accounts on the same events, produced for the most part since the turn of the last century. These differ, the only similarity often being that they take a position on the biblical account, ranging from seeing it as basically accurate to total rejection. As these scholars do not agree on an alternative presentation to the one we have in the Bible, I will present the biblical account of the Israelite conquest of the Holy Land. At the same time, I will provide the reader with an idea of the debate regarding the historical authenticity of this account.

Motives for the destruction

In order to comprehend the motives for the destruction described in the Bible, it is important that we understand that we are dealing with a time when the *Weltanschauung* of people differed significantly from ours. In ancient times, people lived in a mythological universe, a universe ruled by gods and goddesses. The influence of these deities permeated all areas of personal and community life. Supernatural forces had control over health or sickness, influenced the weather, and determined fruitfulness. In wars, they supported one community of believers against enemies who usually had other gods. In other words, in ancient times humans perceived the gods as having a central role in determining the well-being of the individual and of the community of which he or she was a member. Religious sacrifices and other means of homage were intended to avoid punishment and solicit the support of the supernatural world, enabling the individual and the community to lead a successful existence.

Most ancient societies were polytheistic; that is, they believed in a number of gods. These might be the gods of a particular tribal community or of a city-state. In addition, people had their personal god to whom they could relate in their special way. In polytheistic societies, gods tended to fall into two larger categories: munificent and punitive. Much of the life of ancient peoples revolved around religious practices that would help them avoid punishment from punitive deities and elicit the support of beneficent ones.

The Israelite God, Yahweh, differed in several ways from the deities of most ancient societies. Whereas most ancient societies had a number of deities who were either rewarding or punitive, Yahweh was seen to embody both of these characteristics: he could either reward or punish. Israelite society, therefore, centered on gaining the rewards of Yahweh and escaping his punishment. Yahweh was seen to be unlike all other gods. At times he was seen as the one supreme God who ruled the universe. At other times he was seen to be the only living God, with all other gods being mere representations of wood or stone. At other times he was seen as being the only genuine God, with other gods and their followers being little more than imposters or tempters seeking to woo the Israelites away from the true religion. In this regard, Yahweh was perceived to be a jealous God who punished those who deviated from their worship of him. Indeed, his followers believed that he at times went to the extreme of utterly destroying those who deviated from the rules of behaviour he had established for mankind. At the same time, he rewarded those who followed his rules and carried out the religious practices demanded of them. It was the attempt by the ancient Israelites to meet the demands of Yahweh whom they saw as all-powerful and as bountiful in his rewards as he was severe in his punishment, which led to the destruction of the idolaters. To ensure that they follow his commandments, Yahweh demanded the following:

> When the LORD your God brings you into the land which you are entering to take possession of it, and clears many nations before you, the Hittites, the Gir'gashites, Amorites, the Canaanites, the Per'izzites, the Hivites, and the Jebusites, seven nations greater and mightier than yourselves, 2 and when the LORD Your God gives them over to you, and you defeat them; then you must utterly destroy them; you shall make no covenant with them, and show no mercy to them (Deut. 7:1-2).[4]

Yahweh had chosen the Israelites as his own people, a people elected to worship him. In return, he would love and reward them. However, his gifts were conditional. Receiving these was linked to the destruction of other peoples. Thus:

> 6 For you are a people holy to the LORD your God; the LORD your God has chosen you to be a people for his own possession, out of all the peoples that are on the face of the earth. 7 It was not because you were more in number than any other people that

the LORD set his love upon you and chose you, for you were the fewest of all peoples; 8 but it is because the LORD loves you, and is keeping the oath which he swore to your fathers, that the LORD has brought you out with a mighty hand, and redeemed you from the house of bondage, from the hand of Pharaoh king of Egypt. 9 Know therefore that the LORD your God is God, the faithful God who keeps covenant and steadfast love with those who love him and keep his commandments, to a thousand generations, 10 and requites to their face those who hate him, by destroying them; he will not be slack with him who hates him, he will requite him to his face. 11 You shall therefore be careful to do the command-ment, and the statutes, and the ordinances, which I command you this day. 12 And because you hearken to these ordinances, and keep and do them, the LORD your God will keep with you the covenant and the steadfast love which he swore to your fathers to keep; 13 he will love you, bless you, and multiply you; he will also bless the fruit of your body and the fruit of your ground, your grain and your wine and your oil, the increase of your cattle and the young of your flock, in the land which he swore to your fa-thers to give you. 14 You shall be blessed above all peoples; there shall not be male or female barren among you, or among your cattle. 15 And the LORD will take away from you all sickness; and none of the evil diseases of Egypt, which you knew, will he inflict upon you, but he will lay them upon all who hate you. 16 And you shall destroy all the peoples that the LORD your God will give over to you, your eye shall not pity them; neither shall you serve their gods, for that would be a snare to you (Deut. 7:6-16).

The destruction

The destruction of the idolaters was motivated by the desire to avoid Yah-weh's punishment and establish what might be called the next best thing to Paradise. The biblical accounts of the different campaigns to destroy the idolaters vary in detail. More detailed accounts might stress the power of Yahweh to act on behalf of his people. Thus, in the case of Jericho, the writer attributes the conquest essentially to the work of Yahweh:

15 On the seventh day they (the Israelites) rose early at the dawn of day, and marched around the city in the same manner seven times: it was only on that day that they marched around the city

seven times. 16 And at the seventh time, when the priests had blown the trumpets, Joshua said to the people, 'Shout; for the LORD has given you the city. 17 And the city and all that is within it shall be devoted to the LORD for destruction; only Rahab the harlot and all who are with her in her house shall live, because she hid the messengers that we sent. 18 But you, keep yourselves from the things devoted to destruction, lest when you have devoted them you take any of the devoted things and make the camp of Israel a thing of destruction, and bring trouble upon it. 19 But all the silver and gold, and vessels of bronze and iron, are sacred to the LORD; they shall go into the treasury of the LORD.' 20 So the people shouted, and the trumpets were blown. As soon as the people heard the sound of the trumpet, the people raised a great shout, and the wall fell down flat, so that the people went up into the city, every man straight before him, and they took the city. 21 Then they utterly destroyed all in the city, both men and women, young and old, oxen, sheep, and asses, with the edge of the sword. 24 And they burned the city with fire, and all within it; only the silver and gold, and the vessels of bronze and of iron, they put into the treasury of the house of the LORD (Josh. 6:15-21, 24).

In the case of the conquest of Ai, the Israelite leaders took a more decisive role in the conquest:

10 And Joshua arose early in the morning and mustered the people, and went up, with the elders of Israel, before the people of Ai. 11 And all the fighting men who were with him went up, and drew near before the city, and encamped on the north side of Ai, with a ravine between them and Ai. 12 And he took about five thousand men, and set them in ambush between Bethel and Ai, to the west of the city. 13 So they stationed the forces, the main encampment which was north of the city and its rear guard west of the city. But Joshua spent that night in the valley. 14 And when the king of Ai saw this he and all his people, the men of the city, made haste and went out early to the descent toward the Arabah to meet Israel in battle; but he did not know that there was an ambush against him behind the city. 15 And Joshua and all Israel made a pretence of being beaten before them, and fled in the direction of the wilderness. 16 So all the people who were in the city were called together to pursue them, and as they pursued Joshua they were drawn away from the city. 17 There was not a man left in Ai or Bethel, who did not go out after Israel; they left the city open,

and pursued Israel. 18 Then the LORD said to Joshua, 'Stretch out the javelin that is in your hand toward Ai; for I will give it into your hand.' And Joshua stretched out the javelin that was in his hand toward the city. 19 And the ambush rose quickly out of their place, and as soon as he had stretched out his hand, they ran and entered the city and took it; and they made haste to set the city on fire. 20 So when the men of Ai looked back, behold, the smoke of the city went up to heaven; and they had no power to flee this way or that, for the people that fled to the wilderness turned back upon the pursuers. 21 And when Joshua and all Israel saw that the ambush had taken the city, and that the smoke of the city went up, then they turned back and smote the men of Ai. 22 And the others came forth from the city against them; so they were in the midst of Israel, some on this side, and some on that side; and Israel smote them, until there was left none that survived or escaped. 23 But the king of Ai they took alive, and brought him to Joshua. 24 When Israel had finished slaughtering all the inhabitants of Ai in the open wilderness where they pursued them and all of them to the very last had fallen by the edge of the sword, all Israel returned to Ai, and smote it with the edge of the sword. 25 And all who fell that day, both men and women, were twelve thousand, all the people of Ai (Josh. 8:10-25).

In the case of Hazor, we also have a longer account, probably because of the significance of this battle in the conquest. Thus:

When Jabin king of Hazor heard of this, he sent to Jobab king of Madon, and to the king of Shimron, and to the king of Ach'shaph, 2 and to the kings who were in the northern hill country, and in the Arabah south of Chin'neroth, and in the lowland, and in Naphoth-dor on the west, 3 to the Canaanites in the east and the west, the Amorites, the Hittites, the Per'izzites, and the Jeb'usites in the hill country, and the Hivites under Hermon in the land of Mizpah. 4 And they came out, with all their troops, a great host, in number like the sand that is upon the seashore, with very many horses and chariots. 5 And all these kings joined their forces, and came and encamped together at the waters of Merom, to fight with Israel.

6 And the LORD said to Joshua, "Do not be afraid of them, for tomorrow at this time I will give over all of them, slain, to Israel; you shall hamstring their horses, and burn their chariots with fire." 7 So Joshua came suddenly upon them with all his

people of war, by the waters of Merom, and fell upon them. 8 And the LORD gave them into the hand of Israel, who smote them and chased them as far as Great Sidon and Mis'rephothma'im, and eastward as far as the valley of Mizpeh; and they smote them, until they left none remaining. 9 And Joshua did to them as the LORD bade him; he hamstrung their horses, and burned their chariots with fire.

10 And Joshua turned back at that time, and took Hazor, and smote its king with the sword; for Hazor formerly was the head of all those kingdoms. 11 And they put to the sword all who were in it, utterly destroying them; there was none left that breathed, and he burned Hazor with fire. 12 And all the cities of those kings, and all their kings, Joshua took, and smote them with the edge of the sword, utterly destroying them, as Moses the servant of the LORD had commanded (Josh. 11:1-12).

Unlike the above, most accounts relating to Joshua's exploits in the conquest of biblical Palestine are presented in summary form:

28 And Joshua took Makke'dah on that day, and smote it and its king with the edge of the sword; he utterly destroyed every person in it, he left none remaining; and he did to the king of Makke'dah as he had done to the king of Jericho.

29 Then Joshua passed on from Makke'dah, and all Israel with him, to Libnah, and fought against Libnah, 30 and the Lord gave it also and its king into the hand of Israel; and he smote it with the edge of the sword, and every person in it, he left none remaining in it; and he did to its king as he had done to the king of Jericho.

31 And Joshua passed on from Libnah, and all Israel with him, to Lachish, and laid siege to it, and assaulted it: 32 and the LORD gave Lachish into the hand of Israel, and he took it on the second day, and smote it with the edge of the sword, and every person in it, as he had done to Libnah.

33 Then Horam king of Gezer came up to help Lachish; and Joshua smote him and his people, until he left none remaining.

34 And Joshua passed on with all Israel from Lachish to Eglon; and they laid siege to it, and assaulted it; 35 and they took it on that day, and smote it with the edge of the sword; and every person in it he utterly destroyed that day, as he had done to Lachish.

36 Then Joshua went up with all Israel from Eglon to Hebron; and they assaulted it, 37 and took it, and smote it with the edge of the sword, and its king and its towns, and every person in it;

he left none remaining, as he had done to Eglon, and utterly destroyed it with every person in it.

38 Then Joshua, with all Israel, turned back to Debir and assaulted it, 39 and he took it with its king and all its towns; and they smote them with the edge of the sword, and utterly destroyed every person in it; he left none remaining; as he had done to Hebron and to Libnah and its king, so he did to Debir and to its king.

40 So Joshua defeated the whole land, the hill country and the Negeb and the lowland and the slopes, and all their kings; he left none remaining, but utterly destroyed all that breathed, as the LORD God of Israel commanded. 41 And Joshua defeated them from Ka'desh-bar'nea to Gaza, and all the country of Goshen, as far as Gibeon. 42 And Joshua took all these kings and their land at one time, because the LORD God of Israel fought for Israel. 43 Then Joshua returned, and all Israel with him, to the camp at Gilgal (Josh. 10:28-43).

Warfare such as this led to the almost total annihilation of the original inhabitants of ancient Palestine, who fell into the hands of Israelites led by Joshua. The only peoples spared were those who were able to trick Israelite leaders into believing that they did not occupy territory being reserved for the worship of Yahweh. This was the case of the inhabitants of Gibeon, who, when negotiating their surrender, deceived the Israelites into believing that they had come from far away. The Israelites therefore deviated from Yahweh's command and accepted their peaceful submission. However, the Gibeonites were enslaved, becoming "hewers of wood and drawers of water for the congregation" (Josh. 9:21).

The biblical record as a historical account

How historically accurate is this narrative? Written down several centuries after the Israelites first took possession of biblical Palestine, the account was undoubtedly condensed and altered as it was passed from generation to generation. Moreover, the Book of Judges presents a somewhat different version of the Israelite conquest of biblical Palestine than do other books in the Old Testament. Albrecht Alt and the German school of biblical scholars conclude from the different accounts presented in the Bible that there was no military conquest of Canaan by the Israelites, but rather a gradual and pacific penetration.[5] Other biblical scholars take issue with Alt's interpretation. William Albright has used archaeology to try to determine the accuracy of the biblical record, in particular the Book of Joshua.[6]

Ever since modern topographical research methods began to be used in archaeological studies more than a century ago, scholars have endeavoured to locate the cities the Bible mentions as having been destroyed by Joshua and to identify the "destruction layers" from the twelfth and thirteenth centuries BC that might be attributed to the Israelite conquest. Confirming the Israelite conquest of Canaan archaeologically became one of the major priorities of the biblical archaeology movement led by William Albright and his followers from about 1925 to 1970. They adopted almost exclusively the conquest model presented in the Book of Joshua.[7] Albright's basic premise was that the biblical account was correct and that all he had to do was find evidence of the different cities destroyed in biblical Palestine and date them and he would thereby prove the historical accuracy of the biblical record. Albright found much evidence to support the account rendered by the Book of Joshua.[8] Archaeologists such as G. Ernest Wright, John Bright, and Yigael Yadin, who shared Albright's objectives, also found evidence supporting the view that the Book of Joshua presents a fairly accurate account of events. On the basis of his findings, Yigael Yadin argued that the biblical narrative, in its broad outline, tells us that during a certain period the nomad Israelites attacked many of the city-states of the Holy Land and destroyed them. They set their strongholds on fire and slowly replaced them with new unfortified cities. However, they were unable to dislodge certain cities, which continued to exist in the midst of the invaders.[9]

Biblical scholars such as Craigie, who sought to bring together the biblical with the archaeological record, reached the same conclusion. He takes the view that the results of archaeological work may illuminate the background of the biblical story, filling in the gaps in the text.[10] This view is also expressed by Baez-Camargo, who argues that the traditional view of the Israelite conquest of Canaan as a single, extensive campaign led by Joshua has been called into question by scholars who use the archaeological record to explore the biblical account. The increasingly accepted theory is that the Israelite invasion followed two main routes: one from the south, for which archaeological evidence is somewhat uncertain, and the other through the east (led by Joshua, and best described by the biblical account), across the Jordan and then towards the north.[11]

Until the 1970s, Albright's approach to biblical criticism held a dominant position, particularly in North America, where his views regarding the historicity of the Book of Joshua tended to be broadly accepted. Thereafter, a new generation of archaeologists gained prominence, which was inclined to reject Albright's view that archaeology was somehow the handmaiden of biblical scholarship, relegated to the task of expanding on the biblical record. Nor were they interested in exploring the massive destructions on which Albright and his group concentrated, but rather sought to examine the archaeological record of everyday life.

Building on findings of archaeologists who take issue with Albright and his school, Dever proceeds to construct his own theory as to the historicity of the Book of Joshua and the origins of Israel.[12] He argues that the biblical account in the Book of Joshua may have come down to us as a record of the "house of Joseph." He adds that "these newcomers" to Canaan may have passed through Transjordan, entered Canaan via Jericho, and "intruded forcefully" into central Palestine. Such a route would explain some of the conquest narratives in the Book of Joshua. He goes on to say that in time the story of the house of Joseph became the story of "all Israel" because it was the only extant record. As an illustration, he suggests that the landing of the *Mayflower* might have become the story of all Americans if it had been the only record retained relating to the landing of Europeans in America.[13]

The landing of the *Mayflower* is not a mere story but is based in fact. Applying Dever's analogy to the Book of Joshua suggests that the biblical accounts of these conquests are also not mere stories but also have a basis in fact. From this perspective, Dever's account isn't all that different from that of Craigie or Baez-Camargo, who argue that different tribal groups contributed to the biblical record and that, in its broad outline, the archaeological record essentially supports the account presented in the Book of Joshua. Of course, Dever calls these accounts mere "origin stories," written to show Yahweh's work on behalf of his people.[14] He does not seek to resolve the question of the extent to which these stories are based in fact. At the same time, he does admit that it is difficult for archaeologists to ascertain the belief systems of ancient peoples and that archaeologists are not equipped to be palaeo-theologians.

Dever has not been the only one drawing particularly on archaeological evidence to discount or improve upon the biblical record.[15] Among scholars working in the field, one of the most scholarly rigorous has probably been Israel Finkelstein, who in *The Bible Unearthed* shows quite convincingly that the original creators of the biblical account were wrong on numerous occasions in identifying the location where destructions occurred. They were often wrong in identifying the time when the destruction they mention occurred. Also, they overemphasized the significance of a particular person or event. Furthermore, creators of the biblical record were very much influenced by the environment in which they found themselves, including their religious beliefs and the aspirations of rulers at the time when the Bible was first committed to written form.

Finkelstein not only criticizes the biblical record, but also builds on

Albrecht Alt's peaceful infiltration theory to present his own account on how the Holy Land was established. This presents a number of problems (See Appendix A), and demonstrates that although archaeology has been quite successful in pointing out shortcomings of the Bible as history, it has been less successful in presenting a satisfactory alternative account on the establishment of the Holy Land. In part, this stems from the archaeological method itself. Dark argues that the material past does not speak for itself; it speaks only through the beliefs, ideas, and frame of reference of the archaeologist.[16] Commenting on the usefulness of archaeology in Bible criticism, Boling states that what archaeology can do for biblical study is provide a physical context in time and place. Inscriptions and other evidence are of exceptional importance for biblical background and for occasional mention of biblical places and names. The remainder of the archaeological record, however, leaves room for interpretation, which is very much influenced by the beliefs and attitudes of the people doing the interpreting.[17]

Furthermore, although archaeology can provide us with considerable information on the material past as this relates to the Bible, it has been less successful in providing us with information on the beliefs of the ancient Hebrews. The main source in this regard has been the Bible. This, in turn, reflects the religious beliefs of the people who left us this record and their views regarding the role Yahweh played in the life of his people. Boling informs us that, when writing the Book of Joshua, the writers drew on a variety of older sources.[18] This could help explain why we find different and, at times, seemingly contradictory accounts of the conquest. Nor do such contradictions necessarily deny the factual basis of the conquest as described in the Book of Joshua. To reach a conclusion in this regard, it would probably be more sensible to look at the overall biblical account, which shows that the destructions described in the Book of Joshua did not constitute isolated incidents, but rather were part of Israelite practice for a prolonged period.[19]

The above suggests several things. It suggests that Joshua's attempt to wipe out the original inhabitants of biblical Palestine was not an isolated incident but part of a prolonged effort. It suggests that some of the people escaped each killing spree by the Israelites, with some surviving until, eventually, they or their descendants were enslaved. Craigie argues that if the historian's task were simply to resolve the tension inherent in the biblical narrative, it could be argued that the Books of Joshua and Judges give complementary, but considerably oversimplified, pictures of the history of Hebrew conquest and settlement. The Book of Joshua provides an overview of a major military campaign that brought the Israelites into the Promised Land. At the same time, however, Hebrew control was restricted to a few areas. The summary and the beginning of Judges and the narratives that follow present an account of a more prolonged period of consolidation after the initial conquests.[20]

What concerns us in this study are the motives of the people who "intruded forcefully" into biblical Palestine. Although written from the perspective of the belief system of the people of the time, the Book of Joshua provides us with an insight into the motives driving the invaders to take possession of the land they conquered. We are told in this account that the goal of the invaders was to slaughter all the people who did not believe in Yahweh and were not members of the Tribes of Israel. Although we cannot ascertain from both the biblical and the archaeological record to what extent the invaders followed these directives, we can say that, from the evidence they had, the writers of the Book of Joshua concluded that the invaders had followed these directives. We are also informed why they followed these directives: they saw in this a way of ensuring that the Israelites would receive the blessings of Yahweh and avoid his punishment.

The historicity of the biblical account also becomes evident when we look at patterns of conquest followed by other ancient peoples. To an extent, the destruction of the idolaters follows a pattern of conquest and destruction pursued by other ancient groups, with the Israelite tribes being but one of the nomadic groups taking possession of the city-states that had been established around them. In ancient times, conquest in itself gave the conquerors absolute power over the conquered. Initially, the conquerors used this power to sacrifice to their gods any captives taken in war. Such a practice was common, for example, among the early Sumerians and Greeks.[21] It was also common among groups related to the Israelites, such as the Moabites, who appear to have continued such sacrifices longer than the Israelites.[22] In time, though, more practical motives won out and the conquered would generally be enslaved rather than killed. However, patterns varied across groups. Thus, the ancient Hittites tended to focus on negotiation rather than conquest. Cities that submitted willingly could negotiate conditions of surrender. In these cases, the Hittites concentrated on seeking allies rather than subjugating a population. If a city chose to go to war rather than submit, it was destroyed and its territory was dedicated to the thunder god, and its inhabitants dispersed as serfs among Hittite nobles.[23] The Assyrians were at the other extreme. Although a city could negotiate conditions under which it would submit, the Assyrians would cruelly slaughter most of the people who resisted conquest so as to terrorize future target groups, discouraging them from resisting Assyrian expansion.[24]

Variations of these patterns were evident among other groups. Thucydides describes the encounter between the ambitious Athenians and the Malians who resisted them. The Athenian speech to the Malians, in Thucydides' account, gives insight into Athenian motives and actions:

> We on our side will use no fine phrase saying . . . that we have a right to our empire because we defeated the Persians, or that we have come against you because of the injuries you have done us —a great mass of words that nobody would believe. . . . You know as well as we do that, when these matters are discussed by practical people, the standard of justice depends on the equality of power to compel and that in fact the strong do what they have the power to do and the weak accept what they have to accept.[25]

According to Thucydides, the Athenians did not press the siege seriously. Due to some treachery inside the city, the Malians surrendered to the Athenians, who put to death the grown men and sold the women and children as slaves. Subsequently, Athens sent out five hundred colonists to inhabit the place.

Writing of Rome, Fustel De Coulanges states that its soldiers made war not only upon other soldiers, but also upon an entire population - men, women, children, and slaves. A war might cause an entire people to disappear, and change a fertile country into a desert. It was by virtue of this law of war that the Romans extended an uninhabited cordon around their city. Of the territory where the Volscians had twenty-three cities, they created the Pontine Marshes; the fifty-three cities of Latium disappeared; in Samnium, the route take by Roman armies was less recognized by what remained of their camps than by the unpopulated landscape.[26]

An example of the Roman pattern of conquest at its extreme is the destruction of Carthage at the conclusion of the Punic Wars in 146 BC. Prior to the city's destruction, the Romans gave the Carthaginians the choice of vacating their city, which the Romans would then destroy, or war. When Carthage refused to surrender, the Romans attacked and conquered the city, killing many of the Carthaginians in the process. Following this, the city was torn down, the territory where it had stood was sown with salt, and its people were sold into slavery.[27]

In some cases, Israelite patterns of conquest were not dissimilar from these examples. This was the case where the conquered did not occupy territory which the Israelites had reserved for the worship of their deity. Thus, we read in Deuteronomy:

> 10 When you draw near to a city to fight against it, offer terms of peace to it. 11 And if its answer to you is peace and it opens to you,

then all the people who are found in it shall do forced labour for you and shall serve you. 12 But if it makes no peace with you, but makes war against you, then you shall besiege it, 13 and when the LORD your God gives it into your hand you shall put all its males to the sword, 14 but the women and the little ones, the cattle, and everything else in the city, all its spoil, you shall take as booty for yourselves; and you shall enjoy the spoil of your enemies, which the Lord your God has given you. 15 Thus you shall do with the cities which are very far from you, which are not cities of the nations here (Deut. 20:10-15).

This practice stood in contrast to the treatment the Israelites under Joshua meted out to peoples who occupied land reserved for the worship of Yahweh. Here the conquest was an integral part of the Israelite religion and the relationship the community had with its deity:

16 But in the cities of these peoples that the LORD your God gives you for your inheritance, you shall save alive nothing that breathes, 17 but you shall utterly destroy them, the Hittites and the Amorites, the Canaanites and the Per'izzites, the Hivites and the Jeb'usites, as the LORD your God has commanded (Deut. 20: 16-17).

Scripture even gives a justification for this severity by placing it in the larger context of war among ancients, when it states: "For it was the LORD'S doing to harden their hearts that they should come against Israel in battle, in order that they should be utterly destroyed, and should receive no mercy but be exterminated, as the LORD commanded Moses" (Josh. 11:20). At the same time, the Israelite conquest of what became the Holy Land was much more destructive than were conquests carried out by other ancients. It was more destructive because of the nature of the Israelite relationship to their God. In this regard there was a major difference between the Israelites and other ancient peoples. No matter whether it were the Sumerians, the Hittites, the Babylonians, the Assyrians or other ancient conquerors, none were commanded to slaughter all the inhabitants on the territory reserved for the worship of their gods. In fact, the opposite tended to be the case. Conquest often meant adding the stable of deities of the conquered to their deities and thereby being strengthened. It was almost as if these deities were seen to represent energies. By assimilating the deities of the conquered people, the conqueror absorbed the energy represented by these deities, making them work on his behalf.

Those who spoke on behalf of the Israelite deity, Yahweh, did not believe their community would be strengthened by the acquisition of other deities. On the contrary, such an act would evoke Yahweh's anger against his people. The idolaters had to be destroyed to minimize the possibility of Yahweh's punishing the Israelites and maximize the possibility of receiving his rewards. Conquerors such as the Babylonians or Romans could destroy a people, or assimilate them through the sharing of deities. The account we have in the Book of Joshua is written from an entirely different perspective. The objective of these invaders, as presented to us from the point of view of the writers, was to totally destroy people who were not members of the Tribes of Israel and followers of Yahweh. The idolaters were to be wiped out so that their territory could become the base for the Israelite God, a God who ruled the universe and had made the Israelites his chosen people. The purpose of the slaughter was ultimately to create a place where the believers in Yahweh could practise their religion without the threat of contamination from non-believers.

This emphasis on total destruction and on linking the destruction to the well-being of a group that saw itself as chosen in some special sort of way makes the wars of Joshua relevant for the study of the holocaust genocide. It presents not only a holocaust-type genocide but also a contextual framework in which it was carried out. Inevitably, it does so in the language and in terms of the concepts peculiar to the time. Despite this limitation, comparing and contrasting the dynamics that led to the events described in Deuteronomy and the Book of Joshua with those leading to more recent mass destructions could well provide insight into modern genocides that have been identified as holocausts. The information we have from the more recent past may, in turn, shed light on the biblical record.

2
The Witch-Hunts in Europe

Trevor-Roper sees a close similarity between the persecution of the witches during the late Middle Ages and the war Nazi Germany carried out against European Jewry. Just as the witches were blamed for society's problems during the Middle Ages, Jews were blamed for the problems facing German society in the early part of the twentieth century. As with witches, an image was created justifying the slaughter of the Jews.[1] The same argument is made by Adolf Leschnitzer, who considers the witchcraft mania of the Middle Ages as having been similar to the anti-Semitism in nineteenth-century Germany. He finds parallels between these two events in the following areas: economic and physical insecurity; projection of anti-social impulses onto a demonized defenceless group; cruelty in battling the demonized group being combined with the endeavour to deprive it of its possessions.[2] Norman Cohn argues that the link between persecution of the witches and that of the Jews was established in particular through the propaganda leaflet entitled "The Protocols of the Elders of Zion." Anti-Semites, in particular the Nazis, used the document to paint a picture of the Jew out to control the world.[3]

To understand why the witch-hunts occurred, we must first examine what Europeans during the late Middle Ages meant when they accused someone of being a witch and practising witchcraft. Witchcraft for early modern Europeans almost invariably meant the performance of maleficent rather than beneficial magic, with the Latin term *maleficia* being used to describe such magic. Witches, however, were not merely seen to be performing *maleficium* or harmful magic. They were also considered to have entered into a relationship with the Devil, the enemy of God and the personification of evil. From this perspective, witches were not only considered to be practising sorcery, but were also perceived as paying homage to the Devil, the source of their power to do magic.

This view of the witch was developed largely by churchmen and lawyers, who drew on Christian theology, canon law and certain philosophical ideas for their theories. In these, special significance was placed on the demonic pact, entered into when the Devil met with his recruit in physical form. In this encounter, the witch renounced her baptism, promised to serve the Devil in the present life and give him her soul on death in return for material advantages and magical powers. In addition, Christian witch theorists were convinced that no witch operated alone. It was believed that witches assembled at midnight meetings in which they worshipped the Devil, received his orders and had sexual intercourse with him or his subordinates. The belief that witches entered into a pact with the Devil essentially altered earlier European beliefs regarding witchcraft. In earlier times, people believed witches could practice either maleficent or beneficial magic. The pact with the Devil abolished the distinction between white and black magic and made them both evil.[4] Levack notes that this Christian European view of witchcraft, which combined *maleficium* and diabolism (Devil worship), was very different from the view of witchcraft in other societies. The belief of late medieval demonologists that the witch was a member of a large sect of flying magicians worshipping demons was unique to European medieval society. It evolved as medieval theologians defined both the Devil and the witch.[5]

The initial accusation that a person was practising *maleficium* usually came from below, that is, from family members or neighbours. Thus, a person might be accused of using sorcery to make someone ill or to cause death. The association of such acts with diabolism, however, developed as the accused proceeded through the legal system of lawyers, judges and magistrates. In these instances, torture was used to force the accused to admit that his or her actions involved not merely *maleficium* but also diabolism.

According to Hughes, the witch-hunts began after the image of the Devil had been well established by the church fathers. The Dominicans, in particular, spread the message that witches, who represented the Kingdom of Satan, threatened the Kingdom of Christ.[6] Further impetus to the witch-hunts was given by the Papal Bull of 1484, which was directed not only against witches but also against heresy in general. To make the Bull effective, judges were appointed with the power to investigate accusations. Two such judges were Father Jacob Sprenger, of Bâle, and Father Heinrich Kramer - both Dominicans - who were the Chief Inquisitors for Germany. In about 1490, they produced a book, the *Malleus Maleficarum*, in which they outlined the process of searching for witches. They described how to recognize witches and how to exterminate them. At the same time, the *Malleus* claimed that those who denied the reality of witchcraft were heretics. Like many of their contemporaries, Sprenger and Kramer believed that the Devil and his agents existed and had to be defeated if the Christian Church were to survive. Hughes sees them as highly principled men, differing little from the judges of Communist or Nazi courts, who were equally confronted with heresy against the political creeds of a later time. If they had a sin, it was that of absolute faith, absolute conviction as to the righteousness of their cause.[7]

The *Malleus* was only one of many treatises on witchcraft at that time. These provided instruction on how to detect a witch, warned of the danger of witchcraft and sought to convince people of its existence. They provided an important base for the witch hunts in that they helped persuade especially those in control of the judicial machinery that people accused of witchcraft were not merely practising magic but were doing so through allying themselves with the Devil, the enemy of Christ and his Church.

The witch-hunts erupted when these elites became convinced that the individual witches were not merely harming their neighbour by magical means but were rejecting the Christian faith and through this were undermining Christian civilization.[8] The devil in this regard was seen not only as the enemy of Christ but also as the central figure in a new religion. Bossy argues that such beliefs set the base for transforming the crime of witchcraft from that of *maleficium* to Devil-worship.[9] People came to view supposed practitioners of witchcraft as idolaters who not only could cast spells but also paid homage to the Devil and had renounced the Christian faith. This view of the witch helped transform what were often local persecutions of individuals into a crusade against witchcraft.

This view of the witch developed in large part from evidence obtained from people accused of witchcraft through the application of torture. This in turn was abetted by the introduction of inquisitorial trials into the European legal system. Before the thirteenth century, European courts made use of an accusatorial system of justice. In this system, a person launching a criminal action was also involved in prosecuting it. Following a formal public statement by the accuser, a judge would decide on the validity and justification of the accusation, with the decision of guilt or innocence being left to God in the more difficult cases. In these instances, the accused might be required to carry a hot iron a certain distance or put his hand into scalding hot water, whereupon the judge made his decision regarding guilt or innocence on the basis of the effects.

At the beginning of the thirteenth century, Western European ecclesiastical and secular courts increasingly began to make use of Roman law in their practises. It was felt that Roman law, which had been discovered in the eleventh and twelfth centuries, would be more effective in dealing in particular with hidden crimes such as heresy. Referred to as inquisitorial, the new system eventually replaced the old system during the thirteenth, fourteenth and fifteenth centuries and by the sixteenth century was in use throughout Continental Europe. Although the system was also in use in England, it did not have as pronounced an effect there because jurors rather than court officials made the final decision regarding guilt or innocence.

While facilitating the prosecution of all crimes, the inquisitorial procedure proved particularly useful in trials involving heresy and witchcraft. Under the old system, the plaintiff could himself become liable to criminal prosecution if his charges were malevolent and were dismissed as a consequence. As the new system didn't make the plaintiff responsible for the actual prosecution of his case, it permitted someone to denounce a suspect before judicial authorities with little risk to himself. Also, the new system placed the entire judicial process under the control of officials once the initial charge had been laid, with the judge and his subordinates being given a wide range of powers, including the application of torture, to investigate a complaint and determine guilt or innocence.

The use of torture had previously been tried in European jurisprudence. Its unreliability as a means of establishing guilt or innocence, however, had caused the Church to prohibit its application before the middle of the thirteenth century. With its revival in the latter part of the thirteenth century, legal authorities, therefore, devised rules and procedures governing its administration. However, as witchcraft was considered to be an exceptional crime, such rules tended to be relaxed or ignored in these trials. Types of torture applied included the *strappado*, which involved leaving a person hanging with his hands tied behind his back. Instruments of compression were used, including thumb screws, leg screws and head clamps, which served to compress a particular part of the body so as to force a confession. The following provides an idea as to the type of torture applied to "persuade" the accused to confess. This is a translation from the German of a note from the shaky hand of Burgomaster Johannes Junius to his daughter, dated 24 July 1628. He writes:

> Many hundred thousand goodnights, dearly beloved daughter Veronica. Innocent have I come to prison, innocent have I been tortured, innocent must I die. For whoever comes into the witch prison [at Bamberg] must become a witch or be tortured until he invents something out of his head—God pity him, bethinks him of something. I will tell you how it has gone with me. . . . And then came— God in highest Heaven have mercy— the executioner, and put the thumbscrews on me, so that the blood ran out at the nails and everywhere, so that for four weeks I could not use my hands as you can see from the writing. . . . Thereafter they first stripped me, bound my hands behind me, and drew me up in the torture (By means of a rope attached to the hands tied behind the back,

and carried over a pulley on the ceiling). Then I thought Heaven and Earth were at an end; eight times did they draw me up and let me fall again, so that I suffered terrible agony. The executioner said, 'Sir, I beg you for God's sake confess something, whether it be true or not, for you cannot endure the torture which you will be put to, and even if you bear it all, yet you will not escape . . . '

He begged a day to think, invented a story of a witch meeting, and under threat of further torture named various people as being present, and confessed to various crimes.

> Now, dear child, here you have all my confession, for which I must die. And they are sheer lies and made-up things, so help me God. For all this I was forced to say through fear of the torture which was threatened beyond what I had already endured. For they never leave off with the torture till one confesses something; be he never so good, he must be a witch. Nobody escapes, though he were an earl . . .
>
> Dear child, keep this letter secret so that people do not find it, else I shall be tortured most piteously and the jailers will be beheaded. So strictly is it forbidden. . . . Dear Child, pay this man a dollar. . . . I have taken several days to write this; my hands are both lame. I am in a sad plight. Good night, for your father Johannes Junius will never see you more. July 24th, 1628.
>
> [On the margin]. Dear child, six have confessed against me at once: the Chancellor, his son ... all false, through compulsion, as they have told me, and begged my forgiveness in God's name before they were executed.[10]

When torturing the accused, witch hunters looked for evidence of diabolism, or devil worship. This essentially involved attendance at the Sabbath and a pact between the Devil and the witch in which he or she pledged fealty to him. Both were seen as proof that the witch was an enemy of Christ and his Church. Instead of Christ, the witch worshipped the Devil. Although the Devil, or Satan ("the adversary"), as he was generally referred to during the Middle Ages, assumed a distinct personality only in the latter books of the Old Testament, by Christ's time he had become an important figure in Scripture. Ruling over a host of subordinate demons, he tempted Christ. At the same time, medieval Christians saw him as the main adversary in the titanic struggle between the Kingdom of Christ and that of Satan. This view, combining Christian and Persian beliefs, perceived the world as a battleground between the powers of good and evil.

It was up to people to decide on which side they belonged. Witches, having chosen to side with the Devil, had made themselves the archenemies of Christ and his Church.

When choosing the Devil as his or her master and renouncing the Church, the witch was seen as having undergone a particular ritual. In it, the Devil branded his new recruit, leaving either a visible blemish or an insensible place in the skin to indicate his ownership. Simultaneously, the chrism supposedly given the person at baptism was removed. This pact was generally carried to a conclusion by the Sabbath, essentially the antithesis of the Christian Eucharistic celebration in which believers dedicated themselves to God. During the Sabbath, the witches did everything which the Church condemned as they worshipped and dedicated themselves to the service of Satan. In witchcraft trials, torture was used to determine whether the accused had participated in the Sabbath and to discover who else had participated so that all cult members might be eliminated.

While indicating how a witch was identified, the above doesn't fully explain why the hunts erupted. They would not have been possible without the social and economic conditions prevalent at the time. These included a dramatic rise in the population after a long period of stagnation and decline, with towns multiplying and growing in size. At the same time, there were intermittent outbreaks of the plague and other epidemics, as well as years of crop failure followed by famine. Prices rose. Agricultural and mercantile capitalism were introduced into many areas. These changes, affecting almost every aspect of people's lives, created instability and uncertainty. For a population long used to a fixed order, it contributed to turmoil and confusion. This in turn encouraged people to look for the influence of Satan in the world and be on guard for the activities of his agents, the witches. In this atmosphere, witch-hunting became a means of fighting Satan. At the same time, it helped people maintain psychic and social equilibrium by providing them with simple explanations for their problems and a visible object upon which to vent their frustrations.

The years during which the witch-hunts took place also witnessed profound religious changes. The Reformation, which started in the early part of the sixteenth century, shattered the unity of Latin Christendom. The success of the Protestant Reformation, in turn, encouraged a reform movement within Catholicism. Protestants and Catholics competed against each other to disseminate their vision of the "true" faith. At the same time, desperate to convince people that only they represented the "true" Christianity, Protestants and Catholics accused each other of being heretics and agents of the Devil. This focussed people's attention on the workings of the Devil, and stressed the necessity of purifying the faith by eradicating vestiges of paganism, and suppressing magic as the enemy of religion. This in turn encouraged awareness among people of their own moral transgressions, as well as making them anxious regarding their eternal salvation. Under these circumstances, following the biblical exhortation of Exodus 22:18, "Thou shalt not suffer a witch to live," was appealing to both Catholics and Protestants. The persecution provided both groups with a means of demonstrating to themselves their moral sanctity, which in turn gave them assurance of their own eventual salvation. All these changes, Levack argues, engendered uncertainty and conflict in the communities, which resulted in a general anxiety that encouraged witch-hunting.[11]

Larner also sees other factors contributing to the rise of the witch-hunts, including the rise of the national state and the development of personal religion among the peasantry. In early medieval times, she argues, the personal beliefs of the peasantry were of little interest to the rulers and the fate of their souls was the ultimate responsibility of religious specialists, be these monks or priests. The wandering preachers of the pre-Reformation church, the Reformation, and the Counter-Reformation effectively Christianized the peasantry for the first time. At the same time, the rise of rival versions of Christianity, each with its exclusive claims, greatly enhanced the political usefulness of religion to the rulers of early modern Europe. Churches were used to establish political borders. These events transformed Christianity into a political ideology in the sense that a degree of education was required in order for the finer points of varying dogmas to be absorbed. To establish the legitimacy of a regime, it was necessary that the populace adhere to the correct version of Christianity. In this context, witches provided a negative standard of social acceptability, and persecuting them was part of the process those in power used to define acceptable and unacceptable behaviour and beliefs for their populace.[12] Thus, rulers used the witch, concentrating on his or her image as the enemy of Christianity, to help people deal with their anxieties and at the same time impose conformity of religious practice and belief.

A variety of situations could trigger a witch-hunt. It could start when an individual or group denounced a person for being a witch. In most instances targets were misfits believed to be practising *maleficium*. Charges might arise out of someone's contracting a sudden unexplainable illness, or by a sudden death in the family, with the accusation serving both to explain and to take revenge on the person held responsible. Large hunts might arise when a number of people, each of them seeking revenge for attacks supposedly directed at them or their family, launched a complaint with the authorities. Hunts could also arise when people used accusations of witchcraft against their political enemies, economic rivals or family members. In other cases, people might be accused of Devil worship.

No matter what launched a particular hunt, those prosecuting the person or persons accused of witchcraft invariably shared a common view as to what a witch was, his or her role in society and how to prosecute both the accused and anyone associated with him or her.

Having decided to prosecute a witch, local villagers might denounce the suspect in front of a local court or ask village leaders such as church elders or the local magistrate to start proceedings against the accused. The local elite was generally responsible for the arrest and initial interrogation(s). As they tended to be familiar with demonological theory, it was at this point that notions of diabolism were generally introduced into the judicial process. To find evidence of this, investigators might prick the accused to find the Devil's mark, or even go so far as to apply torture. In most circumstances, these officials did not try the accused. Such actions usually required the approval from higher levels of government, although the final granting authority varied, depending on the degree to which a state was centralized. Once it was decided that a witch case would be heard, judicial officials assumed control of the trial. Judges essentially served as gatekeepers of the witch-hunts, deciding which witnesses to call, whom to have tortured, and which of the witch's alleged accomplices to prosecute. In most instances, they decided whether the accused was guilty or innocent and also imposed the sentence. Thus, while the initial impulse to prosecute came from below, the manner in which the witch-hunts developed was determined from above.

Once a suspect was brought to trial, a hunt could develop into a small hunt, a medium-sized hunt or a large hunt. Small hunts, which were the most common, involved the prosecution of one to three persons. Such hunts tended to be confined to the individuals initially accused. They were most common in England, where the accused tended to be charged for practising *maleficium* and the use of torture by judges to obtain names of accomplices was impermissible. At the same time, jurors rather than court officials decided on guilt or innocence, all of which contributed toward containing the hunts.

Medium-sized hunts, claiming from five to ten people, developed when the investigators didn't restrict their investigations to those initially accused. Common in French-speaking Switzerland and, to some extent, in Germany and Scotland, these generally included the use of torture. Also, second-round accusations took place. However, the process didn't get out of hand because torture was sparely used and non-capital sentences were granted. At other times, judges ran out of further people who could be accused after the main accomplices had been murdered. Also general hysteria among the local populace tended not to be widespread, encouraging the judiciary not to take a case to the extreme.

The large witch-hunts, most common in the sixteenth and the seven-teenth centuries, claimed anywhere from ten to one hundred victims each. They were characterized by a high degree of panic and hysteria. While not confined to Germany, they were most common there. Chain reactions were common in these hunts, with those tried and confessing to witchcraft providing the names of accomplices, who on being tortured to obtain their conviction in turn gave the names of others. In other instances, a large number of names might be obtained from a single accuser or a group of accusers. At other times a large hunt might be little more than the compos-ite of a number of small hunts.

The witch-hunts went through several stages. Richard Kieckhefer provides us with an idea of their development for the period from 1300 to 1500. He argues that, prior to 1300, cases were too rare to indicate a pattern. From 1300 to 1330, people suspected of witchcraft were seldom prosecuted. Trials that occurred (mostly in France, England and Germa-ny) were largely political in nature and involved prominent figures either as suspects or victims. A substantial number of sorcery cases were heard between 1330 and 1375. Politically motivated hunts had virtually ceased, however. Also, diabolism was essentially absent in these hunts. Between 1375 and 1435, the number of prosecutions increased, with charges of diab-olism becoming more common, in particular in Italy. Encouraged through the use of inquisitorial procedures in the lower courts, this development reflected a tendency to identify sorcery with diabolism. After 1435, trials for sorcery not only increased, but also were more likely to be interpreted as involving diabolism. The years 1435 to 1500 are the last period with which Kieckhefer deals. It witnessed the appearance of a large number of witchcraft treatises, which both reflected and stimulated an increase in prosecutions.[13]

Witch-hunts decreased in number during the first part of the sixteenth century, in part because of the initial shock of the Reformation. In addi-tion, the spread of Renaissance scepticism at the time may have contrib-uted to the decline of the hunts. While doing little to destroy the concepts that underlay the hunts, such scepticism attacked the scholastic mentality that was receptive to it. Also, although Protestants were no less antago-nistic toward witches than Catholics, they had not yet established a legal framework to prosecute witches. In Catholic areas, in the first part of the sixteenth century, secular courts were gaining increasingly more control over witch trials, necessitating legal changes before they could fully carry out this function. These developments contributed to a brief lull in the rate of prosecutions.

This situation changed in the latter part of the sixteenth century, with a number of conditions contributing to the intensification of the hunts. The printed Bible with its advocacy that the witch be destroyed became more widely available. Years of missionary work by Protestants and Catholics competing for new converts or attempting to convince existing members to remain within the fold strengthened religiosity, which in turn made people more aware of the immediacy of Satan and his threat to Christendom. To this was added the economic and political volatility of those years, compounded by periodic famines and epidemics, all of which fostered a mood of anxiety which encouraged witch-hunting. As a consequence, the 1550s to the 1570s saw a rise in prosecutions, to be followed by a period of mass trials in the 1580s and the 1590s in some countries, with the period from 1580 to 1650 witnessing the height of the witch hunts.

Witch-hunting expressed itself differently in different areas. Perhaps seventy-five per cent of the prosecutions took place in Germany, France and Switzerland, areas also where the major panics and most large hunts occurred. Most prosecutions took place in France in the early years of the hunts, particularly in the areas bordering Switzerland and Burgundy. These trials were kept under control, however; with France's system of appeals from local courts to the eight provincial *parlements* having a dampening effect on witch-hunting. Also, the central government restrained local and regional courts from going to excess. Eventually it also passed an edict banning all witchcraft cases.[14]

By the late sixteenth century Germany had become the center of the prosecutions. Trials continued in France, including a number of cases involving demonic possession. However, the major trials of the late sixteenth and seventeenth centuries took place in German-speaking lands. There are a number of reasons for this, the most important of which is likely the political weakness of the Holy Roman Empire, of which these lands formed a part. The empire was a loose federation of small kingdoms, principalities, duchies, and territories, each acting as either a sovereign or near-sovereign state. This gave virtual judicial autonomy to relatively small political units. Although the empire supplied the legal code for prosecuting witches, the *Carolina* of 1532, it did not have effective mechanisms for enforcing it, which meant that local or regional courts were entrusted with trying the witches.

Thus, in Germany, local judges and the petty potentates who controlled them, had a latitude in dealing with witchcraft cases that few zealous witch hunters in other parts of Europe possessed. This was in particular the case in the smaller states.[15] Thus, the small *Fürstpropstei* of Ellwangen had no outside force to restrain it when it embarked on one of the most severe witch-hunts in Germany, taking the lives of almost 400 individuals between 1611 and 1618.[16] In Bamberg, unrestrained torture led to the destruction of some 300 people accused of witchcraft between 1624 and 1631.[17] The largest hunt took place in Trier, where at its height a total of 306 witches named about 1,500 accomplices, each accused offering an average of twenty names.[18]

Although German courts seldom had to deal with imperial tribunals, they were required to consult with universities in witchcraft cases. In particular, prior to proceeding with torture and before sentencing, courts were required to request advice from the local university. As universities were instrumental in developing and disseminating demonological theory, this procedure served to encourage rather than hinder the prosecution and destruction of people accused of being witches.

The persecution of witches was on occasion also severe in Switzerland. As Swiss cantons were autonomous, Switzerland didn't have a uniform approach to the hunts. For example, although Geneva experienced panics related to the spread of the plague, it experienced few prosecutions. Pays de Vaud, on the other hand, executed 90 per cent of those tried for witchcraft, with the total number of victims exceeding 3,000.[19]

Witch-hunting also took a heavy toll in smaller territories in west-central Europe, such as Luxembourg and Lorraine. In Lorraine, Nicolas Rémy sent more than two thousand witches to their death during his entire career, and more than eight hundred between 1586 and 1595. In Luxembourg there were 358 executions between 1509 and 1687 and in other parts of the Spanish Netherlands many more.[20]

The Northern Netherlands was the only area in this part of Europe that did not experience extensive witch-hunting. With a population of more than a million, this region executed fewer than 150 witches. It seems that Dutch judges neither believed in the activities described by the demonological literature nor accepted the view that witches were part of a vast diabolical conspiracy. As a result, Dutch Catholic and Protestant ecclesiastics were reluctant to engage in campaigns against superstition. In addition, the energy of the people was focused on gaining independence from Spain, a struggle that was all consuming until it was resolved in 1648.[21] After this, Dutch attention turned from fighting the Spaniards to building their commercial empire.

Outside west-central Europe, witch-hunting was relatively mild and restrained. Of course, all these areas had their panics. However, the hunts were more limited in size and number than in the European heartland. Thus, England had a major witch-hunt in the 1640s, and Scotland experienced a number of major panics in the late sixteenth and seventeenth centuries. Few of these, however, compared in size and intensity to the "holocausts" that occurred in Ellwangen, Wurzburg or Bamberg. There are a number of reasons for this. One was the English use of juries rather than the inquisitorial procedure to try witches, which led to the relatively spare use of torture. This discouraged both the full development of a belief in witches and the expansion of individual or group trials into medium-sized or large hunts. While Scottish justice eventually incorporated some features of the inquisitorial procedure, juries here retained their independence, discouraging witch-hunting by official promotion.

Witch-hunts in Scandinavian countries bore a close resemblance to those in Britain. As on the British Isles, the continental concept of witchcraft was not fully accepted. Scandinavians were generally reluctant to use torture to gain confessions or the names of accomplices. This did not, however, prevent witch panics from erupting in some areas. Denmark was the first Scandinavian country to prosecute witches. In the 1540s, maintaining that in particular those with Catholic tendencies were guilty in this regard, Peter Palladius, the Lutheran bishop of Sealand, started a chain-reaction hunt that cost some fifty lives. To counter similar excesses, the government passed laws in 1547 preventing the testimony of persons convicted of crimes such as sorcery from being used to convict other people, and also permitted the use of torture only after a death sentence had been pronounced.[22] These laws served to discourage large-scale witch-hunts and to minimize the number of convictions.

Prosecutions for witchcraft were somewhat fewer in Norway than in Denmark. Of those tried for witchcraft, only about one-quarter were executed. Here also ideological and legal factors played a role in restraining witch-hunting. Although torture was permitted, its sparse use contributed to diabolism figuring in less than one-fifth of Norwegian witch trials.

Prosecutions for witchcraft began in the 1580s in Sweden. Most of these were for *maleficium*, with few executions as a consequence. A law passed in 1593 required either the testimony of six witnesses or a confession for a capital conviction. The same law stipulated that all death sentences after 1614 be appealed to a royal court in Stockholm. These measures helped to keep witch-hunting in check. Still, as diabolism was not absent and torture was often permitted in witchcraft trials, the potential existed for large-scale hunts.

In 1668 a major hunt, which developed in the Swedish province of Dalecarlia, spread through the northern part of the country. Involving a large number of children among both the accusers and the accused, the hunt began when several children claimed that their parents, neighbours, and older children had taken them to a witches' Sabbath. King Charles XI appointed a number of royal commissions to investigate the accusations, which resulted in several death sentences. In total, more than two hundred people were executed from 1668 to the late 1670s when the panic ended, following confessions by many of the accusers that the charges had been groundless.[23]

Finland wasn't involved in witch-hunting until 1640, when Isaac Rothovius, vice-chancellor of Turku Academy, the first Finnish university, initiated a campaign at the university directed against the practice of sorcery, which he considered to be demonic magic. In the 1660s the full concept of witchcraft appeared in Finnish trials. It was introduced by Nils Psilander, a judge in the Swedish-speaking province of Ahvenanmaa who had been educated at Tartu Academy, where he had become familiar with German judicial thought regarding witchcraft. Between 1666 and 1674 he conducted a campaign against people accused of soothsaying and sorcery, which he interpreted in terms of demonological theory. Although torture was used, sceptical juries kept the hunt from getting out of control.

Witch trials in Finland's Swedish-speaking province of Ostrobothnia were inspired by the witch-hunt in the Swedish province of Dalecarlia. Here charges of witchcraft came mainly from below. Also, as there was no Psilander here to introduce witchcraft theories, the charges against the accused remained essentially those of *maleficia*. With the absence of torture to obtain denunciations, the hunt remained limited.[24]

Countries east of the Holy Roman Empire did not become involved in witch-hunting anywhere to the same extent as those west of its eastern borders. Only Poland of eastern European countries prosecuted witches in great numbers. Here witch-hunting was encouraged by the belief that *maleficium* was practised with the help of the devil, a belief imported from Germany in the late sixteenth and early seventeenth centuries. These views were further encouraged by the fact that the central government had little effective control over the municipal courts, which tried the great majority of witchcraft cases. While throughout the late sixteenth and early seventeenth century witch trials were still within the purview of ecclesiastical courts, by the late seventeenth century local municipal courts increasingly assumed jurisdiction over such trials, and municipal courts imposed much harsher sentences than had the ecclesiastical ones. Witch trials were further encouraged by international conflict brought on by the first northern war against Sweden and Russia (1655-60), which ravaged the country. This enhanced Catholic antagonism toward the Protestant minority, which in turn encouraged witchcraft prosecutions in Poland.[25]

Although Hungary had a history of witchcraft, it was only when Benedict Carpzov's *Practica Rerum Criminalium* became part of Hungarian law in 1696 that Western demonological ideas became readily accessible to Hungarian judges. At the same time, inquisitorial legal procedures weren't introduced into Hungary until the 1580s. All this discouraged witch-hunting. Nevertheless, Hungary experienced occasional hunts. These began in the 1580s with a succession of isolated trials, which at times were accompanied by panic. Thus, accusations of witchcraft were levelled at people who during a drought in 1615 were accused of threatening to use witch-craft to destroy Hungary and Transylvania with hailstones.[26]

The practices of *maleficium* had a long history in Russia. However, un-like in the West where *maleficium* eventually became synonymous with devil worship, in Russia it continued to be viewed as the remnant of an old superstition. This did not mean, however, that the practice of *maleficium* was not prosecuted in Russia. Thus, the eleventh and twelfth century wit-nessed the execution of a fairly large number of Russian men and women for using magic to cause drought. In the middle of the sixteenth century, witches began to be prosecuted in secular rather than religious courts, which resulted in an increase in the number of prosecutions. Forty-seven trials, involving ninety-nine defendants, were referred to Moscow for con-firmation and sentencing between 1622 and 1700. Of the defendants, at least ten were sentenced to death. Some trials, again, did not reach Mos-cow for referral. Thus, a small number of trials between 1656 and 1660 in the town of Lukh led to the execution of five of twenty-five people who had been accused of practising witchcraft.[27]

Although some of the earliest witchcraft trials took place in Italian lands, far fewer people were condemned here for practising witchcraft than in most other areas of Europe. This was also true of Spain and Portu-gal. The main reason for this was the rare application of extreme torture because inquisitors were required to adhere to fairly strict rules of proce-dure.[28] This inhibited the development of extreme, diabolical witch-beliefs and discouraged witch-hunting. Also, while people were accused of prac-tising magic, including love magic and healing, this was seldom seen as indicating they derived their power through a pact with the Devil whom they worshipped collectively. Nor were these magical practices consid-ered to be maleficent. They were to be prosecuted, however, not to protect society from the power of Satan, but rather to correct error and purify the faith.

Hughes calls the persecution of the witches during the Middle Ages a holocaust. Larner calls the witch-hunts during the sixteenth and seven-teenth century a holocaust.[29] Because many of the witches killed were women, Shuttle and Redgrove concluded that the witch-hunts during the Middle Ages were not only genocide directed against a nature religion, but also one directed by anti-sexual, male-dominated Churches against women and women's sexuality. They further argue that witchcraft was a religion, a nature religion whose main proponents were women, and that this genocide was not unlike the slaughter of the Jews in Nazi Germany.[30]

The view that the widespread persecution of witches involved the persecution of a pre-Christian religion first received wide circulation in

1921 when Margaret Murray brought out her book entitled *The Witch-Cult in Western Europe*. Murray's view, however, is questioned by Alan Mac-farlane. Pointing to his study of witch-hunts in Essex, he states that, according to his evidence, Murray's picture of a persecuted witch-cult at the time of the witch-hunts seems far too sophisticated and articulate for the society of the time. Nevertheless, he supports Murray's claim that the accusations against the witches were based on more than mere intolerant superstition.[31]

Similar views are expressed by researchers who see the dynamics of the witch-hunts based, not on the persecution of a pre-Christian cult, but on the image of the witch, created by the religious establishment of the time. Norman Cohn, in his study of the witch-hunts in medieval Europe, argues that in constructing the image of the witch, the persecutors drew on actual experiences with magic, on peasant beliefs regarding magic and witchcraft, and on reports from people who claimed to be witches. These were systematized into a coherent image of the witch by the inquisitors, largely through the use of torture. Cohn characterizes the witch-hunts as an example of a massive killing of innocent people by a bureaucracy acting in accordance with beliefs that, unknown or rejected in earlier centuries, had come to be taken as self-evident truths. The witch-hunts give evidence of the "power of the human imagination to build up a stereotype and its reluctance to question the validity of a stereotype once it is generally accepted."[32]

A similar argument is made by Trevor-Roper, who maintains that the Dominican inquisitors discovered neither a concealed world of demons nor a systematic illusion in witchcraft. Just as in Christianity, there may have been residuals of paganism that survived in witchcraft. It was the inquisitors, however, who manufactured the idea of the witch and the kingdom of Satan, essentially from confessions forced out of people under torture. As such, the witch craze went through two phases. First came social tension and widespread uneasiness regarding the existence of unassimilated social groups who were suspect, not because they were practising sorcery, but because they did not conform to generally accepted beliefs and practices. The stereotype of the witch as the servant of Satan served to explain this deviance. Once created, the stereotype took on its own reality. The second stage of the witch craze developed out of the first in that, once manufactured, the stereotype of the witch and the kingdom of Satan provided a basis for wiping out those who did not conform to the general orthodoxy.[33] Trevor-Roper argues further that throughout the sixteenth and seventeenth centuries people accepted on faith the belief that the Church was engaged in a life-and-death struggle with Satan.[34] The witches were destroyed because they were seen as the representatives of evil, the followers of Satan.

Trevor-Roper, no doubt, overstates his case. As we have seen, extreme beliefs regarding witchcraft, those that identified the witches as agents of Satan, did not develop in all of Europe. They developed in those areas where torture, particularly extreme torture, was used to obtain confessions from the accused. On the basis of these forced confessions, a particular image of the witch was constructed: someone who, together with other witches, had entered into a pact with the Devil and worshipped him. A coherent picture was compiled of the nature of the contract between the witch and the Devil and of the type of worship in which witches were involved. This picture also included a description of the devil-worshipping cult, which was seen to threaten the Christian Church. The most severe hunts took place in France, Germany and Switzerland, in those areas where the witch demonology was most developed and where there were few restraints on court officials who sought to wipe out the people they considered to be the agents of Satan and the enemies of the Christian Church.

Rates of execution reflect the severity of persecution. In regions where fears of demonology dominated, as many as 90 percent of the accused were put to death. This contrasted with executions of just 25 per cent in areas like Norway, where the accused were tried essentially for practising *maleficium*. Differences in the belief systems of the people who tried the witches were the chief cause for these variations. High execution rates were invariably traceable to the link that court officials established between witchcraft and demonology. Those who identified witches as agents of Satan were convinced that, in destroying witches, they were eliminating a Devil-worshipping cult that threatened Christ and his Church.

Larner argues that the witchcraft persecutions in Europe coincided with the period during which Christianity was a political ideology. The witch-hunts continued as long as rulers saw in religion a means of establishing and sustaining their authority. Although Christianity continued to be an important means of social control following the hunts, it lost its political utility to those in power.[35]

One may well ask how many people were destroyed during the witch-hunts. On this point there is wide disagreement among scholars. Hughes claims that some 9 million people were destroyed as part of the war on the witches.[36] At the other extreme, Briggs, who based his work largely on some four hundred witch trials in Lorraine, claims about forty thousand people were destroyed during the hunts.[37] Levack puts the number close to sixty thousand,[38] while Bacon suggests that somewhere between three hundred thousand/two million persons were executed as witches.[39] Starkey points out that the exact number of deaths caused by the witch-hunts can never be accurately known, but she estimates that the number of victims runs into the hundreds of thousands.[40] Larner doesn't even attempt to give an estimate of the number of victims, but endeavours instead to convey the complexity of trying to arrive at a number. One reason for the difficulty is the inadequacy of the sources. We do not know what sources were lost, nor will we ever know of the number of people who died while being arrested or interrogated.[41] Rather than trials for murder, in which court records provide fairly accurate information both on the number of trials and executions, she sees the witch-hunts as exhibiting the characteristics of a smallpox epidemic, for which official state records would be much less reliable.

Whatever the number of victims, the significance of the witch-hunts for purpose of this study lies not in the number of people killed but in the manner in which they were tried and executed. This is particularly true of the people who were accused and tried for practising demonology. In these cases people were ultimately tried, not for what they did, but for what they represented; an image was imposed upon them, spelling out who and what they were. They were tried for being agents of the Devil, enemies of Christianity, and this image was created by the judicial system. In prosecuting and killing people, the prosecutors were destroying an enemy they had created through their own beliefs. Prosecutors acting on these motives killed witches because they believed them to be part of a religion that posed a direct threat to Christ and his Church on earth. There was no room in Christendom for the agents of Satan. In order for Christendom to flourish, the agents of Satan had to be eradicated.

3
Genocide in Turkish Armenia

The almost total annihilation of the Armenians in Turkey took place as the Young Turks sought to transform the Ottoman Empire from an Islamic state to a tribal society. Whereas Islam left room for Christian communities, albeit at a lower status than their Muslim counterparts, there was little room for the Armenians in a Turkish tribal society. This was particularly true during the First World War, when the Young Turks sought to appeal to Turkish nationalism and Islamic militancy to hold at bay the military catastrophe threatening to overwhelm them. In this situation the Armenian outsider became the scapegoat for many of Turkey's problems.

Robert Melson argues that the manner in which the Young Turks defined their national group was at the root of the Armenian genocide, and traces parallels to Nazi Germany.[1] Chalk and Jonassohn see the genocide of the Armenians during the First World War as the first of the modern ideologically motivated genocides, a category into which they also place the Nazi destruction of European Jewry.[2]

Historical background

An ancient people who have lived in the same area for millennia, the Armenians adopted Christianity early in their history, adhering to it despite suffering persecution for their faith from the various groups that overran their homeland. In the Ottoman Empire, despite the second-class citizenship accorded them because of their religion, the Armenians lived in relative peace as long as the empire was expanding. As the empire declined because of its inability to compete with European powers to the west and north, Ottoman rule became more repressive. Armenians and other Christian minorities found themselves more heavily taxed, in part to pay for the lavish expenditures of the sultan's court. Harsh taxation resulted in several revolts, which led to further suppression. European nations intervened, and in 1876 sought to force the sultan to grant minorities more liberties.

He, in turn, resented foreign interference. His half-hearted reforms were therefore short-lived, with the instability accompanying these endeavours exacerbating the general disarray in the empire, where robbery and murder were becoming commonplace.

These events culminated in Russian interference and the outbreak of war between Russia and Turkey in 1877. The Treaty of San Stefano, which concluded the war, granted autonomy to a large Bulgarian state, and independence to Serbia, Montenegro, and Romania. Also, Russian troops were to be stationed on Ottoman soil until the Turks made effective reforms in Turkish Armenia. Britain, however, felt that the Treaty of San Stefano jeopardized its imperial interests and agitated for its revision. At a congress in Berlin in mid-1878, some of the territory lost by the Ottomans was restored to them, and Russian troops were required to leave Ottoman soil immediately. Their departure essentially meant that no reforms would be carried out in Turkish Armenia.

Instead, the Ottoman government became more repressive in its policies, arming Kurdish tribesmen to wreak havoc among the Armenians. Although European powers requested that the sultan put an end to Kurdish depredations, they had become too involved in their own imperial expansions to intervene effectively. Nonetheless, in May 1895 a joint British, French, and Russian plan was forced upon the sultan, which provided, among other things, for the consolidation of the Armenian provinces and the creation of a permanent control commission that would oversee reforms in Turkey. The European intercession, unsustained by force, only made the situation worse for the Armenians. Even as Abdul-Hamid appeared to agree to the reform program in October 1895, Armenians in Trebizond were being massacred. The slaughter of between one hundred thousand/two hundred thousand Armenians and the forced conversion of the population of scores of villages to the Muslim religion was Abdul-Hamid's response to European interference.

In the meantime, opposition to the sultan's rule grew among the Turkish population and led to the formation of the Committee of Union and Progress (CUP), generally referred to as the Young Turks. A revolt among the army units belonging to this group forced Abdul-Hamid to agree to the formation of a constitutional monarchy in 1908. Armenian optimism resulting from this change was to be short-lived. The Young Turk revolution emboldened Austria-Hungary to annex Bosnia-Herzegovina, Bulgaria to declare its full independence, Crete to declare union with Greece, and Italy to use force to assert its claim to Tripoli and the Libyan hinterland. Taking advantage of this chaos, which was accompanied by the further massacre of Armenians, Turkish conservatives sought to stage a countercoup to restore the sultan's authority. At the same time, to solidify its position, the Young Turk cabinet declared a state of siege and suspended normal constitutional rights. In a coup in 1913, the ultra-nationalist faction of the Young Turk party seized control of the government and put in place a regime dominated by the triumvirate consisting of: Enver, minister of war; Talaat, minister of the interior; and Jemal, the military governor of Constantinople.

Turkey's entry into the World War in 1914 essentially extinguished the possibility of resolving the Armenian Question through administrative reforms. Intransigence on this issue was further encouraged by changes in Turkish nationalism. Embraced by the ultra-nationalists among the Young Turks, Turkism envisaged a homogeneous Turkish state based on the concept of one nation and one people replacing the multinational Ottoman Empire. This left little room for minorities such as the Armenians. Their situation worsened when the war turned out to be a catastrophe of unmitigated disasters for the Turks. Rather than blame themselves, they blamed the "traitorous activities" of the Armenians for their defeats at the hand of the Russians. With this, Armenians came to be regarded as enemy agents within Turkey.

The genocide

While the Young Turks laid the institutional, ideological, and social base for modern Turkey, the regime, especially in its later phases, was nothing less than a disaster for the Armenians. In fact, it was the Committee of Union and Progress, headed by Talaat Pasha, minister of the interior, and Enver Pasha, minister of war, that undertook the disarmament and deportation of the Armenians, which eventually led to the destruction of the Armenian people.

Suggestions of Turkish intentions appeared in February 1915, when Armenian troops serving with the Ottoman military were disarmed, demobilized, and organized into labour battalions. They were fed scraps of food, forced to work under inhumane conditions and, should they fall sick, left to die. In other instances, squads of fifty or a hundred men were taken, bound together in groups of four, and then marched to a secluded spot where they were shot.[3] Concurrently, Armenian civilians were disarmed, with each community being required to give up a specified number of weapons. If community leaders did not come up with the number required, they were arrested for withholding arms; if they were able to deliver the required number, they were arrested for harbouring conspiratorial intentions against the government.

Disarmament was followed by deportation. In this, Enver Pasha's Ministry of War oversaw the disarmed labor battalions, while Talaat Pasha's Ministry of the Interior directed the deportation of the civilian population. In particular, in its early stages, to assure the deportations would meet with minimum resistance, emphasis was placed on the arrest and deportation of the Armenian elite, especially the educated, be they writers, lawyers or teachers, essentially all those who had the means or influence to serve as spokespersons for the Armenians, could call world attention to the Armenian plight, or were in a position to organize the Armenians to resist government actions.

With the exception of areas such as Smyrna and Aleppo, the mass deportations of Armenians were countrywide. Patterns of deportation varied, as local officials were allowed some latitude. The few officials who resisted the deportations were removed from office, or rendered ineffectual by the local branches of the ruling party. Although in some regions activity was limited to the relocation of people, and the lives of both men and women were spared, elsewhere "deportations" were essentially massacres. In some areas the men might be massacred and the women forced to convert to Islam. In areas that were of strategic importance due to the proximity of the advancing Russian army, the military authority, with the help of local Kurds, carried out exterminations of the civilian population.

Toynbee describes the common pattern of the deportations:

> On a certain date in whatever town or village it might be ... the public crier went through the streets announcing that every male Armenian must present himself forthwith at the Government Building. In some cases the warning was given by the soldiery or gendarmerie slaughtering every male Armenian they encountered in the streets . . . but usually a summons to the Government Building was the preliminary stage. The men presented themselves in their working clothes. . . . When they arrived, they were thrown without explanation into prison, kept there a day or two, and then marched out of the town in batches, roped man to man, along some southerly or southeasterly road. They were starting, they were told, on a long journey--to Mosul or perhaps to Baghdad. . . . But they had not long to ponder over their plight, for they were halted and massacred at the first lonely place on the road. The same process was applied to those other Armenian men . . . who had been imprisoned during the winter months on the charge of conspiracy or concealment of arms.[4]

Those who were spared had to undergo other horrors. While marched through towns and villages, defenceless Armenians were repeatedly attacked, sometimes by brigands but more frequently by Turkish or Kurdish villagers. Rather than "protect" the deportees, which was what they supposedly had been assigned to do, the gendarmerie from the Ministry of the Interior frequently joined in the attacks.

Armenians deported by rail from the metropolitan centers and the railway zone fared little better. They were packed into cattle cars and were turned out into the open to wait for days and weeks for rolling stock or for the completion of repairs in railway lines. They were forced across the mountains on foot and died by the thousands of hunger, exposure, and epidemics in the concentration camps that grew up along the route. Finally, Toynbee reports, they were marooned with the other exiles in the worst, most remote, desert areas at the disposal of the government, with no food, shelter, or clothing.[5] A German soldier, on hearing of the deportations, in 1916 went to the Armenian camps in Meskene and Aleppo. He described a situation where people were starving to death:

> I saw men gone mad, feeding on their own excrement, women cooking their newborn children . . . people lay apathetically among the heaps of dead and emaciated bodies, waiting for death... Yet all this is still only a fraction of what I saw with my own eyes or what was related to me by friends and travellers, or by the outcasts themselves.[6]

Toynbee comments on the timing and intent of the deportations:

> The months of April and May were assigned to the clearance of Cilicia; June and July were reserved for the east; the western centers along the railway were given their turn in August and September; and at the same time the process was extended, for completeness' sake, to the outlying Armenian communities in the extreme southeast. It was a deliberate, systematic attempt to eradicate the Armenian population throughout the Ottoman Empire, and it has certainly met with a large measure of success.[7]

As is the case with all extensive massacres or genocides, sources disagree on how many people were killed, with those seeking to deny the genocide minimizing the number and those seeking to affirm the genocide often maximizing it. There are no precise figures on the extent of the destruction, which is perhaps natural because the Turkish government is denying even today that this genocide took place. However, Toynbee sought to make an estimate of the number of Armenians destroyed. Using the Armenian Patriarchate figures as a base, he estimated the Armenian mid-nineteenth century population in the Ottoman Empire as standing at 2.5 million. He argued that, by the outbreak of war, this fell to 2.1 million as a result of massacres and emigration. Then, in case the Patriarchate figures may have been inflated, he averaged these figures with those from Ottoman census statistics (which put the Armenian population of the day at 1.1 million) to arrive at the predeportation figure of 1.6 million (the average of 2.1 and 1.1).[8]

He estimated that some 182,000 Armenians escaped deportation by fleeing to Egypt or the Russian Caucasus. He subtracted from the number deported the Armenian population of Smyrna and Constantinople, who had not been deported. He calculated that the refugees plus the population of Smyrna and Constantinople came to a total of 350,000. In addition, he calculated that converts to Islam, as well as the number of Armenian Catholics and Protestants stood at 250,000, who were also not deported. This meant that 600,000 Armenians were spared deportation, while one million Armenians were deported. Of the one million Armenians deported, some 60 per cent were massacred or otherwise destroyed.[9] He concludes:

> We can sum up this statistical enquiry by saying that, as far as our defective information carries us, about an equal number of Armenians in Turkey seem to have escaped, to have perished, and to have survived deportation in 1915; and we shall not be far wrong, if in round numbers, we estimate each of these categories at 600,000.[10]

Toynbee's analysis covers only the winter of 1915 and the spring of 1916. Therefore, it does not take account of what happened to the Armenian deportees in the latter part of 1916. Nor does it consider the fate of the Armenians who were deported from some of the major urban areas after 1916. Aram Andonian presents an idea of the extent of the destruction in this regard:

> Three great massacres took place after 1916. . . . Men, women, and children from Constantinople and the surrounding district, from the Anatolian railway line and Cilicia, were driven into the desert, where they met people from the six Armenian provinces and from the shores of the Black Sea, but this latter contingent consisted only of women, girls and boys of seven and under, as every male over seven had been slaughtered. All these were the victims of the three massacres. The first massacre was that of Resul-Ain, in which 70,000 people were killed; the second took place at Intilli, where there were 50,000 people assembled, most of them

working on a tunnel of the Baghdad Railway; and the third, which was the most fearful of all, at Der Zor, where Zia Bey slaughtered nearly 200,000 Armenians. . . . These figures only give the numbers of people killed by massacre. If we add to their numbers the victims of misery, sickness and hunger, especially in Res-ul-Ain and Der Zor, the number of Armenians who were slain or died in the desert will exceed a million.[11]

Johannes Lepsius also estimates that the Turks killed about one million Armenians.[12] Boyajian suggests that 1.5 million Armenians perished,[13] a figure also mentioned by Dekmejian.[14] Melson suggests that this higher figure may reflect the victims from 1915 to1923.[15] By the latter date, the Armenians had essentially been eliminated from Turkey.

Unlike the massacres of 1894 to 1896, where the connection between Sultan Abdul-Hamid II and the violence was less clear-cut, the deportation and massacres carried out during the First World War were clearly ordered by the CPU under the direction of Enver and Talaat. This may be observed from an interview the American ambassador had with Enver Pasha, in which Ambassador Morgenthau sought to intercede on behalf of the Armenians.

> In another talk with Enver I began by suggesting that the Central Government was probably not to blame for the massacres. I thought this would not be displeasing to him.
>
> 'Of course, I know that the Cabinet would never order such terrible things as have taken place,' I said. 'You and Talaat and the rest of the Committee can hardly be held responsible. Undoubtedly your subordinates have gone much further than you have ever intended. I realize that it is not always easy to control your underlings.'
>
> Enver straightened up at once. I saw that my remarks, far from smoothing the way to a quiet and friendly discussion, had greatly offended him. I had intimated that things could happen in Turkey for which he and his associates were not responsible.
>
> 'You are greatly mistaken,' he said. 'We have this country absolutely under our control. I have no desire to shift the blame on to our underlings and I am entirely willing to accept the responsibility myself for everything that has taken place. The Cabinet itself has ordered the deportations. I am convinced that we are completely justified in doing this owing to the hostile attitude of the Armenians toward the Ottoman Government, but we are the real rulers of Turkey, and no underling would dare proceed in a

matter of this kind without our orders.'[16]

As soon as the Armenian population had been physically removed or liquidated, their lands were taken over by Turks or Kurds. All cultural traces of the former inhabitants, be these churches or place names, were eradicated. Thus ended the Armenian presence in Turkey, remarks Kuper, reduced from a population of about 2 million to less than 25,000 today.[17]

Causes and effects

To explain why the Turks found it necessary to destroy the Armenians, scholars such as Bernard Lewis argue that the Turks were provoked in their aggression, in large part by the circumstances facing them. He states:

> For the Turks, the Armenian movement was the deadliest of all threats. From the conquered lands of the Serbs, Bulgers, Albanians, and Greeks, they could, however reluctantly, withdraw, abandoning distant provinces and bringing the Imperial frontier nearer home. But the Armenians, stretching across Turkey-in-Asia from the Caucasian frontier to the Mediterranean coast, lay in the very heart of the Turkish homeland—and to renounce these lands would have meant not the truncation, but the dissolution of the Turkish state. Turkish and Armenian villages, inextricably mixed, had for centuries lived in neighbourly association. Now a desperate struggle between them began—a struggle between two nations for the possession of a single homeland, which ended with the terrible holocaust of 1915, when a million and a half Armenians perished.[18]

Lewis's suggestion that the Armenians and Turks were somehow equal belies the facts. He implies that both had equal military and political force at their disposal to defend their interests. The fact is that the Armenians had neither a police force nor an army wherewith to defend themselves, never mind the power to conquer the Turks. Nor were they united under one political party or any other social organization. Nor did the Armenians in any way threaten the Turks, as Lewis insinuates, or as a collective group seek to betray the Turks to the Russians in the hope of gaining their independence. Rather, their only realistic alternative was to realize their aspirations within the Ottoman Empire, essentially through achieving autonomy within it. After all, they were too scattered throughout the empire to make independence a realistic option. At the same time, they sought greater government protection from Kurdish depredations. It was self-protection and the drive for greater autonomy and equality, rather than the desire for independence, that motivated them to seek changes within the empire. If the Turks viewed the Armenians as a threat, this perception was due not so much to Armenian actions as to changes in the attitudes of the Turks themselves. Rather than looking at the Armenians, Melson suggests, we should be looking at the Turks to isolate the dynamics leading to the genocide.[19]

Several changes in Turkey had a disastrous effect on the Armenians. One of these was the retreat of the Ottoman Empire from Europe to Anatolia. Turkey's loss of all its European territory between 1908 and 1913, with the exception of a strip to protect the Straits of Istanbul, resulted in the diminution of the multinational and multi-religious character of its empire and left the Armenians as the largest Christian minority remaining under Ottoman rule. At the same time, they were not merely a minority. Despite suppression, they had undergone social, economic, and cultural changes that had culminated in a type of renaissance. In fact, some of the massacres under Abdul-Hamid II had been carried out, in part, to remind them that despite their advances they were still in an inferior position.

The genocide was made possible by the nationalist revolution which the Young Turks had undergone since coming to power in 1908, a transformation that was part and parcel of the broader transformation of the Ottoman Empire. Prior to the defeats of 1908 and 1913, Ottoman rulers had sought to experiment with different ideological systems that could form the base for pulling together the various centrifugal forces in the empire and preserving its unity. One of these was Ottomanism. Supported by the different minorities, including the Armenian Dashneks, as well as by the liberal wing of the Young Turk movement, led by Prince Sabahaddin, it sought to preserve the unity of the empire by recognizing its multi-religious and multi-ethnic nature. To do so, it permitted greater autonomy to the minority *millets*. At the same time, it advocated greater equality for all Ottomans, no matter what their religious or ethnic background. It briefly came into its own after the overthrow of the Sultan in 1908. This short period of hope came to an end following the military defeats that led to the secession of the major Christian minorities from the empire.

The Turks then turned to a pan-Islamic ideology that sought to use the Muslim religion as the basis for the empire's unity. The hope that Islam might serve as a base for imperial unity was dealt a severe blow, however, following the revolt and secession of Muslim minorities, especially in Albania and Macedonia. It was discarded as a means of uniting the empire when, during World War I, many of the Arabs sided with Britain rather than Turkey.

This caused the Turks increasingly to turn to the ideology of pan-Turanism (pan-Turkism) as a means of sustaining the unity of the empire. This was based on the belief that in ancient times there had existed a tribal unity among Turkish peoples, based on race, religion and language. The territory occupied by Turanian people, it was believed, stretched from Constantinople, where their rule was centralized, all the way to China. The Armenians were seen to break up this area of contiguous settlement.

The Pan-Turanists envisaged re-creating this pre-Ottoman and pre-Islamic Turkish Empire in Central Asian lands which they called Turan. As such, they envisaged bringing about the political unification of all Turkic-speaking peoples, no matter whether they lived in Russia, central Asia, Kazan or the Caucasus.[20] Although these aspirations had little chance of being realized, pan-Turanism with its vision of an empire that rivalled the Ottoman Empire in size but had none of its minority problems, intensified Turkish ethnocentrism and made them less inclined to accommodate the needs and interests of non-Turkish minorities.

The most eloquent spokesman of Turanism was Ziya Gölkap, the "father of Turkish nationalism," who advocated the creation of a homogeneous Turkish nation. He defined the nation as "a society consisting of people who speak the same language, have had the same education and are united in their religious, moral and aesthetic ideals - in short, those who have a common culture and religion."[21] He argued that history involved the ceaseless struggle between nations for power and territory. In this struggle, some nations run the risk of physical elimination. Gölkap looked to the distant Turkish past as a sort of Golden Age. He revelled in the military exploits of "Turkish" conquerors such as Genghis Khan and Timur Babur, comparing their times favourably with what he saw as Turkish weakness and decadence in his time.

According to him, the nation had not only a physical but also a moral dimension. Nationalism, as such, was a kind of religion that replaced the belief in God. In his view, every kind of action was permissible for the sake of the nation. This view of the nation, of course, excluded the Armenians and other minorities. Unlike Ottomanism, which accorded minorities a place in the empire and spelled out obligations of the rulers towards them, Turkism placed non-Turkish groups outside the concerns of Turkish rulers, with groups such as the Armenians being viewed as having no legitimate place in Turkish society.

The exclusivist nature of Turkish nationalism, although important, was not the only factor contributing to the genocide. Other factors also enhanced Turkish antagonism towards the Armenians, one being the Turkish view of the Armenians as a "mercantile race." Commerce was an area to which Armenians were attracted because they had little opportunity for advancement in government or the military. By the early years of the twentieth century, Armenians controlled some 60 per cent of imports, 40 per cent of exports, and at least 80 per cent of the commerce in the interior of the empire.[22] Although the vast majority of Armenians were peasants, Armenian dominance in trade led the Turks to view the entire people as exploiters.

Their ethnic and cultural distinctiveness became a problem for the Armenians. The Turkish *millet* system, which granted appreciable autonomy to the Armenians in spiritual and educational matters and allowed them to exercise limited judicial functions, set apart not only the Armenians but also other non-Turkish groups. However, the Armenians were the largest Christian minority that had not yet won its freedom from Ottoman control. Moreover, although dispersed across the empire, the great mass of Armenian peasants lived in eastern Anatolia, which the Turks claimed as the heartland of their nation. A sizable Armenian population also lived across the border in Russia. Irredentist movements among the latter no doubt made Turkish rulers uneasy. This uneasiness would have been intensified by Turkey's catastrophic military defeats during the war. The last comparable defeats had come to an end in 1913, and saw several Christian states being carved out of Turkish territory. The new Armenian Christian state, which would emerge from their present defeats, would arise, not in Europe, but in the heartland of Turkey.[23]

Although the Turkish leaders of the Committee of Union and Progress were not religious fanatics, the declaration at the beginning of the First World War that the country was engaged in a holy war in defence of Islam inflamed religious passion. This made little allowance for the prospect of a Christian state arising in the heartland of Turkey. The very possibility also served to remind the Turks of the long history of conflict between Christians and Muslims, a history evident in the new Christian states of Bulgaria and Serbia, and in the million Muslim refugees who had fled to Turkey during the Balkan wars. The long history of the intervention of foreign nations on behalf of the Christian subjects of the Ottoman Empire arose out of, and was superimposed on, this volatile situation. To this was added the concern that these outside powers were motivated by predatory interests and were intent on dismembering the Ottoman Empire, whose decline was already well under way. The Turks had entered the World War to reverse this trend, but after several disastrous campaigns, they were desperately defending their crumbling state. Kuper says that, under these circumstances, driven by an extreme and exclusivist nationalism, by years of frustration over outside interference on behalf of Christians in the empire, and by the suspicion that the Armenians sympathized with, and were betraying them to, the Russians, the Turks slaughtered the minority group.[24]

All these factors allowed the Turks to link problems facing their state during the First World War to the progress of the minority and to, in turn, connect this minority with an enemy state. The government, therefore, undertook to destroy the Armenians, a goal facilitated by war conditions. The war, including Turkish defeats resulting therefrom, heightened Turkish insecurity. War conditions enabled the government to implement measures to deal with the minority that would have been difficult to carry out in peacetime. The genocide became what Dekmejian calls a "medium of salvation."[25] The Armenians were a scapegoat sacrificed for all the frustrations encountered by the Turks in their desperate attempt to sustain a crumbling empire. At the same time, the Armenian genocide became an assertion of the newly formulated pan-Turanism, serving as a substitute for expansionist aspirations that were being frustrated by Turkish defeats on the battlefield. Simultaneously, it served to certify that any defeats would not result in another Christian state being carved out of Turkish territory, in particular territory the Turks considered to be the very heart of their nation.

4

The Man-Made Famine and Stalin's War on the Enemies of the People

Hryshko describes the famine in Ukraine between 1932 and 1933 as the "Ukrainian holocaust," and characterizes the holocaust as "the systematic destruction of a certain race, class, or nation by offering this group in sacrifice, as it were, to the historic aims of a particular ideology. Thus the word applies to those national or socio-political genocides that are justified by the single-minded worshipping of such an ideology."[1] According to Conquest, the famine during which some seven million people died was part of a larger holocaust that destroyed some eighteen million people between 1929 and 1939. He sees little difference between Nazism and communism, arguing that both were inspired by utopian aspirations and energized by the drive to destroy.[2] While focussing on the famine in Ukraine, this chapter will also explore Stalin's attack on the Communist Party, the Soviet military, and Soviet society in general to isolate the dynamics that may have caused historians to characterize these events as holocausts.

The famine in Ukraine cannot be separated from Stalin's plan to build socialism in one country. At its base was a program of industrialization, to be financed through the sale of agricultural products. To secure the highest profits from the sale of agricultural goods, the state sought to pay peasants as little as possible for their produce and sell it at market value. When peasants responded by decreasing the acreage seeded or hoarding products until they could get a better price, the Communist Party started requisitioning these goods. Lenin had pursued this policy during the early 1920s, when he forcibly took grain from the peasants to feed the urban centers. State requisitions, combined with drought in 1920 and 1921, resulted in a famine in which four to five million people perished.[3] More people would have died had the Bolsheviks not appealed for international aid. A quick response from the United States and Europe helped to stabilize the situation. Conditions were further improved when Lenin ceased his requisitions and allowed the peasants to sell their products on the open market.

The people benefiting most from market sales were kulaks, or better-off peasants. While generally not rich, they had enough land on which they could produce more than they consumed. Private ownership of land, however, did not fit the view of Lenin's successor, Stalin, of how a socialist society should be ordered. Also, as the state often sought to obtain agricultural products at a price that did not cover production costs, the peasants were disinclined to sell to the government. This reluctance was reinforced by the poor quality of the manufactured goods produced by the new state industries that the peasants received in return for their products. This put the government into a difficult position, for without the financial benefits it hoped to reap from the sale of agricultural products, it would be unable to pursue its ambitious program of industrialization. Stalin dealt with this by blaming in particular the richer peasants for the problem, branding them rural capitalists who were ideologically opposed to the Communist Party and its endeavours to industrialize the Soviet Union.[4]

The countrywide terror against the peasantry was thus based on both ideology and power. Ideology demanded that the independent peasantry be destroyed as an economic class; power demanded that the products of the countryside be taken into the hands of the state.[5] To attain these goals, Stalin embarked upon a program which would eliminate the kulaks as a class; replace small private farms with large collective farms; and use War Communism, or the requisitioning of grain and other crops by force, if necessary, to procure the products the peasants, in particular the kulaks, were thought to be withholding.

When Stalin's drive to collectivize Soviet agriculture began in 1929, about 5 percent of peasants were considered to be kulaks. This economic definition of the kulak was essentially meaningless, however. Invented to interpret Soviet agriculture in the context of a Marxian model, the term kulak ultimately had ideological meaning. By defining the kulak in ideological terms, Stalin was able to accuse anyone perceived as standing in the way of his socialist offensive as being, not a human being, but a "class enemy." Kulaks were guilty of the irredeemable crime of having been born into the enemy class or having exhibited the values of this class. Any brutality could be used to eliminate them because they were the symbol of corruption standing in the way of creating the idealized society. Like the Jews under the Nazis, Bullock observes, anyone declared to be a kulak or class enemy was pushed out of society and relegated to subhuman status. As members of an outlawed class or race they were denied all human rights.[6]

The program to eliminate the kulak served a number of practical purposes. Vilifying kulaks as the rural class enemy served to direct the antagonism of their poorer neighbours towards this group, and helped to justify the government's repressive measures against the peasantry. At the same time, making the drive for collectivization a war against the "selfish kulak" helped to recruit other peasants to the cause of collectivization, if for no other reasons than to escape their fate. All people declared to be kulaks, from the heads of the household down to infant children, were to be excluded from the collectives. Some were shot and others deported. Trainloads of kulaks were shipped to the north, the forests, the steppes, or the deserts. Some starved to death or died of disease on the packed trains. Once they reached their destination, the men were separated from their families and sent to labour camps. Many didn't survive the forced marches. Their families were forced to look after themselves in a hostile environment.[7] It is not known exactly how many kulaks were deported during the program of forced collectivization. Bullock estimates that about ten to twelve million were deported, of which about a third had died by 1935.[8] He does not give a figure as to the number of kulaks shot or otherwise killed while villages were being dekulakized.

Meanwhile, the remaining peasantry were being forced to join collective farms, the so-called kolkhoz. The first five-year plan, adopted in the spring of 1929, projected that only about 20 per cent of the peasants would be collectivized during the life of the plan and that this would be accomplished on a voluntary basis, without state violence. Later that year, however, Stalin and the Politburo decided on full-scale collectivization, which was to be spearheaded by the Unified State Political Administration (OGPU) and its heavily armed military units. These units were reinforced by the regular army and eventually by over one hundred thousand urban cadres. The less well-off peasants, who were encouraged to wage war on their more prosperous neighbors, assisted this force locally.

Sometimes serious attempts were made to convince peasants to join the collective farms, but the authorities would brook no refusals. Villages that resisted the intruders were surrounded and machine-gunned into submission. At times whole areas, as in the Dniepropetrovsk region of Ukraine, rose in rebellion, only to be crushed by the Red Army. In many of these cases, peasants who were not killed through mass executions were deported to the Gulag camps and their villages set on fire.

Different cadres of party enthusiasts sought to outdo each other in reaching or exceeding the targets set for collectivization. By March 1930, less than three months into the campaign, more than half the peasantry of the Soviet Union had been driven from their homes onto collective farms. Then Stalin used a tactic he was often to apply later: blaming the excesses of his policies on others. In this case, he blamed the rapid collectivization and the cruelty with which it was being carried out on the party cadres, who in their enthusiasm were exceeding instructions. For a brief period he allowed the peasants to leave their collectives. This respite was short-lived, however, and was followed by an even more vigorous drive to force the peasants to join the collective farms. By 1932, two-thirds of all peasants were collectivized; by 1936 the figure reached 90 per cent.[9]

Soon after the collectivization was launched, another problem arose: the collective farms were not delivering as much grain as the state demanded of them. In 1930, when there had been a good harvest, the delivery of grain had not been a problem. By contrast, harvests in 1931 and 1932 were poor, but the state refused to lower its quota. Famine struck the major grain-growing areas of the Soviet Union. The effects were particularly severe in Ukraine, although not only because it was a major grain-producing area. Stalin despised Ukrainian nationalism,[10] and he took the opportunity of the famine to wage war on Ukraine's rural population, resulting in the "Ukrainian holocaust."

Although the 1932 grain harvest in Ukraine was smaller than average, the state increased its quota by over 40 per cent,[11] dismissing as anti-Bolshevik agitation any requests to lower the amount demanded from the farmers. A new decree declared all collective-farm products such as cattle and grain to be state property. A supplementary decree in August 1932 prescribed ten years' imprisonment or death by shooting for stealing collective farm property. At the same time, the state sent out party activists to take by force any of the grain it had been unable to acquire from the collective farmers.

Party activists, who might include the local teacher, members of the Young Pioneers, or party workers often from the region, broke into people's houses. In some cases, they left some potatoes, peas, or corn for feeding the family, but ideological zealots took not only the food and livestock, but also surplus clothing, ikons, samovars, painted carpets and even metal kitchen utensils, thinking they might be silver.[12]

Particularly in the larger villages, where concealment of such behaviour was easier, party officials used the promise of food to procure women during the early stages of the famine. District bosses might feast on white bread, meat, poultry, canned fruit, wines, sweets, and other luxury items. Employees of the establishments where they were served were issued the so-called Mikoyan ration, which contained twenty different articles of food. Meanwhile, the militia kept the starving peasants away from their doors.

Everyone was brutalized under these conditions. In Poltava province, a woman who was seven months pregnant died after she was beaten for plucking spring wheat. In the same province, a mother of three, seeking to feed her children after the arrest of her husband, was shot by an armed guard while she dug up potatoes in a kolkhoz field at night, and her children later starved to death. In another village of the province, the watchman "activist" beat to death the son of a dispossessed peasant for gleaning ears of corn in the kolkhoz field. In Kiev province, the head of a village Soviet shot seven people, including three children, for gathering grain.

Brigades searched houses every couple of weeks and seized peas, potatoes, and even beetroots from the peasants. People who were not starving aroused suspicion. One activist, after spending a long time searching the house of a peasant who had failed to swell up, finally discovered a small bag containing a mixture of flour and ground bark and leaves. He poured the contents into the village pond. Brigadiers carried both the dying as well as the dead to the cemetery to avoid an extra trip. Children and old people lay in the mass graves for several days still alive.

The government wasn't satisfied with merely using party activists to confiscate grain from the peasants. Under pressure from Moscow, the Ukrainian government passed a decree on 20 November 1932 that stopped all payment of grain remittances due to kolkhoz peasants for their "labor days" until the grain delivery quota had been met. Less than three weeks later, a further decree of the Ukrainian Soviet government and the Central Committee of the Ukrainian Communist Party accused six villages of having sabotaged grain deliveries. In punishment, sanctions were imposed on them, which included halting the supply of goods they received, removing all visible supplies from their cooperative and state stores, as well as purging them of all counter-revolutionary elements.

More measures followed. Villages that could not meet their quotas were literally blockaded. Whole districts were shut off from commercial supplies until they increased their grain deliveries. Eighty-eight out of a total of 358 districts in the Ukraine were punished in this way, punishment that was frequently followed by deporting the inhabitants of the "blockaded" districts to the north.

Despite the party's efforts, at the end of 1932 only 4.7 million tons of grain had been delivered - less than three-quarters of the quota. Stalin and the party did not regard this kindly, and once again put pressure on the Ukrainian authorities. During a joint sitting of the Moscow Politburo and Central Executive Committee in November 1932, Stalin blamed anti-Soviet elements and sabotage for the failure of grain deliveries. The Soviet mouthpiece, *Pravda*, called for a resolute struggle against the kulaks, especially in Ukraine. Other Soviet officials also blamed kulakdom: kulaks who had not been deported, well-off peasants inclining to kulakdom, kulaks who had escaped from exile and were being hidden by relatives who were traitors to the interests of the toilers. Once more the call was for war on the "class enemy."[13]

The peasants tried to survive in a variety of ways. Inadequate threshing, to hide grain in straw, was tried on a number of collective farms where farm leaders were sympathetic, but this proved to be an inadequate source of food. Some peasants put small quantities of grain into bottles, which they sealed with tar and hid in wells or ponds. As the government would confiscate grain taken to the local nationalized mill, local artisans constructed "hand mills." Although the constructor and user were arrested when these were found, the Ukrainian Communist Party press reported that some 200 of these domestic millstones were discovered in one month in one district and 755 in another.[14]

People made bread from nettles or from sunflower oil cake soaked in water, together with millet and buckwheat chaff and a little rye flour to hold the mixture together. Porridge might be prepared from one weed and biscuits from another. As it often contained whole grains, horse manure was used to prepare meals. Over the early winter people ate the remaining chickens and other livestock, followed by dogs and cats. Acorns were collected from under the snow and baked into bread, sometimes with a little bran or potato peelings added.

People were starving, and grain was available to feed them, often within miles of where they lived. Local granaries held stocks of "state reserves" for emergencies such as war, with the famine being considered insufficient reason to have it released. In some regions, warehouses were full of grain. Large heaps of grain piled up at a railway station in Poltava Province were starting to rot, but continued to be guarded by the Unified State Political Administration (OGPU) against the starving local people. Also, in the vicinity of the collective farms, butter was processed and prepared for export in plants to which only officials were admitted. In one area, several thousand tons of potatoes were kept under guard even after they had begun to rot, when they were transferred from the Potato Trust to the Alcohol Trust. However, they remained in the field until they were useless even for the production of alcohol. Officials blamed such waste on kulak sabotage, be this on the steppe, in the grain elevators or in the stores.[15]

Peasant protests tended to be spontaneous and uncoordinated, partly because of the physical weakness of the people. Moreover, the OGPU, which had networks of secret collaborators in the villages, used threats and blackmail to discourage resistance. Nevertheless, occasional riots occurred, even at the height of the famine in 1933. Thus, peasants of Novovoznesenske, Mikalov Province, attacked a grain dump near the end of April that was already rotting, only to be machine-gunned by OGPU guards. In another area, hungry villagers looted a grain warehouse in May 1933. Too weak to carry the corn home, some died on the way back while others were arrested the next day. Many of these were shot, while the remainder were given five- to ten-year sentences.

Driven by the fear of starvation, peasants left their villages to search for food, drawn by rumours that there was bread elsewhere, for example in Russia. Some were able to evade the border guards who sought to prevent the Ukrainian peasants from crossing into the neighboring republic. If peasants returned with bread and then were caught at the border, they were arrested and the bread confiscated. The OGPU also sought to prevent the starving from entering the Polish and Romanian border areas, resulting in hundreds of the inhabitants in frontier regions being killed while trying to cross the Dniester into Romania. Despite the danger, one estimate is that as early as mid-1932 almost three million people were on the move, crowding railway stations, trying to get to the towns or to any other place where they might find food.[16]

Until the final climax of famine in spring 1933, the majority of peasants tried to make do with makeshift edibles in the hope of surviving until the next harvest or until government relief arrived. Those who had personal property of value tried to sell it for food. Although it was difficult for a peasant to leave his village legally, many were able to reach Kiev or other centers because restrictions on movement were not effectively enforced. There, wives of officials, who had large rations, would market their surplus food at local bazaars to obtain the peasants' valuables at bargain prices. Peasants also flocked to the *Torgsin* ("Trade with Foreigners") stores in nearby villages, which accepted only foreign currency and precious metal or stones as payment. Here, golden crosses or earrings would buy a few kilograms of flour or fat, with a silver dollar purchasing perhaps fifty grams of sugar, or a cake of soap, and two hundred grams of rice.[17]

Instead of providing help for the starving peasants, the All-Union Central Committee adopted a special resolution in January 1933, charging Ukrainian officials with failure in their grain collection program. Thereupon, Stalin sent Pavel Postyshev, accompanied by a new head of the Ukrainian OGPU, V.A. Balitsky, to Ukraine to Bolshevize the Ukrainian Communist Party. Postyshev replaced 237 secretaries of Party district committees and 249 chairs of District Executive Committees. The OGPU also purged veterinarians, blaming them for high livestock mortality. About a hundred veterinarians were shot in Vinnytsia province alone from 1933 to 1937, many because horses had died of a fungus in the barley straw. In other instances, meteorologists were arrested and charged with falsifying weather forecasts in order to damage the harvest. At a different level, in March 1933, thirty-five civil servants from the Commissariats of Agriculture and State Farms were shot for damaging tractors or committing other acts of sabotage.[18]

In 1933, in Odessa and in Donets province over 40 per cent of collective farm chairs were removed, usually replaced by Russians. By the end of

1933, many of the leading party officials in Ukrainian villages were Russian. At the same time, at least forty thousand to fifty thousand people were sent to strengthen the rural Communist Party in Ukraine. Thus, in 1933 the provincial party committee and the provincial komsomol committee of Dnipropetrovsk province sent a combined force of nearly four hundred special collectors down to the district of Pavlohrad, which consisted of thirty-seven villages and eighty-seven collective farms. The Communist Party was being thrown into the struggle against the starving peasantry.

Although people had been dying all winter, death on a mass scale really began in early March 1933. People had swollen faces, legs and stomachs, and ate mice, rats, sparrows, ants, earthworms. They ground bones and leather into flour or cut up old skins and furs to make noodles. When the grass sprouted, they dug up the roots and ate the leaves and buds. They consumed dandelions, burdock, bluebells, willow root, and nettles. To keep the body from swelling, thereby prolonging survival, snails were boiled and their juices consumed, while their gristly meat was chopped fine, mixed with green leaves and eaten. In the Kuban and southern regions of Ukraine, people at times survived by trapping marmots and other small animals. Fish could be caught in some areas, though people could be sentenced for fishing in a river near their village.

At times, the desperate attempt at survival ended in death. Many people suffered from dropsy and died from starvation shortly after eating wild plants such as orach, sorrel, or nettles. In a village in Vinnytsia province the death rate was so high during the second half of May as a result of this, that a kolkhoz wagon had to be set aside to transport the dead to the cemetery each day, where bodies were thrown into a common grave.[19]

At the same time, people who could still move left the villages to search for food, in particular when the end of bread rationing came in April and stores were again opened in the towns. People who couldn't reach the cities gathered around the railway stations. At a small town in the Donbas, a railwayman reported families begging round the station and being chased off; by the spring of 1933, however, they arrived in ever-increasing numbers, and "lived, slept, died in streets or squares."[20] Peasants who were unable to reach the stations went to the railway lines to beg for bread from passing trains, from which a few crusts were sometimes thrown.

In large cities such as Kiev there was no famine for those who had jobs and ration cards, but only a kilogram of bread could be bought at a time, and supplies were inadequate. Queues half a kilometre long were common outside stores. People would each get a few hundred grams of bread, with hundreds at the end of the queue receiving nothing but tickets or chalked numbers on their hands to present the next day. Peasants flocked to the cities to join these queues or to buy from those who had managed to get bread. To avoid the roadblocks that had been set up to stop them, they would crawl through swamps and woods. The few, perhaps one out of ten thousand, who managed to get to the city, were seldom rewarded for their efforts; they starved to death in the city rather than at home.

In the towns, people hurried about their affairs as starving children and old people crawled among them, hardly able to beg. Dnipropetrovsk was overrun with starving peasants. One railway worker estimated that perhaps over half of the peasants who reached the Donbas in search of food "were living their last days, hours, and minutes."[21] In Kiev, Kharkov, and other major centers local authorities routinely went round the town during early mornings to clear away the corpses of those who had died during the night; it was not uncommon for the dying to be collected and thrown into graves together with the dead.

Peasants who managed to stay alive after reaching the city faced expulsion. In Kharkov, special operations were undertaken every week or so by the police with the help of squads of party members, to round up the starving peasants. One eyewitness described a police raid on several thousand peasants who had joined breadlines; they were put in railway wagons and transported to a pit near the station, where they were left to starve.[22]

Of a Ukrainian farm population of between twenty and twenty-five million, about four to five million died during the famine.[23] The casualty rate varied considerably by area, and even village, from 10 to 100 per cent of the population. The highest death rates occurred in the grain-growing provinces, where about one-quarter of the people died, although figures were higher in many villages. Elsewhere, death rates were lower, usually between 15 and 20 per cent. In northern Ukraine, a beet-growing area, it was lowest, partly because the forests, rivers, and lakes held animal and vegetable life that could be consumed.[24]

To avoid a diagnosis of starvation, doctors, who were state employees, recorded all sorts of causes of death, including "sudden illness." By the winter of 1932-33, death certificates were no longer filed. No word about the famine was allowed to appear in the press or elsewhere. People who referred to it were subject to arrest for anti-Soviet propaganda, and usually sentenced to five or more years in a labour camp. A lecturer at an agricultural school remarks how she was forbidden to use the word "famine," though food was insufficient even in town, and in one neighbouring village no one was left at all.[25]

Stalin's campaign against the kulak and peasant enemy of the people was followed by a more extensive campaign of terror, which included an attack on the Communist Party itself. Following Lenin's death in 1924, the party was divided as to how to attain the communist utopia. Stalin, who emerged as victor in the power struggle following Lenin's death, wanted to focus on transforming the Soviet Union into a socialist society, using Marx's writings as a guide to action. Of course, Marx had not outlined a plan for creating such a society. The Politburo did not have a unified strategy as to how to obtain this objective, nor did Stalin have a program for transforming the Soviet Union into a Marxist society. Rather, his strategy involved the use of massive propaganda campaigns designed to portray him as the visionary constructing the hoped-for utopia. More important, however, was his use of the secret police and other agencies of the state to push forward programs, even though these were often contradictory and in conflict with each other, through sheer terror and brute force.[26]

In the process of transforming Soviet society, Stalin transformed both the larger society and the Communist Party in whose name, in theory at least, these changes were being carried out. In this, his campaign of terror served several purposes. First, it overcame criticism and opposition to his policies within the party. Second, it served to root out the colloquium-like structure of the party leadership, forcing a move from single-party to a single-ruler state, with Stalin controlling the interpretation of Marxist dogma as well as its application when it served as a blueprint for transforming society. This approach was reinforced by Stalin's paranoid tendencies, which led him to believe he was a great man facing hostile and treacherous enemies engaged in a conspiracy against him, intent on destroying him if he did not destroy them first.[27]

In preparation for his first major attack on the Communist Party establishment, Stalin reorganized the secret police, which was part of the People's Commissariat for Internal Affairs or NKVD. The Special Section of the Central Committee became more active. Headed by A.N. Peskrebyshev, Stalin's personal secretary, the section functioned as Stalin's private secretariat, spying on all party and state agencies, including the NKVD. In December 1934, Sergei Kirov, a member of the Central Committee of the Communist Party, was murdered. Although Leonid Nikolayev, a misfit who failed to keep an official post to which he considered himself entitled, carried out the murder, evidence suggests that the killing was made possible with the co-operation of the NKVD under instructions from Stalin.[28] Stalin, however, presented the attack on Kirov as a threat to the country, its leaders and the revolution. The state-controlled press circulated stories about unscrupulous Trotskyites, foreign agents and anti-communists colluding to destroy the Soviet Union. Hysteria swept the country. So-called Japanese spies were arrested in the eastern part of the country. In Leningrad alone, about forty thousand alleged plotters were arrested. Two members of the Politburo, Grigori Zinoviev and Lev Kamanev, who were implicated by Nikolayev in Kirov's death, were re-arrested, tried, and convicted of "moral responsibility" for the murder. A decree was issued, specifying that persons accused of "preparing terrorist acts" should be investigated immediately and that executions should follow directly after conviction, with no appeal and no right of defence. This decree, Westwood remarks, was carte blanche for murder.[29] In the executions that followed, non-communists suffered the most, but former party members and party members who had once supported factions opposing Stalin were also arrested and deported to the Gulag. By the end of 1935, several hundred thousand workers, civil servants, and officials had been arrested and deported. In the meantime, Stalin strengthened his position in the Politburo by appointing his supporters to key positions.

Towards the end of 1935, the Central Committee declared the mass purge to be over. A new purge began in early 1936 with the goal of encouraging a general revolutionary vigilance against hidden enemies. Most of those expelled from the party were sent to the Gulag camps. There is also a report that Stalin ordered five thousand of the "oppositionists" already in the camps to be shot.[30]

In mid-1936 the so-called Great Purge began, with the Central Committee informing party organizations that too many enemies of the people were still at large, and pressing that these be unmasked. In the denunciations and mass accusations that followed, people were accused of all sorts of traitorous activities. Once accused, they were seldom found innocent. They lost their jobs and were usually deported to Gulag labour camps of low survivability; subsequently their families and associates were also "unmasked" as enemies of the state. Such treatment was not reserved for party members; a peasant woman who was discovered to have a portrait of Trotsky hanging among her icons was likewise arrested and sent to the camps.[31]

Between August 1936 and March 1938 almost all leading members of the Bolshevik old guard went on trial for plotting against Stalin and/or Lenin. They were accused of being counter-revolutionaries, and enemies of the working class who had traitorously aligned with foreign capitalists. The arch-villain instigator of these traitorous activities was seen to be Leon Trotsky, who had been Stalin's main rival to succeed Lenin. He, and anyone who had been associated with him, were accused of being traitors.

Using the services of the NKVD, Stalin subjected party members to interrogations in which torture was used to obtain confessions. Sensational trials in August 1936 resulted in party faithful admitting to plots against Stalin and other members of the Politburo. A press campaign was initiated to demand the death penalty for the traitors. Following their trial, the accused were either shot or sent to the camps.

In January 1937 seventeen other former supporters of Trotsky were tried, even though they had expressed regret over their error of judgment after it became clear that Stalin would defeat Trotsky. Thirteen were executed and the rest sent to the camps. In March 1938 Nikolai Bukharin, Aleksei Rykov, and Nikolai Krestinsky, all former members of Lenin's Politburo, as well as Genrikh Yagoda, the former leader of the NKVD, and seventeen others were tried. They were accused of Trotskyite counter-revolutionary activities, an anti-Stalin conspiracy, espionage for Germany or Japan, or industrial sabotage. At the show-trials that followed, some were sentenced to death; the remainder were sent to the labour camps. In commenting in *Pravda* on the sentences, Stalin wrote that the Soviet Union was encircled by hostile powers whose agents, recruited from Trotskyites hiding behind Bolshevik masks, had penetrated all party, government and economic organizations and were engaged in espionage and destruction, not stopping short of murder. To alter this situation, the party had to undergo ideological re-education from the top to the bottom.[32]

With the arrest and expulsion of Bukharin and Rykov, the Central Committee had lost all power to restrain Stalin. Thereafter, he could order the arrest of any colleagues without consultation or appeal to the Committee. This in turn brought a tenfold increase in the number of arrests between 1936 and 1937. Through these, Stalin not only destroyed any existing opposition but also ensured that no future opposition to him was likely to arise.

While still completing his subjugation of the Communist Party, Stalin also moved against the army, which he perceived as a possible source of danger to him. Prior to this move, he had strengthened his own position with the NKVD by appointing one of his henchmen, Nikolai Yezhov, to head it, which had led to the execution of some three thousand members of the NKVD. On 11 June 1937, it was announced that nine of the leading figures of the Red Army High Command had been arrested on charges of conspiracy and treason. Another announcement the next day stated they had been tried and executed. Further trials and executions followed, accompanied by expulsions from the Communist Party of not only those found guilty but also their wives and children. The NKVD also initiated a series of arrests throughout the officer corps and political commissars of the Red Army, Navy, and Air Force.

A second wave of trials that began in the spring of 1938 reached its climax in July when the naval commander-in-chief, Admiral Orlov, and no fewer than six army commanders were shot, along with eighteen political figures. At the same time, the Far Eastern Command was also savaged. The military purges eliminated three of the five Soviet marshals, thirteen of the fifteen army commanders, and others in the upper echelon of the army. Between May 1937 and September 1938, 36,761 army officers and over 3,000 navy officers were dismissed. Ultimately, between 1937 and 1941, a total of 43,000 officers at battalion and company commander level were arrested and shot, or sent to the camps, or permanently dismissed from office.[33]

In conjunction with the attacks on the officer corps, the terror included an intensification of the purges of the party, governmental and industrial elites of the country. This resulted in 90 per cent of the members of regional or city committees and of the central committees of the republics being expelled from office between 1937 and 1938.[34] At the same time that the most active party workers were rounded up and either sent to the camps or shot, the heads of leading industrial enterprises were replaced by party elements loyal to Stalin. Quotas were fixed on the number of Trotskyites, spies, and saboteurs that each district was required to produce and either deport to the camps or shoot. A local triumvirate was set up, consisting of the regional head of the NKVD, the first secretary of the Communist Party, and the chair of the Soviet Executive Committee. Stalin advised that all party secretaries at all political levels should select two replacements for themselves. Such an edict, no doubt, convinced officials that failure to deliver the required number of enemies would result in themselves being liquidated.

Apart from ravaging the leading elements in the Soviet Union, Stalin also eliminated millions of other people, both party members and ordinary citizens. Some were shot, while others died in NKVD camps. These included managers, administrators, army personnel, one-time Stalinists, foreign communists, including the entire leadership of the Polish Communist Party, Russians who had returned from service in the Spanish Civil War, ex-Mensheviks, and ex-Socialist Revolutionaries. As the wave of denunciation spread, so did the variety of victims. Workers were not spared. Locomotive engineers, for example, were shot both for not driving their trains fast enough, and thus were accused of "sabotage" of the plan, and for driving them too fast, and thus were accused of "wrecking" by causing engine wear and excessive fuel consumption. While some people denounced enemies to prove their virtue and vigilance, others did so to settle old scores. Once denounced, the victim could do little, and his family and friends automatically became suspect.

If the purge had continued past 1938, it would eventually have made every Russian a prisoner, observes Westwood.[35] It was not unknown for interrogators and the prisoners they recently sentenced to find themselves in the same camp. At times, intended victims in outlying areas were spared arrest when the officials who had been sent to arrest them were themselves arrested before they could find the other victims. With industry and agriculture in disarray, and nervous breakdowns and heart attacks becoming a mass phenomenon as citizens listened apprehensively in the small hours for the dreaded knock at the door, Stalin called a halt to the purges. He blamed Yetzhov and the NKVD for the excesses, an action that justified eliminating Yetzhov and replacing him with Lavrenti Beria. Although Beria swept out the top posts of the NKVD, as Yetzhov had done before him, the pace of arrests began to slacken.[36]

The scale of destruction during Stalin's consolidation of power is staggering. The old Communist Party had been liquidated: four-fifth of its members in 1939 had joined the party after 1930. Robert Conquest estimates that, in addition to the some eighteen million people destroyed between 1929 and the beginning of 1939, including those destroyed by the famine, about six million were still in jail or labour camps in 1939. These figures do not include those executed, dying in the camps or imprisoned during the years 1939-53.[37]

During the war years, new groups were targeted as enemies. After Hitler invaded the Soviet Union in 1941, hostility turned towards different nationalities identified with Nazi Germany. Expelled from their homes, persecuted, and forced into slave labour, they suffered massive losses. The first group targeted were Soviet Germans, who were systematically rounded up and shipped to the Russian interior. While Soviet Germans were targeted because of their national origin, other groups suffered because they were accused of being pro-German or co-operating with the Nazis. Their expulsion began soon after their territory was recaptured or again was firmly under Soviet control. Thus, in 1944 the Balkars, Chechens, Ingush, Karachy, Kalmyk, and Crimean Tartars were expelled from their homes. All these groups essentially became part of the Gulag system where they suffered massive losses.

Dynamics contributing to destruction

When attempting to explain the massive destruction in the Soviet Union, in particular under Stalin, Courtois points to the Russian tradition of authoritarian rule. He cites the examples of Ivan the Terrible and Peter the Great, arguing that they, especially the latter, used cruelty to transform Russian society.[38] Courtois also points to the Russian revolutionary tradition, which aimed to transform society through the use of violence.[39] Commenting on the influence of this tradition on Stalin, Volkogonov states that the excesses of Stalin were a product of Stalinism, which he calls an earth-centered religion demanding people's undivided faith.[40] He sees in Stalinism the Russian revolutionaries' love of radicalism, which was manifested in their readiness to sacrifice everything in the name of an idea. Stalin, above all, proclaimed that everything was permitted for the sake of an idea.[41]

We may get an insight into how Stalinism led to genocide by looking more closely at the evolution of Marx's ideas as developed by the Bolsheviks. Marxian concepts, when applied to the study of society, have provided significant insights into the relationship between social organization and the manner in which people make their livelihood. At the same time, Marxism is an ideology that justifies social action. The Hegelian dialectic, which envisages history as evolving through stages marked by the struggle between opposites, forms the core of this ideology. History is seen as developing like the dialectics in an intellectual argument wherein there is a thesis, an antithesis and a synthesis. That is, the thesis engenders the antithesis and the two merge again to form a synthesis. Applied to historical development, Marx saw capitalism growing out of European feudal society. As it developed, capitalism became more powerful and the two came into conflict. This conflict eventually led to the triumph of capitalism over feudalism. This resolution did not necessarily lead to the destruction of feudalism, but rather to a synthesis that placed power into the hands of the capitalists.

Just as feudalism gave rise to capitalism, capitalism led to the rise of its own antithesis, namely the working class. Marx predicted that the new class would come into conflict with the class that had given rise to it. Competition between capitalists would lead to increased impoverishment of the working class. Eventually, Marx predicted, the working class would rise up against the capitalists and take power. The change resulting from this struggle would be categorically different from the merger of feudalism and capitalism. The triumph of capitalism had meant that capitalists controlled the means of production. Under these circumstances, the state was necessary to permit the owners of the means of production to control the workers. Marx saw this state of affairs as contributing to many of the injustices he witnessed in European society. Marx predicted that once the workers took control of the state apparatus away from the capitalists, the state would disappear, because the people who did the work would also own the means of production. The state would no longer be needed to keep the workers in place. With the state's disappearance, many of the social injustices in nineteenth-century capitalist society would vanish.

Marx predicted that the socialist revolution would soon break out in countries like Germany and England, where the working class was both large and aware enough to seize power from the bourgeoisie. He didn't predict when these revolutions would come, nor did he state how the overthrow of the bourgeoisie would take place. He did not think that these revolutions would necessarily involve violence. Indeed, he believed that, in countries such as Holland or England, the revolution could be carried out without bloodshed. Marx claimed that this revolutionary change was inevitable, and he encouraged workers to strive towards this goal.

Lenin, when adopting Marxism as an ideology, took Marx's ideas one step further by stressing the role of the leadership who would guide the proletariat. While Marx makes mention of such leaders, he does not spell out their role. Combining Marxism with the Russian idea of the revolutionary as a transformer of society, Lenin made the Russian revolutionary the agent who would usher in the utopia Marx had prophesied. This revolutionary would not only lead the proletariat but also would play an active role in bringing about the socialist revolution. Lenin knew that Russia wasn't ready for the socialist revolution in 1917. However, the Bolsheviks seized power, justifying this with the explanation that Russia was the weakest link in the European capitalist structure. With this link broken, the entire house of European capitalism would come crumbling down.

By making the leaders of the proletariat the driving force in the revolution, Lenin transformed Marxism into a program of action with a strong moral purpose. Marx had already laid the groundwork for this transformation. His capitalists were not merely the owners of the means of production. Capitalism, which they controlled and from which they benefited, was responsible for much of the evil in society. The Marxian proletariat were not merely workers; they were also the element that would usher in a new world of justice and equality.

In this sense, social categories were also moral categories, with classes being agents of evil or of a higher truth. By encouraging the proletariat to overthrow the bourgeoisie, Marx was also encouraging them to overthrow the agents of corruption and create a new moral order, the socialist society. Taking up this cause, Lenin spelled out the role that the leaders of the proletariat would play in this transformation. Inspired by Lenin, the Bolsheviks, a small group of revolutionaries, seized power in Russia and proceeded to transform the country into a Marxist society.

In this, the workings of the dialectic were frozen; that is, Marxism, rather than being an explanation of historical change, became essentially a justification for labelling different segments of society. Human development, rather than evolving from the economic relationship between people, was replaced by human volition - essentially the drive of revolutionaries to transform society according to an abstract image. Thereby, Marxism was essentially reconceptualized in terms of the old Judeo-Christian concepts of the forces of light in conflict with forces of darkness. For the forces of light to flourish, the forces of darkness had to be eradicated. While there was evidence of this occurring under Lenin, it is quite clear that, under Stalin, a theory explaining social evolution, promising hope for the suppressed, was transformed into a program of action that saw the forces of light (the proletariat) working to obliterate the forces of darkness (the bourgeoisie). Commenting on this, Berdyaev writes:

> The communist is defined psychologically chiefly by the fact that for him the world is sharply divided into two opposed camps- Ormuzd and Ahriman, the kingdom of light and the kingdom of darkness, without any shading. This is almost a Manichean dualism which at the same time commonly makes use of a monist doctrine. The kingdom of the proletariat is the light kingdom of Ormuzd; the kingdom of the bourgeoisie is the dark kingdom of Ahriman. To those who belong to the kingdom of light everything is permissible for the annihilation of the kingdom of darkness.[42]

Of course, the proclivity to divide the world between forces of good and forces of evil in conflict with each other reaches deep in the Judeo-Christian tradition. The wars that the Israelites fought with the idolaters were cast into the framework of the Sons of Light battling the Sons of Darkness.[43] Christians battling the witches certainly saw themselves as agents of forces of light battling agents of Satan, the prince of darkness. For the Russian Bolsheviks, those agents identified with the good were the proletariat, or the Russian working class.

Berdyaev argues further that Soviet patriotism is largely Russian patriotism; that is, in Bolshevik communism we have the "identification of two messianisms, the messianism of the Russian people and the messianism of the proletariat."[44] In this conceptualization, Berdyaev adds, the "Russian working class and peasantry are a proletariat; and the proletariat of the whole world from France to China is becoming the Russian people--a unique people in the world."[45]

These people did not include those elements in the Soviet Union who were thought to be opposed to the proletariat. In particular, they did not include those people who were seen to threaten both the proletariat and Russian nationalism.[46] Just as an image of the idealized group had to exist, the Bolshevik communists also created an image of its opposite: the enemies of the proletariat, or, more specifically, individuals or groups on whom this label could be fixed. We see here the re-emergence of the dynamics of the witch-hunts of medieval Europe, albeit with a different enemy. Once the dynamic dialectic of Marxism became frozen in time and space with the success of the revolution in Russia, what had been an abstract explanation took concrete form in social reality. Whereas this reality made all groups identified with the proletariat (as defined by those in power) good and ideal, groups identified with the enemies of the proletariat became Satanic and evil.

This conceptualization laid the basis for the war against the enemy of the people. As Courtois points out, this conceptualization, imposed by the communist leadership, led to a situation where civil conflict of everyday life was put into the context of total war, a war that was carried out at all levels of society and in all areas of life.[47] This context shaped the characterization of the enemy, in terms of placing him at the opposite extreme of the forces of righteousness. It also shaped the language used to describe this enemy and determined the manner in which he was treated.

Stalin targeted different types of enemies of the people. One was the individual heretic or the party deviator from Stalinist Marxism. Stalin eliminated these people because he considered them a threat to his quest for power or because he saw them as deviating from the correct interpretation of Marxism, namely his own. Rigged trials determined that they were fifth columnists, Trotskyites, Fascist spies, or some other type opposed to true Marxism and its drive to forward the goals Stalinists defined as those of the proletarian revolution. On the basis of evidence obtained through the use of torture, the guilty persons were often condemned to labour camps or killed. People associated with them were seldom granted even such a semblance of a trial before they were shot or expelled to the camps.

Party heretics weren't the only people identified as enemies. People might be targeted because they belonged to groups that were associated with the old regime, or were seen to embody characteristics that had to be eradicated to create the communist utopia. They could be seen as harming Stalin's endeavour to create a socialist society. Others were identified with an outside enemy such as Nazi Germany. In this instance, entire ethnic groups rather than members of a social class tended to be targeted as an enemy and treated accordingly.

Insight into the relationship between dehumanization and the destruction of people identified as enemies may be gained by looking at the motives driving party activists who became involved in requisitioning food from Ukrainian collective farmers during the famine. Writing of the time when he and others broke into the homes of collective farmers to take the last of their food, Kopelev states that he and his comrades were the fanatical followers of a new creed, the only true religion—scientific socialism. The party promised to bring not merely eternal salvation but to create an earthly paradise for humankind. With the works of Marx, Engels and Lenin as holy writ, and Stalin the infallible high priest, the party was greater than any church. In whatever he and his comrades did, Kopelev was convinced, he was taking part in the creation of a new, a purer society.

Any means justified the attainment of this goal, be this lying, stealing, or even the murder of hundreds of thousands and even millions of people, all those who stood in the way of attaining utopia.[48]

To justify depriving the collective farmers of the last of their grain, the peasants were associated with a class that had to be eliminated if the socialist utopia was to be realized. Ilya Ehrenburg, commenting on the struggle against the peasantry, writes that the Communist Party justified its acts with the concept of class essence: even though most of the peasants had lost their wealth, they remained the enemy. Said Ehrenburg: "Not one of them [the peasants] was guilty of anything, but they belonged to a class that was guilty of everything."[49]

The Ukrainian peasantry were attacked not only because they were the enemy class, but also because they were the backbone of the Ukrainian nation. Hryshko argues that, for the Russian or Russophile communists who dominated the Soviet Union, the nationalities problem was always integrally linked to the peasant problem. In particular, Stalin made this connection, seeing the peasantry as constituting the backbone of a national movement. This was true especially for the Ukraine. Stalin's attack on the Ukrainian peasantry, therefore, was an essential part of his attempt to destroy the Ukrainian national identity.[50]

The image of Ukrainian peasants as rural backward people, as nationalists and petty capitalists, all combined to make the Bolsheviks place them in the role of enemy of the people. They belonged to the degenerate old order, as did Ukrainian nationalism.[51] They certainly could not stand in the way of building the communist utopia. These peasants belonged to a world, a state of mind, and a state of existence, which had to be eliminated if the new society were to come into being. Their class had to be destroyed if the communist utopia were to be realized. Dolot writes:

> It had been proclaimed that the kulaks must be destroyed as a class. No pity and no mercy were to be shown them. The kulaks were not to be regarded as human beings. The Party propagandists invented the most derogatory names for them, calling them vermin, hyenas, sharks, snakes and the like.[52]

Commenting on this same subject, Vasily Grossman writes that, for party activists, the so-called kulaks were pariahs, untouchables, vermin; they were repulsive, and had no souls. Therefore there was no pity for them. Killing them was considered to be like wiping out vermin. "In order to massacre them," he adds, "it was necessary to proclaim that kulaks are not human beings, just as the Germans proclaimed that Jews were not human beings."[53]

Such categorization grew out of an ideological system and the endeavor to shape society according to it. First came the system and the attempt to implement it in the social environment through force, under the guidance of an authoritarian leader. The system was perceived as ideal and those who sought to implement it were ennobled by it. Anyone perceived to be in opposition was identified with a class of people that had to be eliminated for the ideal society to be created. Although they were characterized by different names at different times and in different situations, they had one thing in common: when they were targeted, they were identified with an enemy that had to be eliminated for the ideal society to come into being. This justified killing them, enslaving them, dehumanizing them. Such attitudes fuelled the destruction of human life in the Soviet Union under Stalin, a destruction that several scholars have identified as a holocaust.

The question of numbers

Moreso than in many other cases, the question of numbers is extremely problematic in the case of Stalin's holocaust. There are several reasons for this. First, the Soviet leadership, in particular under Stalin, sought to suppress information that reflected badly on the regime. As a police state, in which the government had extensive control over the lives of people, it had the means of not only suppressing but also manipulating information. In the case of people sent to the Gulag, it eliminated anyone who sought to document his or her experiences and let the world know about the destruction of life in the Soviet work camps.[54] In the case of the famine, people who even mentioned the situation were incarcerated.

Second, the Soviet leadership sought to manipulate information in its interest. Thus, in the case of the famine, it invited western journalists and other people sympathetic to the communist cause to the country, gave them tours that were strictly monitored, and then encouraged them to deny that the famine was occurring. At the same time, with the rise of Hitler in Germany, western leaders, looking at the Soviet Union as a possible ally, were loath to criticize Stalin and his excesses.[55] In some cases, journalists and other people sympathetic to the Soviet Union were given special privileges by Soviet authorities for reporting sympathetically on the regime. One of the most well known journalists in this regard was Walter Duranty of the New York Times. Although he knew about the man-made famine and its destructive effects, he nevertheless adhered to the Soviet government line and denied its existence to his readers.[56]

Soviet leaders were able to manipulate the news because they could hide what was actually going on behind the larger communist-versus-capitalist conflict. To many people in the West, Soviet communism was part of a noble experiment of the worker state. They believed Soviet leaders were endeavouring to create an ideal classless society, in contrast to the problem- plagued societies in which they found themselves. Soviet society was trying to bring about the demise of the corrupt capitalist system and initiating the glorious future for which humankind was destined. Any criticism of the Soviet Union and its leadership was therefore nothing but capitalist propaganda to protect the existing order by discrediting the Soviet system. Stalin was able to use not only these views but also the people who held them to dismiss as propaganda any reports critical of his actions.[57]

Given the ability of the Soviet regime to suppress and manipulate information, scholars and other interested parties viewed with hope the opening of the Gulag archives after the collapse of the Soviet Union in 1991. At last, they would be able to determine the extent of the devastation carried out under Stalin. Unfortunately, rather than providing reliable answers, the information from the archives initiated a new debate. Some scholars accepted the information provided by the archives at face value, suggesting that higher estimates prior to 1991 were influenced by the Cold-War mentality.[58] Other scholars suggested that statistics in the Gulag archives might have been manufactured. At the same time, a closer examination of the data obtained by researchers in the archives shows the records have significant gaps in information. Also, information provided is at times contradictory. Furthermore, researchers who had been given access to these files often did little critical analysis of the data.[59]

The problems that the Gulag archives present to researchers who accept them at face value may be seen when one looks at the information they hold on Soviet Germans (see Appendix B). This example shows that Gulag archives are, at times, unreliable. It also indicates that figures sometimes deliberately obscured what was actually happening in the Gulag.

Deliberate obfuscation was probably practised in record keeping relating to other peoples kept in the camps. At the same time, research carried out since the opening of the Gulag archives suggest that the treatment of camp inmates was as inhumane as suggested in works published prior to the opening of the Gulag archives. This becomes evident, for example, in the case of the Kolyma camp system, examined by Robert Conquest in the 1970s (see Appendix C for a summary of his findings). Conquest's findings that this camp system was extremely destructive to human life are corroborated, for example, in Ralf Stettner's extensive work on the camps, published in 1996, and in Małgorzata Giżejewska's work on the Kolyma camps, published in 1999.[60]

Weighing the available evidence, one can accept as realistic Conquest's claim that Stalin's war on the enemy of the people took the lives of some eighteen million people prior to the outbreak of the Second World War. Although extensive research still has to be done to determine the nature of the different Gulag camps, one can conclude that the death rate in camps such as the ones belonging to the Kolyma camp system ranged from 50 to 80 per cent. The most recent information we have on the famine between 1932 and 1933 suggests that four to five million people died during these years in Ukraine.[61] The death rate for the different nationalities expelled by Stalin was also extremely high. For example, about one-third of Chechens and Ingush perished. The death rate was higher for Soviet Germans, some 42 per cent of whom perished,[62] and higher still among the Crimean Tartars, whose losses were at about 46 per cent.[63]

In conclusion, several points may be made regarding the mass destruction of human life under Stalin. Stalinists justified the violence and destruction as instruments to create an idealized society. The violence was directed against a category of people who were seen as standing in the way of this transformation. At different times, different peoples were slotted into the category of the enemy. Once targeted, they could be killed, expelled to the Gulag, or otherwise mistreated. Once targeted, they were identified with a category of being that had to be eliminated for the idealized society to exist.

Several factors have made it difficult to gain an objective assessment of the extent and the nature of the destruction carried out under Stalin. One was the nature of Stalin's totalitarian regime, which made it possible for him both to suppress and manipulate information about events. This was made easier by Stalin's ability to recruit Western opinion-makers who were sympathetic towards the Soviet system. At the same time, the larger communist-capitalist conflict enabled Stalin and his sympathizers to paint as propaganda any attempt to expose what was actually occurring in the Soviet Union. Despite this, enough evidence has come to light to prove that Stalin's war on the "enemy of the people" led to a vast destruction among groups so targeted.

5

The Destruction of European Jewry

According to Ernst Nolte, Hitler's attack on European Jewry involved conceptual constructs similar to those that motivated Stalin's attack on the kulak in the Soviet Union. Both aimed at the eradication of an enemy group, with the Bolsheviks defining this enemy in class terms and the Nazis identifying him in biological terms.[1] This similarity is also pointed out by Courtois, who states that the Nazi goal of creating a pure race parallels the communist goal of creating a pure class. Both of these radical goals were exclusivist, but in different ways and to a different degree; the Nazis declared that the Jews shouldn't exist and the communists declared that the capitalist bourgeoisie shouldn't exist.[2]

Other scholars have noted that the Nazi persecution of the Jews had its basis in the Christian tradition. For example, Trevor-Roper, Leschnitzer, and Cohn have traced parallels between the Christian zealotry of the European witch-hunts and the Nazi war against the Jews.[3] Likewise, Elie Wiesel regards the holocaust as the outgrowth of anti-Jewish beliefs and attitudes of Christians in Europe.[4] Hyam Maccoby states that the attempt by the Nazis to destroy the Jews has its base in Christianity. He sees little that was new in the Nazi vilification of the Jew. The individual cruelties of the Nazis, while horrific, were similar to Cossack massacres of Polish Jews. The Nazi episode was, thus, not an ahistorical explosion of evil but part of the Christian war against Jews, which dated back to the Middle Ages.[5]

Although Yehuda Bauer agrees that the Nazis drew on Christian traditions for their image of the Jew, he maintains that their anti-Semitism was, in many ways, a perversion of Christian symbols. Anti-Semitism was part of a pseudo-religion that, although inspired by Christian symbols, subverted and changed them completely. Using these symbols in a sacrilegious way, modern anti-Semitism, and especially Nazism, was able to transform terms and associations familiar to the Christian mind. In this transformation, the Holy Trinity of Father, Son, and Holy Ghost was transformed into the State, the Race, and the Spirit of the *Volk*. The Jew became the Devil and the Fuehrer the Saviour who would deliver his people from the anti-Christ.[6]

Frei sees the Nazi policy on race, including the settlement of the so-called Jewish question, and on population and health, as the monstrous product of a comprehensive vision of the "renewal of the *Volk*."[7] Fischer argues that the real essence of National Socialism was to produce a racial, rather than a social, revolution. If National Socialism had a genuine revolutionary thrust, it resided in its efforts to transform Germany biologically and to replace class with race.[8] Friedlander sees in particular eugenics, with its emphasis on "race hygiene," as laying the base for the destruction of the handicapped (who were considered to have a life not worth living) and the destruction of outsiders such as Gypsies and Jews.[9]

There is not as much difference as may appear at first glance in the range of these interpretations of Nazi policies toward the Jews. Perceived differences are largely a reflection of which aspects of Nazi policy scholars chose to highlight. The fact of the matter is that different aspects of this policy were closely intertwined. Basic to all of Hitler's goals was the trauma he experienced as a result of Germany's defeat in World War I. He saw the Jews as the beneficiaries of this defeat and blamed them for bringing it about. His objective was not merely to undo the results of the war but also to place Germany in a position where it would not again be defeated. Accordingly, he launched a plan for German expansion into Slavic lands to the east of Germany. Because the Nazis saw Slavic peoples as inferior, they had no scruples about displacing them. Following conquest, Slavs with Aryan features were to be absorbed into the German nation, while others were essentially to serve their new Aryan masters. Hitler ascribed to a social Darwinist view of society and interpreted history as a great arena in which peoples engage in ruthless competition. In this competition, the stronger or more able individuals and nations win, while those who are less able and weaker lose and are crushed.[10]

To ensure that Germans would win and secure their new territorial base, Hitler sought a moral and physical transformation of the German people. This transformation would be attained through a *Volksgemeinschaft* in which German physical characteristics and moral nature could be nurtured and safeguarded. For the Nazis, the physical and moral were closely entwined, with both based on one's biological make-up. This view drew its inspiration from contemporary eugenic theories that were rooted in the social Darwinism of the late nineteenth century, with all its metaphors of fitness and competition, and its emphasis on the survival of the fittest. Eugenics flourished after the popularization, at the turn of the century, of Mendel's theory that the biological make-up of organisms is determined by certain inherent factors later identified with genes. The application of

Mendelism to human beings reinforced the idea that we are determined almost entirely by our "germ plasm," which is passed on from one generation to the next and overwhelms environmental influences in shaping human development. Eugenicists believed that heredity contributed to poverty and criminality; bad genes rather than social influences were the basis for criminal or immoral behaviour.

By the same token, positive characteristics were also hereditary. The Nazi eugenics program had as its goal improving the biological strain of the German people, and this included eradicating influences that would interfere with this goal. Thus they embarked upon a program to wipe out Germans who had physical or mental defects, in particular those passed on through heredity. Patients were killed in gas chambers disguised as shower rooms or in mobile vans into which carbon monoxide was pumped. Fischer states that by August 1941, when such killings stopped, 70,273 people had been exterminated.[11] The cleansing of the German nation also involved a moral cleansing. Homosexuals were killed, not only because they were considered degenerate but also because their lifestyle interfered with the Nazi goal that Germans have as many children as possible. Rector estimates that at least 50,000 homosexuals were eliminated by the Nazis, either by execution, in the work camps, or in the gas chambers.[12] While he may overestimate the number of deaths, others support Rector's observations regarding their fate. Commenting on the same subject, Friedländer states that during the Nazi period some 15,000 homosexuals were incarcerated. How many died in the camps is unknown, but according to one Dachau inmate, these prisoners were quickly and systematically exterminated by the SS.[13]

Gypsies were another persecuted group. The Nazis viewed them as not doing productive work and as habitual thieves and criminals. Moreover, it was believed that in particular the *Mischlinge,* the offspring of a union between a German and a Gypsy, inherited these negative characteristics, and would pass them on to their children. It was a matter of faith that whatever negative characteristic the *Mischlinge* had came from the genes of the Gypsy partner.

The Nazis devised various solutions to deal with the "Gypsy problem." Prior to the war, these policies were largely of a legal nature and included preventing intermarriage between Gypsies and Germans, restricting the movement of Gypsies, and forced emigration. During the war, Himmler briefly entertained the idea of setting up a reservation for the "racially pure Sinto and Lalleri Gypsies." In the end, most German Gypsies were sterilized, shot, or sent to concentration camps, where many of them were killed[14] to prevent their negative characteristics from being passed into the German gene pool.[15] Gypsies were treated in a similar fashion in countries under Nazi control, where they were either killed outright, starved to death, or sent to concentration camps. Particulary in the war against the Soviet Union, Gypsies were frequently killed by the *Einsatzgruppen* because they were seen as spies and agents of the world enemy, the Jews.[16]

The Jews were also viewed as contaminating the German gene pool with their physical degeneration, lack of productivity, and criminality.[17] In part, they were killed because the Nazis wanted to prevent these characteristics from being passed on to the German people. However, Nazi motives for killing the Jews went far beyond this consideration. Commenting on Nazi policy regarding eugenics, Friedländer states that while there were similarities between Nazi eugenic policies and their policies regarding the Jews, these differed in their origins and aims. Whereas eugenics aimed to enhance the purity of the *Volksgemeinschaft*, the segregation and extermination of the Jews—though also a process of purification — was mainly a policy directed against an enemy seen as endangering the very survival of Germany and the Aryan world.[18] While both the Gypsies and Jews were targeted because Hitler did not want their characteristics mingled with the German gene pool, the Jews were also singled out because they were considered to be a world power who sought to keep other peoples enslaved to forward Jewish ends. In Hitler's view, the Jews used both Marxism and capitalism to subvert and undermine other peoples in order to ensure their own success. Hitler saw the Jew as being very much like a disease that can infect a whole society just like a germ can infect a body.[19] The poisonous nature of the Jews was transmitted both through their values and their genetic make-up. The Jew was the enemy who had to be eliminated in order to achieve the transformation of the German people and win them their rightful place among nations.

Hilberg describes the Nazi attack on the Jews as a process that involved the Jews being defined, separated from surrounding peoples, and eventually killed.[20] Gilbert also sees the Nazi attack on European Jewry as going through stages: legalized discrimination, forced emigration, resettlement and forced ghettoization, elimination of Jews by killing squads, and the final solution.[21] Legalized discrimination against the Jews was intended first to separate the Jews from the surrounding German community and then to force them to emigrate. Attacks on German Jewry began immediately after the Nazis took power. They invaded apartments, offices, and stores to arrest Jews and other groups identified as the enemy. Passed on 7 April 1933, the Law for the Restoration of the Civil Service sought to remould the civil service by cleansing from it suspect elements, including communists and Jews. A subsequent definition identified a person with one Jewish parent or grandparent as being of "non-Aryan" descent. On the basis of these laws, Jews were expelled from the civil service, the only exception being those who had been in the civil service prior to World War I, or who had fought at the front for Germany (or one of its allies), as well as those whose fathers or sons had died in the German cause.

A series of laws and administrative orders between April and October 1933, excluded Jews from such occupations as assessors, jurors or commercial judges. On 25 April the Law Against the Overcrowding of German Schools and Universities limited the enrolment of new Jewish students in institutions of higher learning to 1.5 per cent of total new applicants. In the same month, new laws restricted the practice of Jewish doctors and lawyers. The establishment of the Reich Chamber of Culture, in September, served to limit the number of Jews in entertainment and cultural enterprises, whether in art, theatre, or film. In July, the Law for the Repeal of Naturalization and Recognition of German Citizenship cancelled naturalizations that had been taken out between 19 November 1918 and 30 January 1933. This law was aimed primarily at eastern European Jews who had entered Germany during the Weimar period. In September, Jews were forbidden from owning farms or engaging in agriculture. Under the aegis of Goebbels's Propaganda Ministry, Jews were barred from belonging to the Journalists' Association and from being editors. Later changes in the law allowed Jewish editors and journalists to work, but only for the Jewish press.

A brief pause in anti-Jewish legislation came in 1934 when the Nazis turned to internal party problems, and the SA was purged. In 1935 the attack on Jews recommenced, beginning with an increasing number of hate articles appearing in Goebbels's *Der Angriff* (The Attack) and Streicher's *Der Stuermer* (The Attacker), that called for the total exclusion of Jews from German life. When, in early 1935, Hitler made it mandatory for every young man in Germany to serve in the Wehrmacht, fully Jewish men were barred from serving.[22] Other countries did not let these measures affect their relations with Nazi Germany. In June 1935, Germany began negotiations with France regarding economic co-operation. That month, also, it signed the German-British Naval Agreement. Soon after, the Nazis passed the Nuremberg Laws, which spelled out in legal terms behavioural patterns towards Jews that the Nazis were already following in practice. These laws defined a Jew as anyone descended from at least three grandparents of the Jewish faith. A Jewish *Mischling* was anyone descended from one or two grandparents who were fully Jewish. The laws outlawed marriages between Jews and people of German and "kindred blood." They forbade extramarital intercourse between Jews and Germans and also forbade Jews to employ in their households German women under the age of forty-five.

With the annexation of Austria on 13 March 1938, the Jewish population under Nazi control increased by about 190,000. Most of the Austrian Jews lived in Vienna, where they were employed primarily in advertising, manufacturing, and newspaper publishing, as well as in the legal and medical professions. Prior to the *Anschluss*, many Austrian Jews had been politically active, in particular as Social Democrats who opposed anti-Semitism and fought for the equality of all peoples. By 1934, however, the Social Democratic Party had been outlawed and most of its leaders were in jail or exile.

The entry of German troops into Austria was accompanied by the arrest of political opponents of the Nazis and by attacks on Jews, with Jewish stores and offices being broken into and their occupants beaten or arrested. The process of transforming the Jew from a citizen to an outsider whose existence was barely tolerated, which had taken five years in Germany, was accomplished in Austria within a few months. At the same time, Jewish property was confiscated. Within a few months, 83 per cent of the handicrafts, 26 per cent of the industry, 82 per cent of the economic services, and 50 per cent of the individual businesses owned by Jews in Vienna were taken over.[23]

In the meantime, the campaign against Jews in Germany continued. Laws passed in March 1938, deprived German Jewish communities of the right to act as legal personalities. A law against "hiding" the identity of Jewish businesses was enacted a month later. As of September 1938, Jewish doctors were forbidden to treat Aryans, and later that year Jewish lawyers were forbidden to practise law. On 5 October 1938, a law was passed requiring all Jewish passports to be marked with the letter "J" (Jude, Jew), a procedure adopted at the suggestion of the head of the Swiss Alien Police, who was concerned with the number of Jews fleeing to Switzerland.

To prevent the return of Polish Jews in Austria or Germany, in March 1938 the Polish government passed a law declaring that Polish citizens who had not resided in Poland for five consecutive years would be deprived of their citizenship. This act affected a considerable number of people: 56,480 of the 98,747 non-German Jews in Germany were Polish nationals. When on 6 October 1938, the Polish government declared that it would deny citizenship to anyone who had not renewed their passport by 29 October1938, the Gestapo put some 18,000 Polish Jews on special trains heading for the Polish border. Although officially denied entry into Poland, many were forced across illegally by the Gestapo, with many of them ending up in Camp Zbaszyn, named after a Polish border town near which it was located. Upon receiving a letter from his father telling him what had happened to his family in Zbaszyn, Hershel Grynszpan, a student living in Paris, went to the German embassy in that city to kill the German ambassador. Instead, he killed Ernst von Rath, a third secretary of the embassy.

The Nazis used the death of von Rath as a pretext to launch a massive attack on German Jewry. Goebbels incited the SA (*Sturm Abteilung*) and thousands of party members to burn synagogues, loot Jewish shops, and attack Jews. Ninety-one people were killed in the violence. In addition, Jews had to pay an indemnity of one billion Reichsmark for the death of von Rath, and hand over insurance benefits for their destroyed property. The "voluntary Aryanization" of Jewish businesses was ended. Jewish firms could now be forcibly sold or liquidated, after which Jewish employees in these businesses lost their jobs. By the beginning of 1939, only Jewish organizations could employ Jews. The Nazi objective was to force all Jews to leave Germany. To achieve this goal, Jews in concentration camps were released, providing that arrangements could be made for them to leave the country. Under these conditions, the German Jewish population, which had stood at about half a million in 1933, had shrunk to about half that by 1939.[24]

With the German invasion of Poland in the fall of that year, a further million and a half Jews came under German rule. However, the outbreak of war, which included a British naval blockade of Germany, and the restriction of all but military traffic within Germany, made the forced emigration of Jews virtually impossible. At the same time, Nazi policy towards the Jews became more extreme. Fischer believes that the war was responsible not only for the intensification of Nazi persecution of Jews following its outbreak but also for what became the final solution.[25] He bases his view on remarks made to the Czech Foreign Minister on January 21, 1939, in which Hitler threatened the Jews with annihilation should war break out.[26] Commenting on this statement as well as others made by Hitler, Friedländer argues that Hitler's comments were more tactical than is suggested by Fischer. On the one hand, it was blackmail. Believing that the Jews had power over governments in their respective countries, Hitler used his threats to force them to dissuade other countries from going to war against him. At the same time, he wanted to drive the Jews out of Germany. Therefore, the threat of extermination was one possibility among others, "neither more nor less real than others."[27] Gilbert also suggests that Nazi policy towards the Jews was not fixed by the outbreak of war. It was certainly Hitler's policy to rid Germany of the Jews. Changing situations, including the outbreak of war, altered the steps taken to achieve his goal and led, ultimately, to the final solution.[28]

Although analysts disagree as to whether the outbreak of the Second World War brought about the introduction of the final solution, they agree that war intensified Nazi attacks on European Jewry. This policy was particularly evident in the vicious "pacification" of the Jews in Warsaw following an uprising in response to the Nazi invasion. Reviving the medieval concept of the ghetto, the Nazis expelled Jews throughout Poland from their homes and forced them to live in restricted areas far too small for the population. Anyone trying to leave or smuggle food into the ghetto faced execution. Food rations were imposed with the intent of forcing Jews to work for the Germans in order to sustain themselves.

The German victories in Western Europe between April and June 1940 brought Jews living in these regions under Nazi control. They were subject to civic disabilities, with their civil rights being essentially non-existent, and were required to wear a yellow star on their clothing, as they had in medieval times, to identify them. As in Germany and occupied Eastern Europe, their property was gradually taken away and the professions were closed to them. However, their lives were generally safe.[29] Some were able to flee to neutral countries such as Spain or Switzerland and others were able to emigrate. The quick victory on the western front raised the possibility of France ceding the island of Madagascar to the Germans, who would then expel all Jews to that local. Entertained by the Poles during the 1930s to solve what they saw as their Jewish problem,[30] the suggestion was put forward by the Nazis as possibly being included in a peace treaty with Britain and France. It was abandoned when Britain did not make peace. The Nazis, in turn, having secured the western front, excluding Britain, launched Operation Barbarossa and invaded the Soviet Union.

Bullock argues that the invasion of the Soviet Union in 1941 radically altered Hitler's war aims. Unlike in the west, where he had limited objectives, Operation Barbarossa launched a racist-imperialist adventure that had two main objectives: gaining *Lebensraum* which would lay the basis for his one-thousand-year Reich and at the same time eradicating Jewish Bolshevism.[31] War was hereby transformed into a crusade that envisaged saving Europe from the dark forces of Bolshevik communism. This change transformed not only the military conflict but also Hitler's war against the Jews. The conflict in France had made the Madagascar plan, with its focus on expulsion rather than immediate elimination, a possible means for getting rid of the Jews. Such an alternative was barely possible in a crusade that envisaged the enemy as the embodiment of the forces of darkness. It is not surprising, therefore, that under these circumstances eradication rather than expulsion should come to the foreground in Hitler's solution to what he saw as the Jewish problem.

The Nazis first used *Einsatzgruppen* to eliminate the Jews in the Soviet Union. *Einsatzgruppen* dated back to Hitler's annexation of Austria and Czechoslovakia, where they served essentially as security forces. At the time of the Polish campaign, about two thousand SD (*Sicherheitsdienst*) and police officials accompanied the regular army in order to look after security matters in the conquered areas. They seized Communist Party archives, drew up lists of suspect groups or organizations, and rounded up saboteurs. They also, at times, shot Jews, communists, and other elements considered to be hostile. It was not until after the invasion of the Soviet Union, however, that these groups became killing squads used in the widespread destruction of Jews.

Killings started with the murder of Jews of military age. By August and September of 1941, the *Einsatzgruppen* began to murder women and children, and shortly thereafter started destroying entire Jewish communities.[32] Their aim, Gilbert argues, was to destroy Jewish life altogether. Jews were rounded up in eastern Poland, Lithuania, Latvia, Estonia, Ukraine, and western Russia, taken to isolated areas, and shot. The killing was facilitated by the involvement of local police and paramilitary groups, in particular in Ukraine and Lithuania. In Bessarabia, Moldavia, and parts of southern Russia, the killing was carried out by the Romanians.

Gilbert notes that, in 1941, four solutions were used to solve the Jewish problem. In German towns, officials expelled Jews to the cities to enable them to declare their locality free of Jews. In parts of Western Europe under German control, Jews could still emigrate, providing they were citizens of a neutral country or married to such citizens. In parts of Poland that had not been annexed to Germany, Jews were confined to ghettos, where they were forced to work in factories manufacturing clothes for the German army. In the part of the Soviet Union under German occupation, the mass murder of Jews was in progress.[33]

Gerlach addresses the question of when the mass murder of Jews in the Soviet Union was expanded to include the murder of all the Jews of Europe. He maintains that this decision was made in December 1941. To argue his case, he points to the general inconsistency of Nazi policy regarding the killing of Jews prior to this date. In Poland, for example, there were no systematic mass murders of Jews except in Galicia, which had belonged to the Soviet Union until June 1941. In *Reichsgau Wartheland*, which had been annexed from Poland, the mass murder of Jews began in several areas at the end of September and the beginning of October 1941. The move towards the total destruction of Lithuanian Jews was already underway by August 1941.[34]

The deportation of German Jews to the east began in the middle of September 1941. In the middle of October, transports of Jews from Germany, Austria, Bohemia, and Moravia were being sent east, and French Jews were notified that they, too, would be sent east.[35] In September and October, observes Gerlach, the move towards the total destruction of European Jewry became increasingly evident. In Soviet areas, the total destruction of European Jewry had already begun. In Belarus, the western Ukraine, and *Warthegau*, selective mass destructions of people considered to be useless for work had taken place. These developments, adds Gerlach, caused some historians to maintain that the decision to eliminate Soviet Jews was reached in July and August 1941, and the decision to eliminate the Jews in other parts of Europe was reached in September or October 1941, or perhaps earlier.[36]

Gerlach argues that if one looks at the destruction of Jews, in particular German Jews in the latter part of 1941, there appears to be inconsistency in policy, with some Jews sent east being killed while others were allowed to stay alive.[37] One problem the Nazis faced was reaching a consensus as to who exactly was a Jew, in particular as this related to mixed marriages and their offspring. In addition, the inconsistency can also be attributed to the fact that Hitler had not yet reached the decision to totally destroy all the Jews of Europe. Gerlach argues that Hitler did not take the decision to annihilate all Jews until the United States entered the war; the directive was passed on to major Nazi functionaries during a meeting on 12 December 1941. Himmler made a note on 18 December regarding Hitler's instructions and stated that it was Hitler's view that the Jews should be executed as partisans.[38] Placing this note into the context of other events, Gerlach maintains that the instructions could not have referred to Soviet Jews; the murder of Jews in the USSR was well under way. Furthermore, as there were an insignificant number of Jewish partisans in 1941, Gerlach continues, the note had to refer to the destruction of European Jews in general.[39]

Gerlach points to a number of events that brought Hitler to this decision. The main one was the beginning of war with the United States.[40] Gerlach refers to the statement made by Hitler in January 1939 in which he threatened to wipe out European Jewry if Jewish international finance should plunge Germany into another world war. As the war in Europe expanded to include the United States on 11 December 1941, the conflict had truly become a world war. As such, the decision to destroy all Jews was consistent with an earlier threat. With the United States a belligerent, Hitler had the excuse to fully implement a decision he and other members of his party already had in view. Once the Americans had joined the Allies, Jews had lost their value as a bargaining chip. The threat of destroying European Jews could no longer serve as a deterrent to hostilities with the United States. Also, the entry of the United States into the war and the German failure to take Moscow in 1941 raised a serious problem for the Germans: the possibility of all-out war on two fronts, and of having to fight a war against partisans, in which Jews would play a leading role. The Jews would have to be destroyed to prevent this from occurring.[41]

Gerlach's dating of the Nazi decision to murder all Jews is somewhat problematic, in particular as it relates to the mass murder of Jews in the

Soviet Union. He deals with this problem by stating that the Nazi decision to murder all Jews in the Soviet Union must be considered separately from the murder of Jews in the remainder of Europe.[42] But why should this be the case? One could as easily argue, using Gerlach's evidence, that the decision for the mass murder of Jews was made with the invasion of the Soviet Union. Gerlach states that this couldn't have been the case because Hitler refers to murdering Jews as partisans in December 1941, when there were as yet no partisans, and that the decision to murder all European Jews was made in December 1941 to punish Jews for the war's expansion and as a precautionary measure.

However, it would be much more logical to argue that these precautionary measures began at the time of the invasion of the Soviet Union, or shortly thereafter. One reason for this was the nature of the all-out war that, as Bullock makes clear, Hitler expected to fight when he launched Operation Barbarossa.[43] Another was the nature of the early victories. Thus, Browning sees a connection between Hitler's all-out attack on the Jews and his anticipation of an easy victory on the eastern front.[44] However, Browning's argument that Hitler was motivated essentially by the "euphoria" of an easy victory in his policy towards the Jews is a little simplistic. While Hitler anticipated an easy victory, he likely also expected partisan activity - activity that he expected to be spearheaded by Jews. Thus, the use of *Einsatzgruppen* before there were appreciable numbers of guerrillas could be explained as a pre-emptive strike against anticipated partisan activity. This would help put into context Nolte's observation that the Nazi war on the Jews in the Soviet Union was both an anti-guerrilla campaign and a genocidal war.[45] Himmler's diary entry of 18 December 1941 may therefore refer, not to a new approach to dealing with the "Jewish problem," but to the intensification and expansion of a campaign begun in the Soviet Union to include all of Europe.

The Wannsee Conference in January 1942, Gerlach argues, dealt not only with the definition as to who was a Jew (in particular as this applied to German Jews) but also with the decision reached by Hitler in December 1941, to murder not only Soviet but all European Jews.[46] According to Fischer, the Conference was called by the Nazi leadership to implement the final solution; that is, to murder all the Jews of Europe. Jews were to be rounded up and sent to "transit ghettos" in the east and then transported farther east for eventual destruction.[47]

Fischer, Gerlach, Bullock and Browning, although disagreeing on specifics, suggest that Hitler was the prime initiator of Nazi policies regarding the Jews. Other scholars, while not de-emphasizing Hitler's role, point to additional factors as contributing to the final solution. When examining the destruction of Jewry in Galicia, Sandkühler found that directives from

Berlin played a role; at the same time, he also found local factors of significance. These included the anti-Jewish orientation of some Ukrainian anti-
communist elements. Such individuals did not need the urgings of the
Nazi hierarchy to destroy the Jews, whom they themselves identified with
Bolshevism. Sandkühler points to the Nazi hierarchical structure and how
attempts by individuals to move up this ladder influenced the destruction of Jews. He also suggests that the shared belief among Nazis that the
Jews represented everything antithetical to what was decent in German
life meant that direction from some central authority would have played a
minor role in motivating the Nazis to destroy the Jews.[48]

Klein assigns even more influence to local and situational factors. The
construction of death camps at Chełmno or Bełżec, he argues, resulted
from decisions made by local *Gauleiter* rather than from an overall plan
to destroy European Jewry. He takes a similar approach to Hitler's decision to implement the final solution, suggesting that Hitler made the
decision to destroy the Jews about 17 December, when angered by news
reports about the expulsion and mistreatment of the Volga Germans.[49]
Thus, Klein doesn't believe that the final solution resulted from an organized plan carried out once Hitler made the decision to destroy the Jews.
Rather, it resulted from an array of circumstances. One of these involved
events that elevated Hitler's anger towards the Jews to the point where he
decided to destroy them rather than wait for the end of the war to settle
them outside Germany's boundaries. Another was the behaviour of local
Nazi leaders who shared Hitler's antipathy towards the Jews, seeing them
a symbol of all negative aspects of German life. It was the coalescence of
such factors, rather than a planned program of action, Klein suggests, that
led to the final solution.

It is not the purpose of this account to isolate the exact causal factors
that led the Nazis to implement the final solution. Rather, the intent is to
illustrate that a whole series of conditions arose during the war that influenced the nature and the extent of the Nazi attack on European Jewry.
Historians may emphasize one causal factor or another. They may or may
not see links between the different events. The fact remains that at one
point between 1939 and 1942 a number of situations arose that caused the
Nazis to implement a program of mass destruction to deal with the Jewish
question.

According to Bullock, the final solution brought together four programs with which the SS already had experience: the concentration camp
system, euthanasia gassings, *Einsatzgruppen* operations, and methods of
forced resettlement involving the movement of large numbers of victims
who were kept in ignorance of their fate.[50] The euthanasia program had
already made an exception for Jewish patients, who did not have to meet

any of the ordinary criteria, such as incurable diseases or mental deficiency, to be subjected to "mercy killings." Thus, from April 1940, Jews who were inmates of German mental hospitals were killed essentially because of their ethnic origin.[51]

Friedlander argues that the euthanasia program, that is, the killing of Germans who were considered to lead lives not worth living, served as a model for the gassing of both Jews and Gypsies. The success of the euthanasia policy convinced the Nazi leadership that mass murder was technologically feasible, that average men and women could be recruited for carrying out such murders, and that the bureaucracy could be depended upon to co-operate in the undertaking. Gassing was, therefore, a logical alternative to the use of *Einsatzgruppen*. It was less public, less cumbersome, and wouldn't require the recruitment of a large number of killers, thereby decreasing the possibility of involving people who couldn't bear the psychological stress of carrying out the murders.[52]

At first the SS and police used travelling vans to gas people. Eventually, Himmler's men realized that it was more efficient to bring the victims to a central place. The first killing center became operational in December 1941 near Chełmno, in eastern Poland. There, Jews from the nearby Lodz ghetto were gassed in mobile vans by means of engine exhaust fumes. The first death camp that used stationary gas chambers was set up at Bełżec, also in eastern Poland. Operational by the spring of 1942, the gas chambers were under the direction of Dr. Christian Wirth. Architect and chief exterminator of Bełżec, he was one of about one hundred people who had been transferred from the euthanasia program to the death camps in Poland.[53]

The systematic roundup of Jews began almost immediately following the Wannsee Conference. Working through satellite governments or occupation administrations, the German authorities sequestered Jewish property and liquid assets. Regardless of bad weather, Allied bombings, or urgent needs of the Wehrmacht, Jews were herded into sealed freight cars and dispatched eastward, most of them going to the death camps, Auschwitz, Bełżec, Sobibor, Treblinka, or Majdanek. Here, early methods of using exhaust fumes from diesel engines gave way to hydrocyanide (prussic acid), in the belief that it would be more effective in killing people than diesel gas.

Testimony from Kurt Gerstein, chief "disinfection" officer in the Department of Hygiene in the Waffen-SS, provides insight into the mindset of the people who operated the system. He had been ordered by Adolf Eichmannn's office to help transport prussic acid secretly to the Bełżec concentration camp. There he witnessed an attempted extermination under the direction of Dr. Wirth in which the diesel engine refused to fire.

Wirth was beside himself with embarrassment because of the malfunction in the presence of visitors. Horrified by the prospect of the mass murder, Gerstein lied to Wirth, telling him that the prussic acid he had brought with him was no longer usable and had to be buried. He later claimed that the only reason he stayed in his position was to work against the extermination and to bear witness to mass murder.

People not marked for immediate extermination were placed in work camps. Most work consisted of manual labor in quarries or brickyards, but at some of the larger camps, like Auschwitz, prisoners worked in a cement plant, a coal mine, a steel factory, a shoe factory and in the large I.G. Farben plant, which produced synthetic rubber. At all the camps rations were inadequate and the quality of the food atrocious. The daily food allowance, usually given to the prisoners after they returned from work, included a watered-down soup and a little bread, augmented by an extra allowance of margarine, a slice of sausage, a piece of cheese, or a bit of honey or watery jam. Such fare did little to help prisoners survive while they were required to do heavy labor. Emaciation set in quickly and was followed by loss of energy and a general feeling of apathy. People wasted away because of the excruciatingly hard labor, poor nutrition, harsh punishment, and unsanitary conditions that caused frequent epidemics. Prisoners no longer able to work were invariably destined for gassing.

Some countries or puppet regimes set up by the Nazis willingly participated in the destruction of Jews while others sought to counter Nazi efforts. Commenting on Serbia, Bennett states that the country remained more or less quiet until close to the end of the war. Because of these conditions the puppet regime under Milan Nedić was able to wipe out Serbia's Jewish community far more efficiently than the pro-Nazi Ustašas were able to do in Croatia.[54] In Hungary, Jews found some degree of protection until Hitler deposed Admiral Miklos Horthy in October 1944 and set up a puppet regime that he could fully control. Himmler's men then descended on the country, rounding up Jews.[55] The Nazis also halfheartedly experimented with a new technique of selling Jews to the west. Largely as a result of Nazi duplicity and the indifference of western governments, this plan never really worked. Sweden was one of the few countries to render effective aid, sending Raoul Wallenberg to Hungary to assist Hungarian Jews to emigrate to Sweden. Unfortunately, this effort reduced the mass of deportations only marginally.[56]

Nevertheless, the death camp killings tapered off somewhat during the last two years of the war. Triska attributes this to Germany's need for labor to support its war effort.[57] Kren and Rappoport are more specific, tracing the shift in policy to the SS department of economic affairs. Maintaining that concentration-camp prisoners and the remaining Jews should not be immediately destroyed but rather put to use in SS-owned factories or rented out to other industrial enterprises as slave labor, SS economic planners persuaded Himmler to slow down the killing. Yet, the killing was never completely halted until the Nazi defeat, because rival leaders in the internal security department kept pressing for completion of the final solution.[58]

The number of Jews killed can never be precisely known. Estimates range from three million to six million. Fischer considers Raul Hilberg's estimate as closest to the truth.[59] Fischer's breakdown by country is given in the following Table.

Jews killed per country

Poland	up to	3,000,000
USSR	over	700,000
Romania		270,000
Czechoslovakia		260,000
Hungary	over	180,000
Lithuania	up to	130,000
Germany	over	120,000
Netherlands	over	100,000
France		75,000
Latvia		70,000
Yugoslavia		60,000
Greece		60,000
Austria	over	50,000
Belgium	over	24,000
Italy (including Rhodes)		9,000
Estonia		2,000
Norway	under	1,000
Luxembourg	under	1,000
Danzig	under	1,000
	Total	5,113,000

The question has been asked: who carried out the genocide and how widely was it known? Goldhagen argues that "ordinary Germans" shared the "eliminationist anti-Semitism" of the Nazi leadership and therefore willingly executed the policy of exterminating the Jews.[60] Birn and Finkelstein question Goldhagen's thesis, maintaining that his argument is more fiction than fact, reached by an extremely selective use of the sources. On the basis of such evidence he then proceeds to implicate all Germans in the Nazi destruction of European Jewry.[61] Likewise, Sandkühler questions Goldhagen's thesis and suggests that any examination of the relationship between attitudes and the eradication of the Jews should not confine itself to Germany but also include other European countries. In his examination of the final solution in Galicia, Sandkühler often found Ukrainian anti-Semites more eager in the task than Germans who became involved in the killing of Jews.[62] Hilberg suggests that all leading officials of the SS and also railway officials who prepared trains for the death camps knew that Jews were sent there for destruction.[63] Nolte takes issue with this, arguing that the very success of the Nazi plan was predicated on the fact that no one knew more than what he had to know. In this, the Nazis were aided by the nature of modern society and its focus on specialization in which people are taught tasks in their specialized area without being made aware of how each part fits into the whole.[64]

Considering these different views, Friedländer probably provides the most accurate interpretation of German public attitudes towards the Nazi policy on Jews. Commenting on the 1930s, he states that most Germans, while to some degree anti-Semitic, did not insist on anti-Jewish measures, and certainly not on the extreme implementation of such measures. Most "ordinary Germans" acquiesced to the segregation of Jews and their dismissal from the public service. Some sought to benefit from the Nazi dispossession of Jews and expressed satisfaction over their humiliation. Outside party ranks, however, there was no mass demand that the Jews be expelled from Germany or that a program of violence be launched against them. "The majority of Germans accepted the steps taken by the regime and looked the other way."[65] No doubt, this was encouraged by anti-Semitic attitudes in the community as well as by a lack of concern for people perceived as outsiders. It would also have been encouraged by fear that they themselves would become targets if they opposed Nazi methods. Another reason, Frei argues, is that people were mesmerized by the speed with which the Nazis brought about Germany's economic resurgence and its rise in international status. Many became caught up in the drive to construct the *Volksgemeinschaft*. At the same time, the demands of their jobs (following years of unemployment), the relentless drive by the party that people become involved in the ever-expanding array of Nazi organizations, as well as the pressure of balancing all this with their personal lives, dissuaded people from criticizing the regime.[66]

While the above may give insight into the attitudes of "ordinary Germans," it doesn't explain why certain Germans became involved in killing Jews. Fischer suggests that to understand the motives of these people, it may be helpful to look at individuals who became involved in operating the death camps. He identifies two types of murderers: those who gave the orders—the "desk murderers" such as Hitler, Himmler, Heydrich, Müller, and Eichmann, and the people who did the actual killing—Höss, Wirth, Mengele, the *Einsatzgruppen,* and the concentration camp guards. He sees few sadists among them. Rather, he argues that individuals like Himmler or Eichmann saw themselves as decent people involved in important work serving a noble cause. Addressing an SS group in Posen in 1943, Himmler referred to the annihilation of the Jews as a necessary and noble task: "To have stuck this out and—excepting cases of human weakness—to have kept our integrity, this is what has made us hard. In our history, this is an unwritten and never-to-be written page of glory."[67] Another Nazi high official involved in the killings of Jews, Odilo Globocnik, insisted: "if there is ever a generation after us which is so weak-kneed that it does not understand our great task then the whole of National Socialism will have been in vain. On the contrary, in my view bronze tablets ought to be buried, on which it is reported that we had the courage to carry out this great work which is so vital."[68]

Fischer finds a clue to what motivated men like Eichmann or Himmler in their rigid, robotic personalities. They were true believers with all the strength and intensity that accompanies the will to believe. Their intensity of belief and rigidity insulated them from alternative information and prevented them from seeing the world from any perspective other than their own. In order to commit murder, they divided the self into two independently functioning halves—the cold-blooded killer, and the good doctor, family man, or conscientious employee. Guilt was avoided by transferring conscience to the "Auschwitz self" that justified murder as racial hygiene.

Fischer's view is that these men killed out of conviction. They repressed one part of the self in order to allow the murderous self to operate. They then asserted that the killing was in essence a healing process - that for Germany to live, its enemy had to die. For Fischer, this killing-healing syndrome was most evident among concentration camp doctors. Like those who burned the witches, they believed that by killing they were actually healing. He gives as example the case of a Nazi physician, Dr Fritz Klein, who, upon being asked how he could reconcile his murderous activity with his Hippocratic Oath, replied that as a doctor his goal was to preserve life. That is why he would treat a gangrenous appendix in the human body no differently than a gangrenous appendix such as the Jew in the body of mankind: he would remove them both.[69]

Friedlander, who examined the motives of different killers, from camp administrators to the people who removed the corpses from the gas chambers, found that ideology motivated only some of the participants. Moreover, even some of those who were ideologically motivated participated in the killings to advance their careers, for economic gain or to avoid being sent to the front. Others, in particular those at the lower end of the killing hierarchy, were not ideologically motivated, but rather became involved in the killings to forward their economic or career objectives, or to avoid going to the front.[70]

Friedlander further maintains that Nazi policies regarding the Jews must be seen in the wider context of Nazi killing operations against handicapped individuals and the Gypsies. Ideology, which envisaged competition in which only the fittest triumphed, linked the three killing operations, all of which aimed at cleansing the gene pool of the German nation. The collaboration among different segments of the bureaucracy also established links. The killing units that had murdered handicapped people were also involved in annihilating Jews and Gypsies, frequently using the same technology. Indeed, personnel trained in this technology were often transferred from one killing operation to the other.[71]

Nolte mentions other influences that may have motivated the Nazis. He suggests that the war and the manner in which it was fought played a role in Hitler's war against the Jews. He sees these changes in warfare resulting essentially from two influences. One was Bolshevism, which targeted an entire group as the enemy to be destroyed. The other was the alteration in European warfare itself. Nolte explains how, since the First World War, European methods of warfare altered from war being fought against armies to war being fought against total populations.[72] Both, Nolte argues, influenced Nazi behaviour.

One could well argue, of course, that the changes in warfare Nolte describes merely reflected the transfer to the European theatre of a type of war that Europeans had been fighting against Native peoples elsewhere for hundreds of years. As Lal states, the methods of warfare that facilitated the final solution may have been new to Europe, but they had been experienced by Native peoples coming into contact with Europeans for some five hundred years.[73]

The change from war fought by professional armies to one fought by and against total populations led not only the Nazis but also the Allies to commit genocide, Nolte argues. He sees evidence of total war and its genocidal nature in the massacres during Bromberger Bloody Sunday, in which Poles murdered several thousand citizens of German ethnic origin; in the German bomber attacks on Polish cities; in the destruction of some seven hundred thousand German civilians through Allied bomber attacks; in the expulsion of peoples such as the Volga Germans and Crimean Tartars under Stalin; and in the killing of Germans by Poles, Czechs, and Serbs towards the end of, and after, the war.[74]

It is not difficult to sustain Nolte's argument that these events were genocidal in nature. That the expulsion and subsequent treatment of Soviet minorities under Stalin during the war were genocidal in nature cannot be denied. The extent of the mortality that accompanied the expulsion of the Chechens and Ingush, the expulsion of the Soviet Germans, and the Crimean Tartars was mentioned in Chapter 4. Kuper places the destruction of German civilians during bombing raids, in particular the bombing of Dresden, into the category of genocides of international warfare. Another example is the murder of German civilians towards the end of the war and after the war by Poles, Czechs or Serbs. As the American scholar DeZayas makes clear, these people were killed because they were German.[75] These mass killings were of a magnitude that they could be considered genocides. For example, of the some two hundred thousand Donau Swabians who fell under Yugoslav rule after the retreat of the Germans, about half were killed.[76] These mass murders fit into Smith's category of retributive genocide, which is based on the desire for revenge. To an extent, these killings were also similar to the slaughter of the Armenians by the Turks; in both cases, the targeted group was a minority that had become identified with an enemy power. These attacks were also similar to the ethnic cleansing that Stalin initiated when he expelled Soviet Germans and other minorities in the Soviet Union from their homes during the war. With both Soviet Germans and the Germans in central Europe, expulsion was combined with slave labour and other punitive measures that took the lives of people.

While arguing that the genocide committed by the Nazis occurred at a time when warfare was becoming increasingly genocidal in nature, Nolte nevertheless concludes that Hitler's genocides fit into a different category than the destruction of civilian life carried out by any of the Allies during the war. This difference is derived, on the one hand, from the policy of unrestrained national egoism that was behind the drive for *Lebensraum*. Under this policy, Slavic peoples were to be replaced by Germans in vast areas of Eastern Europe. As the Germans moved east, mistreatment and the wanton destruction of peoples resulted. Another difference was, of course, Nazi policy towards the Jews whom the Nazis targeted as their enemy and at different times threatened to destroy prior to embarking upon their program of annihilation.[77]

It is difficult to disagree with the conclusion that such policies made the Nazi genocides different from those of the Allies. At the same time, Nazi war aims regarding the Jews differed from their aims regarding other peoples. It was only in relation to their Jewish policies that what Friedländer calls "redemptive anti-Semitism"[78] played an important role. Prior to the advent of the Nazis, redemptive anti-Semitism combined early Christian antagonism towards the Jews with *völkisch* beliefs about the organic nature of the *Volk*. The Nazis elaborated on these views, portraying the Jew as embodying the worst features of Bolshevism and capitalism. Drawing on old conspiracy theories, such as those spread by *The Protocols of the Elders of Zion*, they believed that the Jews were intent on conquering the world. Eugenics of the time served to give the moral or socio-political threat of the Jew a physiological dimension. As well, Hitler not only expanded on earlier elements of redemptive anti-Semitism but also made it a program of radical action. In this process, the Jews were dehistoricized and transformed into an abstract symbol of evil that threatened their equally metahistorical, symbolic opposite, the Aryan race.[79] This conceptualization made the Nazi war on the Jews not only a war against another people but one in which the Nazis saw themselves as the forces of light out to destroy the forces of darkness. For the forces of righteousness and regeneration to survive and prosper, the forces of corruption and degeneration had to be destroyed.

6
Genocide in Cambodia

Not unlike the Bolsheviks under Stalin in the Soviet Union, the Khmer Rouge under Pol Pot in Cambodia sought to build a communist utopia. However, unlike Stalin, who focussed on industrialization, Pol Pot sought to establish his utopia on Cambodia's agricultural base. At the same time, he sought to completely transform society. Violence and force were the main means of achieving the transformation and attaining the ideological vision. In this process, destruction became intricately linked to the transformation, resulting in what Chalk and Jonassohn describe as "an almost pure case of ideological genocide."[1]

Background

Situated in the southwest part of the Indochinese peninsula, Cambodia borders on the east and southeast with Vietnam, on the northeast with Laos, on the southwest with the Gulf of Thailand, and on the west and northwest with Thailand. With only one quarter of its land suitable for agriculture, rice, its staple crop, is grown on 85 per cent of its cultivated land. It rarely experienced famine and, together with South Vietnam, has been considered one of the major granaries of Indochina. In fact, since the 1920s, it generally has been able to export hundreds of thousands of tons of rice annually, while still retaining an adequate food supply for its population.

When the Khmer Rouge came to power, the majority of Cambodians were farmers, fishers and craftspeople. The Khmer, one of the earliest people to settle in the area, constituted between 80 and 90 per cent of the population. With the exception of a few Christians, they were adherents of Theravada Buddhism, a religion brought to the area from India a millennium ago. In addition to the Khmer, there were Chinese, descendants of people brought over several centuries ago by Khmer monarchs as artisans or intermediaries in the small commercial sector. After the Chinese, the most significant urban minority were the Vietnamese. Numbering more than three hundred thousand in 1970, they were for the most part descendants of immigrants who settled in Cambodia during the nineteenth century. Some also came during the period of Vietnamese political domination, while others were brought in by the French during the colonial era to serve as administrators and tradespeople. Among the remaining minority groups, the most prominent were the Muslim Chams, who, when the Khmer came to power, made their living primarily from fishing or agriculture.

Prior to the South Vietnamese invasion of Cambodia in the 1970s, most Cambodians lived in small villages, where the vast majority were owner-cultivators. Only about 10 per cent of Cambodia's population lived in urban areas of 10,000 or more inhabitants. Phnom Penh, Cambodia's capital, was the country's major city, with about 480,000 inhabitants. Chinese entrepreneurs, for the most part merchants and moneylenders, controlled the country's urban life. Traditionally, the Khmer exhibited little animosity towards them, viewing the higher standard of living of the Chinese as a part of a foreign culture rather than a product of exploitation. The Khmer tended to be more hostile towards the Vietnamese, an animosity that dated back to Cambodia's early history and the decline of the Khmer empire.

This powerful Khmer kingdom, with its splendid capital of Angkor, had once been the strongest and culturally most advanced civilization of mainland Southeast Asia, controlling at various times territory from the Burmese border to the South China Sea. In time, subject peoples such as the Vietnamese and Thais rebelled, and in 1444 the Khmer were forced to flee Angkor. For the next two hundred years the Thais and the Khmer were in almost continuous warfare with each other. Greatly weakened through this, by the beginning of the seventeenth century, Khmer kings were forced to depend for protection on either Siam (Thailand) or Vietnam. Indeed, by the mid-1800s, Vietnam exercised control over the country. This continued until 1863, when France declared a protectorate over Cambodia.

Retaining the main administrative posts for themselves, the French recruited Vietnamese to fill lower positions in the civil service and the police force, which served to deepen existing tensions between the Cambodian and Vietnamese communities. Because Cambodia occupied a peripheral area in the French colonial system, the French made little effort to exploit its resources or interfere with its way of life. This meant that Cambodian traditional society remained essentially intact. At the same time, industrial development was neglected, making the country dependent largely upon its agricultural base. During the Second World War, Japan occupied

Cambodia and declared it independent, setting up Norodom Sihanouk as king in 1941. Although France was able to re-establish its colonial administration after the war, it didn't have the resources to sustain its position. In 1953 it acceded to demands for independence from the royal house of Cambodia led by Prince Sihanouk.

Upon gaining independence, the government concentrated, among other things, on developing Cambodia's educational system. Between 1953 and 1969, school enrolment grew rapidly, climbing from 300,000 to about 1,000,000 at the elementary level, from 6,000 to 120,000 at the secondary level, and from less than 200 to 9,000 at the university level.[2] Many of the future Khmer Rouge leaders were beneficiaries of this system and were among the first Khmer sent to study in Paris. In France, these students came under the influence of French communists and absorbed the ideas of Chinese and Russian communist leaders, ideas that would later be used to diagnose and cure the ills of their homeland.

On returning to Cambodia, many of them worked as teachers. Their open criticism of the corruption in Prince Sihanouk's government resulted in persecution by the prince's security police. In response, several of the most radical chose to go underground to mount a revolutionary struggle against the regime. Their numbers remained miniscule until 1970, when Lon Nol, head of the Cambodian army and police, led a coup that overthrew the government of the still popular Prince Sihanouk, who fled to China. The underground rebels consolidated to resist the regime and, during the next five years, organized themselves under the name Khmer Rouge. Strengthened by Prince Sihanouk's popularity with the peasants and helped by the Vietnamese communists, their ranks swelled with an influx of peasant recruits. By the mid-1970s they made up a fighting force of some 68,000 strong, while the Communist Party grew to some 14,000 members.

In the meantime, Lon Nol's position was weakened by constant clashes with North Vietnamese units protecting the Ho Chi Minh trail, Hanoi's vital supply route to South Vietnam. He also became more deeply embroiled in the war in Vietnam when he allowed a force of 20,000 Americans and South Vietnamese to enter Cambodia to clear out North Vietnamese forces that were taking advantage of Cambodian neutrality to find sanctuary in the eastern part of the country. Following this, massive bombings of rural areas by the Americans led to a flood of refugees who crowded into the cities. The population of Phnom Penh alone rose from about half a million to over two million within five years.

Military action destroyed crops and disrupted communications, making the Lon Nol government ever more dependent upon the Americans to feed its people and support its military power. Corruption was rampant.

From Peking, Prince Sihanouk urged the Cambodians to rise up against the military government. His appeal was particularly effective among the peasantry. By tradition loyal to the monarchy, they were also alienated from the Lon Nol regime and its supporters, who consisted for the most part of the urban upper class comprised of leading civil servants, officers, large traders and the intelligentsia, with whose support the Lon Nol administration had come to power. On 17 April 1975, after a prolonged siege, Khmer Rouge forces under Pol Pot overran Lon Nol's troops and captured Phnom Penh, thereafter changing the name of the country to Kampuchea.

The genocide

There is little in Marx's writings to suggest that Russia in 1917 or Cambodia in 1975 were ripe for a proletarian revolution. Both societies were predominantly agricultural, rather than industrial. Nevertheless, the Bolsheviks and the Khmer Rouge seized power and sought to transform society. To justify their revolution, the Khmer Rouge imposed a Marxist model of socialism on Cambodia. In doing so, they made a number of assumptions. First, they assumed that the Cambodian agricultural community was hierarchically structured. In a speech in 1977 celebrating the achievements of the country's Communist Party, Pol Pot blamed rural injustices on landlordism, a phenomenon that fitted his theories more than it did the reality of the country. He made reference to only two provinces, Svay Rieng and Battambang, where landlordism constituted an important feature of the rural landscape, to justify his national program of collectivization. At the same time, he ignored the fact that most Cambodians were indebted to Chinese moneylenders who were the actual owners of their land, because "smashing the landlords" and taking their land fitted the class war that the communists wanted to wage.[3]

As such, the drive by the Communist Party of Kampuchea (CPK) to stage a revolution did not spring from a study of Kampuchean social conditions, but rather from the CPK's conviction that Kampuchea was in need of a communist revolution. If the right conditions did not exist, the problem could be overcome by revolutionary fervour. The absence of a proletariat was not seen as an impediment. Having no true proletariat in Kampuchea, the communists identified young children and poor peasants with the proletariat.[4] In a sense, their actions were not unlike those of Stalin in creating what he considered a revolutionary situation when he wanted to collectivize Soviet agriculture. Unlike Stalin, who identified the more affluent peasantry as the capitalist enemies of the people, Pol Pot and his communists identified elements of urban society as capitalist enemies of the people.

Immediately upon seizing power in 1975, the Khmer Rouge emptied the cities and forced the urban dwellers into the countryside. In part, the regime was motivated by the desire to develop Kampuchea's agricultural base, upon which they hoped to build the country's future.[5] The decision to evacuate the cities also sprang from the CPK's anti-urban ideology. Since 1968 the party had waged an armed struggle from the countryside with a peasant army whose class enemies, in theory at least, lived in cities and large towns. Townspeople, the Khmer Rouge believed, had exploited the peasantry for millennia, building comfortable lives for themselves on the backs of peasant labourers. Like drones, they exploited but gave nothing in return. The Khmer Rouge was also suspicious of the morality of cities. They tended to believe that, by choosing to stay in the towns, from which Lon Nol derived much of his support, these men and women had become enemies of the revolution. If they were driven into the countryside to work on the land, they might perhaps become useful. If not, the revolution would proceed without them. The common feeling among the Khmer Rouge was "Keeping [urban dwellers] is no benefit; losing them is no loss."[6]

While emptying the cities was intended as a break with the past and a move forward to a new beginning, it also served more pragmatic objectives. The Khmer Rouge saw the urban centers as possible areas of opposition. Removing people from the cities would deprive potential opponents of a natural base, thereby hindering them from organizing. This goal was further forwarded in that the new people were prevented from taking their possessions with them, thereby "proletarianizing" them. In the process of emptying the cities and forcing their occupants to go to the countryside to plant rice, dig canals, and perform other agricultural tasks, the Khmer Rouge also carried out a program of cleansing. Thus, they executed thousands of leading civil servants and officers of the old regime. People considered to be corrupted by their education, whether lawyers, doctors, or teachers, were killed, because they were perceived as being the opposite of the new type of person the Khmer Rouge sought to create.[7] Such people had been spoiled by a corrupt regime and couldn't be reformed, and therefore had to be physically eliminated from the brotherhood of the pure.[8] This corresponded to slogans the Khmer Rouge broadcast over radio: "What is infected must be cut out," and "What is rotten must be removed."[9]

Little effort was made to integrate urban dwellers who were not killed and who survived the forced transfer into the rural setting. Rather, they were labelled *prasheashon thmei,* or "new people." At the same time, the regime sought to incite hatred toward these "lackeys of the capitalist imperialists"among the *prasheashon shah*, the country people. A two-tier legal system was implemented which gave preference to rural people, who were also provided with slightly better food. Unlike the new people, these were also allowed to cast ballots for members to the representative assembly of the people during the communist-style election held on 20 March 1976.

In time, the two groups were sub-divided. As part of the process of collectivization, peasants were divided into "poor peasants," "landed peasants," rich peasants," and former traders. Among new people, non-officials and people with little education were separated from intellectuals and previous civil servants. The latter two were gradually purged, purges which after 1978 included women and children, so that the group eventually disappeared.[10]

Hoping to build Kampuchea's future on its agricultural base, the Khmer Rouge plan was to bring about a massive increase in the country's agricultural output, in particular its rice production. The objective was to first systematize Kampuchean agriculture and expand its light industry. After this would come the construction of heavy industry.[11] To achieve this goal, the population was challenged to raise rice production from about one ton per hectare, which had been the norm since 1970, to three tons per hectare. New land, much of it unsuitable, was broken to grow rice. At the same time, the regime sought to increase rice production from two to three crops per year.

The Kampuchean constitution of 1976 stated that a prime right of all its citizens was the right to work. In particular the new people were to see few other rights. The workday was generally eleven hours long. However, during competitions among villages, workdays often stretched to eighteen hours. There were few days of rest, with some locals abolishing such days altogether, while others filled them with interminable political meetings.

Often rejecting the application of new technology and the advice of technical experts, the peasants in charge of projects and their Communist Party masters often embarked on schemes doomed to failure. While some of the dikes constructed at that time remain in place today, others were washed away with the first flood, on occasion drowning workers in the process. However, as criticism was viewed as an attack on the regime, few people with technical skills dared suggest alternative approaches. At the same time, the communist intellectuals, who originated largely from urban centers, insisted on uniformity. Thus, in some situations dikes dividing rice fields were destroyed to make sure all rice paddies were one hectare square. Rice varieties that had been developed locally to meet local conditions were often scrapped to impose uniformity throughout a given district.

To increase the all-important rice production, fruit trees were cut down, thereupon destroying birds that kept insects in check as well as providing alternative food supplies. At the same time, the work force was divided in a manner that interfered with production, with people divided by age groupings with seven-to fifteen-year-olds, or people of marriageable age, working separately. At the same time, within each group, specialists were often trained only in specific tasks, making it difficult for them to respond to the different situations that might arise on the field.

To transform Cambodia's economy, the Khmer Rouge closed down markets, stopped salaried employment, and abandoned money as a means of exchange. To alter people's thinking and behaviour, they outlawed many existing practices and forced people to adhere rigidly to new ones. Practising the Buddhist religion was forbidden, and many monks were killed because they were considered to have too much influence over the people. The survivors were forced to work in the fields or at other collective projects. Strict rules for behaviour were laid down governing style of dress, haircuts, vocabulary, leisure and sexual relations, to name but a few areas. Parents had little control over their children. Rather, children controlled themselves and were encouraged to enlighten their parents. Marriage, which had required parental permission, now had to be approved by the heads of the boys' and girls' groups in the village. Parents were to honour their children, who were considered as having been unsullied by the corrupt past of the adults. The children, in turn, were to derive their knowledge from the workers and peasants, believed to be the source of all knowledge.

To carry out postwar tasks, personal likes or dislikes and even the idea of individual rights were crushed by the weight of revolutionary duties and the class interests of the peasants as interpreted by the party establishment.[12] Perceiving their objective of eradicating traditional Cambodian society as a kind of war, the Khmer Rouge encouraged the continuation of wartime solidarities, aggression, and patriotism. Their combatants (*yothea*) repeatedly launched new offensives (*vay samrok*) in agriculture and against existing or perceived enemies (*khmang*).

Although the CPK sought to establish equality by abolishing jobs, it put power into the hands of the young and the poorest, which contributed to the formation of a new hierarchy. This hierarchy no longer expressed itself in terms of money, possessions, or pre-revolutionary titles. Rather, those with power and status in the CPK had access to three commodities that most of the population lacked: food, weapons, and information. Violence was inherent in the very nature of this society. Even prior to the Khmer Rouge victory, the Communist Party recruited and indoctrinated thirteen- and fourteen-year-olds. When emerging from the indoctrination camps, these children were fiercely antagonistic to parental authority, religion, or anything else associated with the old ways. At the same time, they relished the power the Khmer Rouge had bestowed upon them, which included the opportunity to bully and even kill people.

Many of the new people found it difficult to adjust to a status where they were directed, "ridden, and kicked" both by the young and by uneducated people whom the revolution had placed over them. Animosity, distrust, and violence were further encouraged by the lack of communication among the different levels of power, with those at the top commanding and everyone else obeying.[13] Khmer Rouge attempts to transform society, including their endeavour to discredit Buddhism, eroded traditional legal or community sanctions against violence. Simultaneously, they encouraged aggression by making it a virtue to use terror, ostensibly as a temporary measure, to forward the revolution and eradicate Party enemies.[14]

The regime often spoke of "contradictions" (*tumno'h*), suggesting that conflict rather than the synthesis between opposites energized and gave life to the revolution. The regime's own relationship with most Kampucheans represented a contradiction of another kind. Ostensibly, the revolution had been carried out in the interest of the masses(*mahachon*). At the same time, at the individual level, revolutionaries were to be continually on guard against the people. Although the regime declared in 1975 that all Kampuchean society was composed of only one stratum—the worker-peasants—everyone was urged to fight against the "class enemies," who were compared to microbes (*merok*). However, these enemies were never clearly defined, which gave the party center maximum freedom to attack any enemy it chose as it guided the revolution, created the new society, and purified, or sorted the good from the evil.[15]

Although the Khmer Rouge claimed that "99 per cent" of the masses supported the revolution, people were warned that its enemies permeated every level of society, including CPK ranks.[16] Because traitors were often perceived as being people of urban background,[17] this made the new people especially vulnerable. Not only were they considered completely useless to the new Cambodian society, they were also perceived by the Party as the enemy who could be eradicated for even the slightest hint of opposition to the revolution. Anyone who stood in the way of the revolution was to be crushed beneath it.[18]

A whole number of "crimes" could result in immediate execution or imprisonment. Thus, stealing food was often followed by capital punishment. Marauders were frequently beaten to death on the spot and left to rot where they died to serve as an example to others.[19] Repeated visits to family members were often treated as a crime because these involved missing workdays, and could be followed by incarceration or immediate execution. Sexual relations outside of marriage were systematically punished with death. Insubordination, defeatist remarks or failure to complete tasks could designate one a counter-revolutionary and result in execution or imprisonment.

Death might also result from a hard blow, the lack of medical care, or chronic malnutrition. Unexplained disappearances at the hands of local party officials were commonplace, with summary executions being endemic to the Khmer regime. This was caused in part by the young fanatics who had been placed in positions where they could regulate people's lives. People were killed for the most minor provocation, be this for displeasing the person in power or for even minor infringements of rules.[20]

At the same time, the new people, deportees from the cities, were frequently forced to work land that was not only unsuitable for farming but also infested with disease-carrying insects.[21] This was the case in Pursat, for example, where new people were made to carve villages out of malarial forest. In these cases death from starvation, disease, and overwork were all too common.[22] Ponchaud states that a large portion of those deported appear to have succumbed as a result of mistreatment and the conditions under which they were forced to work.[23]

Khmer Rouge policies brought famine to Kampuchea. Initially, many of the new people had accepted the need to work to feed themselves and had achieved increased agricultural production after they were placed on the land. This willingness faded after the 1975 crop was harvested and the villagers saw most of it hauled away by government trucks to undisclosed destinations. As famine took hold of the country, rather than feed the people, the Party sought to drug them into forgetting their problems with the opiates of shrill triumphalist rhetoric and monotonous, interminable political meetings.

Daily rations were continually reduced. Prior to 1975, an adult would, on average, have consumed some 400 grams of rice daily, the minimum required for a normal diet. Although rations varied by area, once the soup kitchens became common in 1976, Kampucheans were fed a daily diet of watery rice soup containing little more than a spoon of rice per person. According to Ponchaud, Kampucheans should have been receiving from 2.7 to 4.4 tins of rice per day to avoid malnutrition and its long-term effects. The ration for most of the country, however, was one tin of rice (180 grams) per person every two days. Despite this, the Khmer Rouge refused foreign help. When UNICEF offered its assistance to help care for Khmer children, the regime responded that the Kampucheans had everything they needed. In addition, the Khmer Rouge refused to accept a planeload of medicine offered by the French government.[24]

Survivors of the period report that Khmer Rouge supervisors threatened to execute new people who were starving if they picked the fruit in areas where this was still growing in abundance. When supervisors relented and allowed workers to consume this fruit, they were forbidden to share it with those who were already too sick to work. Becoming sick was all too often interpreted as malingering or as an attempt to interfere with the Party's work plans, and thus perceived as counter-revolutionary. People were permitted to stop working only when they were sent to hospital, where food rations were reduced by half. Because of under-nutrition and the infectious illnesses rampant in hospitals, being sent there was the equivalent of a sentence of death.[25] Khmer Rouge officials and soldiers, however, ate well. Their attitude seems to have been "We went hungry for five years. Now it's your turn."[26]

Ethnic groups came under attack. Sliwinski calculates that some 38.4 per cent of Cambodia's 400,000 Chinese were killed at this time, as were also 37.5 per cent of its 300,000 Vietnamese.[27] They became targets not only because of their ethnicity but also because they were concentrated in urban centers. The Chinese also were vulnerable because they were better off than most Cambodians.[28] The Vietnamese, again, were often treated as hereditary enemies. Measures taken against them included a directive from the Party Center on 1 April 1977 that required all Vietnamese to be arrested and handed over to the central security forces. This at times led to the detainment and destruction of anyone who spoke Vietnamese. In addition, in the province of Kratie, which bordered Vietnam, being Vietnamese could lead to arrest and destruction.[29] The Vietnamese also suffered in that many of them were Catholics. Of these, some 48.6 per cent disappeared under the Khmer Rouge.[30]

Of indigenous minorities, in particular the Cham suffered. Numbering some 250,000 in 1970, they were generally considered part of the peasant group because they were active primarily in agriculture and fishing. However, they were at times reprimanded for being overly involved in commerce. As they were seen to be excellent warriors, the Khmer Rouge courted them in the early stages of the "war of liberation." However, in 1973 an attack was launched against their Islamic religion, with mosques being destroyed and prayers banned in the liberated zones. Attacks became more intense and widespread after 1975. Korans were collected and burned and mosques were destroyed or turned into warehouses. The Cham were also forbidden to speak their language and forced to take on Khmer customs. At the same time, they were forced to eat pork. Unlike most Cambodians, the Cham sought to fight back, which resulted in their being massacred, an example being the village of Trea, where the Khmer Rouge, according to a refugee report, annihilated the villagers after they rebelled in November 1975. After 1978, the Khmer Rouge began to systematically exterminate a number of Cham communities, including women and children. Treatment such as this resulted in a drastic decline of the Cham. According to Sliwinski, their population was reduced by 40.6 per cent under the Pol Pot regime.[31]

Khmer Rouge violence stemmed not only from their endeavours at social transformation but also from the attempt by the Communist Party leadership to concentrate power in its hands. When the Khmer Rouge replaced the Lon Nol regime the party was internally fractured, with a great deal of power being held by its regional and its military leaders. Army units under the control of the latter made them, to a large degree, independent of orders from the Central Committee. It was only in July 1975 that the diverse military units were united into a single national army. Still, following this development, the regional secretary of the Party Committee exercised the real power in regions where the Central Committee's influence was limited or non-existent.

In an effort to centralize power, Pol Pot and those closest to him conducted widespread purges of party officials at the regional and local levels. Centralization of political power also had economic consequences. Sharp reductions in food rations had to be made as an ever-larger share of the produce was transferred to the state distribution organization. Hunger led to rebellion. The foreign minister of Democratic Kampuchea, Ieng Sary, admitted that between 1975 and 1978 there were at least seven coup attempts.[32] The most serious of these to the Pol Pot leadership came from the eastern zone, near the Vietnamese border. It was ruthlessly crushed by troops loyal to the central government. Following their defeat, some of the rebel leaders fled to Vietnam, where they organized the Kampuchean National United Front of National Salvation (KNUFNS).[33]

Other people, however, were not that fortunate. Once the government regained control of the eastern zone, it condemned to death those living in the region, describing them as "Vietnamese in Khmer bodies." Out of a total population of 1.7 million, from 100,000 to 250,000 were massacred. In some villages, people were almost totally wiped out. Those surviving were transferred to other areas, where they continued to be killed, including women and children, original peasants and new people. Of some 3,000 people from the eastern zone that had been settled in one commune in the northwest, a mere hundred remained at the time of the Vietnamese invasion.[34]

The prison system also served as part of the killing process. Of course, the Khmer Rouge claimed not to have prisons, because prisons were seen to be a remnant of the corrupt old order. So, like the Chinese, they had what they called re-education centers. The Chinese, however, took re-education quite seriously and went to great length, for example, to demonstrate to the prisoners that the state had a right to imprison them. As a result, Chinese prisoners by comparison were fairly well treated.[35] In Cambodia, by contrast, torture was systematic and prisons, or re-education centers, were used primarily to destroy people.

A variety of peoples were incarcerated in such centers, including thieves, anyone who had transgressed the puritanical sex mores the regime sought to enforce, or anyone who had complained about mistreatment or had ridiculed the Khmer Rouge or any symbols representing them and their rule. People who had lied about their previous profession were imprisoned as were also those who had concealed compromising aspects of their past history, as for example a lengthy stay in the West.

Food rations for prison inmates were minuscule— sometimes a single box of rice for forty prisoners. There were no medical facilities and overcrowding was endemic. Average life expectancy under these conditions was about three months, with very few people getting out of prison alive.[36]

Prisoners were divided according to those who were condemned to die slowly and those who were executed immediately. How one was slotted depended upon the reason for incarceration: whether one had broken a law, had impure social credentials, had openly expressed dissatisfaction with the regime, or had participated in a conspiracy. The focus on conspiracy came into vogue in particular as the evidence mounted that the Khmer Rouge endeavour to construct a rural communist utopia would end in failure, resulting in Party leaders putting the blame on sabotage and traitors in the pay of foreign agents. They sought these traitors not only among people they viewed as suspect (the new people), but also among their own leadership. Regional leaders who resisted some of the party's more extreme measures were forced to confess, under torture, that they were agents of the Soviet KGB or the American CIA. They were forced to divulge the names of their fellow conspirators. Mythical networks of spies and traitors were invented by the interrogators. In such cases, torture was frequently applied to force the accused to name accomplices. Where admissions seemed promising regarding future convictions, detainees were moved up to the next level of prison. Thus, one could be moved from the local reform center to the district facility, to the main zone prison and up to the central prison at Tuol Sleng. Regardless of the level reached, the outcome tended to be the same. Once he had no further information to impart, the prisoner was killed.

There were hundreds of prisons across the country, with the number of detainees increasing gradually. While in 1975 there were barely 200, by 1976 there were 2,250, more than 6,330 in 1977 and 5,765 for the first part of 1978. The prison population increased despite the rapid elimination of those already in the system, be this through torture, starvation or general mistreatment.

Thus, an old school building simply known in code as S-21 claimed 20,000 victims. Most prisoners died in prisons such as this, with only 2 or perhaps 5 per cent of all prisoners passing through to the main prison of the Khmer Rouge, that of Tuol Sleng. A sample of the lists found at Tuol Sleng provides an idea as to the type of people killed while incarcerated by the Khmer Rouge. The list includes names of 1,000 Khmer Rouge soldiers, 324 factory workers, 206 officers of the pre-revolutionary army, 113 teachers and professors, 87 foreigners, 148 highly educated Khmer who had returned from overseas to serve their country and 194 students, doctors and engineers.[37]

In the Tuol Sleng prison in Phnom Penh nearly twenty thousand opponents of the Party leadership, or often those only thought to be opponents, lost their lives after brutal interrogations and forced confessions. Tuol Sleng, with its evidence still intact, fell into the hands of invading Vietnamese in January 1979 when the Kampuchean Communist Party leadership fled. This put to an end the Khmer Rouge experiment to establish a rural communist utopia in Cambodia.

Kiernan, who made a survey of the destruction rates among different groupings of the population, estimates that about 1, 500,000 Cambodians lost their lives during the rule of the Communist Party of Kampuchea.[38] Sliwinski, using demographic techniques, speaks of a little more than two million dead.[39] Of course, the precise number, as in all cases of genocide, will never be known. Examining the different estimates arrived at by scholars, Margolin concludes that Sliwinski's estimate, considering the methodical manner in which he arrived at his figures, was reasonable.[40] The degree of destruction varied for the different groups. Thus, officials of the old regime were either directly killed or later died in prison.[41] Educated people such as teachers and lawyers were killed, essentially because they were targeted as enemies or were seen as beyond redemption.[42] Sliwinski estimates that 82.6 per cent of officers in the republican army and 51.5 of people with higher education perished.[43] In case of the Chinese, it wasn't their ethnic background as much as their concentration in urban centers and their economic status that targeted them for attack. Vietnamese suffered both because of their ethnic background and their religious affiliation. Of domestic groups, in particular the Cham suffered, in part through the Khmer Rouge endeavours to assimilate them, but also because of their religious background.

Of urban people, about 41 per cent of the former inhabitants of Phnom Penh died; 28 per cent of the inhabitants of Kompong Cham (another densely populated region) died, and about 10 per cent of the people of

Oddar Mean Chhey died while forced to work the land.[44] This suggests that inhabitants of cities most closely tied to the old regime, such as Phnom Penh, were especially targeted for drastic treatment.

Survival among urban dwellers sent to rural areas was also influenced by where people were sent. Being sent to a wooded or a mountainous zone meant almost certain death, as these regions required that additional work be done to make them productive. In the meantime, the regime had identical production quotas for all regions. Also, as can be seen in the case of the Cham and the severity with which the Khmer Rouge suppressed rebel movements in the eastern zone, rebellion was severely punished, as was also any indication that one was opposed to the Khmer Rouge and their endeavour to transform Cambodia into an agrarian Marxist utopia. Violence was the main method used to bring about this transformation. Commenting on the mass destructions carried out by the Khmer Rouge, Ponchaud describes these as resulting from the application of an ideology pushed to the limits of its internal logic.[45]

7
Similarities and Differences

When looking at ideological genocides that analysts have described as holocausts, it becomes clear that, in some respects, each was unique. First, each of the genocides discussed in the preceding chapters was an expression of its time and place. The perpetrators in each case used their particular constructs to spell out their special status and identify the group(s) to be annihilated. Second, the methods of destruction also differed, ranging from death by sword, gun, or gas, to starvation and overwork. Third, the motivating belief systems differed. The Israelites mentioned in the Book of Joshua and the Christians who targeted the witches were motivated by religion, while the other groups were inspired by ideological systems. Nonetheless, these ideologies and religions operated in similar ways. Not unlike the traditional religions of Christianity and Judaism, the ideological systems presented a pathway to salvation. Rather than offering salvation through belief in the sacred, they offered salvation through philosophical truths, whether Marxism or social Darwinism. Like religions, these ideologies had their sacred texts, including *Mein Kampf* for the Nazis or Marx and Engel's *The Communist Manifesto*.

Although both Marxists and National Socialists rejected the religious beliefs of their youth, the Darwinian process of natural selection embraced by the Nazis and the Hegelian dialectic that underlay the class conflict subscribed to by Marxists tended to operate in the same mysterious way as the traditional God. In each case, the prime mover had a punitive as well as a rewarding side. The genocides committed by these groups were carried out to help ensure that they would reap the rewards rather than the punishment of their particular prime mover.

Some of these genocides were what one might call "firsts." The slaughter of the idolaters mentioned in the Bible is the earliest report I have come across where a group undertook to totally eradicate a people from a large territory so as to establish a base for its tribal god. The destruction of the kulaks and the enemies of the people in the Soviet Union were part of the first endeavour to transform a country into a Marxist utopia. The destruction of the witches, particularly the large hunts in France, Germany and Switzerland, differed from the persecution of witches in non-Christian cultures: in the former, witches were prosecuted not merely for practising *maleficium* but because they were believed to belong to a cult of Devil-worshippers. The National Socialists are not the first example we have where social Darwinism contributed to genocide. As we shall see from the examples of genocide in the Americas and Australia, beliefs in social Darwinism contributed to the slaughter of the Aboriginal peoples of the New World. Nonetheless, the Nazis were the first to use social Darwinism as a basis for creating an ideological system that would justify a massive program of eugenics, involving selective breeding, the destruction of "undesirable" people within the in-group, and the attempt to destroy out-groups believed to transmit undesirable characteristics through their genes.

What are the implications of these similarities and differences for the categorization of these genocides as holocausts? Of pertinence here is Bullock's response to the so-called *Historikerstreit* (the historians' fight), fought in Germany during the 1980s, which dealt largely with the question of whether the Nazi destruction of European Jewry differed significantly from the destruction of human life carried out under Stalin. His stance was that the inhumanity and excesses of the Stalinist repression were as "unique," in different ways, as those of the Nazis.[1] That does not, however, cancel out the uniqueness of the Nazi final solution. Nor, one might add, does the uniqueness of the Nazi or the Stalinist genocides cancel out the uniqueness of the European witch-hunts or the destruction of the idolaters.

The debate that broke out in France following the publication of *Le livre noir du communisme* in 1997, regarding the differences between Nazism and communism, does little to alter this observation. However, Besançon, one of the most thoughtful and impartial contributors to this debate, raises a very important point. He argues that the emphasis on the uniqueness of the destruction of European Jewry essentially has a religious base. For the Jews, the focus on uniqueness is part of their attempt to understand this event in the light of their relationship to their God. Through this tragedy, what is God saying to them, his chosen people? Christians view this event as unique insofar as they view the Jewish people as a unique people, the people of God. Besançon argues that the idea that the holocaust suffered by the Jews is unique stems largely from the uniqueness of the victims. He adds, however, that this conclusion makes logical sense, ultimately, if arrived at within the context of Jewish and Christian faiths. And that is why, Besançon maintains, the belief that the destruction of European Jewry is unique is not universally accepted.[2]

Besançon's point of view is highly significant. One can very well see how the view that the holocaust suffered by European Jewry is unique grew out of the religious context Besançon describes. Problems arise, however, when this argument for uniqueness, arrived at largely on the basis of religious belief, becomes a basis for describing a historical event. This does not mean that the destruction of European Jewry was not different from other genocides and unique in this way. However, as Besançon argues, each historical event is unique and non-repeatable.[3] Yet, there is a difference between arguing that a historical event is unique and arguing that this uniqueness sets the event apart and into a special category all its own. The attempt by Katz to do this, and by implication to minimize the destruction of Native peoples in the Americas, caused Churchill not only to dismiss Katz's argument but also to claim that those who argue that the genocide suffered by European Jewry is in a category all its own are insensitive to the suffering of other peoples.[4] Bullock concludes, as did many of those who took part in the *Historikerstreit*, that the issue of "uniqueness" is an unsatisfactory focus in the debate.[5] The same can be said of the French debate, which, like the *Historikerstreit,* all too often says more about people's ideological positions than about the events under scrutiny. The emphasis on the uniqueness of any genocide described as a holocaust detracts from more important questions: What were the dynamics that led to these genocides? What do these genocides tell us about people and society?

When one looks at the dynamics that led to the genocides explored in the preceding chapters, patterns readily emerge that offer insight into the forces that caused one group to seek to eradicate another. These patterns provide insight into the conditions that led to these massive destructions. With one exception, all of the genocidal societies under examination had just emerged from, or found themselves in, a social environment of war and turmoil, which no doubt led to a decreased appreciation for the value of human life, strengthened the inward-looking nature of these societies, intensified paranoidal tendencies, and encouraged aggression towards people identified as the enemy. The Israelites, after enslavement in Egypt and years in the desert, had returned to what they saw as the land promised to them, a land inhabited by peoples who did not worship Yahweh. Their return was marked by almost continuous warfare between the followers of Yahweh and the non-believers, warfare in which Yahweh proved his superiority over the gods of other people by granting the Israelites victory. The genocidal slaughter of the idolaters was a part of violent conquest.

The National Socialist movement in Germany grew out of the defeat of Germany in the First World War, the Treaty of Versailles, and the social and economic turmoil that followed the war. This turmoil was accompanied by a disintegration of traditional values. Like other peoples involved in the Great War, the Germans had felt their cause to be just and right. Thus, losing the war put all traditional beliefs and values to the test. Under these conditions, a number of social movements arose to offer a new vision, National Socialism being only one such movement. The National Socialists came to power in part because of the inability of the ever-changing governments of the Weimar Republic to cope with the massive unemployment that, in addition to other problems, faced Germany during the Depression. They were helped in their rise to power by the bungling German Conservatives, who had hoped to use Hitler but were outwitted by him, and also by Stalin, who had opposed an alliance between the German Communists and German Social Democrats. Stalin had mistakenly believed that the Nazis and the German Right would discredit themselves soon after seizing power, thereby preparing the way for a seizure of power by the German Communists. But once in power, even in a minority position, the National Socialists quickly destroyed opposition to their party and imposed their will upon the nation.

The Russian communists came to power during the First World War, largely because the Russian military defeats during the war discredited the old regime and unleashed the many discontents that, to that date, had been contained through the use of force. The communists were carried to power through the discontent of two social groups in Russia at the time of the revolution: urban workers and the rural peasantry. As the urban working class was relatively small in Russia in 1917, it was, ironically, essentially the desire of the peasantry for their private plot of land that enabled the communists to gain and hold on to power.

The Turkish destruction of the Armenians was carried out during the First World War, which came on the heels of a prolonged period of military and economic decline that had deprived the Turks of most of their European possessions. The genocide in Cambodia followed years of struggle against foreign powers, including the French and the Japanese. The only mass destruction that did not follow a period of military conflict was the European witch-hunts. Carried out over several hundred years, from the fourteenth to the seventeenth centuries, the witch-hunts became more intense, however, during periods of warfare or general social tension.

Although some of these mass destructions occurred while these societies were not militarily engaged against an external enemy, conflict nevertheless played an important role in all of them. This is evident in particular in the witch-hunts and the communist war on the enemies of the people. In these cases, the ideological framework that both the witch-hunters and the communists imposed on their environment interpreted everyday life as a struggle against the enemy. This was true especially of the communists. As Courtois points out, under the communists the civil conflict of everyday life was put into the context of total war that was carried out at all levels of society and in all areas of life.[6] This context shaped the conceptualization of enemies, who were placed at the opposite extreme of the forces of righteousness that targeted them; it also shaped the language used to describe these foes and helped determine the manner in which they were treated.

In all the examples under consideration, the genocidal group was endeavouring to escape a situation that it considered intolerable. The Israelite followers of Joshua had come out of bondage in Egypt and saw in the destruction of the idolaters the promise of establishing and retaining their own state. The Christians who hunted witches they considered to be Devil-worshippers were motivated not only by the drive for religious conformity but also by the fear that, if they did not go to extremes, all of Christendom would eventually be destroyed. The Nazis, for the most part veterans of the First World War, had lived through Germany's defeat and post-war impotence, and much of their drive to power was motivated by these experiences. The Young Turks were trying to revitalize the Turkish Empire, which was crumbling under their feet. The Bolsheviks wanted to put behind them the state of abject poverty in which much of the Russian working class and many of the peasants found themselves before the revolution. The Khmer Rouge hoped to pull Cambodia out of its Third World status by vitalizing its agricultural base, whereon, in turn, they sought to construct the communist utopia.

The excesses of each of these groups were fed by their successes, which no doubt nurtured the belief that their aspirations were attainable. The Israelites described in the Book of Joshua had escaped from Egypt and had withstood the vicissitudes of the desert, which included wars against idolaters. These successes were attributed by them to their faithfulness to Yahweh. In fact, the destruction of the idolaters was intended to help ensure further successes. The witches were prosecuted by secular and church authorities who had succeeded in imposing their views on the majority of the people under their control. The people who were burned as witches were often individuals or small groups who did not fit the common mould. The Bolsheviks had not only held on to power in Russia during the civil war that raged between 1917 and 1921, but had also brought about a significant transformation of Soviet society. Stalin's attack on the Ukrainian kulaks, the Communist Party establishment, and other enemies of the people was part of an organized attempt to continue this success and realize utopia in the Soviet Union. The Khmer Rouge seized power after defeating the Lon Nol regime and sought to bring to Cambodia what they saw as communist successes in the Soviet Union and China. Many of the Nazis had been veterans of a war in which they felt victory had been unjustifiably snatched from them, and the regeneration of the German nation was intended to undo the defeat and ensure that it would not recur. The Armenians were slaughtered as part of an attempt to mould Turkey into a tribal unit and thereby regain its lost imperial glory.

In all of these societies, control tended to be vested, not in the group as a whole, but in a small minority. The societies were elitist. Power lay in the hands of the theocracy in the society described in the Book of Joshua, in the religious or secular rulers in late medieval Europe, in the Young Turks in Turkey, in the National Socialists in Germany and in the Communist Party in both the Soviet Union and Cambodia. In all the cases, the leadership formulated or interpreted the basic ideology to which it sought to have the remainder of society adhere. In biblical Israel, the theocracy interpreted the Laws of Moses and sought to ascertain the will of the Lord. Having done so, it endeavoured to have the people adhere to the laws and live according to the will of Yahweh. In medieval Europe, the Church hierarchy formulated policy, a tendency that did not change even with the Reformation. Only the hierarchical structure of the Christian Church changed, with the Protestant biblical scholars interpreting scripture and then using the existing power structure of the state to impose their views of scripture upon the remainder of society. Existing power structures, in turn, used biblical scholars to expand their authority over their subjects.

In the case of the communists in the Soviet Union and Cambodia, the Communist Party and its leadership decided on the correct interpretation of Marxist doctrine. Once the correct ideological stance was decided upon, ideology was translated into programs of action. In the Soviet Union the genocide took place at a time of crisis in the leadership of the Communist Party. Decision-making power shifted from the party to the leader, and Stalin emerged in many ways as a type of fascist dictator.[7] The same dynamics were at work in Cambodia where the destruction of people was encouraged by recurring purges that served to put authority increasingly into the hands of Pol Pot and those closest to him.

In each of the above examples, the genocide was carried out at a time when the leadership of the genocidal group was seeking to establish or to ensure the survival of a certain ideological system in the social environment. In many respects, they were seeking to transform the society they dominated so that it would become the concrete representation of an ideal spelled out by their particular ideological system. With the exception of the ideology of the Young Turks, the ideologies under consideration illustrate a basic similarity in that they all tended to be rooted in what the Jungian psychologist Erich Neumann calls the "old ethic." Neumann states that

> the old ethic is, basically, dualistic. It envisages a contrasted world
> of light and darkness, divides existence into two hemispheres of
> pure and impure, good and evil, God and the Devil, and assigns
> man his proper task in the context of this dualistically driven uni-
> verse.... The individual is now essentially split into a world of val-
> ues, with which he is required to identify himself, and a world of
> anti-values, which are a part of his nature and can in fact be over-
> whelmingly strong, and which oppose the world of consciousness
> and values in the shape of the powers of darkness.
>
> The dualism of the old ethic, which is specially marked in its
> Iranian, Judaeo-Christian and Gnostic forms, divides both man,
> the world, and the Godhead into two tiers—an upper and a lower
> man, an upper and a lower world, a God and a Devil. This dichot-
> omy is effective on the practical level in spite of all philosophical,
> religious or metaphysical declarations of ultimate monism. The
> actual situation of Western man has been essentially conditioned
> by this dichotomy right up to the present day.[8]

This worldview and the proclivity to see the world in terms of opposing
extremes of good and evil characterized all the groups under consideration except the Young Turks. The latter had a romanticized view of their
own group that was given expression in the writings of Ziya Gökalp, for
example. Gökalp sought to transform Turkish nationalism from a religious to a tribal base, making it a rallying point not only for Turks but also
for Turkic-speaking groups outside the country's national borders. Gökalp
declared Turkish tribal society at the time of the great Turkish warriors to
be morally superior to Ottoman society at the beginning of the twentieth
century. Yet, Gökalp's ideal of Turkish tribalism never expressed the extreme elitism that formed the basis of the self-definition of all the other
groups under discussion.

The leaders of all the other groups were consumed with the need to
identify their particular group with the forces of light and to think of it as
elect or special. This notion of being chosen or elect was part of a broad
philosophical or religious system of beliefs that tied the aspirations of
these groups, and their struggle to realize their goals and destroy their
particular pariah, into the larger history of humankind. The followers of
Joshua believed that they were chosen from among nations by the one true
God to follow and worship Him. This view had its basis in the promise by
Yahweh to Abraham, and later to Jacob, that he would bless them above
all others and make them the founders of a great people. Bertrand Russell

argues that Christians took from the Israelites the idea that God favoured a particular group above others. For Jews, the idea was embodied in the Chosen People and for Christians the elect.[9] Russell argues further that an integral part of both belief systems is the doctrine that "all religions but one (namely their own) are false and evil."[10] No doubt, Russell is unfair to generalize about either Judaism or Christianity in this way. One can safely say, however, that both the believers described in the Book of Joshua and the witch-hunters who prosecuted the witches as the agents of Satan viewed all religions except their own as evil.

The National Socialist view that the Germans were a special people grew out of a conglomeration of ideas, hopes, and emotions welded together by a radical political movement in a time of crisis. Bracher sees a number of influences shaping this view, including the nationalist ideas of Fichte, which, formulated at the time of Germany's struggle against Napoleon, postulated the German people's special mission and pre-eminence as a nation.[11] This idea was taken up by romanticist political writers such as Adam Mueller, Wolfgang Menzel, Richard Wagner, and Paul de Lagarde, who delved into Germany's medieval tradition to show that Germans were a unique people with a great destiny. Developed when social Darwinism was at the height of its influence, these ideas frequently fused cultural pre-eminence with racial superiority.[12]

The Stalinist and the Khmer Rouge elitist vision had its basis in Marx's prediction of a proletarian utopia: the proletariat would seize power and usher in a paradise of righteousness and social justice. Crime, poverty, and other evils endemic to capitalist society would cease to exist. The Bolsheviks in Russia and the Khmer Rouge in Cambodia saw themselves as being on the righteous side of the historical struggle described by Marx. They were the vanguard of the morally unsullied proletariat who had risen, and would ultimately emerge victoriously, against the corrupt and corrupting bourgeoisie. They were agents of change, partaking in history to usher in the ideal society that Marx had prophesied.

Although the leadership of each group used different arguments to establish that their particular group constituted the elect, the essential structure of these arguments was similar. No matter what the specifics, the result was that each group believed itself pre-eminent, no matter whether chosen to be "the elect" by Yahweh, by Christ, by the evolutionary process, or by the Marxian dialectic. The notion of being chosen elevated the group above common humanity and, therefore, made it an agent of a greater truth, a truth according to which it sought to re-order society.

With the exception of the Turks, who tended to be driven by the frustration resulting from the decline of their empire, all of these genocidal societies were what Popper calls ascetic and utopian in their aspirations.[13]

They focused on some idealized vision. The asceticism and utopianism of these societies were given expression especially in their moral vision. The moral vision of the Israelites led by Joshua was closely integrated into their religious practices. Religious leaders prescribed specific religious rituals designed to approach as well as to pacify Yahweh. At the same time, they sought to force believers to adhere to certain moral codes, in particular those revealed by Yahweh to Moses. It was assumed that, by adhering to the prescribed moral codes, one could attain a stature superior to that of the non-believers.

The Christian persecutors of the witches sought to establish and perpetuate the living Church on earth. This Church was involved in a massive struggle in which the forces allied with good, with Christ and God, were aligned against the forces of evil, embodied by the witches. The Church fathers prescribed rituals by which to approach the divinity, represented by the Holy Trinity. At the same time, the Church fathers interpreted scripture to direct their adherents towards the ways of the Lord. Both secular and sacred powers were called upon to enforce conformity with prescribed codes of behaviour.

When the Bolsheviks seized power in Russia during the First World War, they were driven by an ideology that foresaw the demise of the state and, with it, the end of social evils endemic to a capitalist society. Realizing that Russia was not yet ripe for a socialist revolution, Lenin justified Bolshevik actions by arguing that Russia was the weakest link in the European capitalist system, a link that, once broken, would bring the capitalist order toppling down all over Europe. Initial hopes that this might be brought about through the social upheavals that occurred in various Eastern European countries immediately after the war were unrealized. This had little effect, however, on what Lenin perceived as the "historic role" of the Communist Party: leading the proletariat to victory over its enemy, the imperialist bourgeoisie. At the same time, the Bolsheviks sought to build socialism in the USSR, a goal that came into focus in particular under Stalin.[14]

In this process, Marxism was increasingly transformed from a theoretical explanation of social change to a moral cause, a utopian vision inspiring a revolutionary group seeking to transform society. Their objective was to create not only a new society but also a new type of human being. Only after the demonic forces standing in the way of the communist utopia had been eliminated would an environment be created that would nurture this new type of person. Unlike the Nazi ideal of a new being who would function successfully in the dog-eat-dog world of social Darwinism, the communist new being would evolve in some linear fashion to a higher degree of perfection. This view ultimately has its base in the Enlightenment, which saw humankind evolving towards a higher degree of awareness. Yet, unlike the ideal human of the Enlightenment, who was nurtured by learning and an expanding awareness, the new being the Marxists sought to create was the final product of a process that would destroy the class enemy and bring to fruition the communist utopia.

Despite its claim to scientific rigour, Marxism ultimately finds its driving force in a vision of society cast into the mould of age-old Judaic and Christian eschatological aspirations. This society would be free of the suppression and crime that characterized the world in its fallen state. As Cohn points out, integral to the post-1917 revolutionary approach to the problem of creating the ideal Marxian society in a world that did not fit Marx's ideals, was a solution common to millenarians: to destroy those elements identified as the enemies or perverters of whatever was idealized.[15] These impulses motivated not only the Bolsheviks in the Soviet Union, but also the Khmer Rouge in Cambodia.

Unlike the communists, and true to the Judaeo-Christian and Rousseauian view of the fall of man, the Nazis idealized a vague primeval state of vitality and innocence in the past. This they found in German traditional society, in the *Volksgemeinschaft*, before it was "perverted" by Jewish influence. The *Volksgemeinschaft*, in their view, was a collectivity united by blood and a common tradition, both of which found unity and expression in the *Führer*. Nazis sought to bring about this *Volksgemeinschaft* by a number of means, including selective breeding and the destruction of morally and physically decrepit elements standing in the way of the ideal type, through *Gleichschaltung*,[16] through demagoguery that Jung saw as appealing to the German primitive,[17] or through Nazi rituals that, as Cassirer remarks, served to lull asleep people's power of judgment and critical discernment, and their feeling of individual responsibility.[18]

The ultimate goal was to re-create a modern form of the tribal community. The reconstitution of this community and, through it, the German type, would improve both the racial and moral characteristics of Germans.[19] These Germans would control the Thousand Year Reich, which would be large enough to meet its own needs without fear of a foreign threat. As such, the National Socialist goal was not merely to transform German society, but also to gain for this society the territorial base that would help it thrive and prosper.

It appears that the manner in which a group cast itself influenced the stereotype it created of its enemy. Unlike the other groups under discussion here, Turkish self-definition, as well as their view of the group they sought to destroy, was not rooted in an abstract cosmology that identified their interests with a universal force. Comparing the Nazi view of the Jews and the view that the Committee of Union and Progress of the Young

Turks had of the Armenians, Melson states that the Turks were national-ists who found it necessary to destroy the Armenians because they stood in the way of a Turkish state that stretched from Anatolia to Central Asia. By contrast, the National Socialists found it necessary to destroy the Jews because they resembled a contaminating disease, threatened to control the world, and sabotaged Nazi efforts to create a new world order. Killing the Jew was part of a process to purify and redeem the elect group.[20]

The Turkish view of the Armenians is different not only from the Nazi view of the Jews, but also from the Israelite view of the idolaters as de-scribed in the Book of Joshua and from the communists' view of their ene-my. The goals of the Young Turks were specific. The Armenians who stood in the way of a Turkish tribal state had to be destroyed, but they were not seen as a contaminating force from which the Young Turks had to save the elect group. In contrast, all the other genocidal groups identified their enemy with some larger process of contamination. For the Israelites under Joshua, the idolaters embodied the negative forces that had the potential to contaminate the elect. The idolaters did not worship Yahweh and did not belong to the tribes of Israel. They lived on territory that the Israelite theocracy sought to reserve for the followers of Yahweh. The idolaters had to be destroyed to prevent the perversion of the rituals and other worship patterns involved in satisfying the demands of Yahweh. The idolaters were also a symbolic representation of what Yahweh defined as reprehensible; killing them was justified as Yahweh's punishment upon them.

To the Christians who killed the witches because they were agents of Satan, the antithesis of the Christian was the representative of Satan. At the time of the early Israelites, both the elect and their opponents saw themselves as being earth-centered. It could well be argued that the main justification for the slaughter of the idolaters was to establish a locale on earth that Yahweh could claim as his own. The Christians' conceptualiza-tion of the witches, as well as of themselves, might be seen, in contrast, as other-world-centered, that is, centered in a world of heaven and hell, of God and Satan. This conceptualization was influenced by a number of traditions. In discussing these, Russell writes that "later Judaism had already learnt to believe in life after death, but the Christians gave a new definition to Heaven and Hell, and to the ways of reaching the one and escaping the other."[21] Developing this view, he states that Persian dualism was absorbed, but with the addition that pagan gods were little more than varying representations of Satan.[22] Persian influence also nurtured the Christian view that the world was the battleground between the forces of good and evil. Within Persian religious beliefs, the forces of good were led by Ahura Mazda and those of evil by Ahriman. Black magic was worked with the help of Ahriman and his followers in the world of spirits. The

Christian Satan is a derivative of Ahriman.[23] In keeping with this concep-tualization, medieval Christians believed that the followers of Satan had supernatural powers such as the ability to fly by night or to cause infer-tility or disease. Their role was considered malevolent, in contrast to the forces of good with which the true believers were allied. Morally, witches were characterized as being opposite from the Christians; witches trod on the cross as a sign of their rejection of Christ and his Church, and they were sexually licentious.

The enemies of the communists were the bourgeoisie, a generally vaguely defined group that included anyone who was perceived as pos-ing a threat to the proletariat and to communist aspirations to establish the ideal society. In Stalinist Russia and in Cambodia under the Khmer Rouge, the leadership decided who belonged to the bourgeoisie, the group that had to be eliminated for the proletariat to prosper. As in the case of the witches, trials were at times used to determine who in fact was an enemy of the people. In both cases, community networks were used to identify the enemy, whether the witch or the bourgeoisie. Also, in both cases, tor-ture was instrumental in locating new enemies who, in turn, were pros-ecuted and then punished or destroyed.

During the famine in the Soviet Union and the mass executions in Cam-bodia, court procedures were discarded. Whole segments of the popula-tion were identified as possessing detestable capitalist characteristics. The language used to describe them, essentially slogans of war and revolution, established the pariah as the people's enemy who had to be conquered and as a corrupting remnant of an old order that had to be eliminated for the proletariat to prosper.

Nazi ideology also slated for destruction the groups that were seen as contaminating, particularly the Jews. Bracher states that the Nazi image of the Jew grew out of a stereotype perpetuated in German society through the popular literature that identified the Jews with corrupt, urban, com-mercial values. These values were contrasted with glorified virtues of the simple rural life. Nevertheless, despite their negative stereotype, it was possible that, as the ideals of the Enlightenment spread, the Jews would gradually have been integrated into the German nation. However, as the optimism of the Enlightenment crumbled under the onslaught of *völkisch* nationalism, the belief in the eternally demoralizing Jews took root. Their assimilation came to be assumed impossible, with religious differences being interpreted in terms of fundamental moral differences. The rise of biological anthropology, which saw human beings as a product of their genes, worked to transform the Jewish stereotype still further, and reli-gious, moral, and cultural differences came increasingly to be interpreted in racist-biological terms. The negative characteristics of the Jews came to be seen as passed on not merely by their culture or religion but by their very being. This view, Bracher argues, laid the groundwork for the Nazi attempt at extermination.[24]

Except for the Armenians, all scapegoated groups in the cases under study were identified with characteristics and value systems essentially opposite from those espoused by the leadership of the genocidal group. Motivated by religious and tribal impulses, the followers of Joshua saw the communities organized around the worship of alien deities as the enemy. Motivated by tribal instincts and the memories of a war lost that they felt they should have won, the Nazis chose as their main enemy a group they perceived as unjustifiably having usurped power. Stalinism, a synthesis of Russian nationalism and Marxist utopianism, targeted as its enemy the Ukrainian kulak, who was seen to threaten the proletariat and Russian nationalist aspirations. In the larger schema of things, Stalin himself eventually became the embodiment of the drive to build the Marxist utopia, and anyone perceived as a threat to him or his goals came to be classified as an enemy of the people and was treated accordingly. The Khmer Rouge saw certain members of the bourgeoisie as too corrupt to be integrated into the classless society they hoped to build. At the same time, they eliminated any elements, including party members, who stood in the way of transforming Cambodian society in the image of the Marxist utopia as perceived by Pol Pot and those closest to him. Motivated largely by religious impulses, the persecutors of the witches concentrated on destroying followers of Satan, the enemy of God and Christ.

In many respects, each of the genocides under discussion was part of a revolutionary transformation of society. The Young Turk revolution had pragmatic goals, with the Armenians being wiped out to create a Turkish tribal state and prevent the further break-up of Turkey. The other revolutionary transformations served to rid the world of the contaminating influences that thwarted a process of regeneration and purification. The pariah groups were identified with this thwarting process, and the battle against them was undertaken in a much larger context: the forces of light battling the forces of darkness, the forces of good fighting the forces of evil.

In all cases under study, including that of the Armenians in Turkey, the scapegoated groups participated in or interacted with the society that declared them pariahs. Although the idolaters described in the Book of Joshua were not part of the social system of the Israelites, interaction between the two groups had been sufficient for the Israelite theocracy to conclude that the idolaters posed a danger to Israelite religious practices. Jews were important in all areas of German economic, political, artistic, and scientific life, and Armenians played an important role in the economic life of the Ottoman Empire. The witches were non-conformists who did not fit into the mould of orthodox Christianity. The enemies of the people in both the Soviet Union and Cambodia were identified with the corrupt old order. These enemies might be Ukrainian peasants who were perceived as being a little richer than their neighbours, people identified with the old order because of their education or other attributes, or people perceived as standing in the way of bringing about the Marxist utopia.

Each group was viewed as powerful enough to negatively affect the society that targeted it for destruction. Clearly groups such as the idolaters, the Jews in Germany, the Armenians in Turkey, the kulaks in the Soviet Union, and the urban educated class in Cambodia had some power. There is no evidence to show, however, that any of them had the power to achieve the things of which they were accused. The Armenians did not have the power to bring about the defeat of the Turkish army by the Russians. Nor did Joshua's idolaters, the witches, the Jews, or the enemies of the people have the power to corrupt the respective societies of which they were a part. It might be said that any power held by the pariah group was largely attributed to it by the genocidal group: it was rarely real power.

Each genocidal society made use of conspiracy theory to give evidence of the danger posed by the pariah. Basic to this theory is the belief that problems in society are caused, not by mistakes the group itself is making, but by outside malevolent forces thwarting its efforts. Because these conspiratorial forces carry out their workings in all sorts of secretive ways, their real power can never be established. This mystification helps to establish as self-evident the belief that these forces are powerful, so powerful that they can prevent anyone from ever knowing the true extent of their influence.

Unlike the Young Turks, who had tangible goals, the people committing genocide in each of the other cases had comparatively elusive goals; they aspired to perfect their society on the basis of a particular utopian image. They aimed at an image of the ideal, in particular a moral ideal. At the same time, they identified their target groups with some abstraction of evil. They projected onto their target group what Jungians call "man's shadow."[25]

The basic problem in each of these cases lay in overestimating humanity's ability to fit an abstract ideal. They also overestimated the influence that an ideology or an idealized social system could have on shaping human beings. Rather than adopting a realistic perspective on the society they idealized, each leadership sought to ignore the darker side of their own idealized group and then pointed to a group they held responsible for undesirable traits, situations, or circumstances in which their society found itself and to an outside power contaminating the idealized group or thwarting the goals of its leadership.

The Israelites in Joshua's time were convinced that the idolaters would contaminate their religious practices, a conviction rooted in their religious beliefs and in the socially deterministic views regarding human behaviour held by the theocracy in power. Killing the idolaters became part of gaining Yahweh's rewards and avoiding his punishment. The same essentially religious orientation influenced the Christian view of the witches. In the nineteenth and early twentieth centuries, despite the general decline of religious values, the belief that individuals or groups could be contaminating was encouraged by the application of the medical model to diagnose psychological or social illness. This model had a profound impact on social theorizing at the turn of the last century and influenced various psychoanalytic theories as well as other theories attempting to explain individual and group behaviour.[26] Basic to this medical model is the view that individuals, as psychic units, as well as groups, can be diseased, much as a body can become diseased from harmful influences acting upon it. Individuals or groups who are diseased can, in turn, contaminate others with whom they come into contact. These views formed an integral part in particular of the theoretical framework applied by Bolshevik communists and National Socialists when pointing out root causes for society's ills.

In contrast to the other genocidal groups, the Young Turks used views such as these to shift the blame for Turkish defeats on the Russian front from themselves to the Armenians. All the other genocidal groups, while also blaming the pariah group for their own failings, cast their net much wider and explained their war against their particular pariah in the context of a much larger struggle between good and evil, between the forces of purification represented by the genocidal group and the forces of corruption represented by the pariah.

Whether a pariah group was targeted for partial or total destruction was, in all these situations, determined by a number of factors. One was the manner in which the pariah was stigmatised. Another was the role played by the pariah in the genocidal group's overall objectives. The Young Turks did not see the Armenians as being some sort of disease or vermin that had to be eradicated so that the Turkish tribal group could thrive. The Young Turks wanted to punish them for their supposed support of the Russians. At the same time, the Armenians were destroyed because they stood in the way of Turkish expansionist aspirations and, on the other hand, to prevent the further subdivision of the Turkish Empire should its military efforts end in total disaster.

In all the other cases, where the genocidal groups were pursuing much more grandiose objectives (to create or to retain a version of, if not the perfect society, then at least the best possible society on earth), pariah groups were associated with ideas and ideals thwarting the attainment of these goals. They became negative abstractions, infectious illnesses that had to be cut out, or diabolical forces that had to be eliminated. It was the image of the pariah as contaminating or corrupting that caused the genocidal groups to lay such stress upon its eradication. The realm of Yahweh as envisaged by Joshua's followers had no room for the idolater. Those building the kingdom of Christ had no room for the followers of Satan. The Nazis had no place for the vilified Jew, nor did the communist utopia have room for the enemy of the proletariat. In each instance, the pariahs ceased to be people and became forces of moral decrepitude threatening some ascetic or utopian vision of society. This negative stereotyping had its basis ultimately in the eschatological aspirations of the leadership of the genocidal group and the linkage between these aspirations and the pariah group. The same drive that pushed the genocidal group to realize its eschatological aspirations also drove it to eliminate the perceived enemy.

Negative stereotyping in these instances operated in different ways. In both the case of the devil-worshipping witch and the bourgeois enemy of the people, negative categories were established that had no readily identifiable counterpart in the social environment. Either category was a fairly malleable abstraction spelling out the type of people who had to be eliminated for the aspired-to society to be created. Nevertheless, once actual people were slotted into either category, they could be tortured, they could be destroyed. They could be treated in this way because, once categorized, they were deprived of their humanity. They became a type that had to be eliminated for the idealized society to come into being, and eliminating this type became an integral part of creating the aspired-to society.

The case was somewhat different for a group that was directly targeted for destruction, as was the case of the Jews who were killed by the Nazis and, to some extent, of the Armenians killed by the Turks. There was a major difference, however, between the Jews and the Armenians. The Armenians who were Muslims were considered to be redeemable and were not killed. In the case of the Jews, the very nature of the Jew was considered to be corrupting and therefore the entire group had to be eliminated. In a sense, the Nazi case is most similar to the situation of the idolaters, as described in the Book of Joshua. Just as it was impossible for the Jew to become a part of the German people through a process of conversion, it was also impossible for the idolater to become part of the Israelite community. In both cases, the creation of the idealized society was associated with the elimination of the target group. Under the Nazis, elimination became synonymous with genocide in particular between 1941 and 1943, when getting rid of the Jews meant killing as many of them as possible.

In the case of the idolaters and the Jews, where groups readily recognized in the social environment became the embodiment of characteristics that made them worthy of destruction, emphasis was on the elimination of all members of the group, regardless of age or sex. In the case of the witches or the bourgeois enemies of the people, where it was much more difficult to establish a link between the abstract group intended for elimination and actual people, perpetrators placed less emphasis on the total destruction of the actual groups who at different times were targeted for attack. Difficulties in identification also made the categories of who was or who wasn't to be attacked much less rigid. At the same time, the leadership of the elect had much more influence on who was to be placed into the category of people slated for elimination, with different groups being persecuted at different times.

When one looks at the genocides under study, one finds that with the exception of the Turkish example, they follow a fairly consistent pattern. The leadership of the other genocidal societies saw their group as elect. It was not merely special in some way; more importantly, it stood above all other peoples. This special status had been given to it by some force in the universe or by social or human evolution. The leaders of these genocidal societies proceeded to create a type of society that corresponded to their particular view of the ideal. This involved a total restructuring of society, in essence giving society a new base, in a sense a new moral basis. On the other hand, these societies also aspired to create a new type of person. The new morality and the new person who would emerge from this transformation would serve as proof of the superiority of the society that was being created. While endeavouring to build this new society, the leadership tended to see faults with the society around it. At the same time, it, of course, encountered difficulty in building its new society. Rather than question its basic premises, the leadership targeted some outside group as the cause of all its problems. Creating the new society became identified with fighting this pariah group, with the struggle eventually leading to the attempt to wipe out the pariah group. This struggle tended to take place at the cosmic level. It involved a struggle between the sons of light battling the sons of darkness. Creating the new society became identified with completely obliterating the sons of darkness.

Considering the differences between the genocide in Turkey and the other ideological genocides described as holocausts, it appears, as Neumann suggests, that the holocaust is largely an outgrowth of the Judaeo-Christian tradition. This tradition spilled over into countries such as Cambodia largely because of the influence the West had on these countries, be this through the spread of communism or Western-style nationalism. The Turkish genocide also illustrates that a genocide similar to the holocaust can be carried out without necessarily being rooted in what appears to be the basic holocaust model. In the Turkish case, Turkish nationalism, as defined by the Young Turks, served to exclude the Armenians and defined them as outsiders. In a state of crisis during the First World War, when Armenians were identified with the enemy, exclusion and suspicion of the outsider led to genocide. However, the broader extremes, the typecasting in terms of corruption in conflict with regeneration, or peoples of light in conflict with peoples of darkness, that appear basic to the Nazi case, the destruction of the idolaters and of the witches, or the communist war on the bourgeois enemy, are absent in the Turkish genocide, as is also the extreme emphasis on the total elimination of the pariah and linking this to the emergence of a new, idealized society. Therefore, the Turkish example, while partially fitting the holocaust model that applies to the other ideological genocides under study here, cannot be seen as a holocaust.

However, the holocaust model fits all the other accounts described here, including the one presented in Deuteronomy and the Book of Joshua.[27] Thus, for four out of five genocides under consideration, the term "holocaust" may be seen as a suitable description. Further insight into the nature of the holocaust genocide may be gained by examining genocides described as holocausts as the Old World conquered the New.

PART II

COLONIALIST GENOCIDES AS HOLOCAUSTS

European expansion into the New World had a devastating effect on the Native peoples of these regions. Genocide, as well as disease, warfare, geographic removals, and the destruction of a traditional way of life, contributed to the decimation or, in some cases, total destruction of Native groups.[1] Epidemics had the most disastrous effect on Natives: European typhoid, smallpox, and measles were the major killers, while African malaria and yellow fever contributed significantly to the destruction of Native peoples in the lowlands of South America.[2] Between 1524 and 1526, hemorrhagic smallpox killed tens of thousands of Incas in Peru.[3] Preceding Pizarro's first voyage to Peru, the outbreak was likely caused by germs carried by the trade route from the West Indies or Mexico, where contact with Europeans was already established. Diseases introduced from Europe also had a disastrous effect on the Native peoples trading with New France. Thornton estimates that the Huron lost one-half to two-thirds of their population between 1634 and 1640 as a result of smallpox and other epidemics.[4]

Evidence suggests that, in some instances, Europeans intentionally spread diseases among Native peoples. McNeil states that American settlers from time to time may have deliberately encouraged the spread of smallpox among the Indians.[5] The best-documented example of the British military using biological methods to subdue the Indians fighting in defence of their lands involved British officers stationed at Fort Pitt giving a handkerchief and blankets from the local smallpox hospital to Delaware Indians in an attempt to suppress a military alliance of Native peoples that had been organized by the Ottawa leader, Pontiac, in the 1760s.[6] Sir Jeffrey Amherst, commander-in-chief of the British forces in North America at the time, instructed his subordinate, "You will do well to try to innoculate (*sic*) the Indians by means of blankets as well as to try every other method that can serve to extirpate this [execrable] race."[7] Although there is no conclusive evidence showing that these attempts at germ warfare succeeded,

Thornton observes that the Delaware, the Mingo, and the Shawnee were soon gripped by a smallpox epidemic.[8] In 1765, the Native revolt was ended by negotiation.

Churchill, when discussing the Pontiac example as well as other cases, concludes that the intentional spread of disease was used both to reduce the fighting capacity of Native peoples as well as to extirpate them.[9] Stannard maintains that the diseases that decimated the Native peoples in the Americas were only a prelude to human catastrophes that followed "on the killing grounds."[10] By concentrating on diseases, analysts have created the impression that the destruction of tens of millions of people as Europeans conquered the Americas was merely the sad, inevitable, and unintended consequence of human migration and progress. Stannard calls this the soft side of anti-Indian racism that serves to exonerate individuals, parties, and nations. Disease and genocide were interdependent forces, each feeding on the other, both working together to drive Native societies to the brink, and often over the brink, of total extermination.[11] Stannard concludes that these dynamics were operative in bringing about holocausts in both Spanish and British America.

In the following chapters, I will explore the motives that caused the European conquerors to destroy Native peoples in Spanish and British America. In the case of the British, I will look at the Thirteen Colonies, the United States and Canada. As France controlled much of the territory prior to the British conquest of what became Canada, I will look at French colonial policy towards the Natives. To gain further insight into the dynamics that led to genocide in Newfoundland and the United States, I will also examine the dynamics that led to the destruction of the Aborigines in Australia. My objective is to explore the forces that caused Stannard to describe the destruction of Native peoples in Spanish and British America as holocausts.

8
The Destruction of Native Peoples in Spanish America

This chapter explores Stannard's argument that the destruction of Native peoples by the Spaniards constituted a holocaust. From the outset, I must admit that I find his position somewhat problematic, largely because of his statement that this holocaust was the result of the Spaniards using genocidal means to advance economic goals.[1] He fails to clarify, however, what a genocidal means is and how it differs from genocide. This lack of clarity is exacerbated when he argues that the destruction of Native peoples by the Spaniards constituted a holocaust.

Having raised these reservations, I nevertheless acknowledge that Stannard's analysis of the destruction of Native peoples in the Americas is one of the most scholarly probing works on this subject. In this chapter, I will present the main thrust of his argument and then return to the questions I have just raised. Stannard argues that the Spanish decimation of Native Americans was a holocaust because its dynamics were similar to those that led to the destruction of European Jewry. These similarities were rooted in the Christian attitudes and racial beliefs of Europeans. In accordance with Elie Wiesel, who argued that the Christian tradition encouraged a frame of mind that allowed the destruction of European Jewry to take place, Stannard posits that these same beliefs contributed to the annihilation of Native peoples.[2] Moreover, according to Stannard, European racial ideas allowed the European conquerors to view the Amerindians they encountered in the New World as a lower form of being. Such attitudes justified their denigration, enslavement, or destruction.[3]

Stannard sees evidence of a holocaust in the indiscriminate slaughter of Native peoples, in their mistreatment following their enslavement by the Spaniards, and in the drastic reduction of the Native population of South and Central America following the arrival of the colonizers. He makes comparisons between the treatment of the Jews and these Aboriginal peoples to illustrate how the dynamics that led to the destruction of European Jewry had a similar effect on the Amerindians.

According to Stannard, the Spaniard's indiscriminate slaughter of Native peoples began with Columbus's second voyage to the New World, in 1494. Accompanied by ferocious dogs that had been trained to disembowel human beings, the heavily armed Spaniards forced the Arawak, the Native peoples of Hispaniola, where Columbus first established himself, to supply them with food, slaves, and gold. The newcomers killed indiscriminately, as if for sport. Some of the Arawak fled as far as Cuba, but they were not able to escape the Spaniards, who killed most of them and enslaved the rest. Quoting Bartalomé de Las Casas, Stannard gives firsthand evidence of the Spanish pitilessly slaughtering Native peoples. Thus, after cutting off an Indian's hand, except for a shred of skin from which it was left dangling, they would send him off, saying "Go now, spread the news to your chiefs." They placed bets to determine who was better at slicing off heads or cutting bodies in half with one blow. This served not merely to satisfy the Spaniard's lust for torture and destruction but also to convince the Native of his utter helplessness in the face of the conqueror.

In one killing spree, which began in the village of Zucayo, where the Natives had earlier prepared a feast for the conquistadors, Las Casas reports that the soldiers killed over twenty thousand people. Stannard also quotes a Dominican friar, who reported that the Spaniards tore an infant from an Indian woman's arms and flung it to their hungry dog, which devoured it before the mother's eyes.[4] Again, he quotes Las Casas, who stated that the Spaniards took pleasure in inventing all kinds of torture. For example, they built a long gallows, low enough so that the toes of those hanged touched the ground, thus preventing the victims from dying of strangulation. The Spaniards then proceeded to hang thirteen Natives at a time in honour of Christ. While the Indians were still alive, the Spaniards ripped their bodies open with their swords to expose the entrails.[5]

Such acts were carried out not only in Hispaniola but elsewhere as well. Once they had wiped out most of the Native peoples in Hispaniola, the Spaniards hunted down Natives in Bermuda and Cuba so that they might enslave them. To help systematize the enslavement of Native peoples, Columbus introduced the basis of what would evolve into the *encomienda* system. This system put Native communities under the control of Spanish masters who were free to work their subjects in any way they wished. During its early years, this system contributed to the death of millions of Amerindians, through both mistreatment and overwork under terrible conditions.

Any slave who dared escape was hunted down with mastiffs. If not killed on the spot when caught, the escapees were put on trial and punished harshly to discourage others from escaping. Las Casas estimates that only 10 per cent of the enslaved Natives survived to the point where they were dismissed because they were too broken to perform further work. Again quoting Las Casas, Stannard gives a first-hand account of the Spaniards beating, kicking, and otherwise mistreating Native people to force them to work, and how the enslaved, crushed by horses, cut to pieces by swords, attacked by dogs, and suffering all kinds of other tortures, abandoned themselves to their fate with no further struggle, their spirit broken.[6]

In a mere two years, the population of Hispaniola fell from eight million to between four and five million, and by 1535 the Native population of Hispaniola was essentially extinct. Stannard compares this annihilation to twentieth-century genocides, and concludes that no modern genocides came close to destroying as many innocent people as the Spaniards did in Hispaniola and other Caribbean islands.[7]

Similar excesses characterized Spanish behaviour on the mainland. To provide insight into this, Stannard details, for example, Cortés's conquest of Tenochtitlán, Montezuma's capital, during the conquest of Mexico. The conquest began with a feast in honour of the god Huitziloppochtli, to which the conquistadors had been invited into the city. During the celebration, the Spaniards suddenly fell upon the unsuspecting Aztecs. They began by decapitating and cutting off the hands of all the singers and dancers, upon which they slaughtered the other Indians present. Trying to escape, the Natives rushed to the exits of the courtyard, only to be cut down by the Spaniards guarding these. Others sought escape by climbing the courtyard or temple walls, while still others threw themselves among the slain, feigning death. This, however, was of little help to them. The Spaniards hunted all of them down, killing anyone found alive.[8]

Despite heavy losses, the Aztecs were able to regroup and force the Spaniards out of Tenochtitlán. The Spanish, however, had by then infected them with smallpox. While smallpox wreaked havoc among the population of Tenochtitlán, Cortés reorganized his forces and destroyed smaller towns around the city. Then he again marched on the capital. After a prolonged siege, the Spaniards destroyed both the city and most of its people, enslaving the few who were left. Tenochtitlán was no more.[9]

Cortés wasn't the only Spanish adventurer seeking to enrich himself by destroying another people. Again quoting Las Casas, Stannard mentions the destructions carried out by Spanish troops under Alvarado, who devastated a kingdom more than four hundred and eighty kilometres square, which was even more populous than the kingdom of Mexico. Between 1525 and 1540, the invaders killed more than four million people, and then continued to destroy those who were still left.[10]

Stannard uses statistics to show the extent of the destruction wrought by the Spaniards. Within seventy-five years of the Spaniards' arrival, the population in central Mexico fell by almost 95 per cent, from more than

25 million in 1519 to about 1.3 million in 1595. Wherever the Spaniards went, consequences were the same. In western Nicaragua, 99 per cent of the people were dead within sixty years of the Spaniards' arrival. In western and central Honduras, 95 per cent of the people were killed in half a century. By 1542 Nicaragua was robbed of as many as half a million of its people who were caught and enslaved, to be worked to death. Between 1514 and 1530, some two million Indians were killed in Panama. Stannard observes that, across the length and breadth of Mexico and down into Central America, the Spanish conquest meant the sudden and near total disappearance of populations that had lived in the region for thousands of years.[11]

Native people in other areas of South America experienced the same fate. The Inca Empire covered virtually the entire western coast of South America and contained some nine to fourteen million people prior to the arrival of the Europeans. Smallpox and other epidemics preceded Pizarro's invasion of the region. Sickness was followed by slaughter during the conquest and mistreatment following the conquest. This included dogging, a favourite sport of the Spaniards, which involved hunting Native people as if they were wild game. As a result, 95 per cent of the population was destroyed long before the close of the sixteenth century.[12] Stannard quotes a statement by Alonso de Zorita noting that the Spaniards had a saying to the effect that it was easy to find one's way from place to place in territories the Spaniards conquered or ruled, because the paths were marked with the bones of the dead. There were certain birds that, when an Indian fell, fed on the remains; these birds appeared in profusion whenever the Spaniards made an incursion into a territory, or claimed an Incan mine.[13]

If outright killing didn't kill off the inhabitants, then they were destroyed by the conditions under which they were forced to work. As described by Stannard, reducing the Native to chattel involved a rather ludicrous ritual. In theory, each time the Spaniards encountered any Natives, they were to read them a statement proclaiming the truth of Christianity and demanding they swear immediate allegiance to the Pope and the Spanish crown. If the Indians refused or hesitated, the Spaniards were permitted to make war on them in any manner. They could deprive them of all they possessed and enslave them, adults and children alike. In practice, the Spaniards did not even follow this procedure. First, the Indians were manacled; then their rights were read to them in Spanish, which, of course, the Natives did not understand. Finally, they were driven off to be enslaved.[14]

Once enslaved, mainland Natives were treated in a manner that had already decimated the original inhabitants of the Caribbean islands. For example, forced to work in the gold mines or to pan gold in the rivers, they had their hands cut off if they didn't deliver the amount of gold demanded of them. As long as there seemed to be an endless supply of Indian labour, the Spaniards found it more economical to work slaves to death rather than treat them humanely. The life expectancy of slaves working in mines or plantations in Peru during these early years was not much more than three or four months, which, Stannard notes, was about the same time that a labourer working in Auschwitz survived.[15]

Such mistreatment, Stannard argues, continued until most of the Native population in Spanish America had been wiped out. It was terminated only when the Spaniards realized that the destruction of the Natives would have a detrimental effect on their own well-being. In the meantime, somewhere between sixty and eighty million Native people had been destroyed by the end of the sixteenth century.[16] Although many of these were killed by diseases brought over by the Spaniards, others had been intentionally slaughtered or had died as a result of the inhumane treatment suffered at the hands of the conquerors. Inhumane treatment, of course, magnified any of the effects diseases had in destroying Native peoples.

Despite such mammoth destruction, Stannard considers this annihilation to have been a by-product of conquest and enslavement, a genocidal means to an economic end and not an end in itself.[17] Other scholars are even more explicit, arguing that the destruction of Native peoples by the Spaniards can't be considered a genocide. Chalk and Jonassohn, for example, state that, in spite of much evidence of Spanish brutality towards the Indians, genocide (deliberate killing with the intention of destroying the group), played an insignificant part, if any, in the Spanish conquest of the New World.[18] Commenting on the destruction of the Arawak in Hispaniola, which has frequently been viewed as the prime example of Spanish cruelty in the Americas, Cook and Borah conclude that although they did not suffer a genocide, the Arawaks of Hispaniola were "for all practical purposes extinct."[19]

Insight into why these authors reached this conclusion may, perhaps, be found by looking more closely at the "extinction" of the Arawak in Hispaniola. After conquering the Indians in the central part of Hispaniola, Columbus imposed upon each chief a tribute of gold that was to be collected every three months. By the end of his third voyage, in 1500, the system of tributes had been extended to the Indian province of Xaragua at the western end of the island. When Bobadilla replaced Columbus as governor of Hispaniola in 1500, the new governor demanded that each chief contribute a certain number of Indians to work in the Spanish gold mines. Two years later, Bobadilla's successor, Ovando, ordered all the Indians of the island (including those of the easternmost province of Higuey, which had never been conquered) to be used in this manner, thus establishing the dreaded *encomienda* system, whereby Indian men on the island were distributed among the Spanish colonists to work in the gold mines or on the plantations of their masters for six to eight months of the year.

Although, in theory, the *encomienda* system was to operate for the benefit of the Indians, providing them with the opportunity to acquire Spanish culture and the Christian religion in return for supplying a moderate amount of labour, in practice the system was badly abused. The Indians were overworked and ill-fed. Although the Arawak did not accept this treatment without a struggle, the conquistadores easily put down the rebellions, often with great cruelty. While working for the Spaniards, many Arawak starved to death; others committed suicide. Mothers killed their children to spare them the lot of their fathers. In addition, smallpox further decimated the population. By 1535, only a few Arawak were left on the island, and the colonists imported Africans, and Indians from other parts of the Caribbean to replace them.

Rouse sees the *encomienda* system and the mistreatment resulting therefrom as the main reason for the destruction of the Arawak of Hispaniola. Moreover, he argues that similar forces led to the destruction of the Indians in Puerto Rico and Jamaica, which the Spaniards settled in 1508 and 1509 after the conquest of Hispaniola. The Indian population in the Bahamas was destroyed before 1600 as the result of slave raids undertaken by the colonists of Hispaniola to replenish the diminishing supply of Indians on that island.[20]

Chalk and Jonassohn and Cook and Borah do not consider the destruction of Native people by the Spaniards genocides because the Spaniards targeted the Natives for enslavement rather than destruction. In their view, a genocide can only be committed if the perpetrator targets a group for destruction. Churchill examines this aspect of the definition of genocide, pointing out that its use may have more to do with endeavours by power groups using the definition of genocide for their own ends (whether to focus on a particular genocide or to deny other genocides) than it does with an attempt to understand the dynamics that lead to genocide.[21] While presenting a cogent argument, Churchill perhaps fails to give sufficient weight to one advantage that this limited definition has, namely, that it tends to be fairly straightforward and relatively simple.

The trouble with simplicity in this case is that it tends towards the simplistic. When one looks at the cases under study, one finds that several steps precede any targeting of a group. In the case of an ideological holocaust, the target group is first defined as evil or contaminating. Having imposed this label on the pariah, the leadership of the genocidal society proceeds to destroy the group so defined. When one looks at the destruction of Native people in Spanish America, a pattern is evident as well. The group carrying out the destruction defines the target group in a way that serves to dehumanize it. In this case, the group is not viewed as a pariah that must be destroyed but rather as less than human. Defining Native people in this way and treating them accordingly led to the total destruction of some groups and massive decimation of others.

Let us take this one step further. Those who make expressed intent an integral part of the definition of genocide argue that X group is guilty of genocide when leaders responsible for the group's actions state that they will work Y group to death and then proceed to translate this expression of intent into action, thereby bringing about the destruction of a great many members of Y group. They also say that X group is not guilty of genocide when they force members of Y group to work under conditions that lead to the destruction of a vast majority of them just so that they can get the maximum work out of them. Only one motive seems to matter. X group may have worked members of Y group to death because they considered them to be lower type beings there solely for exploitation. In this case, members of Y group were not intentionally targeted for destruction. However, the value system that X group brought to the situation contributed to the deaths and in fact caused them. This is dismissed as a causal factor contributing to genocide by those who argue that explicitly stated intent to destroy is the prime criteria which should be applied to determine whether a genocide has been committed.

There is a certain validity to this argument. Chalk and Jonassohn choose direct targeting as their criterion for determining whether a genocide has been committed because they wish to avoid cases where mass deaths resulted, for example, from the spread of disease as a consequence of mass migration.[22] This is perfectly reasonable. It is necessary to consider motives when determining whether or not a genocide has been committed. But how logical is it to apply the direct targeting rule to all cases? Let us look at an example. Chalk and Jonassohn mention the case of Portuguese missionaries who destroyed a great many Native peoples in their endeavours to minister to them.[23] Looking at the case within the confines of the direct targeting criterion, one would have difficulty considering this case a genocide. Yet, in examining the treatment of Native people by Iberian missionaries, Churchill does just that, arguing that these missions were just another way through which the Iberians mistreated and destroyed Native peoples.[24]

Churchill's argument suggests that, while motives must be considered, one must also look at how motives are linked to action. How does this relate to the Spanish case? The government in Spain rationalized that enslavement was in the interest of the Native. In the actual situation, the *encomienda* system was largely an extension of the conquest. As Gibson states, it was closely associated with slavery and an outgrowth of the general assumption that the conquered Indians could be treated as the encomendero's private property.[25] Enslavement and mistreatment resulting therefrom led to the massive destruction of Native people, and such treatment continued until most Native peoples had been wiped out. If one does not consider only motive, but the entire context that led to this destruction, it could well be argued that the massive Spanish destruction of Indians in the Americas constituted a genocide. It certainly would constitute a genocide if one were to accept Ben Whitaker's recommendation that the United Nations include acts of advertent omission in its list of acts of genocide.[26] It would be considered an act of genocide if the United Nations were to accept Churchill's elaborate definition of genocide.[27] Until greater agreement is reached both by scholars and governments as to what constitutes a genocide, little can be done, however, other than to suggest that the definition of genocide as it has been applied by many of the researchers to the Spanish American situation needs further examination and re-evaluation.

In this context, this debate raises another significant point. Stannard appears to agree with scholars who argue that while the destruction of the Arawak, for example, was a tragedy of enormous proportion, it was not a genocide. At the same time, however, he maintains that it was a holocaust, because of the similarities between this destruction and that of the Jews: namely, the forces of racism and religious bigotry that lay at the root of the Nazi destruction of European Jewry also led to the annihilation of Native peoples by the Spaniards. In essence, Stannard suggests that a holocaust is not necessarily genocide.

9
Clearing the Land of the Indian in the Thirteen Colonies and the United States

Churchill argues that, prior to the arrival of the Europeans, there were some nine to twelve and perhaps as many as eighteen million Native people in North America. Most of these lived in what is today the United States. By 1900, the Bureau of Census reported that the Native population in the United States was a little over 237,000. Churchill attributes this decimation in part to disease, which was at times used to deliberately destroy the Native. He sees genocidal wars, in which Indians were indiscriminately slaughtered, as contributing to the destruction. More important, he sees this decimation as resulting largely from the mistreatment of the Native population by the European invaders, in particular by the English, who followed a policy of driving Native people from their ancestral land, killing them indiscriminately, and then replacing them on the land with their people.[1] Indians who refused to move to reserves, where they were routinely cheated of life's necessities by dishonest agents, were often simply exterminated.[2] Together these forces resulted in the almost complete eradication of Native people from the United States.[3]

Written from a Native person's perspective, Churchill's *A little matter of genocide* provides insight into a dimension of the American experience that has received little attention. Churchill shows how the growth and development of the American Empire went hand in hand with the destruction of the Native population. It is not the purpose of this study to describe in detail the destruction of Native peoples in the United States; rather, this chapter will present examples that illustrate the patterns of these mass destructions. The objective is to determine the extent to which the evidence supports Stannard's argument that, while the holocaust in Spanish America was characterized by people being targeted for despoliation and enslavement, the holocaust in British America was characterized by Natives being directly targeted for destruction.[4]

Genocides committed against the Aboriginal people of what is now the United States predated the establishment of the American republic. Here, we will examine only one genocide from this period—that directed

against the Pequot. This is not to say that the Pequot were the only nation extirpated during the colonial period. Genocide played a role in the
elimination of Native tribes in Connecticut, the Carolinas, Florida, and
Virginia.[5] Commenting on the destruction of Natives in Virginia, for example, Thornton remarks that the "colonists were instructed to root out
the Indians...[and] this is pretty much what they did.[6]

The attitudes of the Puritans towards Aboriginal peoples are fairly representative of other early British settlers in the Americas. They did not
recognize Native claims to the land. At different times, they viewed the
Indians as a nuisance and a pest. Thus, following a battle in 1675 in which
the colonial militia was seriously mauled by the Narragansett Indians,
Captain Winthrop, a Puritan, wrote a poem in which he prophesied that
God in his wonder would exterminate the Indians, whom Winthrop compared to flies, rats, and lice.[7] Attitudes such as these meant that the English colonists looked forward to the decimation of the Native people. Observing the speed with which Aboriginal peoples were being wiped out
by diseases brought to America by the Europeans, the Pilgrims noted that
God was sweeping away the Natives so as to make room for newcomers.[8]
Comparing prevailing English, French, and Spanish attitudes towards the
decimation of the Native people through disease or war, Thornton observes that, while the religious element among the French and Spanish
deplored the deaths, the English, religious or otherwise, seemed to look
upon the decimation of the Natives as evidence of God's favouring "His
chosen people."[9]

Destruction of the Pequot

Descendents of nomadic hunters who had arrived in the region 10,000
years prior to the arrival of Europeans, the Indians of New England depended on hunting, fishing, and agriculture to survive. Utilizing their environment according to the season, they hunted in the winter, fished in
the streams and cleared their fields in the spring, cultivated and fished in
the summer, and harvested their fields and hunted in the autumn. Before
the settlement of the Europeans, the Algonkian-speaking people of New
England probably numbered more than 100,000 between the Kennebec
River and Cape Cod. The most numerous among them were the Abenaki,
Narragansett, Pequot, Pawtucket, Massachuset, and Wampanoag. They
all had been in contact with Europeans for generations, in particular with
fishermen who dried their catches and engaged in trade.

English exploration and attempts at settlement occurred in the early
seventeenth century but didn't fare very well. One problem was that the

French had already established permanent settlements in the area and were involved in reciprocal trading relations with Native peoples. Moreover, the English adopted a more militaristic stance than the French, which included attacking and kidnapping coastal Indians and selling them into slavery. However, a factor other than treatment of the Native population paved the way for a permanent English presence in New England. This was disease. In 1616, English fishermen unintentionally infected the Indians in the area with a virus against which the Natives had no immunological defence. Thousands died, with the area from Massachusetts Bay to Plymouth Bay being particularly hard hit. Entire towns were swept away or abandoned. When the Pilgrims arrived in 1620, they came to an area that had suffered catastrophic population losses a few years earlier. Thus, land became available at the same time as the Native's ability to resist European encroachment was severely impaired.

The first few years of contact between Indians and the new settlers were fairly peaceful. A local Wampanoag who had been kidnapped by an English ship captain in 1614 and sold into slavery to the Spaniards, but then had escaped and made his way back to New England, helped smooth contact between the Pilgrims and Native peoples in the area. Also, the Wampanoag were on unfriendly terms with the neighbouring Narragansetts and hoped to gain English support in this struggle. Relations between the English and the Wampanoag became strained, however, when about sixty non-Pilgrim newcomers settled near the Pilgrim colony. They stole grain from the Massachusetts, mounting attacks that resulted in several deaths. When the Puritan mass migration began in 1630, relations between the Puritans and the Native population, while under stress, were still relatively peaceful. This was encouraged by the rivalry among the Native groups, which prevented them from uniting against the newcomers. The Puritans, while publicly committed to interracial harmony, privately prepared for the worst. They trained all men in the use of firearms, prohibited Indians from entering Puritan towns, and sought to prevent any firearms and ammunition from falling into Native hands.

This uneasy state of affairs was exacerbated by a number of factors. Smallpox struck the eastern Massachusetts in 1633 and 1634, killing thousands. For the Puritans this was proof that God had intervened on their behalf at a time when they were seeking new areas of settlement for their increasing population. Like other Europeans, the Puritans believed that Christians were everywhere entitled to dispossess non-Christians of their land. Also like other Europeans, the Puritans subscribed to the theory of *vacuum domicilium*, which claimed that unsettled land could be forfeited to those who would settle and cultivate it. They maintained, therefore, that the Indians had no right to any land they roamed rather than settled.

At the same time, epidemics had very much reduced the area of land occupied by the Indians.

The relationship between Puritans and Indians was also complicated by the Puritan sense of mission, which was to tame and civilize the wilderness, including the people who occupied it. Seen to be lacking Christian piety, purposefulness, and the work ethic, Aboriginal people were considered to be the counter-image of civilized Europeans. Rather than simply Christianizing Native people, the Puritans dealt with this perceived inadequacy by attempting to bring them under Puritan civilian control. While many of the smaller bands of eastern Massachusetts, weakened by disease or fearing stronger neighbours, accommodated themselves to these legal strictures, the stronger tribes did not. This was true, in particular, of the Pequot.

The direct cause for the outbreak of war between the Puritans and the Pequot was the murder of two ship captains and their crews. Blaming the Pequot, the Puritans used this as a pretext to attack the unsubmissive Pequot, sending a joint Connecticut-Massachusetts force against them. In the war that followed, the Pequot were able to withstand the English until the latter surrounded a Pequot village on the Mystic River in May 1637. The English and the Narragnasett, whom the English had succeeded in recruiting as allies, attacked before dawn. They set fire to the Pequot wigwams and then retreated. Because the Pequot warriors were at another village, most of the people fleeing the fire were noncombatants. Yet these women and children were killed, either by the fire or the Puritans lying in wait for them. The war continuing, some captured Pequot were sold to other tribes, and others shipped to the West Indies to be enslaved. Ultimately, the Pequot resistance was broken. Most of the remaining Pequot were then killed either by the colonists or at the insistence of the colonists. Churchill states that before the Puritan war on the Pequot was over, at least two-thirds of the Pequot had been killed. The surviving were absorbed by the Mohegans.[10]

Commenting on the destruction of the Pequot, one Puritan militia captain wrote that, at Mystic Fort, "God laughed his Enemies and the Enemies of his People to Scorn, making them as a fiery Oven . . . [and] filling the Place with Dead Bodies."[11] At the Treaty of Hartford, in 1638, the Pequot nation was declared dissolved. Two generations later, a pillar of the Puritan ministry, Cotton Mather, reiterated: "in little more than one hour, five or six hundred of these barbarians were dismissed from a world that was *burdened* with them."[12]

Nash argues that the destruction of the Pequot, which proved for the Puritans their political and military ascendancy, came in response to the anxiety and disunity that had become widely diffused throughout the colony. The Pequot war broke out following three years of intense internal discord, centered around challenges by Roger Williams and Anne Hutchinson to the power of the magistrates. These challenges were not only of a theological nature but also concerned the distribution of political power, economic policy, and competing land claims of English settlers in Massachusetts, Connecticut and Rhode Island. With their settlements embroiled in controversy, Puritan leaders warned against God's anger being kindled against his people for corrupting "the City on the Hill." The Puritan determination to destroy the Pequot, and the violence manifested at Mystic Fort, Nash concludes, was fuelled by land hunger reinforced by self-doubt and guilt that Puritans could "expiate" only by destroying their enemies, whom they also saw as enemies of God. As such, "dead Pequot were offered to God as atonement for Puritan failings."[13]

The Destruction of the Yana and other Indian tribes in California

The history of the United States, after it gained its independence from Britain in 1776, is a history of white settlers displacing Indians from their own territory. Aboriginal people stood little chance of stemming the flow of settlers, behind which stood an army with some of the most advanced weaponry of the time. By orders issued to the army in 1799, white squatters were to be granted "all the humanity which the circumstances will possibly permit."[14] Hagan describes the effect of such orders: "For Army officers in a civilian-dominated military establishment this was sufficient warning. If Indian and white interests conflicted, the Indian was sacrificed."[15]

Moore argues that few American leaders wanted to annihilate the Indians. Yet, politicians at the state and local levels adopted policies that subordinated Indian lives to their political aspirations, and to the land hunger of white settlers and ranchers.[16] Chalk and Jonassohn argue that, supported by the electorate, American political leaders became accomplices in the killing of Indians by failing to protect them from settlers in their territory and by deporting them to reserves and then not providing them with the necessities they required to sustain themselves. Furthermore, they "insisted on harmful acts of commission and omission long after it became clear that their policies emboldened the most unscrupulous settlers, who—left unhindered by the force of law and order—went on to destroy essential Indian food supplies, to kidnap Indian women and children, and to murder peaceful Indians with impunity."[17] All these influences are evident in the destruction of the Southern Yana and other tribes in California.

Although first contact likely occurred decades earlier, it was not until 1848 that white settlers on the California-Oregon trail crossed into northern and central Yana territory. Farther south, the Lassen trail, which came into use in 1849, transversed Yahi Yana territory. Established in 1851, Noble's Road became one of the main roads bringing miners and settlers into northern California. Although the southern Cascade foothills were initially little affected by mining and settlement, in particular the use of the foothills as grazing lands for livestock brought the Yana into contact with the early settlers. Captain John Fremont's attack on a peaceful gathering of Indians (who likely were Yana) on Bloody Island in the Sacramento River in 1846 marked the first hostility between the two groups. The Yana retaliated on occasion by murdering a few whites. They also began to raid cabins as it became increasingly more difficult for them to obtain adequate food. In response, the settlers massacred the Yana, at different times killing more than thirty of them. Following the 1867 massacre of 45 or more individuals on Dye Creek, there weren't enough Yana to bury the dead and the bodies remained on the ground. Within twenty years, the Yana population had fallen from 1,900 individuals to probably less than 100.[18]

Ishi, the last living member of the Southern Yana, was "caught" in the California mountains and given a home in the Museum of Anthropology of the University of California. The curator of the museum, Professor A.L. Kroeber, and his wife, Theodora, befriended him and, in the process, gained insight into Ishi and his people. Ishi belonged to a Southern Yana tribe that, in 1865, was practically exterminated during a massacre perpetrated by the settlers. The five survivors took refuge in Deer Creek Canyon in Tehama County, with 1870 being the last recorded time that anyone had seen them.

The experiences of Ishi and his people are related to us primarily from the point of view of the people who destroyed them. Although Theodora Kroeber's and Robert Heizer's account[19] is sympathetic to Ishi's experiences and those of his people, it nevertheless presents these experiences from a white person's perspective, as does Theodora Kroeber's less formal discussion of the same subject.[20] At the same time, Kroeber used her knowledge of both Ishi and his people to present an account of what it must have been like to undergo the destruction he and his people experienced. As we have so few records of what conquest and destruction must have been like from the perspective of Native Americans, Ishi's observations may give us an insight into this experience. Ishi recounts:

When mother was as big as Tushi, the hills and the river-valley were filled with people. There were other worlds too, to the south and east and north and west. . . . Last night Elder Uncle said only

Yahi were left in the hills when I was born. And three turnings of the moon ago, when Elder Uncle brought us to Tuliyani, there were not even any Yani left but us.

The next morning, Timawi and Ishi were bringing in wood for the watgurwa fire and Ishi asked, 'Why could not the People turn away the other saldu [white people] as Grandfather turned away the first ones?'

Timawi answered, 'There were too many of them; they came too fast. So Elder Uncle says, Grandfather says it was because all saldu carried firesticks and hunted the People, meaning to empty the hills of us.'

'Why then were not all the Yahi killed as were the others?'

'I think it was because your father learned to fight the enemy. And once he learned this, they stopped coming over the ridge trail and through Yahi country since they might be shot down by the arrows of the wanasi. Your father taught the People—not only the wanasi, but the old, the children and the women—to hide at the back of dark caves, under piles of leaves, in the middle of a clump of poison oak or spiny manzanita. He showed them how to lie face-down beside a trail, sometimes with a rock to hide them, sometimes with nothing. Horses might pass almost over them without their being discovered.

'He and the good swimmers learned to stay for a long time under water against a boulder, or to swim into the shade where they could come up to breathe as a bullfrog does, and go under without being seen. The wanasi with your father even learned to go behind waterfalls while saldu searched and then gave up the search because they could not see them behind the water.'

'Tell me what else my father did.'

'I heard him say in the watgurwa, 'Jupka and Kaltsuna gave us no weapons for fighting men, but the saldu do not have a magic which turns the straight-flying arrow from their hearts; it may enter as it enters the deer's heart.'

'Did my father's and the other wanasi's arrows enter the hearts of many saldu?'

'Not many, not enough; the Yahi were the hunted ones. But many times, your father drew the enemy away from the villages, from the women and children and Old Ones who were without bow and arrows. He did this by showing himself, he and his wanasi, by leaving signs where they had made a fire. But they kept out of range of the saldu firesticks. I remember one time when they were gone for more than two moons. Your father led a large party of saldu around the foot of Waganupa to the far side. In all that time, saldu did not kill a single Yahi, did not take a single scalp. Finally, your father turned south and left the saldu well outside the Yahi World and so came safely home with all his men. Aii-ya! If I had been of a size to go with him! To have shot my arrows into the enemy.'

'And then what did my father do?'

'You have heard Elder Uncle say, 'One man cannot forever hold against twenty saldu with firesticks.' That is what he tried to do at Three Knolls Village where he fell.'

And then again:

Twenty saldu and more, hidden behind the three knolls attacked the village at dawn while everyone in the houses slept. I remember my father hiding my mother and me in the trees behind the house. People screamed; the thunder of firesticks filled the air; and there was the smell of burning. Shooting from the shelter of the house wall, my father fought the enemy. It was his bow against twenty firesticks, and some saldu were among those who lay dead on the village paths.

More saldu were hidden down the creek. One of them shot and my father fell—here—in front of his house. Mother ran to him and dragged him into the brush. No one saw her through the smoke. She and I lay beside my father on our faces all day. She says I did not move or cry or speak. I think I slept some of the time.

At last it was dark and the saldu left. Elder Uncle and Grandfather found my mother and me, here, beside my father, and they took us to Tuliyani. I remember Elder Uncle's carrying me in his arms and I remember Mother's crying. All the way down the canyon my mother cried and when we were in Tuliyani, my mother and my grandmother cried all that night and for many days and nights. I shall not forget the tears of my mother, nor those of my father's mother.[21]

Of course, the Southern Yana were not the only Native people to suffer genocide at the hands of American settlers. Miller and Chalk and Jonassohn consider the treatment of the Northern Yuki Indians of Round Valley in northern California to be a genocide.[22] About 3500 Yuki Indians inhabited Round Valley when the first Americans arrived there in 1854.[23] Because, under California law, kidnappers couldn't be tried unless a white eyewitness testified against them, American frontiersmen began seizing

Yuki women and children, either for themselves or to trade with the Spanish Californians. When the three Americans who "discovered" Round Valley left again after having wintered there, they persuaded thirty-five Yuki children to come with them over the mountain, whereupon these were sold into slavery.[24]

The Yuki lived by hunting, fishing, and gathering, and the inflow of American settlers in the 1850s severely depleted their food supply. Nuts, lily bulbs, acorns, and other edibles that Natives had gathered, and which constituted an integral part of their food supply, were increasingly consumed by the settlers' livestock. Nor did moving the Yuki on to reservations help; the settlers grazed their cattle on reservation land. Although the whites recognized that they were preventing the Yuki from continuing their normal way of life, they "preferred to sacrifice the Indians rather than their livestock."[25] Provisions provided by the government were stolen by dishonest agents, who in turn sold them to white labourers working on ranches or operating sawmills owned by the agents. The scarcity of food encouraged the spread of disease. Confining the Yuki to reservations made it easier for settlers to conduct raids to kill the Yuki or capture them and force them into virtual slave labour. The Yuki responded by fleeing into the mountains. From here, they, at times, raided the settlers' cattle herds to keep from starving. In response, the settlers undertook to annihilate them, mounting a number of expeditions for this purpose between 1856 and 1861. A cattle supervisor named H.L. Hall became especially nefarious. His motto was that any Indian found should be killed, and in March 1859, settlers led by him killed about 240 Indians in revenge for the killing of a valuable stallion.[26]

The situation for the Yuki deteriorated still further when, upon receiving a petition signed by a number of leading citizens of the state of California, Governor John P. Weller, in 1859 granted state commissions to a company of volunteers, the Eel River Rangers, to hunt down the Yuki in the mountains.[27] Reports from federal army officers to their superiors, warning them that these volunteers would "hunt the Indians to extermination" and that they had no way of preventing it, were ignored. Also ignored were reports to the Secretary of the Interior in Washington from J. Ross Browne, a Treasury Department agent, who was appalled by the diversion of food intended for Indians on reservations, as well as by the hunting of Indians as if they were "wild beasts." When the state-commissioned volunteers had finished their work, killing all the Indians they tracked down regardless of age or sex, Governor Weller sent his congratulations for doing "all that was anticipated."[28]

By 1880, the Yuki population of Round Valley had fallen to about four hundred people.[29] Special Treasury Agent Browne, in his report to Washington, stated: "In the history of Indian races I have seen nothing so cruel or relentless as the treatment of those unhappy people by the authority constituted by law for their protection. Instead of receiving aid and succour, they have been starved and driven away from the reservations, and then followed into their remote hiding places, where they sought to die in peace, and cruelly slaughtered, till but few are left, and that few without hope."[30]

Thornton considers genocide to have played a role in the decline of the Telowa, a tribe in northwestern California. Direct formal contact between the Telowa and Americans probably first occurred in 1828 and resulted in an epidemic. By the 1850s, non-Indian settlement in Telowa territory had become intensive as a result of gold mining operations. The decline in the Telowa population is generally attributed to diseases such as measles and cholera, as well as to "pseudomilitary engagements." The first killing took place in 1853, during a ceremonial dance, when 450 to 600 Telowa were slaughtered by settlers for alleged theft. During the second massacre, which took place the following year, another 150 Telowa were killed. More Telowa were killed several years later during a battle with settlers. Commenting on these events, a Telowa man stated that not many of their people were left. The only ones to survive were those who escaped into the mountains.[31]

A similar fate was suffered by the Sinkyone, many of whom were killed by white settlers and the US military from the 1850s to the 1870s. A survivor who witnessed the massacre of her family at Needle Rock reports that whites killed her grandfather, mother, and father. They also killed her sister, who was just an infant, cutting out her heart and throwing it into the bush. She was so scared that she hid a long time clasping her baby sister's heart in her hands. Massacres such as this almost eradicated the Sinkyone as a distinct tribe.[32]

The destruction of Native peoples and the treatment of Indians in California

Soon after the Treaty of Guadalupe Hidalgo (1848) ceded the sovereignty over California, Utah, Arizona, and other southwestern territories to the United States, Americans poured into these areas, seizing land from Native peoples both in the interior and along the California coast. The whites' total disregard for the natural environment made it increasingly difficult for the Indians to successfully maintain their traditional lifestyles. Their position was made still more precarious by the new economic order that was beginning to emerge in California. The Spaniards and Mexicans had incorporated the Indians into the colonial economic and social structures and by the time of the American conquest of California, were beginning to treat Amerindians more humanely. Within the Anglo-American system, however, there was no place for the Natives. Indian life, deemed valuable to the Mexicans who had institutionalized Indian labour for wealth, was considered worthless to the Americans. New labour laws kept the Native people in a state of virtual slavery. Indians could be rounded up, made to work, and then turned away to starve when their labour was no longer required.

Conflict between the Indians and white settlers resulted in the so-called Indian Wars. Reporting on these wars to the Commissioner of Indian Affairs, Agent Adam Johnson stated that the majority of tribes were kept in constant fear by the indiscriminate massacres of their people for real or imagined injuries.[33] Many were attacked to drive them from their land, sometimes by regular troops as well as by local militias. The following recounts a massacre that followed the killing of two whites by the Pomos. The white men had brutally exploited the Indians at Clear Lake by enslaving them, and many died as a result. In the attack, soldiers equipped with boats,

> went across [the lake] in their long dug-outs, the Indians said they would meet them in peace. So when the whites landed the Indians went to welcome them but the white man was determined to kill them. Ge-Wi-Lih said he threw up his hands and said no harm me good man but the white man fired and shoot him in the arm. . . . Many women and children were killed around this island. One old lady . . . saw two white men coming with their guns up in the air and on their guns hung a little girl, they brought it to the creek and threw it in the water. . . . Two more men came. . . . This time they had a little boy on the end of their guns and also threw it in the water. A little ways from her . . . two white men stabbed the woman and the baby. . . . All the little ones were killed by being stabbed, and many of the women were also. This old lady also told about the whites who hung a man on Emerson's Island. . . . The Indian was hung and a large fire built under [him]. . . . Another . . . was tied to a tree and burnt to death.[34]

The army reported destroying 60 of the 400 Indians on the island, as well as another 75 on the nearby Russian River. Two whites were wounded in these encounters. Indians were also killed to eliminate what the whites considered a nuisance. J. Ross Browne, who investigated the mistreatment of Natives on behalf of the national government, provides this description of a typical militia expedition against Humboldt Indians:

> During the winter of last year a number of them [Indians] were
> gathered at Humboldt. The whites thought it was a favourable
> opportunity to get rid of them altogether. So they went in a body
> to the Indian camp, during the night when the poor wretches
> were asleep, shot all the men, women, and children at the first
> onslaught, and cut the throats of the remainder. Very few escaped.
> Next morning 60 bodies lay weltering in their blood - the old and
> the young, male and female - with every wound gaping a tale of
> horror to the civilized world. Children climbed upon their moth-
> ers' breasts and sought nourishment from the fountains that death
> had drained; girls and boys lay here and there with their throats
> cut from ear to ear; men and women, clinging to each other in
> their terror, were found perforated with bullets or cut to pieces
> with knives - all were cruelly murdered.[35]

Native people lived in constant fear of such incidents, news of which often
predated their direct contact with American settlers. For example, when
the first white people arrived on Wailaki lands in northern California in
1854, the Wailaki had already heard reports from trading partners and
neighbours of kidnapping, raiding, and killings directed against other
tribal groups. Consequently, they tried to keep out of harm's way by hiding in the mountains. Such a move exposed their land for expropriation,
leaving them with little means of sustaining themselves except through
stealing. As a result, many of them were slaughtered by the white settlers.[36]

The state and federal governments subsidized the destruction of Indians by reimbursing "private military forays" for expenses incurred in
such undertakings. Almost any white man could raise a volunteer company, outfit it with guns, ammunition, horses, and supplies, and be rea-
sonably sure that the state government would honour its vouchers. The
California legislature passed acts in 1851 and 1852 authorizing the payment of over $1,100,000 for the suppression of Indian hostilities. In 1857
the legislature issued bonds amounting to $410,000 for the same purpose.
Congress eventually reimbursed the state for nearly all the bonds issued,
thereby subsidizing the murder of Indians.[37] Bancroft states that the so-
called Indian Wars in California were essentially an attempt at the whole-
sale slaughter of Native peoples.[38] Churchill states that, even after official
bounties were ended, private businessmen established their own bounties
and continued paying them until a number of Native tribes in the northern part of the state were entirely extinct.[39]

The introduction of a reservation system did little to improve the position of Native peoples. In 1854, Edward F. Beasle gathered together some two thousand Indians to establish the Tejon Reservation on fifty thousand acres of land near the southern end of the San Joaquin Valley. Other reservations were established soon after. The reservation system, however, was riddled with corruption. Beasle was dismissed for not keeping financial records, and another official, Treaty Commissioner Wozencraft, was charged with irregularities in his purchase and delivery of beef to starving Indians. These men were replaced by even more corrupt officials who used their influence to settle white families on Native land, an action that drove off the Indians. Thievery and mismanagement by administrators kept the Indians in a state of destitution. Starvation was not uncommon, hastening the demise of the Native population. The Huchnom, for example, suffered such harassment from the white settlers that they became extinct while on a reservation.[40]

Examples showing the destruction of Indians as they were being cleared from other areas of the United States

The destruction of Native peoples was not limited to the southwest. The Cherokee Indians of the southeast were among the first tribes to feel the effects of settler pressure to clear the trans-Appalachian region for white settlement. Attempting to adapt themselves to the demands of the new society, a segment of the Cherokees settled down to farming on permanent homesteads. They adopted a new constitution and a new legal system modelled on the American Constitution and on aspects of Indian law. However, they were expelled to a reservation despite this, perhaps because they proclaimed themselves an independent nation and simultaneously claimed sovereignty over Cherokee lands in Georgia, Alabama, North Carolina, and Tennessee. Claiming authority over the Cherokee and their lands, the state of Georgia ordered the tribe to move. Although the US Supreme Court in *Worcester vs. Georgia* (1832) ruled in favour of the Cherokee, President Andrew Jackson ordered that they move west of the Mississippi, to the "Great American Desert."

Troops were stationed at various points throughout Cherokee country where stockade forts were erected for gathering and holding the Indians in preparation for removal. Troops were sent out to seize and bring in the Indians. People were abruptly seized from their homes and fields. They had no sooner left their homes when these were looted and the livestock driven off by the people following on the heels of the soldiers. Indian graves were robbed of silver pendants and other valuables that had been buried with the dead.

While most Cherokee did not resist being driven from their homes, there were some exceptions. One old man named Tsali, "Charley," exasperated by the soldiers who were prodding his wife with bayonets to hurry her along, sought to talk the men closest to him into trying to escape. Not understanding Cherokee, the soldiers remained unaware of what was transpiring until they were attacked by warriors who wrenched the guns from them. One soldier was killed in the attack and the rest fled, while Charlie and those with him escaped. Hundreds of others also succeeded in escaping. When he was unable to apprehend the escapees, General Scott, who supervised the removal, promised them that they would have their cases heard by the government, on the condition that they handed over Charley and those with him for punishment. To save the other escapees, who were having difficulty surviving on wild berries and roots, Charlie and his group surrendered. Thereupon, he as well as three of his family members were shot, Cherokee prisoners being forced to do the shooting to impress upon them that they were at the total mercy of the government.

The forced removal began soon after about seventeen thousand Cherokee had been forced from their homes into the stockades. Organizing the expellees into several groupings, the troops commenced with the removal of some of the Cherokee in early June. They went overland and then by steamer down the Tennessee and Ohio rivers to the far side of the Mississippi, from where they went overland to Indian territory. As this took place in high summer, a great number of people became sick and died. To prevent further deaths, Cherokee chiefs requested that Scott allow them to remove themselves in the fall, when the summer heat had ended. Scott acquiesced, on the condition that, with the exception of the old and sick, who would not be able to move rapidly, they start the removal by 20 October.

Thereupon, the Indians organized themselves into detachments of about a thousand people. With two leaders in charge of each detachment, the removal began in October 1838. Except for the few who took the river route, the vast majority, some 13,000, went overland; with the aged, the ill and small children in the wagons, while the remainder rode or went by foot.

As the forced march continued along what the Cherokee have come to call the "Trail of Tears," ten to twenty people died daily. However, the group continued on, reaching the Mississippi, opposite Cape Girardeau, Missouri, in mid-winter. With the river full of ice, they were unable to cross. Meanwhile, the sick and dying had little more than an overhead blanket to protect them from the elements. Finally they succeeded in crossing and the march continued through Missouri on to Indian territory. Taking almost six months, in the coldest part of the year, the journey was disastrous for the expelled. Hundreds had already succumbed while still in the stockades and "waiting" camps. Others died from sickness and exposure on the journey or soon after their arrival in Indian territory. It is estimated that in total over 4,000 Cherokee died as a direct result of the removal.[41]

Chalk and Jonassohn have assessed the removal of the Cherokee in terms of their own and the UN definition of genocide. They conclude that the removal was not a genocide because perpetrator intent was absent. They add, however, that if one considers the American government's "advertent omission" to preserve Cherokee lives along the Trail of Tears, and accepts a recommendation that had been made to the United Nations that it "include acts of advertent omission in its list of acts of genocide, then an act like the Cherokee deportation would almost certainly be considered an act of genocide today."[42]

Elsewhere, Native people endured similar and even worse experiences. Those who were on reservations with land coveted by the Americans were removed to worse land on almost any pretext. Both the Santee Sioux and Winnebago were forced from their reservation in Minnesota, where they had lived quite well, onto a reservation in the Dakotas. Little Hill, a chief of the Winnebago Indians, describes their situation when they got to the Dakotas:

> After we got there they sometimes give us rations, but not enough to go round most of the time. Some would have to go without eating two or three days. It was not a good country; it was all dust. Whenever we cooked anything it would be full of dust. We found out after a while we could not live there. Sometimes the women and children were sick, and some of them died; and we think many of them died because they could not get enough to eat while they were sick. For the past three years we supposed our Great Father has sent us enough goods, provisions, and money, but we do not think we have got half of it. Sometimes some of the women and children don't get much of what they ought to have, only a piece of calico, or something like that.

And again:

> We are most all naked; the whole tribe. Some of the tribe are more destitute of clothing than we are. We got some goods here now which the Great Father sent us. They are lying in the Omaha warehouse, and we don't know but that the rats have eaten them.

There are a good many women and children who are naked and
cannot come out of their tents.[43]

Little Hill's account illuminates how disease could wipe out a people forced
to live under such conditions. It also makes understandable Stannard's
and Churchill's argument that disease was not an independent variable in
the destruction of Native Americans. Its role in the destruction of human
life must be looked at in the overall context of white-Indian relations.

Indians who did not peacefully accept relocation were removed by force
of arms. Wrone states that, in areas where hostilities existed, the United
States military policy was "to exterminate the Indians."[44] Although such
a statement is too extreme, the evidence shows that the American military
did not hesitate to massacre Indians who resisted removal from their territorial base. Chalk and Jonassohn consider one of the best-known genocidal massacres in American history to have been the result of a conspiracy between Governor John Evans of Colorado, who sought a seat in the
US Senate, and Colonel John Chivington, the military commander of the
District of Colorado, who aspired to a seat in the US House of Representatives.[45] The conflict started when settlers in Denver and the mining camps
of Colorado occupied land that government treaties with the Natives had
allocated to the Cheyenne and Arapahos. Instead of removing the settlers,
upon whose votes those in public office depended, the government attempted to remove the Indians. In February 1861, federal representatives
persuaded a number of chiefs to accept a small reservation in southeastern Colorado. Later, upon realizing the meaning of this treaty, the chiefs
renounced it. Governor Evans informed Washington in November 1863
that the Plains Indians planned to go to war against the white population
in the spring of 1864. Washington thereupon authorized Evans to raise a
regiment, the Third Colorado Cavalry, to subdue the Cheyenne, who were
led by Black Kettle and other chiefs.

Acting on the pretext that the Cheyenne had stolen 175 head of cattle,
Chivington led the Third Colorado Cavalry into the field in November
1864. He instructed his troops to use any means to kill the Indians, to "kill
and scalp all, little and big."[46] When Chivington's volunteers attacked on
29 November, both American and white flags flew over the encampment
of some 700 Indians at Sand Creek, which Chivington had led their chiefs
to believe he would protect. The attackers killed about one-third of the Indians, most of them women and children. They took no prisoners. Robert
Brent, the son of a local trader and a Cheyenne woman, describes part of
what occurred:

I saw five squaws under a bank for shelter. When the troops came up to them they ran out and showed their persons to let the soldiers know they were squaws and begged for mercy, but the soldiers shot them all. There were some thirty or forty squaws collected in a hole for protection; they sent out a little girl about six years old with a white flag on a stick; she had not proceeded but a few steps when she was shot and killed. All the squaws in that hole were afterwards killed, and four or five bucks outside. The squaws offered no resistance. Every one I saw dead was scalped. I saw one squaw cut open with an unborn child, as I thought, lying by her side. Captain Sould afterwards told me that such was the fact. I saw the body of White Antelope with the privates cut off, and I heard a soldier say he was going to make a tobacco-pouch out of them.[47]

Similar treatment was accorded to the Northern Cheyenne during the closing days of the American wars against the Plains Indians. Unable to continue the war in defence of their lands, the Cheyenne had surrendered on the condition that they would not be forced from their homeland in the north. Breaking its promise, the government shipped them south to Indian territory. Here, on a reservation closely guarded by the military, Cheyenne family structures disintegrated. The women were prostituted by the military and drunkenness became rampant. Finally, Dull Knife and other leaders determined to return home in the north, rather than see their people corrupted and destroyed on the reservation, even if it meant fighting their way back. In September 1878, 320 Cheyenne escaped from the reservation. Soon the plains were alive with army and militia units hunting down their quarry. The episode ended with most of these Indians, including women and children, being killed.[48]

The story was repeated with the massacre of the Sioux at Wounded Knee. Following their military defeat, Sioux tribes were forced onto reservations in South Dakota where the Secretary of the Interior and the Commissioner of Indian Affairs sought to "civilize" them. Indian agents attacked the Sioux religion, language, way of life, and kinship system. The usual problem of dishonest agents stealing provisions made hunger a major threat on the reservation and exacerbated the problem of disease. Although the Sioux found some solace in messianic religions, these didn't solve their problems, which were made worse by the pressure ranchers, speculators and land-hungry farmers put on the government to abolish the reservation and open its land up for settlement.

Under these conditions, several leaders emerged in the fall of 1890 who sought to encourage the Sioux to take concrete steps to deal with their problems. Rather than address the issues raised by Sioux leaders, the Bureau of Indian Affairs accused them of fomenting rebellion and turned to the military to have them removed. Thereupon, the army sent in troops to arrest the supposedly rebellious leaders. One regiment halted Big Foot's band, which allegedly was arming for war. Big Foot suggested that the problems at hand be discussed. The soldiers, however, were little interested in discussion. Surrounding several hundred warriors at Big Foot's camp, they began to search them for weapons. Angered by the rough manner in which the search was being conducted, one of the warriors fired a shot. The military responded with a massive barrage, killing or wounding all the warriors. They then turned their cannon and rifle fire on the fleeing women and children. When the shooting stopped several hours later, some three hundred Sioux, mostly women and children, lay dead.[49]

Causes and effects

These examples suffice to provide insight into the dynamics that led to genocide and the destruction of the Native American population and way of life in the United States. Several forces can be discerned behind this violence. One was the drive by individuals to dispossess the Indians and take ownership of their lands. Indians were also killed because, having been driven from their land, they were forced to steal to remain alive. All too often the white man's response was to slaughter the Native to protect his property. Such attitudes fostered individual and group violence by whites against Native people.

In addition to individual and group violence, military campaigns against the different tribes contributed to the destruction of Native populations, first in the Thirteen Colonies and later in the United States and its territories. As with individual and mob violence, the underlying motive for these campaigns was the desire to appropriate Native lands. Once the Native population had been displaced, attacks continued against those who refused to accept the loss of their lands and their new position in a society dominated by the conqueror.

While interpreting the destruction of Native peoples by the Spaniards in South and Central America as a by-product of conquest and Native enslavement, Stannard sees the extermination of the Natives as a primary goal in the British colonies to which he confines his study, namely the Thirteen Colonies and the United States.[50] He sees this goal as having been encouraged by conditions in Britain and in the Americas. It was further reinforced by the beliefs and attitudes British peoples brought to the New World. The Thirteen Colonies contained nothing even remotely comparable to the exportable mineral wealth the Spaniards found in the areas they invaded. Thus, the British had no corresponding need to enslave Native populations. Also, Britain had a larger surplus population than Spain. Although it had a flourishing economy—indeed, one at the threshold of dominating the world economy—Britain still had a large number of desperately poor people. The state sought to improve their condition in life by settling them outside its borders.[51]

Although British first impressions had been largely positive, as among the Spanish, negative views of the Indians of the Americas quickly came to dominate. Like the Spanish, the British believed in the Great Chain of Being, which included a belief in the existence of creatures that were half human, half beast. The Indian's place along this chain was at that ambiguous level where human and beast overlapped. Among other things, the British saw the Indian's near-nakedness as evidence of his bestial nature. Such attitudes were encouraged by British perceptions of the morally and intellectually inferior nature of Native peoples. Hostility was further encouraged by Native reluctance to accept English religious and cultural habits. Thus, Indians were marked as incorrigibly non-European and non-Christian, and therefore as permanently non-civilized in British eyes, all of which served to enhance their less-than-human status.[52]

The British view of property helped to dehumanize Native people. The concept of private property as a positive good and even an insignia of civilization took hold among both Catholics and Protestants during the sixteenth century. Among European Protestants during the Reformation, failure to put property to "good or profitable use" was grounds for seizing European monasteries. The idea of production was a major component of Max Weber's Protestant ethic, and was integral to C.B. Macpherson's ideology of possessive individualism. Basic to this ideology is the belief that a person has a right to the profits derived from his or her labour. In particular, people have a right to whatever land they improve or cultivate. Integral to this view of private property was also the conviction that whoever failed to put land to good profitable use deserved to be dispossessed of it. In practice, this principle of *vacuum domicilium* frequently became the basis for dispossessing Native groups of their land.[53]

These influences also expressed themselves in a more extreme form. Stannard comments on this when he states that the aggressiveness wherewith the settlers took Native land was all too often projected onto the Native. Here we have economic self-interest combined with the Medieval image of the witch, used to demonize the Native, thereby justifying in the settler's mind the depredations committed against Native peoples.[54] The settler, in this context, became an agent of civilization and righteousness carrying out God's judgement against enemies of all that was correct and proper in European eyes.

Unlike the Spanish, who killed an enormous number of people to acquire gold and enslave the Natives, all the English settler wanted was the land. For them, the Indian had no "use value." The British had a homeland bursting at the seams with surplus population, and they felt they needed what, in another language and another time, became known as *Lebensraum*.[55] A much greater number of British than Spanish peoples moved to the New World. Unlike the vast majority of Spanish, the British came with families, and they came to stay.

To the flood of British colonists in what was to become the United States the Indians were largely superfluous. In states such as Virginia, plantation agriculture commenced only after the extermination of most of the Native population, whereupon enslaved Africans were purchased to carry out the work. In most British colonies, however, the colonists did most of the agricultural tasks themselves or with the help of indentured servants. While early Spanish arrivals were rewarded with a large number of Indians to enslave, British settlers were provided with land. This difference in what motivated the Spaniard and the British to come to the New World had a profound influence on how the two groups perceived and responded to the environment and the Native peoples they encountered therein. The Spanish regarded the Native population as theirs to enslave and exploit in the pursuit of wealth while Anglo-Americans regarded them as an impediment to their drive to take possession of the coveted land.

Stannard sees evidence of the Anglo-American drive to dispossess and, in the process, exterminate the Native, at all levels of society in the United States. Antagonism was expressed towards Native peoples by average American citizens as well as by their religious leaders.[56] Similar attitudes and views were expressed by American political leaders such as Thomas Jefferson, who stated that nation- building included pursuing the Indians to extermination or driving them to areas beyond the conqueror's reach.[57] Later, Andrew Jackson urged American troops to root the Indians from their dens and kill Indian women and their "whelps." In Jackson's view, it was no less natural that the Indians should be driven to their graves by white Americans than that one generation should die off to make room for the next.[58] George Washington described the Indians as wolves and beasts who deserved nothing from the white man but "total ruin."[59]

Over a century later, a somewhat similar view was expressed by Theodore Roosevelt, who remarked that the "extermination" of the American Indians and the "appropriation" of their lands was not only inevitable but also beneficial. "Such conquests," he continued, "are sure to come when a masterful people, still in its barbarian prime, finds itself face to face with a weaker and wholly alien race which holds a coveted prize in its feeble grasp." Roosevelt went on to say: "I don't go so far as to think that the only good Indians are dead Indians, but I believe nine out of ten are, and I shouldn't like to inquire too closely into the case of the tenth."[60]

Commenting on the dynamics leading to the destruction of the Indians by British Americans in the United States, Longley remarks that this was an expression of the British American belief that they were God's chosen people. That is, they had inherited the Israelite position as God's elect.[61] In fact, he draws a parallel between the early Israelite dispossession of the Caananites and the American dispossession of the Indians when he states that both the Canaanites and the Indians were seen as being outside the covenant, not among God's especially beloved. "Their lands could be taken, and if they resisted, they could be killed."[62] At the same time, however, to provide the appearance of legality to the dispossession, the Americans signed numerous treaties with the Indians. However, they invariably found an excuse to break these.[63] "In fact," Longley adds, "the progress of American settlement into Indian territory would have proceeded little differently had the declared policy been one of naked and ruthless plunder, without regard to legal niceties."[64] He blames American land hunger. Although American Indian policy may have started out with high principles, these became harder and harder to reconcile with settler land hunger, "which it was government policy to stimulate." Yet the pretence remained that high principles continued to guide American policy and that Indian lands were being acquired through civilized rules. "America not only had to be seen abroad to have kept the faith of the Enlightenment; it had to be able itself to believe it had done so. That demanded some arrangement of the facts."[65] This led Americans to focus on the emptiness of the land,[66] with the continent being seen as wilderness "waiting to be populated and tamed by the bringers of Christian civilization."[67] At the same time, they stressed that in all this the Indians were being done a favour in that they were being exposed to the advantages of American civilization.[68]

Commenting on American policy regarding the Natives, Chalk and Jonassohn state that they considered ethnocide as having been the principal United States policy toward American Indians in the nineteenth century. It was at the core of the Indian removals, the reservation system, the Dawes Act and the schemes for educating Native children at boarding schools after the Civil War. Genocide, when practised, expressed itself in particular through the creation of famine conditions. The mass slaughter of the buffalo, which the federal government encouraged, and its policy of forcing the Natives onto reserves where they could little sustain themselves contributed especially to starvation and with it the decimation of the Indian population. This was further fostered through the use of "terrorizing genocides and genocidal massacres" to crush resistance or even the contemplation of such.[69]

The conclusion reached by Chalk and Jonassohn reflects their view that a genocide has been committed if a group states its intention to carry out a genocide and then commits it. Stannard, on the other hand, argues that the genocides in British America and the United States grew out of the basic belief systems of Anglo-Americans. These beliefs, given expression on different occasions by the American public, and by American religious and political leaders, caused them to dehumanize the Native, drive him from his land and slaughter him. Stannard considers beliefs and attitudes such as these north of the Mexican border as bringing about what he sees as the American holocaust.

10
European-Native Relations in Canada

Does Stannard's observation that in British America the holocaust suffered by Native people resulted from their being directly targeted for destruction also apply to Canada? After all, what is today Canada fell under British rule when France ceded most of its North American colonial possessions to Britain through the Treaty of Paris in 1763. Prior to this, Britain controlled most of Newfoundland. It gained control of the Hudson Bay basin after the establishment of the Hudson's Bay Company in 1670. This all makes the situation in Canada more complicated than it was in the Thirteen Colonies or the United States.

Any examination concerning dynamics leading to the destruction of Native people in what is today Canada must take these differences into consideration. During the early period of settlement, France rather than Britain dominated relations between the different Indian tribes and Europeans in the northern half of North America. This had an influence on the relations which Britain later established with Natives once it took possession of New France. Although relations between the French and the Indians were much better than they were in either the British or Spanish colonies in the Americas, genocide nevertheless played a role in French-Native relations. In Newfoundland, conditions that bring to mind the eradication of the Yana in California, led to the "extinction" of the Beothuks. The Mi'kmaq in the Maritimes were in many respects saved from a similar fate because both the English and the French sought to recruit their support in their struggle for dominance in the area. European-Native interaction was less destructive in the Hudson Bay basin. Except for isolated incidents, there was little conflict between Natives and British traders. Unlike further south, where the drive by British settlers to take over Indian land led to conflict, in the Bay area relations between Natives and Europeans were structured largely by the fur trade in which Natives and Europeans in many ways operated on an equal basis and had a need for each other.

Of course, the focus of this study is to explore situations in which relations between Europeans and Natives led to the mass destruction of the latter. Thus, the chapter will be divided into three sections. One will explore conditions that led to the "extinction" of the Beothuks in Newfoundland. Then I will look at genocide in the French fur-trade empire in the Americas. I will conclude with a brief look at British-Native relations after 1763 when what became Canada fell under British rule. Here I will seek to show how the French tradition, British relations with French Canadians, as well as relations that Britain established with Native peoples, affected European-Native interaction.

The "extinction" of the Beothuks in Newfoundland

Although the "extinction" of the Beothuks does not constitute as clear-cut an example of genocide as does, for example, the extermination of groups such as the Yana in the United States, I include it because of the similarity in the treatment of Native peoples in these cases. The attitudes that led to the destruction of the Yana are also evident among those who destroyed the Beothuks. Furthermore, in both instances people who took over their territorial base slaughtered Natives as if they were animals.

Some scholars deny that the destruction of the Beothuks was genocide. Rowe admits that atrocities of the most barbaric kind were committed against the Beothuks from about 1750 to 1810, during which time an unknown number of Beothuks met their death from the guns of settlers and visiting fisherman.[1] "Nevertheless," he continues, "recognition of the barbaric treatment accorded the Beothuks by a few settlers of the northwest coast does not imply acceptance of the charge that this treatment represented a deliberate, systematic attempt by the Europeans to exterminate the Beothuks."[2] He then implies that because there was no deliberate policy to destroy the Beothuks, natural causes such as disease and famine brought about their demise.

The problem with Rowe's argument is that he attempts to apply a model of genocide that fits, for example, the destruction of European Jewry by the Nazis and concludes that, because the model doesn't fit, no genocide was committed. He is quite right in his statement that settlers, fishermen, and trappers pursued no consistent policy to exterminate the Beothuks. They did, however, persist in attacking and killing these people, and such attacks eventually led to the decimation of the Beothuks, their withdrawal from the coastal areas of Newfoundland, and their final extirpation.

Although early contacts between Beothuks and Europeans (for example, with Jacques Cartier in 1534 or John Guy in 1612) were usually amicable, this changed as the British and French began to settle in Newfoundland. Misunderstandings, conflicting interests over coastal fishing and hunting resources, and Beothuk thefts from fishing boats and white settlements led to mutual hostility. Trappers and fishermen killed the Beothuks not only to protect their property but also for sport. At the same time, the French encouraged the Mi'kmaq to attack the Beothuks.

Increasingly frequent conflict between the Beothuks and Europeans during the seventeenth and eighteenth centuries pushed the Aboriginal people back from the coasts and confined them to the southeastern interior. While Beothuk raids on whites were primarily for tools and equipment they could not otherwise obtain, white raids were essentially for killing Beothuks, and various eighteenth-century reports boast of the murder of tens and even hundreds of the Natives. By 1823, the tribe had been reduced to a handful of survivors through attacks, malnutrition and disease. The Boeothick Institution, formed in 1827, failed to locate any traces of surviving Beothuks. Shanawdithit, one of the last of the tribe to be captured, died in 1829. Her death likely marked the final extinction of the Beothuks in Newfoundland.[3]

Howley, whose work deals largely with British-Beothuk relations, argues that the destruction of the Beothuks can ultimately be traced back to the manner in which they were treated by the main power on the island, the British. To support his case, he uses a number of sources. He draws on journal entries made by Captain George Cartwright between 1770 and 1786, who notes that "our people" might easily have established friendly relations and beneficial trade with the Indians, but "vile murder at first produced a spirit of revenge" that expressed itself through the cruel mistreatment of the Natives by "our" fishermen.[4] Cartwright adds that the British murdered the Natives indiscriminately, in the process destroying their food supplies, canoes and other goods whenever they attacked an Indian encampment, forcing the Natives to flee. These losses at times led to entire families dying of starvation.[5]

Howley also draws on findings from inquiries to support his argument. When responding to queries by a committee appointed in 1793 to examine the trade to Newfoundland, Captain George Cartwright stated that he believed that there had been a considerable number of Natives at one time. However, he did not know how many were left, as they had been "so much chased and driven away" by the fishermen and trappers. The Indians tended to come to white settlements at night to supply their necessities by stealing such things as sails, hatchets, boats, and kettles. Trappers and fishermen, on the other hand, shot Indians for amusement, with some remarking they would rather shoot an Indian than a deer.[6] Cartwright added that during the winter a few years earlier, two men, one of whom he knew personally, went up the Great River Exploits strictly to murder and rob Indians. On reaching the head of the river, they encountered an Indian encampment with some one hundred inhabitants. Opening fire with their long guns, they wounded and killed several Natives. When the others escaped into the woods, some naked and others half dressed, the men robbed the wigwams. They took whatever they wanted and burned the rest. Cartwright concluded that such actions must have destroyed all those who escaped the attack, for they could not hope to survive on snow.[7]

During this same inquiry, the Chief Justice of Newfoundland observed that, unlike the wandering tribes on the continent who roamed from place to place, the Beothuks, and everything belonging to them, were under the complete power of the British, who robbed and murdered them, as well as deprived them of the free use of their shores and rivers. He noted that there was no interaction between "our people" and the Indians except for plunder and murder. If the British found a wigwam, they robbed it of its furs and burned the remainder; if they discovered an Indian, they would shoot him as if he were a wild animal.[8]

Discussing evidence pertaining to the treatment of the Beothuks, Peter Such mentions the "Liverpool Manuscript," which Howley had overlooked in his investigation.[9] It contains a report Magistrate John Bland of Bonavista prepared in 1792, while investigating rumours about the murders carried out by a man by the name of John Peyton Sr., an important fishery owner, and several British trappers and fishermen. The manuscript suggests the group set out to kill Natives to revenge the killing of a man by the name of Thomas Russel, a noted Indian-killer who had been ambushed at his fishing weir and killed by the Beothuks in 1789. The answers provided by Peyton and others suggest they had treated any Indians encountered with great cruelty. The manuscript also recounts the experiences of Thomas Taylor, Richard Richmond, and William Hooper, who went to the Beothuk encampment at Charles Brook to look for some lost nets. As they approached a wigwam, two women ran out of it to hide. A man came out, carrying a little boy. Taylor fired, wounding the man and the boy. Letting the boy fall, the man tried to escape. William Hooper fired again, killing him. They left the wounded boy to die. However, they captured a girl, who later died while in the possession of a Mr. Stone, a merchant.

The manuscript gives further examples of Peyton's killings. Although Bland recommended that the man be expelled from Newfoundland, this was never carried out. Peyton and the trappers continued their slaughter and were key figures in the last years of the Beothuks. Thomas Taylor recounts an incident in which

Mr. Peyton, Millar & myself went three day's journey up the Main

Brook—on the third morning, at day-break, we saw the tracking of an Indian. I looked, but could see none, for by the time I came up he was gone, but soon after we saw a great number of them in the landwash spreading skins. They ran to their wigwams, and we pushed on. They stood together in a large body, near their wigwams and we thought best to fire.[10]

Newfoundland oral tradition reports that, in about 1800, three or four hundred Beothuks were driven onto a long point of land near their favourite sealing site and shot down like deer. The area is still referred to today as "Bloody Reach." Commenting on the incident, Such states that this marked the beginning of the end of the Beothuks. Once forced inland, maritime activities on which their lives depended became virtually closed to them. Hounded on all sides in the inhospitable interior, they sought to survive as best they could. He adds that "John Bland's prediction in 1790 that 'before the lapse of another century, the English nation, like the Spanish, may have affixed to its character the indelible reproach of having extirpated a whole race of people' was to come true much sooner than he predicted."[11]

Insight into the treatment of the Beothuks is provided by another comment by Such. Commenting on Shawnadithit, the last of the Beothuks, he writes that she lived in obscurity as a domestic in Peyton's household in Twillingate. While there, she was shot at twice by Indian killers. Noel Boss, a Métis of English and Mi'kmaq background, boasted that he had killed ninety-nine Beothuks and wished to make her his hundredth.[12]

Marshall comes essentially to the same conclusion as Such and Howley: that the British element in Newfoundland ultimately was responsible for the extinction of the Beothuks. She points to a number of causes as having led to the demise of the tribe. One was British colonial policy, which promoted the appropriation of Native land without assuming any responsibility for the well-being of the rightful owners, a policy supported by the church, which argued that Native people were inferior because they were non-Christian. By gradually taking control of the territory where the Beothuks fished, hunted, gathered eggs, or otherwise made their livelihood, the settlers, fishermen, sealers, and trappers deprived the Natives of their means of survival, and this led to starvation. Desperate, the Beothuks were driven to steal from the Europeans, which led to violent retribution. All these factors, combined with the generally violent behaviour of certain elements among the British population, led to the destruction of the Beothuks.[13] This tragic event was perhaps best summarized by Captain David Buchan, who, during a British Parliamentary inquiry in 1836 into the fate of the Beothuks, stated that the "effect of the 'visitation of civilised and christian men' in Newfoundland had been the destruction of its native population."[14]

Genocide in French colonial North America

As the French dominated the northern half of North America prior to the British conquest of New France, the relations they established with the Amerindian population would undoubtedly have influenced the relationship that their British successor would establish with the Natives. This, in turn, would influence the treatment of Native peoples in Canada. Looking at the French example would also provide insight into the dynamics that led to the destruction of Aboriginal peoples in British and Spanish America and into what Stannard calls the American holocaust.

A number of influences contributed to making French-Indian relations more positive than those that existed in either the Spanish or British colonies. As the French did not settle in great numbers in the New World, and were interested primarily in the fur trade, they were much more dependent than other groups on good relations with their Aboriginal trading partners. Unlike the Spanish, they were not interested in plundering and enslaving the natives; unlike the English, they were little inclined to settle widely on Native land. Furthermore, because the French newcomers were largely single men—unlike the English, who were more likely to emigrate as families—they were much more inclined to intermingle with the Native population than were the English. Indeed, early French colonial policy favoured intermarriage between the two groups as a way to help civilize the Indians. Finally, unlike the Puritans or the Spanish missionaries, for example, who tended to look at Aboriginal religious practices as works of the devil, the French Jesuits working among the Indians sought to slowly change their beliefs rather than eradicate them.[15]

Nevertheless, there is evidence that the French did not hesitate to use genocide when it suited their purposes, as is evidenced by the destruction of the Natchez in 1731. Arriving in the lower Mississippi region in the early part of the eighteenth century, the French sought to gain control of the interior of North America. Hostilities broke out when the Natchez Indians resisted French expansion into their territory. The conflict was characterized by massacres on both sides. In 1731, the French, in co-operation with one of their Indian allies, the Choctaw, destroyed the major Natchez stronghold. Avenging the killing of several hundred of their citizens, the French killed a thousand Natchez and sold some four hundred of them into slavery in St. Dominique. After this, the Natchez ceased to exist as a people.[16]

The French also persistently tried to wipe out the Mesquaki, or Fox Indians, as they were generally called. Following a protracted struggle with the Fox as the French sought to consolidate their position in Wisconsin, the French decided to exterminate them altogether. In September 1730, French troops surrounded about 1,200 of the 1,600 remaining Mesquaki, who had numbered about 4,500 in 1700. After an eighteen-day siege, the starving Mesquaki sought to escape, only to be overtaken by the French and their Indian allies. When the slaughter ended, over 200 warriors and approximately 300 women and children lay dead on the prairie south of Lake Michigan. Most of the remaining combatants, as well as women and children, were taken prisoner. About 50 warriors escaped, only to be hunted down. Those captured were taken back to their enemies' camp, where they, as well as those who had been taken prisoner earlier, were tortured and then burned to death. Of the remaining 450 Mesquaki, some 200 (including women and children) were killed in an attack in 1832 by Huron and Iroquois warriors at the urging of the French.[17] Although this attack did not totally destroy the Mesquaki, they ceased to pose a threat to French ambitions. Churchill argues that the manner in which the French disposed of this nation was a genocide.[18] In contrast, Wrone and Nelson argue that the French actions towards the Mesquaki constituted an attempted extermination but not genocide.[19]

Although the French were in conflict with different Native tribes, in particular the Iroquois Confederacy, there is little evidence that they wiped out or attempted to eradicate other Native tribes as they sought to expand their empire in North America. More so than other Europeans, the French made great efforts to enter into alliances with Native peoples. At this they were fairly successful, causing Morton to comment that a genuine respect and affection existed between the two peoples.[20] Indian support was insufficient, however, to counterbalance the preponderance of power Britain possessed in its colonies to the south of New France. Continuous rivalry between the two European powers led to the defeat of France in North America, with Britain taking control of most of its possessions.

European-Native relations following Britain's conquest of New France

The Treaty of Paris of 1763 gave Britain control not only of New France but also of European-Native relations in the former French possessions. Commenting on the change, Dickason observes: "If the defeat of France in the New World was a bitter blow to French Canada, it was a disaster for many Amerindians, from the east coast to the Great Lakes and even westward."[21] The elimination of France as a power in North America deprived them of their bargaining power between the British and French rivals. At the same time, Britain's Native allies had been led to believe that once the French were driven out, the encroachment of settlers onto their lands would cease. However, after the defeat of France the push by settlers to take over Indian territory intensified, with Native peoples being little able to stop them.

Settler pressure on Native land had already, prior to the conquest, forced Britain to look more closely at its relations with the Indians. Noticing that its lack of a uniform system in land dealings and trade with the Indians had frequently motivated them to ally themselves with France, the Imperial Government had appointed an Indian Superintendent to look after its Native affairs. He ensured that presents were distributed annually among the Indians to maintain good relations. He undertook to protect Indians from fraudulent trade dealings as well as to regulate settler encroachment onto Native lands. However, such endeavours had little effect on the European alienation of Indian lands; nor had they persuaded most Indian tribes to break their alliances with the French. To repay them for their loyalty, France included provisions for the protection of its former allies once it gave up power in North America. Thus, terms of capitulation obtained by the French stated that Natives be treated as soldiers under arms and that they "be maintained in the lands they inhabit." Although the wording of the capitulation was vague, by accepting it Britain obligated itself to pay more attention to Indian land rights. The issue was made more pressing by the Pontiac uprising, which was evoked in part by Native fears regarding settler encroachment on their lands.[22]

To allay Native fears that the British would dispossess them, Britain passed a number of proclamations seeking to regulate relations between Native peoples and Europeans. The most important of these was the Royal Proclamation of 1763. It was supposed to be a temporary measure. However, in particular the approach it outlined relating to the alienation of Indian lands turned out to have important long-term consequences. The Proclamation claimed that King George III had sovereignty over all the lands formerly occupied by the French. It also reserved to Indian "nations" as their "hunting grounds" those territories "to the Westward of the sources of the Rivers which fall into the Sea from the West and the Northwest." While it isn't clear what area this embraced, the Proclamation tended to refer to those areas which at the time were most threatened by white settlement. Also, the Proclamation stipulated that Natives were free to sell their Aboriginal interests in the soil, should the reserve be required for the future settlement of colonists. Such purchases could be carried out by individuals on behalf of the British crown. This in part acknowledged Native territorial rights to their lands. Also, it suggested an orderly process whereby

Natives could alienate their land and make it available for white settlement.

Allen goes a little far when he calls the Proclamation the *"Magna Carta* of native rights in Canada."[23] Equating provisions of the Proclamation, which helped regularize and not make as destructive the alienation of Indian lands under the British as it did in the United States, with the rights received by the Lords under the *Magna Carta* in Medieval England, is rather extreme. Tobias is more to the point when he argues that the Proclamation laid the groundwork on the basis of which the government obtained Indian lands in Canada, both while it was under British rule and afterwards.[24]

The Proclamation influenced this process in several ways. Making the Crown the agency responsible for alienating Native lands, it not only made it more difficult for private persons to cheat the Natives, but also made negotiation at the government level an essential part of the process of obtaining Indian lands. Thus, it set out a procedure "requiring the voluntary cession of Indian lands to the Crown in a public assembly of the Indians concerned. The British Crown thus established its precedent for mutual agreement or treaty, and a binding procedure for the acquisition of First Nations' lands according to British law."[25] This presented not only a process for carrying out negotiations. The written agreement also offered a reference point to which either the British government or Native signatories could refer should either party not live up to conditions of the signed treaty.

Britain's attempts to protect Natives against the land-hungry settlers eventually alienated its colonists. Of course, this wasn't the only reason the Thirteen Colonies rose in rebellion against the motherland in 1775. They also had other grievances. Once the French threat was gone, the Thirteen Colonies were much less willing to contribute to imperial defence and other British ventures. They protested against being taxed while Britain decided how their tax money would be spent. They protested against the Quebec Act of 1774, naming it one of the "Intolerable Acts." One reason for their objection was that it was part of the British attempt to control land settlement in such areas as the Ohio Valley so as to give better protection to Native peoples. The Thirteen Colonies, in turn, interpreted this as a British attempt to prevent their expansion into an area they saw essentially as their back yard.

Once the Americans rose in rebellion in 1775, Britain sought to recruit support not only from French Canadians but also from Native people in its struggle to suppress the rebels. In fact, under these circumstances, Dickason argues, Britain increasingly found itself in a situation in relation to the Indians similar to that in which France found itself prior to the conquest. That is, its policy toward the Indians was very much dictated by its attempt to recruit their support in fighting its major enemy in the Americas.[26] While it wasn't successful in winning over all Native groups to fighting the rebel colonists during the American War of Independence, it did win over some groups, in particular the Iroquois.

For Native peoples, British support was of limited help. The Treaty of Paris in 1783, which brought to an end the American Revolution, essentially ignored the Indians, with no provisions being made for their lands in territory transferred to the Americans. The Americans rejected the British proposal that a separate indigenous state be established. At the same time, Indians that had supported the British cause were forced to flee to British soil, as did white Americans. They became part of the some forty to fifty thousand Loyalists who found refuge on Canadian soil following Britain's defeat by its rebel colonists.

This necessitated that the government find land where it might settle these people. At least some of this land was situated in Native territory in the western part of Quebec. To acquire this land, the government followed the process suggested by the Proclamation of 1763. That is, Aboriginal interest in the land was recognized. At the same time, the government undertook to enter into negotiations with Native occupants to have them sell their interest in the soil. It did so by entering into a series of treaties with Native groups which were in essence land transfers. The first of these transfers were used to provide land for the Loyalists, including Native tribes that had supported the British cause. However, the endeavour to obtain Native land and open it up to general settlement didn't end there. By the 1830s, the Crown had obtained, through treaty negotiations with local Indian tribes, unencumbered title to most of Upper Canada south of the Pre-Cambrian Shield.

The Indians were encouraged to sell their rights in the land for a number of reasons. One was that considerable trust existed between Natives and the imperial government, both of them convinced that it was in their interest to co-operate to keep in check the expansion of the land-hungry United States. At the same time, Indian tribes with which the government negotiated were often few in number and therefore too weak to oppose government demands.[27] Also, despite limited options, treaty negotiations offered the Indians the opportunity to have at least some input into determining their place in the world that was rapidly transforming around them.

This pattern of negotiation continued after Canada became a nation in 1867 and the federal government took over many of the responsibilities of treaty negotiation that had formerly been carried out by the British. Just how this worked may be observed when examining Canada's settlement of its prairie frontier. Here, the Hudson's Bay Company and other fur trade interests had sought to discourage land settlement as long as possible because they saw this as interfering with the fur trade. However, at the time of Confederation, Canada began to look toward expanding into the prairie lands west of Ontario. This expansion was carried out almost totally under the direction of the Canadian government. To initiate the process, it put pressure on the British government that Hudson's Bay Company rights to its land in western Canada be extinguished and that this territory be transferred to Canada. Following this, the Canadian government took a leading role in negotiations with Native peoples to prepare the way for eventual European settlement.

Its approach in this regard was directed by several influences. Observing that the Native wars that at the time were setting the American prairie aflame were costing more money than what Canada's central government had in its budget, Canadian leaders decided on a more peaceful approach to taking possession of Native lands.[28] Also, when acquiring Rupert's Land, or the former Hudson Bay territory, the Canadian Government promised, on behalf of the imperial monarch, to negotiate with its Native people both to extinguish Native title and provide reserves for Native use. It promised Britain that it would honour the provisions of the Proclamation of 1763. Furthermore, Natives themselves insisted on treaty negotiation as a means of guaranteeing their rights. Thus, the Saulteaux in Manitoba and the Ojibwa Indians of the North-West Angle insisted on treaties guaranteeing their rights before Canada even commenced with the settlement of its prairie frontier.[29] In obtaining Native land through treaty negotiation, the Canadian government did not necessarily see itself admitting that the Indians owned the land. Rather, it saw treaty negotiation as part of a process of fulfilling its moral obligations, be this to the mother country or Native peoples, and as a means of avoiding conflict with the some thirty-five thousand Indians on the Canadian prairies.[30]

Negotiations commenced with tribes that occupied territory in Manitoba and then moved further west. For the most part, treaty negotiations were pragmatic affairs. In these, the Indian tribes sought to work out agreements with the federal government that would best help them survive once the buffalo were gone. The government, on its part, was mainly interested in obtaining maximum land for the best price so that it could settle it with farmers from Europe. Thus, Natives and the government often took different positions on the amount of land to be set aside for Native use, or on the amount of aid to be given them to make a start as farmers. They at times disagreed over where reserves should be located, over whether they should be close together or at some distance from each other. Differences were gradually resolved, with the treaties resulting in reserve land being set aside for the particular Native group in question. At the same time, the government agreed to provide Native peoples with a mutually agreed-upon amount of aid to make a start on the land as well as to help them acquire the skills needed to make their living from farming.

A number of factors aided the government in its negotiations. While some tribes resisted the changes, most prairie tribes realized that the days of the buffalo hunt were coming to an end. They also realized that they had to find an alternative way of making a living. Treaty negotiation offered a good means of achieving this. As Long and Dickason state: For Natives in Canada, "treaties provided leeway to adapt, within the framework of their own traditions, to the demands of a changing world. Consequently, in those areas where European settlement was expanding, most of the pressure for treaties came from the Amerindians themselves."[31] In essence, Native peoples often looked forward to treaty negotiations, which would give them some input into shaping the world in which they would find themselves once their traditional means of making their livelihood were no longer available to them.

On its part, the government stressed to Native peoples, be they Cree, Ojibwa, Assiniboine or any other, the limited choices available to them. Not only were the buffalo disappearing but non-Native newcomers would be taking control of most of the lands no matter whether or not a treaty was agreed upon. Natives could resist the incursions through war or they could agree to some form of government assistance to help them adjust to the upcoming changes. Generally the government took up negotiations first with tribes most readily swayed by its arguments. At the same time, it used missionaries, the Metis, who were closely related to the Indians, and other groups to put pressure on the Indians to enter into treaty negotiation.

In particular the North-West Mounted Police (NWMP) became an important factor in persuading the Natives to enter into treaty negotiations with the government and give up land for settlement. Established in 1873, the NWMP took up duties as a law-enforcing agency in 1874. In this regard, they made special efforts to win the trust and confidence of Native peoples. They were helped in this by putting an end to the blatant activities of American whiskey traders who were both exploiting the Natives and contributing to general lawlessness on the prairies. At the same time, NWMP officers made a special effort to win the confidence of tribal leaders.

The government, while seeking to gain the best deal for itself in negotiations, at the same time was open enough to Native demands to help persuade them that negotiation rather than force was the best way to attain their goals. Observing the destruction of Native peoples south of the border, Native leaders, while pressuring the government to obtain the best deal for themselves, did their best to avoid violence as a means of gaining their goals. Despite this, several armed rebellions arose in Canada, led by people who felt themselves threatened by Canada's settlement of its prairie frontier. The first of these was the Red River Rebellion. While apprehensive regarding government intentions, Indians did not take part in the Riel insurrection.[32] The rebellion was precipitated by uncertainty at Red River, created by the power vacuum that emerged during negotiations that led from Hudson's Bay Company control to Canada's assuming control of this territory. At the time of the transfer, both Americans and Canadians sought to take possession of the area. The Canada First Party at Red River, composed largely of English-speaking Canadians from Ontario, was especially vociferous in pushing Canada's claim. Absorption by Canada and the expected influx of settlers that would follow made in particular the French-speaking Metis at Red River apprehensive. They had sought assurances of their rights at Red River several times through appeals to London, but with little success. The uncertainty of the situation during the transfer of Hudson's Bay Company lands to Canada at last brought them to act. Under the leadership of Louis Riel, they seized Upper Fort Garry and in December 1869, proclaimed a provisional government. In the spring of 1870, they organized the territory of Assiniboia and entered into negotiations with the Canadian government so as to safeguard their rights. The government sent in troops to suppress the Metis assertion of power. At the same time, it entered into negotiations with the Red River Metis, agreeing to consider their demands. The negotiations resulted, among other things, in the guarantee of French linguistic rights in Manitoba and also provided for land being set aside for the Metis.

Uncertainty and other problems that evoked the Red River Rebellion also played a role in the North-West Rebellion. Plains Indians, be they Cree, Blackfoot or Assiniboine, had been reduced to near starvation by the disappearance of the buffalo. At the same time, for a number of years the federal government had been enforcing a policy of work for rations, except for the sick and aged. Only "general" famine was seen as a warrant for free rations. The per diem allowance of food for individuals was reduced. Resulting food shortages led to desperate acts, including the killing of cattle and the pillaging of Hudson's Bay stores. Confrontations between Natives and employees of the Indian department over rations threatened several times to erupt in massive outbreaks of violence. Natives appealed to Ottawa. However, Ottawa paid little attention to their complaints.

In the meantime, the Metis in the North-West had difficulty settling down to a farming life and at the same time were anxious regarding their rights to the land they farmed. They sent for Louis Riel, who was in the United States, to speak on their behalf with the government. As soon as he arrived, Riel sought to unite the different groups with grievances to spur the central government to action. In the fall of 1884, he prepared a petition, inviting the Metis, English half-breeds and settlers to sign it. In the spring of 1885, at a meeting in St. Laurent, Saskatchewan, a Revolutionary Bill of Rights was passed that, among other things, asserted that the Metis had a right of possession to their farms and demanded more and better provisions for the Indians. On March 18 and 19, the Metis formed a provisional government and organized an armed force, which soon after occupied the community of Duck Lake. On March 26, the NWMP, supported by citizen volunteers, about one hundred strong, under Police Superintendent Crozier, sought to dislodge the Metis. However, a large Metis and Indian force met the police and volunteers near the village. In the ensuing battle, nine volunteers and three police were killed as well as a number of Metis and Indians.

Immediately after the attack, the government sent out troops to crush the revolt, which it did in the spring and summer of that year. It not only crushed the revolt. It also used the revolt, led and orchestrated in large part by the Metis, as an excuse to further its control over Native groups. The number of police was increased and the movement of Native peoples was restricted. At the same time, intense pressure was applied on tribal groups such as the Cree to take up reservations assigned to them.[33] This included refusal to make food provisions available until they had settled on a reservation. As the buffalo no longer roamed the prairie and the Indians depended on government supplies to survive, this essentially meant using starvation as a pressure tactic. At the same time, trials were held that led to the imprisonment of leaders of the rebellion as well as to the execution of rebels who were proven to have committed murder at the time of the unrest. While making use of intimidation and force, the government also made an attempt to meet the needs of Metis and Indian peoples by addressing issues that had led to the rebellion. At the same time, the government rewarded in particular the Indians who had not taken part in the rebellion.[34]

The rebellion was the last major uprising on the Canadian prairies. Essentially no settlers had participated in it. Some Metis had participated in it, as also did fewer than 5 per cent of prairie Indians.[35] While the Canadian government used force to crush the opposition to its settlement policy, this did not lead to the massive slaughters that characterized the crushing of Indian opposition south of the border. There are several reasons for this. While the Canadian government did not allow opposition to interfere with its settlement plans, it did listen to the people who felt threatened by the changes which land settlement would bring. In fact, it couldn't help but listen. In both the Red River and the North-West Rebellion, the rebel movement or at least its leadership consisted of French Canadian Metis who had no difficulty gaining the support of French Canadians in Quebec. As Quebec support was generally vital for federal political leaders in Canada wishing to retain power, groups that gained Quebec support could certify that their needs would gain attention. Furthermore, the general lawlessness that led to settlers often taking the law into their own hands south of the border never existed in Canada. Observing the violence that often characterized Native-European interaction south of the border, both Native leaders and governments in Canada sought to avoid these extremes. The peaceful negotiation of differences was also encouraged by the control the national government had over the whole settlement process. An integral part of this control was certifying that the law was operative in old areas as well as in new areas of settlement. This was achieved in western Canada largely through use of the North-West Mounted Police. Doing their best to certify that the law operated fairly and was perceived to be operating fairly not only for the new settlers, but also for the Indians and Metis, the NWMP helped to inspire confidence in Canadian government policy.

At the same time, the process involving the negotiation of treaties as well as the treaties themselves contributed to a relatively peaceful transfer of Indian land. The treaties allowed for a process of negotiation with which Natives were comfortable. They allowed Native peoples to state their needs. Of course, they weren't always listened to. Nor were Canadian leaders overly generous in meeting these needs. Rather, they exploited their position of power to assure they got the best deal possible from the different tribal groups. At the same time, both government and Indian leaders seldom let their differences go to the extremes where they saw armed conflict as a means of resolving problems regarding land settlement. The treaties that were negotiated allowed Native people to take an active role in negotiating for themselves the best treaty available to them under the circumstances in which they found themselves. They permitted the government to take control of land that it could then open to general settlement.

Although force played a role in this whole process, in particular during the North-West Rebellion, one can well argue that there were basic differences between the expanding British Canadian settlement frontier and the expanding British American settlement frontier. Overall, in the case of Canada, the frontier expanded in an orderly fashion. This was in large part encouraged by the manner in which settlement was carried out, in particular by the governments involved. That is, government took a leading role in opening the land. In making arrangement for the transfer of land from Native peoples, it generally took some effort to convince Native people that any agreement reached was in their interest. Once land was available for European settlers, the government helped recruit immigrants and settle them. While putting down opposition to settlement, it also adopted measures to assure, as much as possible, that the grievances of those who feared settlement were listened to and that the law which was established could, for the most part, be trusted by all concerned.

In areas of the United States where the expansion of the settlement frontier was most destructive, many of these conditions were not present. Thus, settlement often involved settlers pouring into Indian territory before proper agreements were made to provide for a systematic alienation of land from the Natives. Government officials, rather than addressing the concerns of Native people affected by these actions, in many respects merely became agents of those who sought to dispossess and exploit the Natives. A major culprit in this regard was the electoral system. While rapid settlement at times created conditions that contributed to lawlessness on the frontier, this in itself would not have led to the extremes that led to the decimation of the vast majority of Native peoples in the United States by 1900. It was participatory democracy and the manner in which it operated that made this process particularly lethal. The Native had no voice in this system. He was an object to be exploited, removed or even killed, with rewards often being offered for his destruction. Under these conditions, the entire political system and military establishment in many ways became an agent of those who sought to dispossess, exploit or destroy the Natives.

In Canada, where Natives also had no voice in the political system, several restraints were operative in this regard. One was the tradition of cooperation that had evolved. Both Britain and the Natives saw it in their interest to cooperate to stem the expansionist drive of the American settlers, in particular after the outbreak of the American Revolution. Another was the monarchical system of government, which generally made legislatures less responsive to the popular will than was the case in the United States. This was further encouraged by the composition of Canadian society, in which the fear of offending either the British or French population base dissuaded government from going to extremes. All these factors encouraged the government to consider the interest of the Natives to a greater degree and be less inclined to become associated with forces that in the United States were decimating the Natives. However, this still allowed government to participate effectively in what it deemed to be the national interest, be this in negotiating treaties that would allow Native peoples at least some input in determining their future, or in the larger program of recruiting immigrants from Europe and settling the land. This still led to the dispossession of Natives, of course. It still led to governments at times abusing their power to force Natives to accept agreements that were all too often less than fair to the weaker party.

Having said this, one has also to admit that Canadian land settlement policy operated in a way that allowed Native peoples to express their demands, as well as forced the government to consider the needs of those who perceived their interests as being negatively affected by its settlement policies. All these influences helped create conditions that made the dispossession of Native people less destructive in Canada than it was in the United States. They did so on the one hand by keeping the aggression that lay at the basis of the conquest and dispossession from going to the extreme. At the same time, they made at least somewhat kinder the process of dispossession, thereby helping to restrain the anger that this process would naturally evoke among the Indian population. This restrained the cycle of violence that in the United States served to encourage the destruction of Native peoples.

11
The Fate of Aborigines in Tasmania and on the Australian Mainland

To obtain further insight into the dynamics that led to genocide in British America, it would be helpful to look at genocides committed in other areas colonized by the British, for example in Tasmania and on the Australian mainland. Commenting on the destruction of the original inhabitants of Tasmania, Molony states that although the newcomers had not deliberately engaged in genocide, they had achieved it nonetheless.[1] What Molony means is that, while the British had not deliberately set out to destroy the Natives in Tasmania, they destroyed them by depriving them of their land and, in the process, treating them as a pariah. Native Tasmanians were dehumanized and their destruction was seen as part of the progress of civilization. Such attitudes and actions led to the annihilation of the Aborigines in Tasmania and to their near destruction in other parts of Australia.

In this chapter, I will examine the destruction of Native peoples in Tasmania and then endeavour to place this genocide into the larger context of white-Aboriginal relations in Australia. Although these relations had been friendly at first contact, they deteriorated once whites settled on the island. Conflict intensified with the marked increase in settlement in Tasmania following the Napoleonic wars. The same geographic areas along the river systems attracted the immigrants and also supported a large number of Aborigines, who very early after the arrival of the white settlers expressed their resentment at interference with food supplies and hunting grounds. The Aborigines indicated their disapproval by throwing stones and shaking their spears at the intruders. Up to the early 1820s, attacks were sporadic, although the sealers in the northeast had already begun to abduct or prostitute the women and murder the men. Shepherds, who often kept women chained to their huts so that they could abuse them sexually, had also forced Aboriginal women on the edge of all the settled districts into prostitution.

In the mid-1820s, a number of Aborigines were captured and hanged for killing whites. At the same time, Europeans who had been indescribably brutal to Native women had received only twenty lashes. During the following years, attacks continued from both sides. The press became hysterical about the threat from the Aborigines and, in November 1827, Lieutenant-Governor George Arthur gave instructions for military protection to be given to the settlers. On realizing, however, that the Europeans were the initiators of the conflict, Arthur considered establishing a reservation in the northeast, but abandoned this scheme because of the nomadic lifestyle of the Aborigines.

In May 1828, the *Hobart Town Gazette* carried a proclamation by the lieutenant-governor that he would stem the Aborigines' threat to the life and property of the colonists of Van Diemen's Land (as Tasmania was then known) by establishing military posts along the outskirts of the settled districts.[2] The Aborigines wouldn't be permitted beyond this area, except for their customary annual travel to the coast for shellfish, for which they would require the permission of the lieutenant governor. Arthur's proclamation, however, failed to address the real problem, which was Aboriginal interference with the newcomer's attempt to establish himself on the land and use it as he saw fit. If the Aborigine interfered with this endeavour, he was perceived as a sort of animal pest to be eradicated.

Although the increase in the number of military posts checked the activities of the Aborigines in the winter of 1828, with the coming of spring they again came into conflict with the settlers. In response, at the beginning of November 1828, the government proclaimed a martial law that allowed the settlers to shoot the Aborigines on sight in settled districts. At the same time, search-and-capture parties were initiated, the first one apparently having been led by Gilbert Robertson, the chief district constable of Sorell, who in November 1828 captured five Aborigines near Swanport.

Most such parties, however, were not successful. A search-and-capture party led by a man by the name of John Batman reported that they had sneaked to within fifty feet of a group of Aborigines on the eastern side of Ben Lomond when one of their guns discharged as the owner stumbled against a tree. As the Aborigines ran off, the whites opened fire, seriously wounding two men. They also captured a woman and a child. When they found that the wounded men were unable to walk, Batman killed them. Despite this, the lieutenant governor permitted him to continue pursuing Aborigines into areas not under martial law.

Casualties in the conflict between whites and the Native Tasmanians are difficult to estimate. The *Tasmanian* reported in 1828 that some thirteen Europeans had been killed that year as also had been about an equal number of Aborigines. Many Europeans had also been wounded, with the Aborigines usually targeting huts occupied by one or two men. In February 1829 the *Launceston Advertiser* reported nineteen Aborigines killed and five captured and one European speared.[3] That month, also, a shepherd was speared near Launceston and a ten-year-old boy beaten to death by Aborigines in the Pheasant Hills.

It seemed the conflict would terminate only once one group or the other had been destroyed. In August 1929, employees under Alexander Goldie of the Van Diemen's Land Company were constructing a shed near the Cam River on the northwest coast when they saw some Aborigines. Goldie reported that the Aborigines had come to within two hundred yards of the Europeans before being noticed, and the Natives then started to flee. As the Europeans pursued them, Goldie shot one woman who was running into shrubbery. He rode down another in the bush, who was then killed with an axe. In another case, servants of the Van Diemen's Land Company tried to "take liberties" with Aboriginal women. When their men reacted by spearing a shepherd in the thigh and, continuing the retaliation, killed some company sheep, a punitive expedition was organized. Members murdered some thirty Aborigines and threw their bodies off a cliff.

Although decimated by such means, the Aborigines appear to have decided that if they were going to be wiped out, they would take as many whites with them as possible. They targeted in particular the huts at the outskirts of the settlements, which were generally occupied by two to three men. They pressed their attacks until they had either killed the occupants or were repulsed.

The Colonial Office approved in general of the martial law, convincing itself that the measure would not only benefit the Native people but also ensure the safety of the settlers. Meanwhile, the struggle continued: on the one side Aborigines fighting for the most part with stones and spears and the other side fighting with guns and other modern weaponry. The result was inevitable. Four years after martial law had been introduced, the Aborigines had reached their final stages of destruction. In his report to the Colonial Office, in April 1830, Arthur blamed the Aborigines for the attacks launched against them. Typical in this regard was a report by Isaac Sherwin, who asserted that in the fall of 1829 some forty or fifty Aborigines had attacked him. However, he had seen only four or five of them. He added that he knew of no atrocities committed by whites against Aborigines. He did know, however, that the thatch of his house had been set on fire. He also conveyed the opinion that the Aborigines wanted Van Diemen's Land for themselves. He suggested different ways of solving the problem: Sydney Aborigines or bloodhounds could be used to destroy the people of the island; another alternative was to poison them. Another settler stated that his sheep at Bashan Plain had been speared, and recommended that convicts be used to clear out the Aborigines. They would likely shoot a larger number than they would capture.[4]

With most of the Aborigines destroyed by fire-power, disease introduced by the invaders, and the fatal disruption of their lives and culture, Lieutenant-Governor Arthur decided to deal with the remainder by capturing them and placing them where they would no longer hinder the settlers. Although only about five hundred Aborigines were left, some of them, equipped with firearms, had robbed some settlers. The new plan of action involved capturing the remnants of the Big River, Oyster Bay, and Abyssinia tribes - considered the most savage - or driving them into the Tasman peninsula as beaters might drive game before them. The project, which began on 4 October 1830, captured only one man and a boy during its seven-week operation.

This operation was still underway when a man by the name of George Augustus Robinson initiated his project to save the remaining Aborigines of Van Diemen's Land. A self-made man with a sense of duty, Robinson intended to Europeanize the Aborigines and teach them Christian values. He left Hobart Town for Port Davey toward the end of January 1830, on the first of what were to be six expeditions. He ultimately spent more than four years in the wilderness, inquiring into the condition of the Native population of the colony for the government. In the process, he found out much not only about the cultural traditions of the Native Tasmanians, but also about how they had been mistreated by the Europeans.

Robinson heard of a man who carried in his pack the ears and noses of Aborigines he had slain, exhibiting them as trophies. Employees of the Van Diemen's Land Company told him that they would shoot Natives whenever they could. William Gunshannon, a company employee, boasted about his participation in the massacre of Aborigines. Charles Chamberlain admitted that he, Gunshannon, and two other men had massacred some thirty Aborigines. Aborigines later told Robinson that the company's shepherds had gotten Aboriginal women into their hut, wanting to take liberties with them. Resenting this, Aboriginal men had speared a European in the thigh. In response, the Europeans killed one of their men. Subsequently, Aborigines destroyed some of the company's sheep by driving them over a cliff. Some time after that, the company's men took by surprise a whole tribe, massacred thirty of them, and then threw them off a cliff. Ever since then, Van Diemen's Land natives called the Europeans at Cape Grim *nowhummoe* (devil); when they heard a shot, they said the *nowhummoe* had destroyed another Aboriginal tribe.[5]

Robinson was informed that Aborigines at Minedim, in the Cape Grim district, had shown little hostility until employees of the Van Diemen's Land Company viciously attacked two of their women. One of the women, noticing she was about to be shot, turned away from her attacker, stooping down to protect her child. She had no sooner been felled by the shot than another European ran up to chop her on the neck. When the other woman and her child were captured, the woman was mistreated. The husband of the killed woman swore he would take out his revenge on every European he met.[6]

Reports of other atrocities also reached Robinson. He was told of a shepherd named Paddy Heagon who shot nineteen Aborigines with a swivel gun loaded with nails. At Middle Plains, several men on horseback were searching for stray cattle when they met a tribe of Aborigines. They drove them into a small lagoon, where they shot several. They drove the remainder to the foot of Ritchie's Sugarloaf, where they shot them all with the exception of an old man and a woman. Other reports included that of a shepherd who, seeing the fires of Aborigines at night, went out and shot nine of them. Another shepherd, by the name of Punch, said that a half-caste woman helped with killing Aborigines and that on one occasion a party of the 40th Regiment killed nine or ten. Punch also informed Robinson that Knight, a shepherd killed by the Aborigines, deserved to die because he used to kill Aborigines for sport.[7] On other occasions, Native peoples were poisoned, with hundreds being destroyed in this way.

Robinson collected these reports while he was trying to make contact with the Aborigines and bring them together into an area where they might be safe. His endeavour ended in early August 1834, when he returned to Hobart Town. What were thought to be the few Aborigines still at large, a man, four women and a boy, were brought in by Robinson's son Charles, in the last days of 1834. In late November 1836, George and Charles Robinson came upon a husband, wife and four children near Cradle Mountain, but this little group refused to go to Flinders Island, where Robinson had established his refuge. These were probably the only Aborigines still remaining who were not taken to Flinders Island. No one knows what eventually happened to them, for they disappeared without a trace.

Robinson spent over three years in charge of the Flinders Island settlement. There, he sought to establish the Natives on the land by teaching them how to cultivate the soil and live as farmers. His attempts proved unsuccessful, however, and the last Native man died in 1869 and the last woman in 1876. "Such was one result," Robson concludes, "of the colonization by Europeans of Van Diemen's Land."[8]

Tasmania and the destruction of the Aborigines in Australia

It is rather ironic that, after they were hunted almost to extinction, a mission of mercy should lead to the final destruction of the original inhabitants of Tasmania. Obviously, the annihilation of the original inhabitants had been underway for some time before Robinson undertook his efforts to save the last remnant. Their mistreatment by settlers, whalers, and herders had destroyed their social relationships and livelihood, and had made them fugitives in their own land. Commenting on the destruction, Lyndal Ryan states that the local government considered the "absence" of Aborigines in the colony an indication of its maturity and that the newly responsible governments of Victoria and New South Wales on the Australian mainland, which also had "remnant" Aboriginal populations, shared this attitude.[9]

Judging from the works of Molony, Reynolds, as well as of Evans, Saunders and Cronin, the attitudes towards, and treatment of, Native Tasmanians did not differ significantly from those on the Australian mainland. In both cases, terror was used to subdue Native people. They were poisoned and hunted for sport. Any attempt by Aborigines to assert ownership of their land brought a massive reaction by the invaders.

Molony states that, to the white Australian, the Aborigines were "a scoff and a jest on humanity," and their eradication was virtually assured.[10] In Tasmania, as well as on the Australian mainland, Native people tended to be viewed as "so much black trash" to be transformed into manure at the first opportunity.[11] Popular views that denigrated Native people and justified their slaughter were supported by pseudo-scientific theories popular at the time. As elsewhere, European settlers in Australia embraced the idea of the Great Chain of Being, which placed Aboriginal people one step above animals. Also popular were Darwin's survival-of-the-fittest theory, and pseudo-scientific pronouncements of phrenologists, who measured skulls in an attempt to prove the intellectual inferiority of non-whites. All of these combined to soothe the conscience of those who, for the sake of material gain, decimated an entire race.[12]

Reynolds sees the conflict between Native and settler as resulting from the struggle to possess the land. It stemmed essentially from the failure of the imperial government to define what constituted Native ownership of the land, which in turn motivated the settler to seize Native land at will.[13] Talk by government officials that kindness be shown in the treatment of Aborigines could not hide the fact that, once having made the decision to settle, crushing Aboriginal opposition was an inevitable consequence, regardless of the cost in human lives. Under these circumstances, punitive expeditions were an inevitable government response to Aboriginal resistance, in particular if this resistance raised the possibility of settlers having to give up their farms.[14]

Unable to drive out the invaders because of their technological superiority and, later, numerical superiority, Native people resorted to guerrilla warfare. The invader reacted by terrorizing Aborigines to force them to accept their lot, which included the loss of land. Rather than seeing European action as the cause for the Native's guerrilla warfare, the settler regarded attempts by Natives to assert their land claims as reflecting their violent nature.[15] Throughout, the invader saw himself as the innocent party in this conflict. Such a soothing of the conscience served to justify not only depriving the Native of his land but also mistreating and even killing him in the process.

In some areas of continental Australia, the effects of white-Aboriginal relations were almost as devastating as in Tasmania. In Victoria, the Native population was reduced from an estimated 11,500 in 1834, to 806 in 1886.[16] By 1901, only 271 full-blood Aborigines remained in Victoria.[17] Commenting on the decrease in Aboriginal population, Cannon states that by any standards, this amounted to the "virtual extermination of a race of people, which is commonly known as genocide."[18] Evans, Saunders, and Cronin state that the initial settlement of almost every district of Queensland was accompanied by a period of violence, sometimes brief but intense, at times extended over a longer period, but nevertheless "severe."[19] Reynolds estimates that, in Australia as a whole, 20,000-30,000 Aborigines were poisoned or shot by the white pioneers.[20]

Others died of diseases brought by the newcomers. The destructive influence of disease was enhanced through general mistreatment, which was an integral part of a process that involved the replacement of the Aboriginal inhabitants by the newcomers. These contributed to the widespread and immediate destruction of the original inhabitants and assured that, by the beginning of the twentieth century, only a small remnant of the Aboriginal population remained. The extent of this remnant varied for different areas. In Tasmania, none were left. In areas such as Victoria, some 98 to 99 per cent of Aborigines had been destroyed by 1901.

Tasmania, Australia, and British North America

When one compares the extent of the destruction of Aborigines in Tasmania and Australia in general with the destruction of Native peoples in British North America, one finds much greater similarity between Australia and the United States than between Canada and Australia. This becomes evident when one compares the percentages of Native peoples destroyed in the different areas. To do so, it would be helpful to again note Churchill's observation that there were some 9 to 12 million Native people in North America prior to the white man's arrival, with most of them living in what is today the United States.[21] By 1900, their number had been reduced to about 237, 000,[22] indicating a destruction rate of some 98 per cent. In Tasmania all Native peoples were destroyed and some 98 to 99 per cent of Native peoples were destroyed in areas such as Victoria on the Australian mainland.

Dickason estimates that at the time of first contact some 500,000 Native people lived on the territory that was to become Canada.[23] Canadian population statistics state that there were 127,941 Native people, including Eskimos and Indians, in Canada in 1901. This is a loss of some 372,000 people. Thus, in percentage terms, the Native population in Canada declined by 74 per cent, which is considerably less than the 98 to 99 per cent decline for the United States and Australia.

Similarities and differences in percentage of people destroyed suggest a number of things. They suggest that the very process of being deprived of their land and marginalized had a drastic effect on Native peoples. They suggest that disease, inter-tribal warfare and the wars fought by the United States against Native peoples had a role in the decimation of Indians in both Canada and the United States. At the same time, differences in the percentage of Native peoples destroyed in Canada, the United States and Australia suggest essentially one thing. They suggest that the manner in which British elements in the United States and Australia took possession of Native land had a devastating effect on Native peoples in these areas. One cannot get much closer to a destruction of 98 to 99 per cent of a population without speaking of eradication and extermination.

Reasons for differences in the degree of destruction in Canada and the other areas become evident in particular when one looks at the role of violence in structuring Native-European relations. Evidence of this violence is observable in two main areas: attitudes expressed and behaviour. There is little evidence that British Canadians expressed the extremely aggressive attitudes towards Native peoples which were expressed by some political leaders in the United States or which Molony found existent in Australia. Nor did British Canadians imitate the violent methods pursued by both the Americans and the Australians when taking possession of Native lands. This suggests that violence, once resorted to, encouraged dehumanizing the Native. It also encouraged further violence. Projected onto Native peoples, such aggression served not merely to justify mistreating Native peoples, killing them and taking over their land, but also to legitimize the perpetrator's actions. In this context, Roosevelt's observation that the extermination of American Indians and the expropriation of their lands was a good thing and his suggestion that the only good Indian is a dead Indian[24] may be seen as a more accurate reflection on the Indian experience in the United States than some of us may wish to think. Whether this destruction might be considered a holocaust, as Stannard claims, may be determined by comparing it to other mass destructions under examination.

12
Patterns of Genocide as the Old World Conquered the New

To determine in what respects the genocides carried out in Spanish and British America, as well as in Australia, were holocausts, we need to compare and contrast the dynamics that led to genocide in the different cases under study. All cases were characterized by encounters between Christians and peoples they considered heathens, whites and people of colour, and technologically advanced and relatively backward societies. All these factors affected European attitudes and contributed to the dehumanizing and killing of Native peoples.

Clearly, the Christian belief system affected the Europeans' relations with Aboriginal peoples. Some Christian groups, in particular the Catholic missionary orders, as Gibson suggests, believed it was their duty to convert Native peoples from their heathen beliefs to the Christian faith.[1] Such goals, of course, were not the prime motivation of the people intent on mistreating, despoiling, or killing the people they encountered when they arrived in the New World. Nonetheless, they drew on aspects of the Christian belief system to help them denigrate Native people, justifying enslaving or killing them. One such belief was the Christian view of the Chain of Being. In terms of this conceptualization, the universe was hierarchically structured. At the zenith was God, followed by the Angels. Beneath these came human beings, in particular European Christians. As one went down the Chain of Being, one eventually encountered people who were not quite human and not quite animal; in fact, they might even occupy that realm where the human and the animal merged. Europeans slotted the Natives of the New World into this realm.

Another derivative of Christian beliefs was the European claim that the land they were invading was theirs by right of discovery. This belief, which was rooted in the ancient claim that Christians were everywhere entitled to dispossess non-Christians of their land, encouraged the European to appropriate Native lands. Moreover, the belief was bolstered by European legal theory, in particular the view regarding *vacuum domicilium,* which claimed that land not "occupied" or "settled" went by forfeit to those who attached themselves to it in a "civilized" manner. Arguments such as these were put forth, in particular in the British colonies, to drive the Natives from their land.

These arguments concerning land ownership were encouraged in the British colonies by the fact that Native people tended to not occupy a permanent territorial base but moved, depending on their ability to live off different areas of the land at different times of the year. This pattern did not fit the European idea of ownership, that is, possessing a piece of property and working it or having it worked by others for one's benefit. Their perception that Native peoples did not "own" or exploit the land properly encouraged the Europeans to take possession of it.

In Spanish America, cultural bias combined with religious belief led to the enslavement of the natives. Although the Catholic Church discouraged the enslavement of Christians, it did permit the enslavement of infidels. At the same time, Europeans developed the view that Africans, Indians, and other non-Christian peoples of colour had not descended from Adam and Eve but from lower progenitors. Others argued that indigenous peoples in the Americas, being wild, vicious, and totally irrational, were suited to be slaves.[2] Thus, European views regarding Native peoples and Christian religious beliefs coalesced to allow the conqueror to regard the people they came into contact with in the New World as a lower form of being whom they could treat as they wished.

These attitudes were further reinforced by other cultural or philosophical ideas. For example, European dress codes encouraged the newcomers to look upon the Native's scanty dress as a sign of lack of civilization, even bestiality. In addition, the Christian's ascetic *contemptus mundi* tradition, which saw sexual abstinence as the ideal, encouraged the Europeans to interpret the Native's more liberal sexual practices as an indication not only of a beast-like nature but also as a sign of a fallen state.

In the extreme, these beliefs could lead Christians to view all non-Christians as evil and as agents of Satan. Stannard argues that these beliefs, combined with the Old Testament message that all those who are the enemies of God could be slaughtered at will, were encouraged in particular by the extremes of wealth and poverty existent in their homelands when the Europeans first made contact with the New World. Extremes in social condition encouraged a messianic fervour. This, in turn, encouraged the mistreatment and slaughter of the Natives among those people intent on exploiting them.[3]

Subsequently, as religion came to have less of a hold on European society, science, which in many ways became the measurement of truth and falsehood, was used to justify mistreating or killing Native people. In many respects, social Darwinism reconstituted the hierarchy of the Chain of Being, conceptualizing it in scientific rather than religious terms. Such developments reinforced the Europeans' belief that they were the epitome of civilized beings. At the same time, they regarded the destruction of Native populations as an inevitable process whereby superior beings replaced inferior beings, just as, in the process of evolution, more adaptable creatures replaced creatures less able to adapt. Thus, they were able to explain away moral responsibility by scientific theory.

Technological differences, in particular in weapons of war, also influenced the relationship between indigenous people and the European conquerors. Obviously, the more advanced weaponry of the European made the conquest relatively easy. This was especially the case in the British colonies. Even where Natives were able to obtain firearms, they were dependent upon Europeans for ammunition and maintenance. In addition, guns greatly enhanced the Europeans' position in battle, making it possible for a small number, or even one individual, to face and overcome Natives who, in some instances, were still in the stone age in regards to weaponry.

There was little to protect Native people against European aggressiveness. Although some of the missionaries working among New World peoples protested against the mistreatment, their admonishments went largely unheeded. The central governments in Madrid and London might accept some responsibility for protecting the lives of their new subjects, but these governments were too far removed from the colonies to carry out this responsibility with any effectiveness. Indeed, actions to protect the Natives seldom went beyond rhetoric. In any case, because their imperial or economic interests resided with the invaders, central governments all too readily sided with the forces mistreating, enslaving, or driving the Natives from their territorial base.

The diseases the Europeans brought with them also influenced interaction between Europeans and Native people. These cut vast swaths through the Native populations. At times, Europeans intentionally spread diseases to decimate Aboriginal populations, or to obliterate resistance to white encroachment. For the most part, however, the diseases that decimated the Natives were caused by natural contact. These greatly weakened Native peoples, leaving them less able to resist the Europeans. However, diseases themselves were rarely the source of the genocides or the deaths caused by genocidal means. These were caused by the aggressive actions of one group towards another.

In this regard, interaction between Natives and Europeans was structured by the goals of the invaders as well as by the social systems they established. The Spaniards' treatment of Native peoples was dictated largely by the quest for gold and efforts to enrich themselves by enslaving indigenous populations. Spain was still largely a feudal society in which the majority of people were either serfs or slaves, and it was over-extending its primitive economy with expensive imperial ventures. Gold and silver were no sooner deposited in Spain than creditors drew them away. The only remedy to this state of affairs was to accelerate the appropriation of wealth, and this demanded the theft and mining of ever more New World gold and silver. As the Spanish possessed neither the manpower nor the inclination for mining America's vast store of precious metal themselves, they used Indian labour.

After the initial conquest, the *encomienda* system structured the relationship between Natives and the Spaniards. This system, in theory implemented to help Christianize and civilize indigenous people, in practice served to reward the Spanish conqueror with Native land and slaves. Combined with extreme cruelty during the conquest and the Spanish hunt for slaves, the *encomienda* system constituted a massive onslaught on the Native's way of life and led to the total destruction of some peoples whom the Spaniards conquered. The Spaniards did not set out to exterminate these people. However, the Spanish *encomendero*, believing the Native supply of people inexhaustible, treated the Natives as an expendable source of labour. The result in the case of groups such as the Arawak in Hispaniola was the annihilation of a people.

Having said this, one must add that, although the *encomienda* system operated at first with great severity and cruelty, it at the same time placed Native people into a meaningful social relationship vis-à-vis the conqueror. After all, the Spaniards' own economic well-being depended upon Native labor. Indigenous people were severely mistreated only as long as it was thought that the supply of labour was inexhaustible. Treatment improved after the Spaniard came to the conclusion that Native populations were not limitless. By that time, most Native people had already been killed outright or worked to death.

In the French colonies, it was primarily the desire to eliminate competitors in the fur trade and expand the French fur trade empire that led to the destruction of the Natchez and the near destruction of the Mesquaki. In some instances, slavery was used to achieve these goals, as in the case of the Natchez, but this was dissimilar to what occurred in the Spanish colonies, where plunder and enslavement of Natives was a main goal.

In the British colonies, settlement was characterized by the systematic replacement of Native occupants with British interlopers. Although the Spanish sought to encourage white settlement, this policy was not as successful as it was in the British colonies. Spaniards were disinclined to emigrate, and Spain did not have the surplus population Britain had to draw on. In the case of the French, settlement was deliberately restricted in the interest of the fur trade.

According to Stannard, the settlers' drive to dispossess Native peoples in British America was at the root of the destruction of the indigenous population. Reynolds sees similar goals and attitudes influencing individual and group violence against the Australian Aborigines. Attacks against Natives stemmed from the settlers' underlying assumption that they - not the original inhabitants- had the right to the land, and that the land could be appropriated with impunity. Commenting on the dispossession of the Australian Aborigines, Reynolds states that perhaps the single most important element in the relationship between the colonizers and the Natives was the revolutionary concept of private property that the settlers brought with them from Britain, along with the will and the weapons to impose it in Australia.[4] Settlers arrived in the colonies with the desire to own the land and everything on it "in the most absolute manner."[5] Most of them preferred to drive away any Aborigines they encountered, both for security reasons and to assert their claim of ownership to the land. They prevented, insofar as they were able, Aboriginal hunting and gathering, restricted Aboriginal access to water and severely punished any attacks on their livestock. Reynolds observes that once the land had been seized, and the legal strictures defining property ownership, theft, and trespass had been introduced into the new colony, the efforts of the conqueror went into forcing the Aborigines to accept their position as propertyless and powerless outcasts in a class society. In this context, violence against Aborigines was engendered by the drive to confirm the private ownership of property and impose the social relations of the new order.[6]

Reynolds regards this whole process as an offshoot of the bourgeois revolution that swept over Europe during the late eighteenth and early nineteenth centuries. He sees the possession of land as the center of this revolution, and compares the experiences of the Aborigines in Australia to those of the Scottish highlanders who were forced off their traditional lands by new landowners. He characterizes the settlers as revolutionaries, who were instrumental in Australia in bringing about the complete and violent overthrow of one social and economic system by another, and one mode of production by another.[7]

There is a grain of truth in Reynolds's observations, but there are also certain limitations, which arise out of his attempt to draw too close a parallel between the situation in Scotland and that in Australia. In Scotland, tenant farmers were thrown off land belonging to the lords. In Australia, the government and settlers took over and treated as private property land occupied by the Aborigines. The people in Scotland had somewhere to go after they were removed from the land, namely, to the colonies. The Natives removed from their land had nowhere to go. In Scotland, there is no evidence of landowners and sheep, which replaced the tenant farmers on the land, getting together with the lords to kill tenant farmers who refused to move off the land. There are numerous instances in both the United States and Australia of government and settlers co-operating to eliminate Native people who resisted removal from their territory.

In the Scottish highlands, the revolution Reynolds speaks of was taking place in a rural society where both tenant farmers and landlords were part of the same population. The revolution, which transformed social relations in British America and Australia after the arrival of the Europeans, was not simply an economic revolution. While it involved the replacement of one economic system by another, it also involved the replacement of one racial group by another. This replacement formed part of a process that saw the expansion of the British Empire and the territorial expansion of Anglo-America into the interior of the United States. Integral facets of this expansion were the removal of Aboriginal peoples combined with an immigration policy that encouraged the settlement of the appropriated territory with Britons and other Europeans who could be easily assimilated into the British mould. The removal of the Native population included mass destructions that were genocidal in nature, in particular where resistance to removal was met by state and/or individual aggression to force Natives to accept the new order.

Although there were instances where Natives were replaced by African slaves, far more important was the replacement of the indigenous population through an immigration policy that served to build a new society that was, at its core, white Anglo-Saxon. In this society, land taken from the Natives became the possession of private individuals, who farmed it or used it in other ways that left little room for the original inhabitants. This policy deprived Native peoples of their territorial base and established a society that, because of its colour and attitudes, excluded them from its ranks. This does not mean that half-hearted attempts were not made to integrate Native people into the newly emerging society. The overall thrust of the conqueror, however, was to build an essentially white, British or Anglo-American society that by definition excluded the Native.

Wiebe believes that the whole process involving the dispossession of the Native people and their replacement by Anglo-Americans in the United States was tied into the belief in progress held by white Americans.[8] This concept of progress, in which the destruction of a people and their way of life is simply viewed as part of growth, shows the influences of certain aspects of Western thought. It demonstrates a linear concept of history, according to which humankind progresses from a lower level of being and awareness to a higher level. Such linearity is evident essentially in two areas of Western thought. One is the Enlightenment, which sees human beings progressing from a lower to a higher level of awareness, from a lower to a higher level of humanity as they acquire greater knowledge of the human condition. Secondly, linearity is also an integral part of social Darwinism, which is based on Darwin's ideas regarding the evolution of the species. Progress seen in terms of the destruction of one society and the individuals associated with it so as to make way for a new type of society, the view of progress that Wiebe describes, is ultimately based, not on the view of progress that grew out of the Enlightenment, but on the social application of Darwin's concept of natural selection. It was the prevalence of this view of social Darwinism, in particular in the United States and Australia, which served to justify the destruction of Native people and made elements of the emerging societies look forward to their disappearance. At the same time, it helped to rationalize the excessive violence that, in both these instances, served to drive Native peoples to destruction.

The evidence suggests that the manner in which British elements went about creating an essentially British society and the extent to which violence formed a part of these endeavours influenced the destruction of Native peoples. British elements in Canada, the United States, and Australia were all intent on building what was at core a British society. Yet, this process was less destructive in Canada than it was in the other two countries. Most important in this regard was the existence of conditions here that worked against government becoming an extension of the forces intent on dispossessing and destroying the Natives. As a result, violence had a much less significant role in dispossessing the Native, in creating the new society and in forcing the Native to accept his position therein.

In summary, there is little evidence that the attitudes held by the Spanish, French or British invaders differed greatly. All held the view that Native people, as non-Christians, had little right to the land they occupied. All considered Native people inferior because of their religion, culture, and level of technological sophistication. The French treated the Natives better than did the Spanish or English for several reasons. Unlike the Spanish, their main goal wasn't to despoil or enslave the Indians. When establishing their main territorial base in New France, they brought over people from Europe to work the land. This settlement, which grew slowly, was not as expansionist as the British colonies in the Americas. The drive for expansion in the case of the French came from the imperial government and fur trade interests, both of which were dependent on good relations with the Indians. Being more dependent on Native people, and, in fur trade, interacting with them on a more equal footing than was the case in the British or the Spanish colonies, the French were also generally more tolerant of these people, their way of life, and their religious beliefs.

The Spaniards came to enrich themselves with Indian land and gold and through the enslavement of the Native population. To gain wealth, the Spaniards slaughtered the Natives and mistreated them at will. Insofar as indigenous people survived, they did so largely because they eventually found a place in the slave society established by the Spanish, who, for their own self-interest, in time came to treat them more humanely.

In the case of the British, disregard for the Native's land led to the dispossession of the original inhabitants. This didn't, however, have equally destructive effects in all instances. Thus, dispossession itself and the loss of their traditional way of life had a negative impact on the demography of Natives in Canada as well as in the United States and Australia. However, the destruction in Canada was not as extensive as it was in either the United States or Australia, where excessive violence in the dispossession of Native peoples and forcing them to accept their position as second-class citizens led to their near annihilation. This suggests that there is some validity to Stannard's observation that there was a relationship between the manner in which Native people were targeted in the British colonies and the extent to which they were destroyed. One might even go further and state that it is hard to image that the Native population could have been reduced to the extent that it was reduced in either the United States or Australia without direct targeting having had a role in the decimation.

PART III

A TYPOLOGY OF GENOCIDE

In the first part of this study, I examined the different ideological genocides, comparing and contrasting them to isolate common features. I found that enough similarities emerged in four of these examples to suggest that the term "holocaust" more logically applies to a type of genocide than to a unique case. This type of genocide exhibits certain characteristics: all genocidal groups subscribed to a system of beliefs, or an ideological system, that identified them as elect or special; the leadership of the genocidal group sought to use its particular ideological system to radically transform society; it encountered problems doing so, which it projected onto some outside group; it came to identify the creation of its idealized society with the destruction of this targeted group.

In the second part, I sought to gain insight into mass destructions as European powers expanded into the New World. I looked in particular at mass destructions of Native peoples in Spanish and British America, which scholars have identified as holocausts. To gain better insight into these, I also looked at mass destructions of Native peoples that occurred in Australia and in the French colonial empire in North America.

In Part III, I will compare and contrast ideological genocides described in Part I with the genocides described in Part II to determine whether a pattern emerges that will permit one to speak of a holocaust-type genocide that includes both ideological genocides and genocides committed as European powers expanded into the New World. To determine this, I will compare and contrast dynamics leading to mass destruction in different cases under study. Following this, I will isolate the dynamics that characterize the holocaust-type genocide, identifying its main features and the conditions under which it has occurred. Then I will seek to determine whether there are also other patterns of genocide this study isolates. Essentially, this involves looking at the patterns of destruction that led to the different genocides and determining where they best fit in terms of the typologies developed by researchers to date.

PART III

A TYPOLOGY OF GENOCIDE

13
Ideological Genocides and Colonialist Genocides
Similarities and Differences

All the genocides under study were carried out as part of a pursuit of power. This is clearly evident in the case of genocides committed in the New World. Here the drive to take possession of Native land or to despoil and enslave people was part of a process of acquiring wealth and building empires. This drive to power is also evident in the case of the Nazis, the Young Turks, and the early Israelites. In all these cases, the genocides were part of a drive to expand a group's territorial base. In the case of the communists, the pursuit of power and empire building is most obvious in situations where the interests of the proletariat become identified with a certain national group, with the destruction of a target serving the interests of this group.

There is one major difference between the drive to power as it expressed itself in the European conquest of the New World and in the ideological genocides discussed in Part I. In the case of the former, the genocides were committed almost solely to expand empire, and acquire and exploit resources. While these motives are also evident in ideological genocides, the destruction of the target group in these instances was also part of an endeavour to dominate the thinking of people. This is true in particular with a holocaust-type genocide.[1] Here, targeting and eliminating the enemy were an integral part of the process those in power used to transform the thinking of groups they identified as the elect. In many instances, the destruction of the enemy was an integral part of a process whereby those in power carved out their empires, the extent of which was measured not only in territorial terms but also in terms of the numbers of adherents ascribing to a particular system of beliefs.

In the genocides in the British colonies and the United States, and in the case of ideological genocides, exclusion formed part of the process that contributed to the destruction of peoples. In the case of a holocaust, the idealized society to be created left no room for the contaminating pariah targeted for destruction. Turkish society based on the tribal unit left little room for the Armenians. In British colonies, in particular where mistreatment contributed to the near destruction of the Native population, the Natives' colour and customs, as well as the conqueror's drive to possess Native land, served to exclude them from the emerging new society. Native communities continued to exist at the fringe of the society that was being created, but such communities tended to have a precarious existence. If it served the dominant group's needs, they were removed from their territorial base. In some instances, entire groups were wiped out as a result of this process.

A holocaust and the genocides carried out as the Old World took possession of the New involved an extreme degree of dehumanization of the victim group. In the case of a holocaust, the dehumanization was an integral part of the ideological structure that elevated the genocidal group and portrayed the pariah group as a contaminating or diabolical threat. This stereotyping not only served to dehumanize the pariah, but also drove the genocidal society to annihilate him. The dehumanization of Native people had its roots in the technological, cultural, and religious differences between the Natives and the Europeans, differences that led the colonizer to look upon the colonized as a lower form of being. This being could be despoiled, mistreated or slaughtered at will.

All ideological genocides derived their impetus from an ideological system that identified a particular pariah group. In the case of the Young Turks, the ideology directed them to build a tribal society. In the case of a holocaust, the war against the pariah served an integral part in sustaining and/or realizing a particular ideal in the social environment. In a sense, a holocaust derived its impetus from a utopian vision pursued by a centralized state. This vision had as its basis the pursuit of perfectibility, be this to create a society pleasing to God, a socialist utopia, or some kind of *Volksgemeinschaft* that would be superior both physically and morally to other societies. Genocide was carried out to destroy those elements that were deemed to subvert the endeavours of the genocidal society to attain the perfectibility to which it aspired.

Genocides committed as the Old World took possession of the New were not driven by the pursuit of a single, unilinear, utopian vision. Even in the case of the Puritans, their destruction of the Pequot was not part of an attempt to create a utopian society but rather was driven by the desire for the Natives' land. If any basic force can be isolated as leading to genocide in the New World, it was greed for empire, gold and land.

The French annihilation of the Natchez or their decimation of the Mesquaki was directed at Native tribes who hindered the expansion of the French fur trade empire in North America. In all other cases under study, the genocides were committed as part of a process of radical social transformation.[2] In the case of a holocaust, the drive to social transformation was provided by an ideology that sought to impose some form of the ideal on the social environment. The destruction of the Armenians fed on an ideology that envisaged the creation of a Turkish tribal state. The destruction of Native peoples in the British colonies and the United States were part of a radical transformation in which Europeans sought not only to possess the land held by Native peoples but also to create on this territory a society that was essentially British in nature. In South America, the genocides were part of a process in which the Spaniards plundered Native riches and, at the same time, forced the Native peoples they conquered to become slaves dominated by their European masters.

There is a striking difference between the holocaust, the Turkish war on the Armenians, and the genocides carried out as Europe conquered the New World. In the last case, major empires were seeking new areas of conquest. The genocides were in many respects an expression of the excessive use of power wielded to attain imperial ends. The holocaust-type genocides, as well as the Turkish war on the Armenians, on the other hand, were often destruction wrought by groups that saw themselves in danger of losing power, and genocide was part of a process through which they hoped to revitalize themselves to assure their hold on power. In a sense, fear was the basis for all ideological genocides, including the holocaust-type genocides. Schmookler points this out in the case of the Nazis where he sees the Nazi drive for power as growing out of fear of being the powerless victim, the fear of being at the bottom, with this fear growing out of Germany's humiliation at Versailles.[3] Fear was also a prime motivating factor behind the genocides described in the Book of Joshua, carried out soon after the Israelites had escaped slavery in Egypt, or behind the genocides committed by the communists in the Soviet Union, who saw the socialist revolution as an avenue of escape from the abject poverty in which the Russian lower classes found themselves before the revolution.

In the case of a holocaust, the destruction of the Armenians, and the genocides committed in the New World, in particular in the British colonies and the United States, we have what appear to be two extremes, both resulting in genocide. At one extreme, genocide results from actions of individuals or groups who had few restraints on their pursuit of material gain in an environment that encouraged the despoliation of a target group. At the other extreme is the unfettered state pursuing ideological objectives.

In the holocaust, the state took a leading role not only in attacking the pariah group but also in mobilizing the general public against it. Thus, Stalin decided that the kulak should be targeted as the enemy of the people and then proceeded to recruit the poorer peasants to attack this group.

Hitler targeted the Jews and then sought to recruit general German support for his policy, an example being *Kristallnacht*, in 1938. More specialized recruitment also occurred, as was the case with the *Einsatzgruppen* or the operators of the death camps, which were set up predominantly in the frontier areas rather than in Germany proper so as to better conceal what was carried out in them. The state, as such, essentially initiated, directed, and carried out the destruction.

In the British colonies and the United States, we find the opposite extreme leading to genocide. Although some of the national leaders, in particular in the United States, may have shared the annihilationist sentiments of the local population, the central government did not explicitly sanction the drive to dispossess and kill the Native population. The initiative here came largely from individuals or groups at the local or regional level, who were intent on dispossessing the Native and taking control of his land.

There are some features that make the holocaust as well as the Turkish war on the Armenians more similar to genocides committed in the British colonies than to the destruction of peoples carried out by the French or the Spanish. This is particularly true of the role played by the replacement of peoples or ideas. Whereas the replacement of peoples formed an integral part of the genocides in the Turkish war on the Armenians and in the British colonies, the holocaust-type genocides were carried out primarily to replace contaminating belief systems and behavioural patterns viewed as contaminating with generative systems and patterns. At the same time, holocaust-type genocides were in many respects also part of a process involving the replacement of power elites, or perceived power elites. Even in the destruction of the idolaters, where the genocide involved territorial replacement, the motivating force for the slaughter was ultimately ideological--to remove belief systems and people subscribing to them from the land that the Israelite leadership had selected as the territorial base for their God. It would be wrong, however, to argue that the destruction of the idolaters was motivated only by ideology. It also had practical objectives; clearing away the idolaters provided an area of settlement for the Israelites. As such, the ideological objectives of the genocidal group were linked with its territorial objectives, each being an integral part of the other.

A main difference between a holocaust and the Turkish destruction of the Armenians, or genocides committed as Europeans conquered the New World, is that a holocaust calls for the total elimination of the pariah group. This was seldom the case with genocides against indigenous peoples in the Americas. Here, rather than being directly targeted for elimination, Native groups tended to be destroyed while they were being plundered, enslaved, or driven from their land.

Still, the Europeans did annihilate several Native societies. In the case of the Natchez, this happened after the military defeat of the tribe, following which part of it was slaughtered while the remainder was sold into slavery. In the British colonies and the United States, such massive destructions were part of a prolonged period of violence, at times lasting over several generations. An integral part of the territorial replacement, it led, in some instances, to the complete annihilation of Native groups.

Although calling for the total elimination of a pariah, there is no evidence that a holocaust ever brought about the total destruction of a targeted group or targeted groups. Of course, this is difficult to say when a religious group or a class was targeted. Neither the witches nor the purported enemies of the people in the Soviet Union or Kampuchea differed sufficiently from the society at large to permit one to determine what percentage survived the genocidal onslaughts. Part of the problem stems from the fact that neither the witches nor the enemies of the people were defined in sufficiently concrete terms to allow clear differentiation between them and the larger society.

How, then, should we understand the Nazi case and Katz's view that the Nazis had as their goal the destruction of all Jews?[4] There are several problems with Katz's position. As Stannard and Bull argue, Katz's conclusion imputes a consistency to Nazi policy and action that it never had.[5] In other words, Katz suggests a consistency in Nazi policy that isn't supported by the evidence. Gilbert argues that Nazi policy regarding the Jews evolved from forcing them to emigrate, to ghettoizing them, to using *Einsatzgruppen* to kill them, to the final solution.[6] This progression suggests that the Nazis decided on the mass destruction of European Jewry only during the war. It also indicates that the final solution cannot be separated from the war, in particular from the war on the eastern front. That the war played a significant role in bringing on the final solution is also suggested by Mayer.[7] Evidence further suggests that, had the Nazis achieved the easy victory they had anticipated, they would have expelled the Jews from Europe rather than killed them.[8] It may very well be, however, that the Nazis would have killed all Jews still under their control had the war dragged on inconclusively for a prolonged period. It might be argued that the fact that the Nazis implemented the decision to destroy the Jews of Europe at the time when they had most of the world against them, guaranteed that this goal would not be attained. At the same time, it was the pressure of the war that after 1943 caused them to change their policy from direct killing to one which emphasized the exploitation of Jewish labour.

If one is to use Hilberg's figures as to the total number of Jews killed and accept Heydrich's estimate that there were eleven million Jews in occupied Europe, one can conclude that the Nazis killed about 51 per cent of the Jews under their control.[9] Using Reitlinger's and Benz's statistics, which put the Jewish population of Nazi-occupied Europe in 1939 at about 9.6 million, and estimate the number of Jews killed as being between 5.29 million and just over 6 million,[10] the percentage of Jews killed by the Nazis would be between 55 and 63 per cent.

A better understanding of these percentages and their relationship to the holocaust-type genocide can be provided by comparing them to other groups under study. Of course, statistics in all cases involving genocide are problematic. As Conquest states when looking at death figures relating to the famine in Ukraine and the mass destruction of European Jewry: "We do not have exact figures on population losses—as, indeed, is true even of the Jewish Holocaust. The fact that we are not certain of the human cost within a few million is itself remarkable testimony to the extent of the terror."[11] The problem Conquest points out is exacerbated in that minimizing deaths is, in all these instances, used as part of genocide denial. Therefore, to make my comparisons I have chosen statistics that appeared to me to have been arrived at objectively. In most instances, I endeavour to give both a low and high, in terms of the percentage of a group destroyed.

Thus, during World War II the Nazis destroyed not only a great number of Jews, but also some 66 to 75 per cent of German Gypsies and 75 per cent of Austrian Gypsies.[12] Conquest estimates that a quarter to a fifth of a Ukrainian rural population of between 20 and 25 million died as a result of the famine in 1932 - 1933.[13] While we have no percentage of the number of Russians killed during this period, there is no indication that it came close to these figures. In Cambodia, some 28 per cent of Cambodians were killed, as were 41 per cent of the inhabitants of Phnom Penh, 38.9 per cent of Chinese, and 40 to 50 per cent of Cham.[14] Under Stalin about 42 per cent of Russian-Germans, 46 per cent of Crimean Tartars, and about 30 per cent of groups such as the Chechens or Ingush were destroyed as a result of the conditions into which they were placed or the manner in which they were treated after they were deported.[15] Such destruction is also evident in the case of other regimes that absorbed the Soviet brand of communism. After the war, Tito's forces killed some 50 per cent of Donau-Swabians under their control after they came to power in Yugoslavia with the help of the Soviet Union.[16]

As for the Armenians, if one uses the figure of one million Armenians killed (arrived at by Lepsius) and Toynbee's estimate that 1.6 million Armenians lived in Turkey before the First World War, one arrives at a figure of about 63 per cent of Armenians having been destroyed during the war. Boyajian's estimate that the Turks killed 1.5 million Armenians, which Melson suggests may refer to the number of Armenians killed between 1915 and 1923, leads to the conclusion that 94 per cent of Armenians under

Turkish control were exterminated.[17] The results are not that much less dramatic if other fairly reliable estimates are used, an example being the figures of the American Committee for Armenian and Syrian Relief, which estimated the Armenian population in the Ottoman Empire to have been about 1.8 million prior to the outbreak of the First World War.[18] Using these figures, some 55 per cent of Armenians were killed during the war and 83 per cent of Armenians were killed between 1915 and 1923.

In many respects, the destruction of Native peoples in both Spanish America and in areas of British settlement was much more devastating than most of the destructions mentioned above. Thus, according to Stannard's estimates, the Spaniards destroyed some 95 per cent of the Amerindian population of Spanish America before they decided to treat them more humanely.[19] About 98 per cent of Native peoples were destroyed in the United States by 1900, if one uses Churchill's lower estimates.[20] Even though disease played a role, these figures nevertheless indicate that the manner in which the conquerors of the New World, be they Spanish or British, treated Native peoples, led to massive destruction.

A number of conclusions can be reached from the above figures. Thus, in the case of the Nazis, they killed a greater percentage of Gypsies than Jews, even though direct targeting had a greater role in the destruction of Jews. Ready identification, be this in terms of area of origin, as in the case of the inhabitants of Phnom Penh in Cambodia, or in terms of ethnic identity, had a significant influence on all destructions. Ethnic origin was of particular significance in this regard, with the destruction rate being significantly higher when a majority targeted a minority group for destruction than when it dealt with members of its own ethnicity. Furthermore, the percentage of people destroyed in the Armenian genocide or in the case of Native peoples was significantly higher than in any of the holocaust-type genocides for which statistics are readily available. This suggests that perhaps factors other than expressed intent to obliterate a group or demonization as found in a holocaust play an extremely significant role in the destruction of peoples and affect the extent to which they are destroyed.

Looking at these similarities and differences, in what respect might the destruction of Native peoples be considered a holocaust, as Stannard and Thornton maintain? Because Thornton makes little attempt to explore in what way the destruction of Native peoples in the Americas constitutes a holocaust, it is unclear why he uses the term to describe genocides in the Americas. Stannard, in contrast, makes a detailed exploration of European Christianity and racism, showing how these values were at the root of the destruction both of Native people and European Jewry. In this sense, the destruction of European Jewry is more similar than other holocausts to the genocides committed in the Americas. Thus, while essentially only Christians were involved in the destruction of Native peoples and Jews, both Jews and Christians were involved in following Stalin's orders to deprive the Ukrainian collective farmers of their grain which led to the man-made famine in the Ukraine. Also, the idea of race, though often confused with tribalism and nationalism, played a much more important role in the destruction of European Jewry than it did in the targeting and destruction of pariahs in other holocausts.

Yet, similarities between the destruction of European Jewry and the genocides in the Americas can be overstated. European attacks on Native peoples were motivated not only by Christian values and racism, but also by the fact that Native technology, combined with devastating new diseases, made the Natives a relatively easy target. Native cultural habits and relatively backward technology, especially in weapons of war, also encouraged Europeans to view Aboriginal people as lower forms of being.

Furthermore, the influence of racist ideas on Nazi anti-Semitism can be overstated. It was not only racist ideas that motivated the Nazi to kill the Jew. Whereas the Nazis were going to absorb Slavs with "Aryan" characteristics—Slavs who were blond and blue-eyed—no similar policy was followed regarding the Jews. If only racist ideas had influenced Nazi policy, then this inconsistency would not have existed. What the Nazis did in many respects was to confuse racial with religious characteristics. What we have in the case of the Nazis, in many respects, is traditional anti-Semitism interpreted in terms of racial theory. Therefore it would be wrong to place too much emphasis on the racist dimension as a motivating factor causing the Nazis to target the Jews.

Racial differences between Europeans and indigenous peoples were much greater than between Germans and Jews, and played a greater role in the slaughter of the Natives than they did in the Nazi murder of the Jews. Having said this, it cannot be denied, as Stannard maintains, that both Christianity and racism played a significant role in the Nazi destruction of European Jewry and in the annihilation of Native peoples in the New World.

The question then arises: are these similarities sufficient to allow one to call the destruction of Native peoples by Europeans in the Americas holocausts? To answer this question it may be helpful to look at arguments put forth by researchers who claim that the destruction of European Jewry is different from all other genocides. Katz argues that the destruction of European Jewry is unique because only in this case did the perpetrator call for the total destruction of the target group. Like Bull, Stannard counters this argument by stating that Katz has made up a definition of genocide that doesn't apply even to the Jewish case and then uses it to discuss other genocides.[21] No doubt, Stannard and Bull are correct in their overall observations. However, this does not mean that Katz's statement should be totally rejected. Clearly, the Nazis made a concerted effort between 1941 and 1943 to destroy the Jews. This was particularly true for Jews whose labour they could not exploit. Robert Melson raises a significant point regarding the uniqueness of the Jewish case when he compares the Nazi war on European Jewry with the destruction of the Armenians by the Young Turks. He argues that, while the destruction of the Armenians by the Young Turks was an ideological genocide, as was the holocaust, it was not a holocaust because the Young Turks had specific objectives when destroying the Armenians. The Nazis, on the other hand, destroyed the Jews because they saw them as contaminating and corrupting, the devil himself.[22]

How does Melson's observation apply to the destruction of Native peoples? In each case there was a degree of dehumanization and, particularly in the British colonies and the United States, demonization of the Native people. Beyond this consideration, however, differences outweigh similarities. Ultimately, Native populations were targeted not because they were perceived as a contaminating disease. Rather, in Spanish America the destruction was part of the endeavour to conquer, plunder and enslave the Natives. In the British colonies, the destruction followed from the drive to appropriate the Natives' land and build thereon a society that was British at its core.

Unlike in the holocaust-type genocide, Native people were not placed in an ideological framework that targeted them as enemies that had to be destroyed for the ideal society to come into being or to perpetuate itself. Rather, they were seen as beings that were not quite human and therefore could be killed at random or treated as beasts of burden. They could also be treated as wolves or other vicious animals that had to be cleared from the land for it to be tamed and civilized. These differences—the manner in which the groups were targeted and the role the genocide played in the objectives of the genocidal group—make it difficult to describe the destruction of Native peoples in the Americas as a holocaust.[23]

14
The Holocaust within a Typology of Genocide

Although there are similarities between the genocides committed as the Old World conquered the New and the holocaust type of genocide, a holocaust is distinct enough to allow one to conclude that neither the destruction of Native peoples in the Americas nor the Turkish destruction of the Armenians were holocausts. In terms of the theoretical literature discussed in the introduction to this work, the holocaust can best be classified as an ideological genocide. Roger Smith argues that the ideological genocide is motivated by the desire to impose a particular notion of salvation or purification on an entire society; Chalk and Jonassohn contend that it is driven by the desire to implement a belief, a theory, or ideology in a society.[1]

One may, of course, ask: if a holocaust is an ideological genocide, is an ideological genocide also a holocaust? Melson provides an answer when he concludes that, while the destruction of both European Jewry and the Armenians are ideological genocides, the Armenian genocide was not a holocaust because the Young Turks pursued specific objectives while the Nazi attack on the Jews was part of a cosmology that envisaged the Aryans as the people of light being thwarted in realizing their goals by the people of darkness, the Jews.[2] This emphasis on the morally degenerate characteristics of the group targeted for destruction differentiates the destruction of the Armenians not only from the Nazi war on the Jews, but also from the Israelite war on the idolaters, the Christian war on the witches, and the war of the communists against their enemies. The Nazi case is also similar to these other examples in that all these genocides were undertaken in pursuit of an idealized society, be this the *Volksgemeinschaft*, a society pleasing unto Yahweh, the idealized Christian community, or the communist utopia.

One can well argue that while the concept of a holocaust, as used by the Greeks and then borrowed to describe the destruction of European Jewry by the Nazis as unique, does not apply to the destruction of the Armenians, it can be applied to describe the destruction of the idolaters, the witches, the enemy of the people. All these genocides involved groups that saw themselves as people of the light in conflict with people of darkness. For the light to flourish, the people of darkness had to be eradicated. In every case except the persecution of the witches, the genocides were associated with a powerful personality who was instrumental in either initiating or carrying out the genocide. Like the holocaust practised by the Greeks, these genocides were, in essence, part of a religious ritual. They were carried out as much to create the idealized society as to avoid the consequences if such a society were not created. Even if the holocaust concept were not used, or other words or concepts were used to describe any of these genocides—*shoah*, for example, or the *Holodomor* in the case of the famine in the Ukraine—these genocides have enough in common to illuminate a specific pattern. However, as the term "holocaust" has been broadly used to describe one of these genocides, it is logical that the term can also be used to describe the annihilation of idolaters as presented to us in the Book of Joshua, the destruction of the witches, as well as the extirpation of the enemies of the people in the Soviet Union or in Cambodia.

As a holocaust is one pattern through which ideological genocide expresses itself, it may be described as a subcategory of the ideological genocide. As such, a holocaust may be characterized by the following:

1. A holocaust finds its inspiration in an ideological system. This system is essentially a religious system that is legitimized, ultimately, by the faith of the believers.

2. This ideological system divides the world into extremes of good and evil. Good and evil are seen to be in conflict with each other; to obtain the good, evil must be struggled against and eradicated. In fact, good is defined in such a way as to leave no room for its opposite to exist.

3. The societies in which these beliefs are held are essentially authoritarian. Leadership is vested in a small, essentially theocratic group at whose head is, frequently, a charismatic leader. The leadership interprets ideology and seeks to impose it on the social environment.

4. The theocratic leadership identifies the good with a particular collectivity. This group is viewed as possessing or being capable of possessing the qualities that a particular ideological system idealizes. The collectivity might be a tribal group, a religious group, a social class, or a combination of these. This group is perceived as somehow special, this specialness setting it apart from and above the rest of humankind.

5. The theocratic leadership isolates a pariah group, which it identifies as evil and sees as its enemy. This may be an old social group, which it identifies with the decrepit moral order it seeks to destroy, or it may be a social or racial group it sees as clinging to power illegitimately and thwarting its own drive to power. In either case, the pariah group becomes the concrete representation of ideas or behavioural patterns that the theocratic leadership believes contaminate the society it represents. In this regard, the holocaust type of genocide appears to have two foci: where the ideology serves to make the tribal group special, a tribal or racial group is focussed on as the enemy; where the ideology serves to make the adherents to an ideology special, the pariah is selected primarily on the basis of ascribed attitudes, beliefs, and behavioural patterns.

6. The theocratic leadership seeks to mobilize the elect group to attain goals that will enhance its specialness. At the same time, the leadership launches an attack on the group(s) seen as preventing the elect group from attaining these goals. Taken together, these two objectives constitute a revolutionary situation. In this situation, the leadership seeks to:

   a) re-create society so as to make it an expression of the goals or characteristics being idealized;
   b) consolidate society's support of its leadership;
   c) eradicate those influences that are seen to be thwarting its efforts to make society an expression of the ideal, influences that are seen as corrupting and contaminating and that are projected onto a pariah group.

7. In all these cases, the pariah group is placed into a category of people who must be eliminated for the ideal society to be created. In this regard, the attack on the pariah follows two patterns:
   a) where the idealized group and the pariah group are identified in essentially tribal terms, the focus is on the complete elimination of the pariah from that territory that the leadership of the elect group preserves or covets for its own.
   b) where an abstract category (eg. Enemy of the people) is constructed that does not identify a readily recognizable collectivity in the social environment, then the genocidal destruction is fuelled by the extent to which the leadership of the idealized group can fit individuals or groups into the category of people that have to be eliminated for the ideal society to

be created or to perpetuate itself. In this case, less emphasis is placed on the destruction of the group that is being attacked, in part because it is more difficult than in the case of a readily identifiable group to establish a link between the abstract group to be eliminated and the group under attack. At the same time, the leadership of the genocidal group has much more choice in deciding what enemies are to be targeted. This results in a larger number of groups being placed into the category of the group(s) slotted for destruction than in cases where a tribal group is directly targeted. At the same time, the extent to which any of these groups will be destroyed is influenced by the degree to which a group can be readily identified or by the degree to which it actually fits the abstract category that is targeted for elimination.

One may well ask: what are the prime motivating factors in the holocaust-type genocide that influence the destruction? Looking at the elimination of European Jewry by the Nazis, writers have isolated a number of the main contributing factors. Cohn emphasizes the role of ideology in the Nazi genocide.[3] Davidowicz, while not underemphasizing the importance of ideology, stresses Hitler's pathological anti-Semitism.[4] Hilberg and Arendt emphasize the needs and dynamics of the organizational structure.[5] Horowitz stresses the importance of the totalitarian state.[6] Examining the Nazi genocide, the Turkish genocide, and genocides carried out by the communists in the Soviet Union and Cambodia, Melson, while acknowledging the importance of ideology and other factors, stresses the importance of the revolutionary situation as contributing to both a holocaust and an ideological genocide in general.[7]

Nolte suggests that a holocaust could only occur in a specific historical situation. Looking at the Nazi case, he argues that Nazi behaviour was influenced, not only by Hitler's personality or German nationalism, but also by a war that increasingly used civilians as a legitimate target for military aggression. Nolte also contends that Hitler's attack on target groups, such as the Jews, was influenced by the Bolshevik example of targeting a particular class as an enemy who should be destroyed.[8] Examining the genocides carried out under Hitler and Stalin, Bullock raises the question as to whether it was the personality of the leader, or the ideology, or the historical situation that played the most decisive role. He concludes that a combination of these factors contributed to the genocides.[9]

While the above researchers focus almost exclusively on the Nazi case and, to some extent, on the Stalinist period in the Soviet Union, the same conclusions could be reached in regard to other holocaust-type genocides under examination here. That is, ideology, organizational structure, in particular an authoritarian social system, played a significant role. The same is true of the revolutionary situation, where especially the endeavour to radically transform society played an important role in all the genocides.

Except for the witch-hunts, all these genocides occurred when a group sought to establish its ideological system in the social environment. Nevertheless, a number of preconditions had to be met before the witch-hunts could take place. One was the belief that practising witchcraft was a sign of Devil worship, and that those who practised it were in fact threatening Christ and his Church. Another was some degree of choice, where individuals or groups could accept or reject a particular religious system in a society whose leaders felt threatened by the existence of such freedom. These leaders used their position, as well as a belief system that divided the world in terms of good and evil in conflict with each other, to impose their particular belief system or ideology and crush competing ideologies. Thus, one can well argue that the witch-hunts occurred in Europe only at a time when conditions were similar to the conditions that led to the other holocausts. That is, the witch-hunts were part of an endeavour to establish an ideological system or a system of beliefs in the social environment. Thus, Levack argues that during the witch hunts the Churches Christianized Europe in an unprecedented way.[10] Delumeau goes even further, arguing that it was at the height of the witch-hunts (the period during the Reformation and the Counter-Reformation) that the peasantry of Europe was Christianized for the first time.[11] It can be argued, therefore, that although Christianity was introduced to Europe centuries earlier, conditions leading to a holocaust-type genocide helped crush alternative belief systems and firmly established the Christian faith on the European continent.

The fact that the holocaust-type genocide served to establish the Hebrew faith in biblical Israel, played an important role in firmly establishing the Christian faith in Europe, and played a role in establishing both Nazism and communism, suggests that the holocaust is especially significant in imposing an ideological system on the environment and forcing people to accept it. Thus, in summary, the holocaust-type genocide may be seen as being an integral part of a process whereby an authoritarian leadership imposes a particular ideological system on the social environment. It involves a group that sees itself as the elect of a universal God or Prime Mover, an ideology that divides the world into extremes of good and evil, a society having some freedom to question this ideology, and a leadership that uses this ideological system to impose its own system of beliefs and crush competing ideologies.

15
Colonialist Genocides within a Typology of Genocide

The genocides, and what Stannard calls the destruction of Native peoples through genocidal means that occurred as Europeans conquered the New World, could fit into a variety of broader categories of genocide examined in the introduction of this book. They could fit, for example, into the category Kuper calls genocides committed against Aboriginal peoples, a subcategory under domestic genocides, which arise as the result of internal divisions within a society.[1] These cases of human destruction could fit into the category that both Dadrian and Smith call utilitarian genocides.[2] Genocides in the British colonies and the United States fall into what Fein calls developmental genocides, in which the perpetrator intentionally or unintentionally destroys people who stand in the way of economic exploitation.[3] All the mass killings of indigenous people could fit into the category that Chalk and Jonassohn describe as genocides committed to acquire economic wealth. They see this type of genocide as probably having its roots in antiquity, where the desire for wealth constituted one of the motives driving a city-state or empire to expand. In the modern period, this genocide was associated primarily with the discovery and settlement of the New World.[4]

To some extent, the examples of human destruction carried out as Europeans took possession of the New World could fit into the above categories only because the categories are, in most instances, rather vague. It is not clear, for example, what Dadrian and Smith mean by utilitarian genocide. In Helen Fein's conceptualization, how does development relate to exploitation of raw resources and also to genocide? One advantage of Chalk and Jonassohn's category is that it points to a prime motive—the desire to acquire material goods—that played a major role in the destruction of Native peoples of the New World. It may be of interest, therefore, to explore the effect of the desire to control wealth on the genocides in the different colonial empires.

In the case of the French, who sought to exploit the fur trade, the drive to accumulate wealth had a comparatively minor effect on Native people because it did not greatly alter their way of life. In the Spanish Empire, the conqueror's methods of acquiring wealth had a devastating effect on Natives until the Spaniards realized that the supply of indigenous labour was not inexhaustible. In British colonies and the United States, the invader's quest for wealth had a devastating effect on Native peoples in areas where few restraints were placed on the settlers' drive to take possession of the Natives' land. This left the Natives with few opportunities to make their livelihood. This situation was made worse when they had to turn to stealing to support themselves, such theft was frequently used as an excuse to massacre them.

Are patterns of destruction in the different empires sufficiently similar to constitute a subcategory under the larger category of genocides committed to obtain wealth? To explore the question, it would be helpful to look more closely at the influences leading to the destruction of Native populations in the different empires.

In Spanish America, the following dynamics led to the destruction of Native peoples:

1. a) Christian Europeans coming into contact with non Christians;
    b) a technologically superior society coming into contact with one that was technologically inferior to it;
    c) people of one colour and culture coming into contact with people of another colour and culture.

The above factors led the Spaniards to:
-   think of themselves as superior;
-   use their technological superiority to seize Native wealth and to kill the Natives or enslave them and force them to toil under inhumane conditions.

2. Such actions led to the total annihilation of some groups and the decimation of others where:
-   people were killed indiscriminately in the effort to plunder their wealth;
-   people were killed in great numbers so that the remainder could be enslaved;
-   people were forced to work under conditions that killed many of them or interfered with their ability to reproduce.

In the British colonies, the following conditions led to genocide:

1. a) Christian European society coming into contact with non-Christians who were considered as having little or no right to their territorial base because of their beliefs and way of life;
b) a technologically superior society coming into contact with a society technologically inferior to it;
c) people of one colour and culture coming into contact with people of another colour and culture.

The above led the British to:
- think of themselves as superior;
- denigrate the claim technologically inferior people had to their territorial base.

2. Technologically advanced people used their position to take possession of the land held by the technologically less advanced people.

3. Property that had been communally shared became privately held, with each possessor jealously guarding the right of possession, to the point where owners killed to defend or increase their possessions.

4. Being increasingly displaced from their territorial base, members of the technologically less advanced society were forced to steal from members of the more technologically advanced society. Little able to face the invaders head on, the indigenous peoples resorted to guerrilla warfare.

5. The technologically more advanced society used the stealing and the attacks to further dehumanize members of the technologically less advanced society. People who had at one time been seen merely as inferior came to be seen as vermin or vicious animals that had to be exterminated.

6. The process of destruction and replacement was an integral part of building a new society, which excluded members of the less technologically advanced society, whether for reasons of colour, way of life, or other differences.

7. Being excluded from the emerging social structure had several effects on members of the technologically less advanced society. Serving no useful function in the emerging society, they came to be viewed as a harmful hindrance. No one had an interest in protecting them. Although the central government may have proclaimed it was there to

protect the Natives, it seldom did so because its imperial interests were advanced through replacing the original inhabitants of the land with other people, for the most part its own. Thus, members of the technologically less advanced society were vulnerable to people or groups who exploited and destroyed them at will to take possession of what they owned.

8. The combination of these influences led to the mistreatment and killing of Native people, resulting in the decimation of some groups and the total annihilation of others.

In the French empire, the following conditions led to the destruction of the Natchez and the near destruction of the Mesquaki:

1. a) A Christian European society coming into contact with non-Christians;
    b) a technologically superior society coming into contact with one technologically inferior to it;
    c) people of one colour and culture coming into contact with people of another colour and culture.

The above led the French to:
-   think the Native inferior;
-   lay claim to the territorial base of the technologically inferior society, acknowledging Native claims to the land only insofar as it suited French interests.

2. All these factors contributed to the French destruction of the Natchez and the near destruction of the Mesquaki, tribes who stood in the way of expansion of the French fur trade empire into the North American interior.

Patterns of destruction of Native peoples in the different colonies have the following characteristics in common: European Christians coming into contact with and destroying Native peoples who were different in religion, culture and colour, and were less technologically advanced than their European conquerors. Despite these similarities, it would be difficult to place all these examples of human destruction into one subcategory under Chalk and Jonassohn's category of genocides carried out to obtain wealth. Goals pursued by the different European conquerors, and the effect of these goals, were dramatically different. Also, although the dynamics leading to destruction in the Spanish Empire share certain features with dynamics operative in other colonial empires, it would be difficult to place the mass destructions in Spanish America under a category of genocide. The main reason for this is the disagreement among scholars over whether the mass destructions in Spanish America were genocides. Thus, until changes have been made in the definition of genocide, it is difficult to include the destruction of Native peoples under the Spanish in the same category as the killings that went on in the French Empire and among English-speaking peoples in the New World.

It would be of interest to explore whether the genocides committed in the different colonial empires are similar enough to allow one to cluster these together as a sub-category under the larger category of genocides committed to obtain wealth. In this case, the destruction of the Natchez and near destruction of the Fox in the French colonial empire is insufficient to be indicative of a pattern. It would be difficult to cluster the pattern of destruction in Spanish America under genocide when researchers disagree over whether or not these killings were genocides. In areas of British settlement, genocides were committed often enough and were similar enough to indicate a pattern. This is true in particular of the United States, Newfoundland and Australia. In all these instances, the mass destructions involved the territorial replacement of peoples combined with the drive to possess and defend private property.

It would be of interest to determine whether these patterns of ethnic cleansing can be placed into a specific category of genocide in the manner in which the holocaust can be placed into a category. As already mentioned, dynamics leading to mass destruction in these instances were different from those which led to a holocaust or to the destruction of the Armenians. The dynamics leading to mass destruction in the British colonies also differ in significant ways from earlier examples where empires or city-states expanded to obtain wealth. In ancient times, no matter whether it was the Babylonians or Assyrians, or the Greeks and Romans at a later date, conquest invariably involved the expansion of centralized empires. In the British case, the mass destruction was often motivated by individuals or small groups hungry for the Native's land. Also, in ancient times, conquerors tended to enslave a conquered population. This was true, in particular, of the Romans. The British, on the other hand, wanted to get rid of the Natives and take possession of their land, with the destruction often ensuing from the attempt at elimination so that Natives couldn't interfere with the new order being established.

The British practice of driving people from their territory does have some earlier precedents. Thus, when the Hittite ruler, Suppiluliuma, came to power in 1380 BC, he not only consolidated Hittite power by concluding treaties with neighbouring states, reinforcing these with matrimonial ties, he also founded a dependent kingdom in Syria and installed his son Piya-sili on the throne. He chose Carchemish, the stronghold on the Euphrates, to be its capital, and banished the possibility of resistance by deporting the city's inhabitants and resettling it with Hittites and others whose loyalty was assured.[5] Deported people, in such instances, tended to be dispersed to serve as serfs for the Hittite nobility.

The Assyrian ruler Tiglathpeleser III initiated a major policy of deporting and intermingling captive populations. It seems he did so largely because he thought that the best way of preventing revolts was to uproot what we would now call "national feeling"—the fidelity to local gods and traditions—by mixing together the populations of the empire. Whole towns and districts were depopulated, with their inhabitants re-settled in distant regions. In turn, people brought in from other regions replaced them. While the forced expulsions, no doubt, took a great toll on the lives of people, with many people dying on the endless, sun-scorched treks, survivors were not badly treated. Among the ruins of burnt-down villages, they found a new home as well as a field to plough.[6]

The British practice of clearing other peoples from the land differed in important ways from such earlier practices. One difference was the use of a reserve system that confined conquered peoples to a specific area. Another, more significant, was their replacing a system of collective ownership with one of private ownership of land and resources. Reynolds considers this to be a revolutionary concept, which the settlers brought with them from Britain, along with the will and the weapons to impose it.[7] In this situation, genocide was committed as part of a process in which people sought to gain possession of, as well as hold on to and defend, private property. More so than in the past, one finds examples of the types of genocides committed in the British colonies and the United States in modern profit-motivated society. Thus, when the Brazilian government in the early 1970s undertook to address its problems of chronic poverty by throwing the Amazon region open for settlement, the farmers cleared the land, burning, cutting down or bulldozing away trees with little regard for the boundaries of Indian reservations. Farmers and miners intent on exploiting the land and its resources killed Indians who stood in the way of opening the territory, destroyed the game upon which Native peoples depended, and polluted rivers and streams. As a result, many tribes disappeared from the region, and others were decimated. The Indian population of the new state of Rondônia in this region, for example, dropped from about 30,000 in 1950 to 5,000 in the 1980s.[8]

The Brazilian and the British cases are both characterized by a land-hungry population eager to take possession of a plot of land they can call their own, and by miners and business people out to exploit the resources of the areas being opened. One could well argue that the drive to gain, hold on to and increase private wealth leads to ethnic cleansing and genocide in situations where a population hungry for property and wealth comes into contact with weaker peoples who stand in the way, or are perceived as standing in the way, of satisfying this drive. The original owners are treated as a hindrance to be eliminated just like wild beasts are killed off as farmers turn wilderness into farmland. The pattern of destruction just described has the following characteristics:

1. a) A technologically superior society comes into contact with one technologically inferior to it;
    b) people of one social and cultural background come into contact with people of a different background.

The above are used by the technologically superior society to:
- think itself superior;
- disregard the claim that people with a technologically inferior background have to their territorial base.

2. Technologically advanced people use their technological superiority; in particular in the area of warfare, to take possession of what is held by the technologically less advanced people.

3. Property that had been communally shared becomes privately held, with each owner jealously guarding the right of possession, even to the point where he kills to defend or increase his possessions.

4. The technologically inferior society's resistance to its dispossession is resolved through violence.

5. The process of destruction and replacement is an integral part of building a new society. Because of its values and structures, it is difficult or impossible for members of the traditional society to fit into the new order or to continue their way of life.

6. Being excluded from the emerging social structure has several effects on members of the technologically less advanced society. Serving no useful function in the emerging society, they come to be viewed as a nuisance. This leaves them vulnerable to people or groups who exploit and destroy them at will to take possession of what they still own and who generally mistreat them. Exclusion also leaves the members of the technologically inferior society vulnerable to undernourishment and

disease, which in turn magnifies the destructive effects of mistreatment.

7. Although central governments may express concern at the destruction of the weaker people, they do little to alter the situation because their interests lie with the aggressors. The result is a massive attack on the technologically less advanced group, with members of the technologically advanced group exploiting and destroying members of the weaker group at will.

8. The combination of these influences leads to the partial destruction of some groups and the total destruction of others.

This pattern of destruction occurred often enough and is different enough from other genocides carried out to acquire wealth, that it may be seen to constitute its own subcategory under the larger category of genocides committed to obtain wealth.

Conclusion

Causes, effects, and categories

In this study, I have explored, compared and contrasted specific case studies so as to identify the basic features of a holocaust. I have examined ideological genocides identified as holocausts, including the destruction of the idolaters, the persecution of the witches, the destruction of the Armenians, the destruction of European Jewry, and the annihilation of the kulaks and the enemies of the people in Cambodia and the Soviet Union. I have shown that, while the destruction of the Armenians was an ideological genocide, it was not a holocaust. The other four ideological genocides, the destruction of the idolaters, of the witches, of the Jews and of the enemies of the people in both the Soviet Union and Cambodia are both holocausts and ideological genocides. In fact, the holocaust can be seen as a sub-category under the larger category of the ideological genocide.

As such, it is both less and more than this. That is, it is less than the ideological genocide in that it falls under the larger category of the ideological genocide. It is more, however, in that the pattern of destruction peculiar to the holocaust may be evident not only in the ideological type of genocide. Thus, it may also be evident in other types of genocide, as in genocides committed to obtain wealth in the form of territory held by other groups, an example being the destruction of the idolaters by the Israelites. While a part of this pattern of genocide, it does not, however, lose its basic features, such as its emphasis on planting or sustaining a system of beliefs in the social environment and its emphasis on the total elimination of a pariah in order to achieve this.

The destruction of Native peoples in the Spanish, French and British empires and the United States also exhibits features that characterize the holocaust. Thus, the Christian concept of war and European racism both played a role in the destruction of Native peoples in the Americas as well as in the destruction of European Jewry by the Nazis. Demonization played a role in the holocaust as well as in some genocides in the New World. However, there is a difference between the manner in which the target group was chosen in the case of the holocaust and in the case of Native peoples. While in the holocaust the pariah groups were targeted for eradication because they were seen as infectious diseases or agents of evil, Native peoples were targeted for despoliation because they were seen as not quite human, as occupying some realm where animal and beast merge. They were demonized when they resisted conquest and asserted their claim to their land. While, in case of the holocaust, the genocide was part and parcel of an attempt to impose an ideological system on the social environment, in the case of Native peoples, the drive to destruction was fuelled primarily by the desire to obtain wealth, be this in the form of gold or land. For these reasons, the destruction of Native peoples can be classified more logically, not as holocausts, but under Chalk and Jonassohn's category of genocides committed to obtain wealth.

Whereas all the holocausts under examination logically fit into a sub-category under the ideological genocide, such categorization was more difficult in the case of the destruction of Native peoples. A major reason for this is the disagreement among researchers over whether the destruction of Native peoples by the Spaniards constituted a genocide. The analysis of the patterns of destruction in the different colonial empires led to the conclusion that the only instance where the destruction of Native peoples occurred frequently enough to indicate a pattern of genocide was in the case of the British colonies and the United States. In this case, the genocides had enough in common to allow one to fit them into a sub-category under genocides to obtain wealth.

My analysis of the different genocides suggests that the use of terms such as "holocaust" can help us understand a particular pattern of destruction. At the same time, however, using the term too broadly and trying to impose it on situations in which it doesn't really fit can distort a situation. Thus, there were similarities between the Nazi destruction of European Jewry and the European destruction of the Natives. However, the basic motives for the destruction were quite different. By focussing too much on fitting the destruction of Native peoples into the holocaust category, researchers had not paid sufficient attention to these differences.

By concentrating too much on the holocaust, Stannard, for example, didn't pay sufficient attention to other aspects of Nazi ideology and policy that are similar to beliefs and attitudes that led to the destruction of Native peoples. Nor did he appear to be aware that there were genocides, as for example the genocides carried out by the different communist regimes, that have as much and even more in common with the holocaust genocide than does the Nazi case. In the case of the communists, all the genocides committed more or less fit into the holocaust pattern. In the case of the Nazis, two basic influences motivated them. In one instance, they targeted a group such as the Jews for destruction because they saw them as contaminating. This led to a holocaust. In the other instance, they sought to turn Slavic peoples into vassals or replace them on their territorial base. Here, in particular the influence of social Darwinism is evident.

One may well argue that the similarity between the Nazis and the European conquerors of Aboriginal people lies, not so much in the holocaust, as in the manner in which these groups interpreted and applied, for example, social Darwinism or the Christian view of the Chain of Being to justify territorial replacement, enslavement, or mass destruction. The Christian view of the Native as being at a lower position on the Chain of Being caused some Christians—Spanish, French, or British—to seek to convert the Natives. Those who despoiled or killed Native peoples were driven by a different interpretation of Christianity. In this case, Christian beliefs, including the belief in the Chain of Being, led the Europeans to regard themselves as superior to the New World inhabitants they encountered. This attitude served not only to denigrate the Natives, but also to justify despoiling, mistreating or killing them.

When the Nazis came to power, the influences of the Enlightenment and of different democratic and socialist movements encouraged respect for the individual and for social groupings. Moreover, Christianity had changed sufficiently so that it could no longer be interpreted as it had been by the conquerors of the Americas. However, social Darwinism presented a substitute form of the Chain of Being, though with a different underpinning. Rather than religion, it was based on the late nineteenth century source of truth—Science.

In the British colonies, the settlers coveting Native land had already applied social Darwinism to justify driving the Natives from their land and killing them. The Nazis essentially put this theory into an ideological framework and applied it to the European situation. Whereas the British and the Spanish had seen themselves as superior to the Natives because they were Christian, white, and technologically more advanced, the Nazis saw Germans as superior to the Slavs, not because they were Christian, but because of German achievements in the arts, the sciences, and other areas of endeavour. They believed that they were the purest of the white race. Pride in their particular tribal group and pride in culture led them to place themselves at the top of the Chain of Being, just as the conquerors of the Americas had done. From this supposed superiority, the conquerors drew all sorts of privileges when dealing with their inferiors, particularly the privilege of conquering, destroying, and mistreating them. Thus, the similarity between the Nazis and the European conquerors of the Americas or Australia lies not so much in the holocaust-type genocide as Stannard suggests, as in the manner in which the Nazis interpreted social Darwinism to justify their mistreatment of Slavic peoples and the way the Spanish interpreted concepts such as the Chain of Being and the British interpreted both the Chain of Being and social Darwinism to justify their despoiling, enslaving, or killing Native peoples.

This being said, there were important differences between the way the conquerors of the New World used the Chain of Being or social Darwinism and the manner in which social Darwinism was interpreted and applied by the Nazis. For the former, the belief in the Chain of Being or social Darwinism justified the expansion of empire and the acquisition of wealth in whatever form. The belief in social Darwinism also was at the root of the Nazi drive to expand the territorial base of Germans. Unlike the Spaniards or the British settlers, however, the Nazis were not driven by the desire to acquire wealth. Rather, ultimately they were driven by fear of being eventually eradicated in a world where only the strong survived.

The Nazi drive for territorial expansion was also closely integrated with their beliefs regarding eugenics and race hygiene. Germany was, of course, not the only country where race hygiene became popular. In the 1930s, it was generally accepted in most European countries as well as in North America. Only in Germany, however, did a group come to power that made racial hygiene a national program of action. The Nazis not only coveted new territory but also sought to transform German society, both morally and biologically, to assure that Germans would be able to defend their territorial base. It was this goal of transformation that led to their attempts to destroy people who could weaken the nation either biologically or morally. Hitler considered the Jews to be biologically and morally inferior. At the same time, he regarded them as a world power enslaving other peoples to forward their own ends. Killing the Jews served not only to remove from the German nation a people who were purportedly inferior, both biologically and morally, but also to destroy an enemy standing in the way of national regeneration. Therefore, eradicating the demonized Jew became an integral part of the process of seeking salvation for the German people.

Not only the Nazis but also other groups that sought salvation through a holocaust linked the creation of their particular idealized society with the eradication of a demonized enemy group or groups: the idolaters, the witches, the bourgeois exploiters of the people. In all these cases, the link the genocidal group could establish between its abstract definition of the targeted group and the actual group upon which it could impose these characteristics influenced the extent and nature of the destruction. The ease with which a link could be established, in turn, was influenced by the manner in which the genocidal group defined both itself and the pariah.

Here I might comment on the *Historikerstreit* and the debate in France regarding similarities between the Nazi destruction of European Jewry and the destructions carried out by different communist regimes. I shall address only two problems, both of which relate to the manner in which the debates were intellectually structured. First, while the disputants were debating genocides committed by a Stalinist and a Nazi regime, and invariably applying the term "holocaust" to one or both, few made the effort to explore the term to see what light this might shed on the debate. Few seemed to realize that when an event is described through the use of an abstract term such as holocaust, that event is taken out of its context and placed into a more or less abstract category. Before one can adequately determine whether a certain event can be placed into a specific category, and then compared to other events, one must first determine the nature of the category. Major problems arose from the fact that people were comparing events without specifying what measurements they were using to reach their conclusions.

Another problem in the debates arose from the fact that the disputants concentrated almost exclusively on the twentieth century, comparing and contrasting genocides committed by different, and yet in many ways similar, authoritarian regimes. Little effort was made to place these genocides into a larger context. Doing so would have supplied additional criteria, permitting the disputants to relate the Nazi and communist genocides more fully to the holocaust concept and to each other. At the same time, other examples would have provided further insight into the nature of the genocides being looked at, providing additional criteria for comparison.

In this regard, my study can make an important contribution to this debate. I took some effort to define the term "holocaust," looking both at its origin and the manner in which it was applied to genocide. I also looked at different genocides to extrapolate the features that characterize the holocaust-type of genocide. Furthermore, I place the holocaust into an intellectual and religious tradition that provides insight not only into the Nazi, but also into the communist, genocides.

Having said this, I might add that, just as the Jews were the victims of the Nazi holocaust, the people who were destroyed because they in one way or another fit into the communist category of the bourgeois enemy of the people, were victims of the communist holocaust. That is, they all were victims of a group that saw itself as elect. They were victims of regimes that sought to implant and promote a particular ideological system in the environment and, in the effort to do so, created an enemy who had to be eliminated for their ideal system to be realized. The Nazis as well as the communists under Stalin and Pol Pot used extreme violence to eliminate this enemy.

The people annihilated by these regimes suffered their own particular holocaust. In the case of the communists, the genocides followed a pattern in which the pariah group to be eradicated was not clearly defined, allowing the perpetrators to slot a variety of individuals or groups into the category. Therefore, the genocides resembled the witch-hunts. In the Nazi destruction of European Jewry, the manner in which their pariah was targeted was very similar to the manner in which the idolater was targeted.

By drawing these parallels, I am merely suggesting that every event has a larger context to which it can be related. The event can best be understood by being placed into this context. Only in this way will we be able to understand the dynamics that have led to the human suffering brought on by a holocaust, no matter how it expressed itself. The larger context will also help us explain the reasons for a holocaust. Only by seeking to understand these dynamics will we be able to prevent a recurrence of these events.

In this regard, I might add that, when observing the debates considering similarities between communism and Nazism, I very much had the impression that contemporary Marxists, while they see Hitlerism as an unmitigated evil, consider Stalinist communism at root a noble experiment, albeit one that had gone slightly off course. I embraced this delusion until I probed a little more deeply. Unfortunately, those who still maintain this idea are permitting their hopes for a better world to interfere with reality. A closer examination would reveal that nowhere where Bolshevist communism came to power did the utopia Marx had prophesied come into existence. This is true for Russia, Cambodia, China, and North Korea, as well as for Vietnam. In all cases, these revolutions resulted in a dictatorship and the rule of one party. The revolutions may have been fought in the name of the oppressed, but it was not the oppressed who came to power. Instead, a dictatorship and new political establishment replaced the traditional establishment. These now enjoyed the fruits of privilege. Instead of the proletariat owning the means of production, the government and the party apparatus owned these. Instead of bringing the economic and political equality Marx had prophesied, Bolshevik communism returned us to the time of absolute monarchs. I would even go further than this and argue that both communism and Nazism returned us the theocracies of ancient times where the ruler was divine or semi-divine. Its concomitant was the shrinkage of the importance of individuals as human beings, these being reduced both by the ideological system and by those who sought to impose it on the social environment. In contrast, the significance of the dictator was magnified. The dehumanization that formed part of either process was an integral part of the mass destructions.

Furthermore, the aspirations of both regimes and the manner in which they sought to realize them in many ways bring us face to face with basic issues concerning human moral nature, in particular as this relates to the attempt to shape people to fit some idea of the good or the ideal. Milton deals with this in *Paradise Lost* when he describes Satan as the archangel who is so obsessed with being perfect in his own eyes, with being the best, that he becomes evil. Groups committing holocausts all sought to transform society into some image of an ideal that left little room for the multidimensional nature of what it means to be human, thereby serving to dehumanize both the target and the perpetrator of the crime.

In this regard, further insight into the dynamics of the holocaust may be obtained by exploring Neumann's view that the holocaust is the product of a *Weltanschauung* that divides the world into extremes of good and evil, light and darkness, God and the Devil. One may go one step beyond this and say that the holocaust is an outgrowth essentially of a particular view of God. What all these groups shared was the concept of a two-dimensional God. On the one hand, the God of all these groups punishes; on the other hand he rewards. What all these groups sought to do was avoid the punishment of their particular deity. In many ways, concepts such as the Devil or the people of darkness were mere symbolic representations of forces that could put them in the position of being punished by their particular deity.

This dual dimensional God is an integral part of the Judaeo-Christian tradition. Deuteronomy and the Book of Joshua give evidence of the nature of this dual-natured God. The followers of Joshua destroyed the idolaters to assure they would avoid punishment from this God and be assured of his blessings. In the Christian tradition, the dynamics of reward and punishment express themselves somewhat differently. The conflict between good and evil, which the early Israelites saw as taking place in the temporal sphere, the Christians saw as taking place in the cosmic sphere, as well as at the personal and social levels. Thus, the persecutors of the witches saw the struggle between God and Satan for the soul of man occurring at the community level, where certain individuals, who had sold their soul to Satan, threatened Christianity. Witches had to be destroyed if Christians themselves were to attain salvation.

The Darwinian process of natural selection as interpreted by the Nazis and the Hegelian dialectic as interpreted by the Marxists also operated like a dual-natured god. To be on the losing side of history, according to the Nazis, would eventually result in the nation being crushed and obliterated. The only way to avoid this fate was to certify one had the power to keep on the winning side of the process of evolution. Under Bolshevik communism, the holocaust served somewhat different purposes than it did in the case of the destruction of the idolaters, the witches or Jews. In the latter three, the enemy group was targeted for destruction so as to create the best society possible for the perpetrators. The Bolshevik communists also aimed at creating the best society for their idealized group, the proletariat. At the same time, however, they aimed at creating the ultimate perfect society.

For Bolshevik communism, the triumph of the proletariat was very much like the final battle between the righteous and the antichrist, described in the Book of Revelation, where the perfect society is ushered in through the destruction of the antichrist and all those forces associated with him. History, as we know it, ends because all evil has been defeated. The Nazis did not envisage a similar final triumph for themselves. They saw their elect group as being in a much better position to compete in a Darwinian world where only the fittest survived. The Israelites described in the Book of Joshua also did not envisage an ideal world being ushered in by their destroying the idolaters. They believed they would be in a better position to meet the demands of Yahweh, which in turn would help safeguard the flow of his blessings towards them. The Christians saw in the destruction of the witches a means of creating a society in which they would be better able to serve Christ and thereby save their own souls from perdition.

In many ways, the very view of being elect seems to have been engendered by the dual natured view of god that was held by these groups. On the one hand, these groups believed in a god or force that was universal: that is, this god's workings affected all humankind. On the other hand, each group wanted this universal force to operate in some special way for its own benefit. In order to be granted these rewards, the group had to ascribe to itself characteristics that made it more worthy than any other group of receiving rewards from this universal force. Some groups chose religious beliefs, others chose tribal characteristics or social class, on which to base their specialness. No matter what was chosen, this specialness made them more in tune than other groups with the universal force the group saw as directing human affairs.

Having defined themselves as special people with a divinely ordained mission, they then found it necessary to create a social environment that would allow them to lead a life in keeping with this specialness and would allow them to receive the rewards and avoid the punishment of their particular Prime Mover, be this Yahweh, Christ, the Darwinian process of natural selection, or the Marxian dialectic. In all these cases, the threatened punishment for failure was nothing to scoff at. It might mean the destruction of the group, putting one's soul in danger of perdition or being subject to continual exploitation—all punishments severe enough to make the group in question seek to avoid them at all cost.

These conditions made the struggle for salvation seem even more necessary and the utopian aspirations even more appealing, which in turn encouraged sacrificing the self and others to attain these goals. The problem with the promised utopias in all these societies was that they were cast in a mould in which the realization of the ideal society for the genocidal group was integrally connected to the destruction of other peoples. If the attainment of the goals of one collectivity means targeting another collectivity as an enemy, one can well argue that, sooner or later, these goals will lead to persecution and even to attempts to destroy the enemy group. The problem with these, as all, utopias lies with applying abstract conceptualizations to everyday human affairs. Such endeavours may lead to fruitful results in the field of art, where asceticism opens up endless possibilities. However, when one aims at shaping the human condition the way a piece of art might be shaped, with some image of the ideal in mind, the situation is quite different. What best explains the dynamics in such situations is the concept of Jung's shadow.[1] The ideals aspired to by groups who carried out holocaust-type genocide were so extreme that they left little room for human failings and limitations, which were viewed as an attack upon the ascetic vision. Each group dealt with this situation by projecting the unacceptable part of the self or of the in-group as a whole, onto an outside pariah group. Each genocidal society had initially escaped into a pursuit of the idealized in an attempt to escape from a situation of incertitude and inadequacy. Once having taken this step, the idealized vision itself reinforced the sense of inadequacy and also the drive to attain the ideal as well as the drive to destroy the pariah.

Perhaps the fault lies, not so much in applying abstractions to everyday life, but in the particular abstraction that guided these people. Here I would like to bring up a point raised earlier. When looking at the different elements that bring about a holocaust, whether it is the leader or the bureaucracy, I suggested that perhaps it is the dynamics of all these elements interrelating to each other that bring on the holocaust. I would like to examine this a little more closely, and will begin with a number of questions rather than a statement. Thus, could it be that the various elements that contribute to a holocaust, be it leadership or the bureaucracy, are merely cogs which are put into motion by an ideological structure? That is, could it be that the manner in which these people structured their world played a major role in bringing on a holocaust? Could it be that the view these groups had of themselves as special or elect and the manner in which they decided to go about creating an environment that helped them perpetuate their specialness had a major influence in creating the dynamics leading to a holocaust?

Of course, I don't think having a positive view of oneself or a view that one may be better than other people is the problem. All groups who achieved something display elements of this, be it the Chinese, the Romans, the Greeks or Europeans in general. What differentiates groups that committed a holocaust genocide is that they saw themselves as special, elect, somehow selected for some special role in the history of mankind. Furthermore, they connected this to some ideological system that spelled out their specialness.

This system spelled out a unilinear vision of how the individual life as well as society should be ordered. All the groups encountered problems that put their specialness into question and faced difficulties translating their utopian vision into reality. Their solution wasn't to question either their specialness or their aspirations but to point to some outside group(s) as being the cause of their not being in a situation to which they deemed themselves entitled because of their specialness. The genocide developed out of this process of scapegoating. It wasn't merely the abstract vision that led to the genocide but also the manner in which this abstract vision was imposed on social reality at a time of crisis. More specifically, these dynamics were operative in particular when such an ideological system was first being imposed on the social environment. In this situation, leaders, the bureaucracy or whoever else were, perhaps, mere actors in a play whose conclusion can be foretold from the manner in which the drama was structured.

Of course, one may go too far in pressing the argument that the very idea of being elect and seeking one's salvation through the destruction of another group will inevitably lead to genocide. In all the above cases, other factors were also involved: a leader, or leaders, determined, and in the position, to direct the collectivity towards destroying another group; values in society at large that may not sanction such violence but at least provide a rationale for it; an organizational structure to implement this solution; and a situation where one group has enough power over another to carry out its destruction.

A collection of interrelated group dynamics led not only to a holocaust-type genocide, but to other genocides as well. Here also some motivating factors appear to be more significant than others. In the destruction of Native peoples, greed for gold or for Native lands was a paramount influence. Essentially two different groups pursued European expansion in the New World. Spanish colonial expansion was carried out in large part by the lower and middle echelons of the ruling class, who sought to exploit the resources, including the people, of the New World to enrich themselves, with the Spanish crown using the wealth of the New World to enhance its position in its struggle with other European powers. These circumstances also apply to some extent to the French and British expansion into the New World. However, in the case of the British, the people seeking to enhance their economic position in the New World were largely those experiencing difficulty in the mother country. Individuals or groups seeking to gain or hold on to wealth by despoiling other people committed the genocides in all the colonial empires. However, the destruction, even if motivated by greed, could not have occurred if Native peoples were not first dehumanized, a process facilitated by the influence of concepts such as the Chain of Being or social Darwinism. These influences, in turn, worked together with others, such as the technological superiority of the invaders and the diseases they brought with them.

Here I would like to return to Lal's statement that the suffering experienced by groups such as the Jews or Gypsies during the Second World War had been experienced by Native societies during the past five hundred years.[2] This statement is only partially true. Clearly, Native societies underwent tremendous suffering as a result of conquest. In many ways, this suffering, as Stannard makes clear in his study, was similar to that of groups during the Second World War. However, to draw too close a parallel between the genocides in the New World and the experiences of Europeans during the war would be a disservice to our understanding of the experiences of Native peoples. Although there are similarities between these cases, there are also significant differences. One, as Lal suggests, is that the suffering of Europeans during the war was of relatively brief duration compared to the decades—indeed, centuries—of genocidal policies directed at Native peoples.[3] Another is that, although the suffering of Europeans derived largely from ideological systems promising salvation to a particular group of elect, the suffering of Native peoples resulted largely from people of a different colour and culture, and at a higher state of technological development, suppressing, exploiting, and destroying people of another race and culture at a lower state of technological development, in particular where methods of warfare were concerned.

Undeniably, the Second World War resulted in the massive destruction of peoples. Yet, the combined forces of disease, mistreatment, and slaughter led to a destruction in the New World that, in terms of the percentage and number of people destroyed, has been unsurpassed in the annals of humankind. The expansion of the British in the New World involved the most extensive territorial replacement of one people by another in history. It involved the use of warfare and the massacres of peoples at a stage of technological development vastly inferior to that of the invaders. This resulted in the vast decimation of some Native societies and the total annihilation of others. The slaughter of Native peoples by the Spaniards in the Americas is one of the most massive destruction of innocent lives that the world has witnessed. Unlike the war in Europe, these ravages led to the destruction not only of peoples but to the eradication of dynamic civiliza-tions. Finally, although some Jews could view the worst genocide of the Second World War, the Nazi war on European Jewry, as a test of faith that God rewarded by fulfilling a long-cherished Jewish dream—namely the re-establishment of Israel[4]— the destruction of Native peoples contributed to the fulfillment of no similar dreams.

Despite these facts, the genocides in the United States, the British col-onies, and Spanish America have been given but scant attention in the study of genocide. Some scholars do not even believe that the annihilation of Native peoples in Spanish America constitutes a genocide because the definition of genocide generally applied focuses on direct targeting as its main feature. Such absurdity suggests that there is a major problem with our study of genocide and the definitions we use to guide our analysis.

The present study shows that many interrelated factors influenced the extent to which a group is destroyed in a genocide. Direct targeting is only one of these. The duration of the destruction, the settlement patterns of people targeted, the organizational structure of the group carrying out the genocide, and many other factors played a role. Any future definition of genocide must take into consideration these different factors that can lead to one group destroying another. Such a definition is necessary if we are to use the past to help us understand the present and influence the future.

Lessons to be learned and social action

To determine what lessons may be drawn from these examples of human destructiveness, it would be of interest to look again at features that some or all of these genocides share. A major feature of all these examples is the proclivity by the genocidal society to divide the world into rigid categories, into them and us. Often, these categories also depicted one group, namely the genocidal group, as special. Thus, in the holocaust type of genocide, the genocidal group saw itself as elect, no matter whether chosen by God, Christ, the workings of the Darwinian process of natural selection or the Marxian dialectic. Such elitism is also evident in the case of the European Christian who, no matter whether measured by the Christian Chain of Being or the Darwinian process of natural selection, saw himself at the pinnacle of humankind. The Turks did not define themselves as special in the way these other groups did. Rather, they saw themselves as members of a formerly great empire that, in its decline, was threatened by the world around it.

Just as rigid categories defined the genocidal groups, they also served to define the groups that became the object of aggression. In both cases, these categories served to identify people, not as individuals, but in terms of their group membership. While the Europeans saw themselves at the zenith of the civilized man, they saw Natives they encountered at the opposite extreme, namely at some stage of development where man and beast merged. In the case of the holocaust genocide, while the elect group saw itself above other peoples, the pariahs were seen as vermin, or some contaminating or diabolical force. Again, the categorization was less extreme in the case of the Turks, who typecast the Armenians not only to exclude them but also to depict them as a threat to the tribal community the Young Turks aspired to establish.

As in the case of the Armenians, target groups in other instances were defined in a way so as to direct the aggression of the genocidal group towards them. In the holocaust-type genocide, the target group was not only defined as vile or contaminating, but was also described as standing in the way of the genocidal group's efforts to create the idealized society. Native peoples were seen as less than human. This view of the Natives encouraged the European Christian to treat them as an exploitable resource, or as wild beasts that could be killed in the process of clearing the land.

Such categorization not only provided a justification for the aggressive behaviour of the genocidal group toward its target, but also deprived both the genocidal and the target group of their humanity. Thus, in the case of the holocaust, the genocidal groups were agents of a larger truth battling and wiping out diabolical or contaminating forces preventing them from implanting their ascetic vision in the social environment. In the case of the Young Turks, the ideology made the Young Turks agents of tribal interests battling the Armenian enemy foiling their dream of a Turkic state. In the case of Native peoples, the categorization allowed the Europeans to transform themselves into agents of progress and civilization dealing with people who were little more than beasts of burden that could be enslaved or wild animals that could be killed at will.

To prevent these dynamics from recurring, action must be taken in several areas. In particular, the tendency toward rigid categorization must be discouraged. This inclination is fostered by reductionism, or the proclivity to explain complex situations in simplistic terms. Both are an integral part of any tendency to divide the world and our fellow human beings into categories of good and evil, and to divide people according to those who belong to our group and those who can be slaughtered, enslaved or exploited. Encouraging people to understand individuals and situations in their full complexity, rather than feel threatened by differences, can do much to counter reductionism.

By advocating the acceptance of differences, I do not mean embracing unrestricted individualism, in particular not in the economic sphere. Nor do I suggest that people need to lose their identity or give up all boundaries between self and other or between the different groupings that make up society or humankind. What is important is trying to understand rather than render judgement. The basis for such understanding is an educational system that encourages questioning and the acceptance of ambiguity rather than black-and-white answers, which encourages empathy, tolerance, and an appreciation of self as well as others. Such an educational system could well take its guidance from Christ's simple yet straightforward message: to share, to do unto others as you would have them do unto you, to love rather than to hate, exploit, and destroy. Christ gave this counsel both to the Jews and to the remainder of humanity. People fail to see the wisdom of such counsel when they choose to focus on their uniqueness or on their own problems, when they become obsessed with greed to the extent that they forget that the people targeted for despoliation are fellow human beings.

To deal with the problem of categorization and gain insight into forces leading to genocide, one needs to examine the underpinnings of the belief systems that motivated different genocidal societies. In the case of the destruction of the idolaters and of the witches, absolutist positions were justified by a rigid monotheism that envisaged only one path to salvation and identified different views as threatening and evil. Beliefs as expressed in the Chain of Being and social Darwinism structured the world hierarchically in the manner where they contributed to mass destruction. In particular, pseudo-science had a destructive influence in genocides committed both by the Nazis and the communists. Conquest comments on this in regard to Marxism, arguing that Stalinism, in part at least, was a product of nineteenth-century "scientism," which held that all human action could be calculated, considered, and predicted.[5] Courtois adds that, as in the case of the Nazis, communists used pseudo-science to dehumanize their enemies and prove them inferior. At the same time, they used the language of science to sanitize killing. Killing the enemies of the people metamorphosed into cutting out a disease.[6] Pseudo-science also convinced the communists that theirs was the correct course of action and that a scientifically objective analysis underlay Marx's prophecy regarding the demise of the bourgeois state and the advent of utopia. This certitude helped pave the way for the destructive policies pursued both by Pol Pot and Stalin.

In no other country has the misapplication of science and technology had as disastrous an influence as in Nazi Germany. One reason for this was that Germany was in many ways a center for the development or exploration of these ideas, some of them useful in helping to explain complex phenomena and others simply bizarre. The Nazis did not invent the idea of the unworthy life, although they exploited it by slotting the Jews and the Gypsies into this category to justify killing them. Their euthanasia program grew out of such works as *The Release of Unworthy Life in Order That It Might Be Destroyed* (*Die Freigabe der vernichtung Lebensunwertes Lebens*), published in 1920 by the lawyer Karl Binding and the physician Alfred Hoch. Nazi ideas that groups such as the Gypsies or the Jews were habitually criminal grew out of theories propounded by Cesare Lombroso, whose research in the late nineteenth century led him to claim that the physiology of certain individuals resulted in criminality. He considered criminality to be inherited, and believed that this justified destroying such individuals. The Nazis identified not only individuals but also ethnic groups as having an unworthy life and being inclined to criminality, and then proceeded to destroy them. Like the communists, they used pseudo-scientific underpinnings to justify and at the same time rationalize their actions.

To prevent the misuse of science as applied by these groups, one has to recognize that there was a grain of objective truth in the theories which, for example, the Nazis and communists used to give legitimacy to their ideologies. For example, Darwin made an important contribution towards helping us understand the evolution of species, just as Marx made an important contribution to help us better understand the evolution of societies. However, both the Nazis and the communists turned these insights into systems of faith, distorting them in the process. By inference, however, they referred back to the original observations sufficiently to give the impression their belief systems were derived from an objective analysis of reality. The only way to oppose such pseudo-science is to point out its true nature. Darwin's writings on the origin of species may provide important insights into how different species altered as they adapted to their ever-changing environment. Nevertheless, there is a significant difference between this and the social Darwinist transformation that involved using an insight into the evolution of the natural world into a rationalization justifying the exploitation and destruction of tribal, cultural, or social groups.

It wasn't only faith or pseudo-science, however, that gave movements such as Nazism and communism their appeal. This appeal was derived from the clear, simple answers pseudo-science provided in times of crisis, doubt and uncertainty. But what was the price for such reassurance? These regimes required people to give up their individual power and place it in the hands of authoritarian leaders. In both cases, individuals and societies lost more than they gained. Even the regimes lost more than they gained. Recruiting the support of the Jews, who were prevalent in the sciences, the arts, and many other areas of German life, would have been very helpful to Hitler in his attempt to establish his thousand-year Reich. In his eradication of the kulak, Stalin destroyed the most dynamic elements in society. He may have gained conformity to political orthodoxy, but at the same time he made his society less productive. This was true not only in regard to the collective farms. By destroying the most productive elements in his society, Stalin laid the basis for the disintegration of the Soviet Union, which he had sought to place on a firm Marxist foundation.

The same critique cannot be made of the individuals or groups who used constructs such as the Chain of Being or social Darwinism to justify annihilating Native peoples. Both the Spaniards and the British gained wealth and territory through this destruction. The United States, the most powerful nation on earth today, was established on territory taken from other peoples. It is little wonder that Hitler saw territorial replacement as a method for establishing his own empire.

Although conquering societies and peoples gained through the destruction of Native peoples, the world lost vibrant societies that could have taught us approaches to life that no other parts of the world had to offer. One may also ask whether such a destructive conquest was necessary for the Spaniard to gain his wealth or the British settler to gain his land. Only greed led to these excesses. Peoples in general would have fared much better if a more humane approach had been taken to expand empire or to enrich oneself.

What about the suffering of people who were on the receiving end of other people's aggressiveness? What was life like for people who underwent these horrible experiences? Do we want people to go through these experiences in the future? If we do not, we must understand the conditions in the past that led to mass destruction. In order to learn and understand, we must study society in general, including the genocidal societies. The best place to start in, probably, is with genocides committed by one's own people. As Churchill suggests, the United States can build all the holocaust memorials it wants and flood its schools with information on genocides committed by the Nazis or communists. It hasn't truly looked at genocide until it looks at how it is that land once in the possession of North American Indians is now dominated by English-speaking peoples.[7]

Of course, Churchill goes further than this when he wonders whether at times the endeavour to describe the destruction of Jews by the Nazis as unique and, as such, offering a more important lesson than other genocides, including the annihilation of Native peoples, is little more than an attempt to turn a blind eye to one's own dark past.[8] Understanding genocide begins not with understanding the genocides committed by other societies, and especially not with understanding the genocides of one's enemies. It begins with searching the shadows of one's own past and the past of one's people.

To understand a particular genocide, its causes and effects, it should be examined in detail. Human suffering can best be understood by our examining not only larger historical patterns but also their effect on individuals. To help us in this, we need not only a general history of a particular genocide but also novels, movies, documentaries, memoirs and other personal accounts that provide insight into how genocide affects human beings.

Whereas individual accounts and the historical analysis of one genocide give insight into the human condition in one situation, a comparative approach helps us isolate patterns that, over time, have motivated people to destroy each other. Some of these patterns are evident in the individual genocide. To gain an understanding of these patterns and determine how they operate in shaping human behaviour, it is important, however, to examine the individual case in a broader context. This will help us isolate those features unique to each genocide. At the same time, the comparative approach helps us compare dynamics inherent in one genocide with those in other genocides and thereby isolate conditions and patterns of human behaviour that have led to genocide. This is important if we are to use what we learn from past genocides to determine what we might do to prevent genocide in the future. This future is not static, even though human fears, drives, and aspirations tend to remain fairly constant within the parameters of ongoing change.

When one looks at the different genocides—whether holocaust-type genocides, the ideological genocide in general, or the mass destruction carried out by the conquerors of the New World—one should never lose sight of the fact that the very forces that led to destruction in these instances had other outcomes in other situations. While some Christians destroyed Native peoples, other Christians built schools, orphanages and hospitals, or sought to help them in other ways. The force of nationalism that motivated Hitler encouraged other individuals such as Gottfried Herder to explore other cultures, believing that each group could make its particular contribution to the well-being of humankind.[9] The forces of social justice that motivated the followers of Stalin to slaughter the enemies of the people caused other people to work among the poor.

How is it that similar beliefs can be used by some people for the common good and by others for the most destructive behaviour imaginable? One thing that all the groups that committed a holocaust share, for example, is a situation of crisis where they felt their existence threatened. Clearly one can question how real this threat was. On the one hand, the threat was real enough to make these groups doubt themselves. This was true in the case of Germany, which had just lost a major war, with its impotence further emphasized by the punitive policies of the victorious powers immediately after the war. The Russian communists had for years endured the interference of western powers in Soviet affairs in an endeavour by the West to overthrow communism. While these attempts had come to nothing, they nevertheless resulted in uneasiness among Soviet leaders. It is well known that the witch-hunts increased during times of crisis in Christendom. We do not have enough information to determine what contributed to Israelite insecurity to lead them to destroy the idolaters.

Ironically, at the same time that these powers felt insecure, they were also convinced of their own potential might. Although the Nazis felt that Germany was vulnerable in 1933, they were also convinced that the country could have won the First World War if it had not been for the stab in the back by traitorous elements under the guidance of the Jews. All that had to be done was to eradicate these elements and Germany would be strong enough to attain its place in the sun. Although the communists had a vague uneasiness regarding the western powers, there is little evidence that, until the rise of Hitler, they felt truly threatened. They certainly felt strong enough to face and defeat the enemy on the home front. The powers persecuting the witches never saw them as a threat to their own power. It was the desire of the Church, or secular powers that controlled the Church, to strengthen its hold over the lives and thoughts of the people, that led to the witch-hunts. Despite whatever threats the Israelites described in the Book of Joshua may have felt, they certainly were convinced that, with Yahweh's support, they could hold their position against any groups that might challenge them.

These genocides were solutions adopted by political leaders to meet what they considered to be the needs of their society, or solutions individuals resorted to to meet their personal needs. These needs had some base in reality. To prevent genocide in the future, the existence of such needs must be acknowledged at the social as well as at the personal level. The international community must be structured in such a way as to provide a certain degree of security not only to the powerful and their friends or allies. Also, justice must be done, and appear to be done, not only for the powerful and their friends or allies but also for others.

Failure to attain such justice and security would have a drastic effect on weak nations, who are largely impotent in the face of a more powerful aggressor. Stronger nations, in particular nations who have been major powers and find themselves sliding into a minor power position, are used to having their way. Suddenly they may find themselves in the position where others direct their destiny. Fear and anger would be a natural reaction on their part. The situation would be made worse should they become convinced that their problems were caused not by their own actions but through the mechanisations of some group whom they can blame for their problems.

Some things might have been done in the situation we know best—that of Nazi Germany—to prevent genocide. Prior to the Nazi rise to power, even small changes in the Treaty of Versailles would have given the Weimar Republic a degree of support. France in particular was insistent in pursuing policies of revenge; yet this served simply to strengthen reactionary forces in Germany and discredit the Weimar Republic. A weak Weimar regime was to the advantage of groups such as the Nazis and helped bring them to power. Then, instead of standing up to Hitler, the western powers gave in to all his demands, which served only to whet his appetite.

Of course, in some instances leaders obsessed with power or groups driven by greed or the desire for territorial conquest would be determined to destroy their particular target group, regardless of warnings given. The best way to deal with that situation would be to stand up to them insofar as possible, call their bluff and face the consequences. Such a stance is likely more effective in checking genocidal tendencies before they occur rather than stopping a slaughter once it has started. For this reason, it may be useful to enumerate some of the conditions that make a society vulnerable to genocide. The genocides under study show that a society is most likely to commit genocide when a revolutionary change leads to the founding of a new society and a change in power structures at the national or international levels. A society becomes more likely to commit genocide when a power is threatened with decline, in particular when it seeks to revitalize itself through blaming some outside group for its decline. Furthermore, a situation that has the potential to lead to genocide is created when conflict breaks out between groups that are unequally matched, as happened when Native societies came into conflict with peoples of the British Empire. The invaders labelled the Native as a lower form of humanity and as innately violent. Such labelling served as a justification to attack all members of the group. Thus, when a powerful group defines a weaker one as being made up of terrorists, or stereotypes this group in any other way to justify killing its members indiscriminately, the situation has the potential to lead to genocide. It is important for societies involved in this situation to recognize what they are doing. At the same time, it is important for the international community to recognize this situation and take the necessary steps to protect targeted groups.

Most of the genocides studied here were committed within the confines of a territorial state, as it defined itself, against weaker groups under its control. This raises the question of the extent to which the outside world should stand by while a state undertakes the slaughter of its own citizenry. How sacrosanct is the idea that each state should be free to act as it wishes within the confines of its borders? To prevent a state from turning on its own citizens, an international apparatus should be established and criteria put in place that permit other states to interfere in the domestic affairs of a sovereign state should it embark on a program leading to genocide.

Just as nations need to operate in an environment that provides some degree of security and fairness, the same is true of individuals in regard to meeting their needs, in particular in meeting their economic needs. It was the general impoverishment of the common people in Russia that laid the groundwork for the revolution. The situation was exacerbated by the vast gap that separated the poor from the rich. Earlier, the drive by impoverished Europeans dreaming of their own plot of land and/or wealth in America contributed to the destruction of Native peoples. To discourage people from adopting extremist positions may very well involve eradicating extremes of rich and poor in society and creating conditions wherein the basic needs of all people will be met. This will discourage the underprivileged from seeking to improve their position through desperate means, including escaping into an ideological space where they seek satisfaction of their needs in an unreal, idealized image of themselves.

This study suggests that we consider carefully the relationship between human behaviour and the institutions we create. Individuals shape institutions and in turn are shaped by them. Once established, social organizations provide ideals for individuals as well as structure social patterns regulating their behaviour. The holocaust-type genocides and genocides carried out in particular in the British colonies and the United States illustrate the destructive effects of two very different types of institutions. One is a rigid institutional framework that seeks to transform the individual and society according to some abstract ideal. In the British colonies and the United States, the institutional framework put few limits on individual behaviour in an environment that targeted an outside group for despoliation. The pursuit of an ideal as well as the pursuit of wealth, each in its own environment, gave direction to human aggressiveness. In one case, it was directed towards a demonized pariah group and, in the other case, towards a dehumanized group that could be despoiled.

Not only the authoritarian state can commit genocide. Individuals or groups who are unrestrained in their drive to acquire wealth can also commit genocide. Whereas the major driving force of the holocaust-type genocide was fear and the reaction to it, the major driving force in genocides committed against Native peoples was greed. Of course, the value system that both the Spaniards and the British or American settlers brought with them helped to channel and give direction to this drive to destruction. The system in itself did not cause the genocide. Rather, the values and social system allowed greed to express itself in a destructive manner. This being the case, one can well argue that society should put restraints on this drive so that it doesn't become destructive. With the contemporary trend of placing more and more power into private hands in the belief that doing so will forward the common good, the question of restraining greed becomes particularly important, especially now, when money can move so easily from continent to continent, often earning more money at the expense of poor, powerless people and the environment.

The present study shows that individuals will not hesitate to wipe out another group in the pursuit of wealth. We can therefore legitimately ask: will the people who make economic gain their goal in life give adequate consideration to the needs of people who may be negatively affected through the operation of a laissez-faire economic system? Will the people who make economic gain their goal in life give adequate consideration to what effect their pursuits will have on the ecological system? This study suggests that they will not. Just as governments need to be restrained by a critical citizenry, so, too, do individuals or groups who make the acquisition of wealth their goal in life.

In summary, I am suggesting that the best way to prevent the destructions described in this book from being repeated in the future is to jealously guard our political freedom and that of others and at the same time place restraints on people who make money their primary goal in life. Placing our fate in the hands of extremist dictators who promise us magical solutions to difficult problems may well lead to the destruction of ourselves and our fellow human beings but is unlikely to solve our problems. If we do not put restraints on the drive of people to acquire wealth, individuals and corporations will grow ever more wealthy at the expense of the economically weak. Such a situation will, in turn, encourage conditions that motivate these people to seek their salvation in a Marxist utopia or some other idealized society. Unrestrained pursuit of wealth will also occur at the expense of our natural environment, be this the earth's ozone layer, its lakes, forests or any other aspects of the ecosystem that make our world habitable for both us and other species. At the same time, we must encourage a society that is tolerant of differences. This necessitates finding and following the Aristotelian golden mean between individual freedom and responsibility, finding a balance between individual and group obligations. It means treating everyone and everything with generosity, with a willingness to celebrate both our differences and our common humanity.

Appendix A

Critique of the Biblical Historical Record as Presented by Israel Finkelstein and Neil A. Silberman, in *The Bible Unearthed* (New York, NY: Free Press, 2001).

The main thrust of the argument presented by Finkelstein, who is the main author of this work, is that the predominant segment of the Hebrew Bible was committed to written form at the time of King Josiah (639-609 BCE) of Judah and that early Hebrew history as found in the Bible to a great extent reflects the interests of Judah and its Davidinian monarchy. As part of his argument, Finkelstein dismisses the biblical account of the conquest. He presents various alternatives: the destructions mentioned in the Bible were caused by the Sea People; they resulted from an Egyptian invasion. In a footnote he mentions that they may have been caused by the Israelites.

This does not necessarily disprove the basic biblical account. Nor does it make Finkelstein's account more credible than the biblical one. From the evidence Finkelstein presents, one could well conclude that the people who created the written record were very poor at dating events. Thus, the Israelite attack on Canaanite cities could well have occurred at the time when the Sea People attacked and destroyed the Hittite Empire and weakened Egypt's hold over Canaan. However, Finkelstein focuses on the Sea People or perhaps the Egyptians using military force to assert their dominance. At the same time, he suggests that the Israelites, who in his view were Canaanites who were monotheists, attained their position of dominance without resorting to war. This, however, does not tell us how and why a monotheist theocracy came to dominate the Holy Land. Nor does it correspond to what we know of the manner in which other groups gained dominance in a particular area in the past. Power and the use of force tend to be fairly universal. The biblical record tells us that force was used to assert monotheist dominance. Finkelstein would have to do better than present an updated version of Alt's argument to prove the contrary.

Finkelstein's ignoring the ban, which involved sacrificing an entire group or entire groups to a deity, doesn't abolish the problems the extensive discussions of it, in particular in the early part of the Bible, raise for his account. If mention of the ban in the Bible was the result of a creative flash of insight by a writer of the account, what inspired it? The oblique suggestion that it may have arisen as a possible solution through which Judah could avoid the experiences Israel had undergone isn't sufficient. Why would it arise at a time when Judah's main enemies were using expulsion rather than mass destruction as a means of sustaining their power? Why would the leadership in Judah advocate so extreme a solution at the time when it was in danger of losing control of its territory? If creators of the biblical account were the cynics Finkelstein often suggests, would they want to put such ideas into the minds of their enemies?

In any case, the reforms Josiah undertook are a far cry from the destruction evident in the ban described in the first part of the Bible. The fact that he could undertake these changes without significant protest suggests that they were in keeping with an older, much stronger tradition. Furthermore, the Bible has a much more satisfactory timing of these ideas and/or events than is suggested by Finkelstein. They occurred during the early period, when the idea of sacrificing conquered peoples to the gods would have been much more acceptable than it was at the time of Josiah. At the same time, the Bible also presents an idea of when the ancient Israelites gave up the ban and used other means to deal with conquered peoples. The biblical account, as such, has an inherent logic in it that is less evident in Finkelstein's account.

Finkelstein remarks that the Jews at first differentiated themselves from other peoples by not eating pork (119) and suggests that this later evolved into a full religion. This doesn't tell us how dietary laws led to a coherent religious outlook different from those of Judah's neighbours. Also, while Finkelstein's comment is interesting, it doesn't reflect at all the pattern whereby we have seen other major religions develop. No matter whether we look at Christianity, Mohammedanism, Buddhism, or Zoroastrianism, for example, these all involved a charismatic leader; they all involved this leader spelling out certain principles, etc. In this respect, the accounts we have about the roles of Moses or of Joshua present a picture in the development of Judaism that is much more in keeping with how we have observed other religions develop than does Finkelstein's account. In fact, Josiah's reforms make much more sense when looked at, not in terms of his essentially creating a new religion, but in terms of the whole biblical story of people accepting a particular religion, of gradually falling away from it, and then being brought back through radical religious reforms.

Also, archaeology doesn't provide all the answers and, in fact, at times raises questions rather than provides answers. An example is the First Temple, whose existence Finkelstein acknowledges, despite the lack of archaeological evidence for it (235, 241 for example). I would argue that there is good reason to conclude that the role of war and the ban in the conquest of the Holy Land also can fit into this category. The numerous destructions many of these centers underwent as well as the manner in which recorders of the biblical account created the record as we know it would point in that direction.

Furthermore, in the Bible we have observations on social customs, religious practices, etc. The presence of these details can hardly be accounted for in an account created essentially to further the territorial interests of Judah and the dynastic interests of its monarchy.

Problems are also evident in other areas of the accounts presented by archaeologists such as Finkelstein. They show up in the questionable assumptions they make at different times and in the evidence they accept and reject at different times. They show up in arguments one archaeologist makes to prove his point only to have another archaeologist, coming from a different perspective, using different data or even the same data, showing him to be wrong. I can go on.

We are left with the question: Do archaeologists, such as Finkelstein, make a more convincing case for the past of the Israelites than do the creators of the biblical record? Both present their problems. Looking at the different accounts, we are left with the impression that the early recorders of Israelite history sought to tell the story of their people as they saw it on the basis of what had been handed down to them. This story was influenced by their beliefs, by the environment in which they found themselves, etc. Of course, archaeologists such as Israel Finkelstein show that there are problems with the biblical record as it was handed down to us. At the same time, when archaeologists endeavour to write their own account of the establishment of the Holy Land, they merely demonstrate that the biblical account, despite its limitations, presents much to help convince us of the veracity of the basic thrust of its argument.

Appendix B

The Problem of Numbers: The Soviet German Example

The ancestors of Soviet Germans had emigrated from Germany to Russia over 150 years before the outbreak of the Second World War. Essentially all those who remained under communist rule were deported by Stalin to eastern parts of the Soviet Union in 1941. NKVD statistics show that 1,202, 430 Soviet Germans were expelled in 1941. Their population had fallen to 687, 300 by 1945, a decrease of 515, 130. Statistics for October 1946, which showed a slight increase in the Soviet German population, also showed that while there were 122,336 men over sixteen, there were 296,014 adult women. Statistics for 1948 showed that the number of Soviet Germans in the special settlements administered by the NKVD had suddenly risen to 1,012,754 (Pohl, *Stalinist Penal System* 78-79,81, 83).

How does one explain the extensive decline of the Soviet German population during the war? According to a report issued on 15 November 1948 by NKVD Colonel Shiain, 105, 294 Soviet Germans died, escaped, or had been released from the camps. This accounts for only about a quarter of Soviet German losses between 1942 and 1945 (Pohl 83). On 10 April 1953 Colonel Shiain issued another report on the population dynamics of the special settlements (settlements essentially of minority groups that had been expelled from their homes by Stalin). This document, which covers the years 1941-48, states that of the 3,266,340 people who had been "resettled" by Stalin during the war, 1,266,162 were lost by 1948. The losses were accounted for by 833,102 releases, 309,100 deaths, and 73,960 escapes and other losses (Pohl 83). No ethnic breakdown is given for the releases. At the same time, there is no reference to any large-scale release of Soviet Germans. Most of the people were released so they could join the Red Army to fight the Germans. Because Soviet Germans had been removed from the Red Army after the outbreak of hostilities, it is unlikely that Soviet Germans would have been released for this purpose.

Commenting on Soviet German losses, Pohl states that, in three years of exile, almost half the Soviet German population disappeared. He adds that it is possible that Soviet German losses may have been due to inaccurate counting (82). The above figures, however, suggest more than mere inaccurate counting. They suggest that some of the "general releases" and "escapees" among the NKVD statistics were actually deaths. Pohl suggests as much when he states that death was probably an important factor in the loss of 522,000 Soviet Germans (82). People died because of the conditions under which they were forced to live and work. Pohl observes that long hours of labour combined with meagre food rations led to many deaths. Death rates increased as rations were progressively reduced for failure to meet quotas (76). Beckett reports on the personal experiences of a British communist, who in the turmoil of the war had been accidentally sent into exile in the Gulag where she worked alongside Russian German women. For two years, she was forced to do heavy labour in the copper mines. She never saw the sun. Malnutrition made her half-blind and turned her skin yellow. She was convinced she avoided death only because someone recognized the mistake and had her released (Francis Beckett, "Rosa Thornton: Daughter of British Communist stumbled on to one of Stalin's great crimes," *Globe and Mail* 19 April 2000: R6).

Of course, Russian German men were treated still worse than the women, with it being in particular the men who were targeted for mistreatment and destruction. That would explain the higher proportion of women than men in the 1946 statistics.

How does one explain the sudden increase in the population of Soviet Germans after the war, it almost doubling by 1953 from where it stood in 1945? This increase certainly couldn't be attributed to a sudden rise in birth rates. Moreover, there was little reason for Germans to deny their racial origin during the war and then suddenly return to it after the war, for they continued to be persecuted. A more logical explanation would be that the Secret Police would have counted among Soviet Germans the people who had fled from the Soviet Union during the war and were then repatriated. They could also have added to the figures Germans sent to Soviet labour camps as the Red Army advanced westward.

There is little reason to believe that statistics kept by the NKVD on Soviet Germans differed significantly from those kept on other groups. The magnitude of destruction suffered by Soviet Germans is not reflected in the death figures provided by secret police archives. It isn't even accounted for. Whatever figures are given, they are often ambiguous when examined in the broader context. They also suggest that the NKVD manipulated both their statistics and the population upon which these statistics were based.

Appendix C

Death in the Gulag

There are many reports on the destructiveness of the Gulag camps. An example is the report from the Central Isolation Prison of Bamlag (the Baikal-Amur camp complex in eastern Siberia), stating that some 50,000 prisoners had been tied up with wire, stacked in trucks, driven outside the camp, and shot [Alan Bullock, *Hitler and Stalin: Parallel Lives* (Toronto: McClelland and Stewart, 1993) 506]. More often, however, people died because of the conditions under which they were forced to work once they became part of the Gulag camp system. This was true particularly of prisoners sent to special labour camps. Conquest provides us with an idea of what led to the deaths of people in the Kolyma system in northern Siberia. The Kolyma camp system had a double function: it was designed to get the maximum work out of inmates and, at the same time, to destroy in particular political prisoners (among the most dangerous enemies of the people). [See Robert Conquest, *Kolyma: The Arctic Death Camps* (New York: Viking Press, 1978) 17, 65, 115]. Commenting on the same group, Vogelfanger states that "political prisoners were rarely released but generally died in the Gulag" [Isaac J. Vogelfanger, *Red Tempest: The Life of a Surgeon in the Gulag* (Montreal: McGill-Queen's University Press, 1996) 84].

Political prisoners were eliminated for a variety of reasons in Kolyma. They were shot for insulting guards or for other minor infractions. They were killed by thieves and murderers who had been incarcerated with them, in part, it appears, to torture them (Conquest, *Kolyma* 55-58, 62-63, 79-86). They were killed for not fulfilling their work quotas (*Kolyma* 51-54, 91), even though these quotas were set so high that a healthy, well-fed person would have difficulty fulfilling them (*Kolyma* 48, 125-129). Rations were cut as punishment for not fulfilling one's work quota. Inevitably such a cut in rations eventually led to death (*Kolyma* 145). According to Conquest, the work quota system served a double function: obtaining maximum work out of people and at the same time killing off the prisoners (*Kolyma* 126).

Some people in the Kolyma camps were targeted for especially severe treatment. Conquest reports that any person who had the letter "T" (for Trotskyite) on his dossier was the subject of a special instruction: "During detention forbid all use of post and telegraph. Use only for the hardest labour, report on the conduct of the accused once every three months." This, Conquest adds, "was a passport to death" (*Kolyma* 102). Another targeted group was the *katorzhnik* serving *katorga*, or hard penal servitude (usually with a twenty- to twenty-five year sentence), who were treated worst of all. Nationalists from minority groups fighting for independence were often in this category. They were used only for hard physical labour. They were transported in chains. They lived in barracks and slept on bare boards in three tiers, without straw mattresses or blankets, so that they never dared to take off any of their wet clothes. They were granted a blanket only after three years of good conduct. All contact with the outside world was forbidden to them. Conquest bluntly states: "They did not survive"(*Kolyma* 102). Extrapolating from information from camp survivors, records relating to the shipment of prisoners into the camps, and other sources, Conquest estimates that about one-quarter of inmates died annually in this camp system, for a total of some three million deaths for the years 1932-1953, the year that Stalin died. He calculates both a high and a low estimate of the total number of prisoners, the low estimate being 3.5 million and the high estimate being 5 to 6 million (*Kolyma* 227-228). If the lower figures were accurate, the death rate would be about fifty per cent; if the higher figures were closer to the truth, the death rate would have been 89 per cent. Giżejewska's estimates, largely derived from reports of former Polish inmates in the camps, are even higher. She states that up to 1949 thirty to forty per cent of prisoners died annually in Kolyma. In the more distant camps such as Čukotka and Indirka, the mortality rate was as high as 80 per cent during severe winters. [See Małgorzata Giżejewska, "Die Einzigartigkeit und der besondere Charakter der Konzentrationslager in Kolyma und die Möglichkeit des Überlebens," *Lager, Zwangsarbeit, Vertreibung und Deportation: Dimensionenen der Massenverbrechen in der Sowjetunion und in Deutschland 1933 bis 1945*, ed. Dattmar Dahlmann and Gerhard Hirschfeld (Essen: Klartext Verlag, 1999) 248].

Notes

Introduction

[1] Stephen Katz, *The Holocaust in Historical Context. Vol. I: The Holocaust and Mass Death before the Modern Age* (New York: Oxford University Press, 1994) 28.

[2] Yehuda Bauer, *The Holocaust in Historical Perspective* (Seattle: University of Washington Press) 32.

[3] Frank Chalk and Kurt Jonassohn, *The History and Sociology of Genocide: Analyses and Case Studies* (New Haven: Yale University Press, 1990) 323-377. Although it isn't quite clear, by ultimate ideological genocide Chalk and Jonassohn appear to mean that the Nazi destruction of European Jewry is the most clear or the most extreme example of a situation where the destruction of a people was part and parcel of a program to implant a system of beliefs, or an ideology, in the social environment.

[4] Deborah Lipstadt, *Denying the Holocaust: The Growing Assault on Truth and Memory* (New York: Free Press, 1993) 215.

[5] Wasyl Hryshko, *The Ukrainian Holocaust of 1933*, ed. and trans. Marco Carynnyk (Toronto: Bahriany Foundation, 1983) 109.

[6] Robert Conquest, *The Great Terror: A Reassessment* (Edmonton: University of Alberta Press, 1990) 487.

[7] Vahakn N. Dadrian, "A Typology of Genocide", *International Review of Modern Sociology* 5:2 (1975) 201-212. Also, Richard G. Hovannisian, *The Armenian Holocaust: A Bibliography Relating to the Deportations, Massacres, and Dispersion of the Armenian People, 1915-1923* (Cambridge, MA: Armenian Heritage Press, 1980).

[8] William Schawcross, *The Quality of Mercy: Cambodia, Holocaust and Modern Conscience* (New York: Simon & Schuster, 1984).

[9] Thornton sees the arrival of the Europeans as the beginning of a long holocaust that, "although it did not come in ovens as it did for the Jews," brought ravages, killings, and diseases that, as in the case of the Jews, led to the death of millions. Russell Thornton, *American Indian Holocaust and Survival: A Population History since 1492* (Norman: University of Oklahoma Press, 1987) XV. Stannard calls the destruction of the Native peoples of the Americas a holocaust because he sees both the Nazi destruction of the Jews and the genocides in the Americas as a product of European Christian beliefs and racist ideas. David E. Stannard, *American Holocaust: The Conquest of the New World* (New York: Oxford University Press, 1993).

[10] Norman Rufus Colin Cohn, *Warrant for Genocide: The Myth of the Jewish World-Conspiracy* (London: Eyre Spottiswoode, 1967); H.R. Trevor-Roper, *Religion, the Reformation and Social Change* (London: Macmillan, 1967).

[11] Thus, Anderson describes the *hêrem*, or the ancient Israelite practice, as in the case of the idolaters, of destroying an entire group, as a "holocaust or sacrifice." Bernard Anderson, *Understanding the Old Testament* (Edgewood Cliffs, NJ: Prentice Hall, 1957) 129, 138.

[12] Martin H. Manser and Nigel D. Turton, *The Penguin Wordmaster Dictionary* (Harmondsworth, Middlesex: Penguin Books, 1987): 334. Also, Henry George Liddell and Robert Scott, comp., *A Greek-English Lexicon*, new (9th) edition (Oxford: Clarendon Press, 1961): 1217.

[13] Francois Chamoux, *The Civilization of Greece*, trans. W.S. Maguinnes (New York: Simon & Schuster, 1965) 228.

[14] Raphael Lemkin, *Axis Rule in Occupied Europe* (Washington: University Press of America, 1944) 92.

[15] Lemkin 79-82.

[16] Dadrian, "A Typology of Genocide" 204.

[17] Dadrian, "A Typology of Genocide" 205-211.

[18] Helen Fein, "Scenarios of Genocide: Models of Genocide and Critical Responses," *Toward the Understanding and Prevention of Genocide*, ed. Israel W. Charney (London: Westview Press, 1984) 3-31. Fein essentially divides society into two groups. One group consists of people who are within a society's universe of obligation in an exclusionary social order. Offences against them call forth punishment of whatever kind. On the other hand, crimes committed against the "other," or those outside the universe of obligation, are not socially recognized or labelled as crimes.

[19] Helen Fein, "Towards a Sociological Definition of Genocide," unpublished paper presented at the International Studies Association conference, St Louis, 2 April, 1988: 9.

[20] For Kuper's analysis, see Leo Kuper, *The Prevention of Genocide* (New Haven, CT: Yale University Press, 1985) 148-170.

[21] Roger W. Smith, "Human Destructiveness and Politics: The Twentieth Century as an Age of Genocide," *Genocide and the Modern Age: Etiology and Case Studies of Mass Death*, ed. Isidor Wallimann and Michael Dobrowski (Westport, CT: Greenwood Press, 1987) 24-29.

[22] Chalk and Jonassohn, *History and Sociology of Genocide* 23.

[23] Chalk and Jonassohn, *History and Sociology of Genocide* 29.

[24] Ward Churchill, *A Little Matter of Genocide: Holocaust and Denial in the Americas, 1492 to the Present*, (San Francisco: City Lights, 1997) 424.

[25] Stannard 279.

[26] Churchill 31-80, 424-429.

[27] Churchill 431-437. Churchill makes an important contribution to our understanding of genocide by pointing out the limitations of a definition with direct targeting as its core feature. At the same time, his endeavour to present a more inclusive definition at times presents problems. This becomes evident, for example, when Churchill speaks of degrees of genocide. The concept itself is ambiguous. It

becomes essentially impossible to determine what the nature of the perpetrator's action is when Churchill discusses his concept of "genocide in the fourth degree", which he sees as resulting, not from any direct action, but from the predator's "depraved indifference."

[28] Peter Novick, *The Holocaust in American Life* (New York: Houghton Mifflin Company, 1999) 133.

[29] Vinay Lal, "Genocide, Barbaric Others, and Violence Categories: A Response to Omer Bartov," *The American Historical Review* 103:4 (October 1998): 1188.

[30] Omer Bartov, "Forum Essay: Response Reply," *The American Historical Review* 103:4 (October 1998): 1194.

[31] Stannard, X.

[32] W. J. Eccles, *France in America* (New York: Harper and Row, 1972) 95-101.

[33] Robert K. Yin, *Case Study Research: Design and Methods* (Beverly Hills, CA.: Sage Publications, 1984) 108.

[34] Barrington Moore Jr., *Social Origins of Dictatorship and Democracy: Lord and Peasant in the Making of the Modern World* (Boston: Beacon Press, 1967).

Chapter 1

[1] Norman Rufus Colin Cohn, *Warrant for Genocide: the Myth of the Jewish World Conspiracy and the Protocols of the elders of Zion* (London: Eyre & Spottiswoode); Yehuda Bauer, *The Holocaust in Historical Perspective* (Seattle: University of Washington Press) 9.

[2] Barrington Moore Jr., *Moral Purity and Persecution in History* (Princeton, NJ: Princeton University Press, 2000) 26.

[3] David E. Stannard, *American Holocaust: The Conquest of the New World*, (New York: Oxford University Press) 177-178.

[4] This and all subsequent excerpts were taken from the Revised Standard Version.

[5] Gonzalo Baez-Camargo, *Archaeological Commentary on the Bible* (New York: Doubleday, 1984) 66.

[6] E.M. Good, "Joshua, Book of," *The Interpreter's Dictionary of the Bible: An Illustrated Encyclopedia*, ed. G.A. Buttrick (New York: Abingdon Press, 1962): 993. Also see William G. Dever, "Archaeology and the Israelite 'Conquest,'" *The Anchor Bible Dictionary* 3, ed. David Noel Freedman et al. (New York: Doubleday, 1992): 556.

[7] Dever, "Archaeology and the Israelite 'Conquest'" 548.

[8] William F. Albright, *The Archaeology of Palestine*, rev. ed. (Harmondsworth: Penguin Books, 1956).

[9] Baez-Camargo 66.

[10] Peter C. Craigie, *The Old Testament: Its Background, Growth and Content* (Burlington, ON: Welch Publishing, 1986) 101.

[11] Baez-Camargo 58-66.

[12] Dever, "Archaeology and the Israelite 'Conquest'" 545-558.

[13] William G. Dever, "Archaeology and the Emergence of early Israel," *Archaeology and Biblical Interpretation*, ed. John R. Bartlett (London and New York:

Routledge, 1997) 22-24, 47-48.

[14] Dever, "Archaeology and the Emergence of early Israel" 47.

[15] Others one might mention include Philip R. Davies, *In Search of 'Ancient Israel'* (Sheffield: JSOT Press, 1992); Keith W. Whitelam, *The Invention of Ancient Israel: the silencing of Palestinian History* (London: Routledge, 1996); Thomas L. Thompson, *Biblical Archaeology and the Myth of Israel* (New York: Basic Books, 1999); Philip Davies, "What separates a Minimalist from a Maximalist? Not Much" *Biblical Archaeology Review* 26:2 (March/April 2000): 26-27,72-73; Israel Finkelstein and Neil A. Silberman, *The Bible Unearthed* (New York, NY: Free Press, 2001).

[16] Ken R. Dark, *Theoretical Archaeology* (Ithaca, NY: Cornell University Press, 1995).

[17] G. Boling et al., *Joshua: A New Translation with Notes and Commentary* (New York: Doubleday, 1982), 77.

[18] Boling et al., 54-72.

[19] The record of events of a later date suggests that the endeavour to destroy the original inhabitants of Palestine continued on after Joshua. Thus, we read in Samuel that God commanded Saul to totally wipe out the Amel' ekites, to not spare them, but "kill both man and woman, infant and suckling, ox and sheep, camel and ass," for their opposing Israel on the way to the Holy Land (1 Samuel 15:2-3). After Saul defeated the Amal' ekites from Hav' elah as far as Shur, east of Egypt, he destroyed all the people with the edge of the sword. However, he saved Agog, the king, as well as the choicest livestock. Samuel criticized Saul for not carrying out the Lord's command, for he was to "utterly destroy the sinners," the Amal' ekites, "and fight against them until they are consumed" (1 Samuel 15:18).

David also totally destroyed the original inhabitants he conquered who still remained in the land (the Gir' zites, Gesh'erites, Amal' ekites), while he was hiding from Saul and lived among the Philistines (1 Samuel 27:8-12). It seems such destruction was directed only against the remnant of people who were left following the initial conquest. The Israelites followed a different pattern of warfare with later arrivals, such as the Philistines. In this case, either one group or the other generally sought to enslave its enemy. At the same time, the Israelites sought to drive the Philistines out of the Israelite cities the latter had conquered (See for example, 1 Samuel 4:9-12, and 1 Samuel 7:13-14). Attitudes toward the original inhabitants also changed in time. Thus, we read that at the height of Israelite glory under Solomon, all the people "who were left of the Amorites, the Hittites, the Per' izzites, the Hivites, and Jeb' usites, who were not of the people of Israel—their descendants who were left after them in the land, whom the people of Israel were unable to destroy utterly—these Solomon made a forced levy of slaves..." (1 Kings 9:20-22).

[20] Craigie 266-267. This interpretation is also shared by Baez-Camargo 58.

[21] Yvon Garlan, *War in the Ancient World: A Social History*, trans. Janet Lloyd (New York: W.W. Norton, 1975) 71. Also see T. Jacobsen, "Sumer," *The Encyclopedia of Ancient Civilizations*, ed. Arthur Cotterell (London:Macmillan, 1983): 79.

[22] Whereas for the Israelites the destruction was part of establishing a territory where they would be able to create an environment in which they would be able to worship their God without fear of contamination of other people, the Moabites, who according to the biblical record were the descendants of Abraham's nephew

Lot, viewed the ban, or the destruction of the inhabitants of an entire locality that was conquered, strictly as a sacrifice to their deity. Thus, Mesha, son of KMSH[YT], king of Moab, reports of his having taken Nebo from Israel, following which he slew all the inhabitants, consisting of seven thousand men, women and children, for he had consecrated it to Ashtar-Chemosh. See Gerd Lüdemann, *The Unholy in Holy Scripture: The Dark Side of the Bible*, trans. John Bowden (Louisville, KY: Westminster John Knox Press, 1997) 45. Lüdemann adds that the Moabite inscription, dating from the year 830 BCE, which is very similar to biblical Hebrew, suggests that the Moabite practice of the ban may be attributed to the common background of the Israelites and Moabites (Lüdemann 45-46). While the Moabites were still practising the ban in 830 BC, it appears the Israelites had given up the practice during the reign of Solomon (965-928 BC), for, rather than attempt to slaughter the descendants of the original inhabitants of Canaan, he enslaved them and used them to build the Lord's temple.

[23] O.R.Gurney, "The Hittites" *Encyclopedia of Ancient Civilizations*, ed. Arthur Cotterell (London: Macmillan, 1983): 115. Also see Johannes Lehmann, *The Hittites: People of a Thousand Gods*, trans. J. Maxwell Brownjohn (New York: Viking Press, 1977) 266-267.

[24] A.K. Grayson,"Assyria," *Encyclopedia of Ancient Civilizations*, ed. Arthur Cotterell (London: Macmillan, 1983): 106.

[25]Thucydides, *The Poloponnesian War*, trans. Rex Warner (London: Cassell, 1962) 360.

[26] Fustel De Coulanges, *The Ancient City: A Study on Religion, Laws, and Institutions of Greece and Rome* (Garden City, New York: Doubleday, 1956) 207.

[27] B.H. Warmington, *Carthage* (London: Robert Hale, 1980) 124-127, 196-209.

Chapter 2

[1] H. R. Trevor-Roper, *Religion, the Reformation and Social Change* (London: Macmillan, 1967) 165.

[2] Adolf Leschnitzer, *The Magic Background of Modern Anti-Semitism: An Analysis of the German-Jewish Relationship* (New York: International Universities Press, 1956) 98-99.

[3] Norman Rufus Colin Cohn, *Warrant for Genocide: The Myth of the Jewish World-Conspiracy* (London: Eyre and Spottiswoode, 1967).

[4] Christina Larner, *Witchcraft and Religion: The Politics of Popular Belief* (Oxford: Basil Blackwell, 1984) 88.

[5] Brian P. Levack, *The Witch-Hunt in Early Modern Europe*, second edition (New York: Longman, 1995) 9.

[6] Pennethorne Hughes, *Witchcraft* (Harmondsworth, Middlesex: Penguin, 1965) 167-169.

[7] Hughes 179.

[8] Levack, *The Witch-Hunt in Early Modern Europe* 28-29.

[9] J. Bossy, "Moral Arithmetic: Seven Sins into Ten Commandments," *Conscience and Casuistry in early Modern Europe*, ed. E. Leites (Cambridge: Cambridge Univer-

sity Press, 1988) 229-231.

[10] Dana Carleton Munro, ed., *Translations and Reprints from the Original Sources of European History*, vol. 3 (Philadelphia: The Department of History of the University of Pennsylvania, 1896) 26-28.

[11] Levack, *The Witch-Hunt in Early Modern Europe* 127.

[12] Larner, *Witchcraft and Religion* 90-91.

[13] Richard Kieckhefer, *European Witch Trials: Their Foundation in Popular and Learned Culture, 1300-1500* (Berkeley: University of California Press, 1976) 16-18.

[14] Levack, *The Witch-Hunt in Early Modern Europe* 198-199.

[15] Levack, *The Witch-Hunt in Early Modern Europe* 194-195. It appears that the size of a particular jurisdiction had a significant influence on the hunts. Levack divides Germany into two regions, one which experienced much more intense witch-hunting than the other. Territories that tended to exercise relative restraint were located in the north and the east, where also relatively large states were located. The main hunts occurred in the south and west, where smaller, more fragmented political units were located, including Würzburg, Bamberg and Ellwangen. By contrast, the large south-eastern principality of Bavaria executed comparatively few witches for a political unit its size. Levack concludes that in particular the smaller, more fragmented political units, which no doubt were more insecure and would have given a dominant personality paramount influence, made possible the extremes in which witch-hunts expressed themselves in Germany.

[16] H.C. Midelfort, *Witch Hunting in Southwestern Germany, 1562-1684: The Social and Intellectual Foundations* (Stanford: Stanford University Press, 1972) 98-100.

[17] Christina Larner, "Crimen Exceptum? The Crime of Witchcraft in Europe," *Witch-Hunting in Early Modern Europe*, vol. 3, ed. Brian P. Levack (New York: Garland Publishing, 1992) 3: 82.

[18] Rossell Hope Robbins, *The Encyclopedia of Witchcraft and Demonology* (New York: Crown Publishers, 1959): 515.

[19] Levack, *The Witch-Hunt in Early Modern Europe* 196.

[20] Levack, *The Witch-Hunt in Early Modern Europe* 196.

[21] M.Gielis, "The Netherlandic Theologians' Views of Witchcraft and the Devil's Pact," *Witchcraft in the Netherlands: from the Fourteenth to the Twentieth Century*, ed. Marijke Gijswijt-Hofstra and Willem Frijhoff (Rotterdam: Universitaire Pers., 1991) 37-52.

[22] Jens Christian V. Johansen, "Denmark: The Sociology of Accusations," *Early Modern Witchcraft: Centres and Peripheries*, ed. Bengt Ankarloo and Gustav Henningsen (Oxford: Clarendon Press, 1990) 340.

[23] Bengt Ankarloo, "Sweden: The Mass Burnings 1668-1676," *Early Modern Witchcraft; Centres and Peripheries*, ed. Bengt Ankarloo and Gustav Henningsen (Oxford: Clarendon Press, 1990) 285-317.

[24] Antero Heikkinnen and Timo Kervinen, "Finland: The Male Domination," *Early Modern European Witchcraft: Centres and Peripheries*," ed. B. Ankarloo and G. Henningsen (Oxford: Clarendon Press, 1990) 320.

[25] Levack, *The Witch-Hunt in Early Modern Europe* 216-218.

[26] Levack, *The Witch-Hunt in Early Modern Europe* 218-220.

[27] Russell Zguta, "Was there a Witch-Craze in Muscovite Russia?" *Southern Folklore Quarterly* 40 (1977): 125. Also, Valerie A. Kivelson, "Through the Prism of

Witchcraft: Gender and Social Change in Seventeeth-Century Muscovy," *Russia's Women: Accomodation, Resistance, Transformation,* ed. B.E. Evans, B.A. Engel and C.D. Worobec (Berkeley: University of California Press, 1991) 74-94.

[28] Levack, *The Witch-Hunt in Early Modern Europe* 225-227.

[29] Larner, "Crimen Exceptum?" 80.

[30] Penelope Shuttle and Peter Redgrave, *The Wise Wound: Menstruation and Everywoman* (London: Paladin Grafton Books, 1986) 201.

[31] Alan Macfarlane, "Murray's Theory: Exposition and Comment," *Witchcraft and Sorcery,* 2nd edition, enlarged and revised, ed. Max Marwick (New York: Penguin Books, 1982) 234.

[32] Norman Rufus Colin Cohn, *Europe's Inner Demons: An Enquiry Inspired by the Great-Witch-Hunt* (London: Sussex University Press, 1975) 255.

[33] Trevor-Roper 126-127.

[34] Trevor-Roper 72.

[35] Larner, *Witchcraft and Religion* 90.

[36] Hughes 195.

[37] Robin Briggs, *Witches and Neighbours: The Social and Cultural Context of European Witchcraft* (London: Harper Collins, 1996) 399-400.

[38] Levack, *The Witch-Hunt in Early Modern Europe* 25.

[39] Elizabeth E. Bacon, "Witchcraft," *The Encyclopedia Americana,* International Edition, vol. 29 (1994): 84.

[40] Marion L. Starkey, "Witchcraft," *Collier's Encyclopedia,* vol. 23 (1992): 551.

[41] Larner, "Crimen Exceptum?" 80.

Chapter 3

[1] Robert Melson, "Provocation or Nationalism: A Critical Inquiry into the Armenian Genocide of 1915," *The Armenian Genocide in Perspective,* ed. Richard G. Hovannisian (New Brunswick, NJ: Transaction Books, 1986) 80-84.

[2] Frank Chalk and Kurt Jonassohn, *The History and Sociology of Genocide: Analyses and Case Studies* (New Haven, CT: Yale University Press, 1990) 249-250.

[3] Henry Morgenthau, *Ambassador Morgenthau's Story* (Garden City, NY: Doubleday and Page, 1918) 302-305.

[4] Arnold J. Toynbee, "A Summary of Armenian History up to and Including 1915," *The Treatment of Armenians in the Ottoman Empire: Documents Presented to Viscount Grey of Fallodon, Secretary of State for Foreign Affairs* (London: HMSO, 1916) 640.

[5] Toynbee 642-645.

[6] Tessa Hofmann, "German Eyewitness Reports of the Genocide of the Armenians, 1915-16," *A Crime of Silence: The Armenian Genocide, The Permanent People's Tribunal,* ed. Gerald J. Libaridian (London: Zed Books, 1985) 66.

[7] Toynbee 648.

[8] Toynbee 649.

[9] Toynbee 650.

[10] Toynbee 651.

[11] Aram Andonian, *The Memoirs of Naim Bey*, second reprinting (Newton Square, PA: Armenian Historical Research Association, 1965) xiii-xiv.

[12] Melson, "Provocation or Nationalism" 66.

[13] Dickran Boyajian, *Armenia: The Case for a Forgotten Genocide* (Westwood, NJ: Educational Book Crafters, 1972) 287.

[14] R. Hrair Dekmejian, "Determinants of Genocide: Armenians and Jews as Case Studies," *The Armenian Genocide in Perspective*, ed. Richard G. Hovannisian (New Brunswick, N.J.: Transaction Books, 1986) 87.

[15] Melson, "Provocation or Nationalism" 83.

[16] Morgenthau 351-352.

[17] Leo Kuper, "The Turkish Genocide of Armenians, 1915 - 1917," *The Armenian Genocide in Perspective*, ed. Richard G. Hovannisian (New Brunswick, NJ: Transaction Books, 1986) 52.

[18] Bernard Lewis, *The Emergence of Modern Turkey*, 2nd edition (Oxford: Oxford University Press for the Royal Institute of International Affairs, 1961) 356.

[19] Melson, "Provocation or Nationalism" 69.

[20] Dekmejian, "Determinants of Genocide" 89.

[21] U. Heyd, *Foundations of Turkish Nationalism: The Life and Teachings of Ziya Gölkap* (London: Luzac, 1950) 29.

[22] Kuper, "The Turkish Genocide of Armenians, 1915-1917" 56.

[23] Dadrian mentions this as a fear directing Turkish action. Vahakn N. Dadrian, *Warrant for Genocide: Key Elements of Turko-Armenian Conflict* (New Brunswick: NJ: Transaction Publishers, 1999) 126-27.

[24] Kuper, "The Turkish Genocide of Armenians, 1915-1917" 56-57.

[25] Dekmejian, "Determinants of Genocide" 93.

Chapter 4

[1] Wasyl Hryshko, *The Ukrainian Holocaust of 1933*, ed. and trans. Marco Carynnyk (Toronto: Bahriany Foundation, 1983) 109.

[2] Robert Conquest, *Stalin: Breaker of Nations* (New York: Viking Penguin, 1991) 319-327.

[3] For an account of this famine, see Roman Serbyn, "The Famine of 1921-1923: A Model for 1932-1933?" *Famine in Ukraine 1932 - 1933*, ed. Roman Serbyn and Bohdan Krawchenko (Edmonton: Canadian Institute of Ukrainian Studies, 1986) 147-178.

[4] Nicolas Werth, "Un État contre son peuple: Violence, répressions, terreurs en Union soviétique," *Le livre noir du communisme: Crimes, terreur et répression* (Paris: Éditions Robert Lafont, 1997) 159.

[5] Robert Conquest, *Reflections on a Ravaged Century* (London: John Murray, 1999) 93.

[6] Alan Bullock, *Hitler and Stalin: Parallel Lives* (London: Harper Collins, 1993) 277.

[7] Michael Kort, *The Soviet Colossus: History and Aftermath*, 4th ed. (New York: M.E. Sharpe, 1996) 172-174.

[8] Bullock 273.

[9] Bullock 171-172.

[10] Werth 188.

[11] Orest Subtelney, *Ukraine: A History*, 3rd ed. (Toronto: University of Toronto Press, 2000) 413.

[12] Robert Conquest, *The Harvest of Sorrow* (Edmonton: The University of Alberta Press, 1987) 230.

[13] Conquest, *Harvest of Sorrow* 240.

[14] Conquest, *Harvest of Sorrow* 234.

[15] Conquest, *Harvest of Sorrow* 235-236.

[16] Conquest, *Harvest of Sorrow* 237.

[17] Conquest, *Harvest of Sorrow* 238.

[18] Conquest, *Harvest of Sorrow* 238.

[19] Conquest, *Harvest of Sorrow* 244.

[20] Conquest, *Harvest of Sorrow* 247.

[21] Conquest, *Harvest of Sorrow* 248.

[22] Conquest, *Harvest of Sorrow* 249.

[23] Conquest, *Reflections on a Ravaged Century* 96.

[24] Conquest, *Harvest of Sorrow* 250.

[25] Conquest, *Harvest of Sorrow* 259.

[26] Kort 169.

[27] Bullock 459.

[28] Kort 190.

[29] J. N. Westwood, *Endurance and Endeavour: Russian History, 1812-1992*, 4th ed. (Oxford: Oxford University Press, 1993) 321.

[30] Bullock 476.

[31] Westwood 322.

[32] Bullock 484.

[33] Bullock 489.

[34] Bullock 490.

[35] Westwood 325.

[36] Westwood 326.

[37] Robert Conquest, "Excess Deaths and Camp Numbers: Some Comments," *Soviet Studies* 43:5 (1991): 949-952. Also, Bullock 501-502.

[38] Stéphane Courtois, "Pourquoi," *Le livre noir du communisme: Crimes, terreur et répression* (Paris: Éditions Robert Laffont, S.A.,1997) 799.

[39] Courtois, "Pourquoi" 798.

[40] Dmitrii A. Volkogonov, *Stalin: Triumph and Tragedy*, ed. and trans. Harold Shukman (New York: Grove Weidenfeld, 1991) 549.

[41] Volkogonov 547.

[42] N. Berdyaev, *The Origin of Russian Communism* (Ann Arbor: University of Michigan Press, 1962) 183-184.

[43] Gonzalo Baez-Camargo, *Archaeological Commentary on the Bible* (New York: Doubleday, 1984) 59.

[44] Berdyaev 144.

[45] Berdyaev 144.

[46] Hryshko 19, 110.

[47] Courtois, "Pourquoi" 811-816.

[48] Lev Kopelev, *To be Preserved Forever*, trans. Anthony Austin (New York: J.B. Lippincott, 1977) 11-12.

[49] Quoted in Glen Allen, "The Harvest of Sorrow: Soviet Collectivization and the Terror-Famine," *MacLean's*, 15 December 1986: 56.

[50] Hryshko 110-111.

[51] Miron Dolot, *Execution by Hunger: The Hidden Holocaust* (New York: W.W. Norton, 1985) 35, 46, 104, 210. See also Olexa Woropay, *The Ninth Circle* (Cambridge, MA: Harvard University Press, 1983) 37-40.

[52] Dolot, *Execution by Hunger* 18.

[53] Vasilii Grossman, *Forever Flowing*, trans. T. Whitney (New York: Harper and Row, 1972) 142-144.

[54] Conquest gives examples of doctors being required to falsify death statistics and of people being killed for trying to record their experiences in the Kolyma Gulag camp system. See Robert Conquest, *Kolyma: The Arctic Death Camps* (New York: Viking Press, 1978) 60, 92.

[55] Marco Carynnyk, "Blind Eye to Murder: Britain, the United States and the Ukrainian famine of 1933," *Famine in the Ukraine 1932-1933*, ed. Roman Serbyn and Bohdan Krawchenko (Edmonton: Canadian Institute of Ukrainian Studies, 1986) 109-138.

[56] Marco Carynnyk, "Making the News Fit to Print: Walter Duranty, the New York Times and the Ukrainian famine of 1933," *Famine in Ukraine 1932-1933*, ed. Roman Serbyn and Bohdan Krawchenko (Edmonton: Canadian Institute of Ukrainian Studies, 1986) 67-95.

[57] For a discussion of attitudes and beliefs that made this possible, see Conquest, *Reflections on a Ravaged Century* 124-149.

[58] See, for example, J. Arch Getty, Gábor T. Rittersporn, and Victor N. Zemskov, "Victims of the Soviet Penal System in the Pre-War Years: A First Approach on the Basis of Archival Evidence," *American Historical Review* 98:4 (October 1993): 1017-1049. The writers essentially take the statistics provided by the Gulag Archives at face value, using them to try to settle what they describe as the debate between Cold War Warriors whom they see as attempting to magnify the destructive nature of the Gulag camp system and the "revisionists," who take the opposite view. They use the statistics to argue that the information in the Gulag Archives supports the revisionists. For other perspectives on the debate, see Edwin Bacon, *The Gulag at War: Stalin's Forced Labour System in the Light of the Archives* (London: Macmillan Press in association with the Center for Russian and East European Studies, University of Birmingham, 1994) 24-25. Commenting on the debate regarding numbers, Anne Applebaum presents figures different people have arrived at regarding deaths in the Gulag or resulting from expulsion. At the same time, she presents figures derived from the Gulag Archives. See Anne Applebaum, *Gulag: A History* (New York: Doubleday, 2003) 578-586. She concludes that to date "no completely satisfactory death statistics for either the Gulag or the exile system have yet appeared" (Applebaum, 582). The statistics given in this work must therefore be considered estimates that the author, after looking at the evidence presented in the different sources, considered to be the most reliable.

[59] Otto J. Pohl, *The Stalinist Penal System: A Statistical History of Soviet Repression*

and Terror, 1930-53 (Jefferson, NC: McFarland 1997) 139-141.

[60] See, for example, Ralf Stettner, *"Archipel GULag": Stalins Zwangslager - Terrorinstrument und Wirtschaftsgigant: Entstehung, Organisation und Funktion des sowjetischen Lagersystems 1928-1956* (Paderborn: Verlag Ferdinand Schöningh, 1996) 217-223. See also Małgorzata Giżejewska, "Die Einzigartigkeit und der besondere Charakter der Konzentrationslager in Kolyma und die Möglichkeit des Überlebens," *Lager, Zwangsarbeit, Vertreibung und Deportation: Dimensionenen der Massenverbrechen in der Sowjetunion und in Deutschland 1933 bis 1945,* ed. Dattmar Dahlmann and Gerhard Hirschfeld (Essen: Klartext Verlag, 1999) 245-260.

[61] Commenting on the death figures during the famine between 1932 and 1933, Werth states that the Ukraine paid the heaviest penalty, with at least four million deaths ("Un État contre son peuple" 185). Conquest states that some 4 to 5 million people died in Ukraine as a result of the famine (*Reflections on a Ravaged Century* 96).

[62] Pohl 72-90.

[63] Pohl 116. Robert Conquest, *The Nation Killers: The Soviet Deportation of Nationalities* (London: Macmillan, 1970) 162. There is a discrepancy between the statistics provided by Pohl and Conquest. Using Gulag archives statistics, Pohl states that about 21.5 of the Crimean Tartar population died between 1944 and 1950. Conquest argues that 46.3 per cent of Crimean Tartars were destroyed as a result of the expulsions. The difference in the two figures appears to result from Conquest's estimating Crimean Tartar losses higher, in particular during the expulsions, than does Pohl. Conquest refers to Tartar sources that state that casualties had been heavy during the round-up and the deportation, in particular during the latter. Sources he consulted mention people having been on the train without food for no less than eleven days, with many of the people on board dying of starvation.

Chapter 5

[1] In this context, Nolte describes the Nazi view of the Jew as being a "biologistisch umgeprägte Kopie des socialen Originals." Ernst Nolte, *Der Europäische Bürgerkrieg 1917-1945: Nationalismus und Bolschewismus* (Berlin: Propyläen Verlag, 1987) 517.

[2] Courtois, "Les crimes du communisme," *Livre noir du communisme: Crimes, terreur et répression* (Paris: Éditions Robert Laffont, 1997) 26-27.

[3] H.R. Trevor-Roper, *Religion, the Reformation and Social Change* (London: Macmillan, 1967); Norman Rufus Colin Cohn, *Warrant for Genocide: The Myth of the Jewish World-Conspiracy* (London: Eyre and Spottiswoode, 1967), and Adolf Leschnitzer, *The Magic Background of Modern Anti-Semitism: An Analysis of the German-Jewish Relationship* (New York: International University Press, 1956).

[4] Irving Abrahamson, ed., *Against Silence: The Voice and Vision of Elie Wiesel,* vol. 1 (New York: Holocaust Library, 1985) 33.

[5] Hyam Maccoby, "Theologian of the Holocaust," *Commentary,* 19 Dec. 1982: 34.

[6] Yehuda Bauer, *The Holocaust in Historical Perspective* (Seattle: University of

272   Notes to Chapter 5

Washington Press, 1978) 9.

[7] Norbert Frei, *National Socialist Rule in Germany: The Führer State*, trans. Simon B. Steyne (Oxford: Blackwell Publishers, 1993) 123.

[8] Klaus P. Fischer, *Nazi Germany: A New History* (New York: Continuum Publishing, 1995) 383.

[9] Henry Friedlander, *The Origins of the Nazi Genocide: From Euthanasia to the Final Solution* (Chapel Hill: University of North Carolina Press, 1995) 10-19.

[10] Michael R. Marrus, *The Holocaust in History* (Hanover, NH: University Press of New England, 1987) 13.

[11] Fischer 389-390.

[12] Frank Rector, *The Nazi Extermination of Homosexuals* (New York: Stein and Day, 1981) 120-121.

[13] Saul Friedländer, *Nazi Germany and the Jews*, vol. 1: *The Years of Persecution, 1933-1939* (New York: HarperCollins, 1997) 206.

[14] Friedlander 246-262; 291-294.

[15] Donald Kenrick and Gratton Puxon, *The Destiny of Europe's Gypsies* (New York: Basic Books, 1972) 66-70.

[16] Michael Zimmermann, *Rassenutopie und Genozid: Die nationalsozialistische "Lösung der Zigeunerfrage"* (Hamburg: Hans Christians Verlag, 1996) 371.

[17] George L. Mosse, *Toward the Final Solution: A History of European Racism* (Madison: University of Wisconsin Press, 1987) 217-220.

[18] Friedländer 40.

[19] Nolte 513-515.

[20] Raul Hilberg, "The Anatomy of the Holocaust," *Holocaust: Ideology, Bureaucracy, and Genocide. The San José Papers,* ed. Henry Friedlander and Sybil Milton (New York: Kraus International Publications, 1980) 87-100.

[21] Martin Gilbert, "Final Solution," *The Oxford Companion to World War II*, ed. I.C.B. Deer (Oxford: Oxford University Press, 1995) 364-368.

[22] Brian Mark Rigg, *Hitler's Jewish Soldiers: The Untold Story of Nazi Racial Laws and Men of Jewish Descent in the German Military* (Lawrence, Kansas: University Press of Kansas, 2002) 88. Rigg adds that although so-called half and quarter Jews could serve, they could not hold positions of authority.

[23] Friedländer 242-243.

[24] There appears to be a disagreement as to the exact figures. For example, Fischer *(Nazi Germany: A New History* 499) states that some 503, 000 Jews lived in Germany in 1933, with the number being reduced to 234,000 by 1939. Rigg, on the other hand, gives a figure of 600,000 Jews in Germany in 1933, with 328,167 remaining in Germany by 1939. Rigg, *Hitler`s Jewish Soldiers* 59. The estimates given in the text are based on these figures.

[25] Here it may be helpful to point out that the term *Endlösung* (final solution) had multiple meanings and evolved under the Nazis. In his discussion of the Nazi attack on the Jews, Naimark, for example, gives insight into how the Nazi program of *Endlösung,* or their "final solution," which prior to the outbreak of war concentrated on dealing with what they saw as the Jewish problem through forced emigration, evolved to where the term *Endlösung* took on the meaning generally attached to it now, with the term being synonymous with a program of mass de-

struction. Norman M. Naimark, *Fires of Hatred: Ethnic Cleansing in Twentieth-Century Europe* (Cambridge, MA: Harvard University Press, 2001) 63-81.

[26] Fischer 393.

[27] Friedländer 312.

[28] Gilbert 364-368.

[29] Gilbert 367.

[30] Friedländer 219.

[31] Bullock 747-748.

[32] Christian Gerlach, "Die Wannsee-Konferenz, das Schicksal der deutschen Juden und Hitlers politische Grundsatzenscheidigung, alle Juden Europas zu ermorden," *Werkstatt Geschichte* 18 (1997) 9.

[33] Gilbert 367-369.

[34] Gerlach 9.

[35] Gerlach 10.

[36] Gerlach 10.

[37] Gerlach 12-15.

[38] Gerlach 22-31.

[39] Gerlach 22.

[40] Gerlach 24-25.

[41] Gerlach 27-31

[42] Gerlach 42.

[43] Bullock 747-748.

[44] Christopher Browning, "The Euphoria of Victory and the Final Solution: Summer - Fall 1941," *German Studies Review* 17 H. 3 (1994): 473-481.

[45] As Nolte makes quite clear, this view was influenced as much by the perception the Nazis had of the Jews as it was by social reality. Nolte 511-513.

[46] Gerlach 34-40.

[47] Fischer 505-506.

[48] Thomas Sandkühler, "Die Ingangsetzung der "Endlösung" im Generalgouvernement am Beispiel des Distrikts Galizien, 1941/42," *Lager, Zwangsarbeit, Vertreibung und Deportation: Dimensionenen der Massenverbrechen in der Sowjetunion und in Deutschland 1933 bis 1945,* ed. Dattmar Dahlmann and Gerhard Hirschfeld (Essen: Klartext Verlag, 1999) 435-458.

[49] Peter Klein, "Die Rolle der Vernichtungslager Kulmhof (Chełmno), Belzec (Bełżec) und Auschwitz-Birkenau in den frühen Deportationsvorbreitungen," *Lager, Zwangsarbeit, Vertreibung und Deportation: Dimensionenen der Massenverbrechen in der Sowjetunion und in Deutschland 1933 bis 1945,* ed. Dattmar Dahlmann and Gerhard Hirschfeld (Essen: Klartext Verlag, 1999) 459-481.

[50] Bullock 755.

[51] Bullock 746.

[52] Friedlander 284-286.

[53] Fischer 502-504.

[54] Christopher Bennett, *Yugoslavia's Bloody Collapse: Causes, Course and Consequences* (New York: New York University Press, 1995) 48. Milan Nedić was the Quisling leader of the Serb puppet regime set up by the Nazis. He accepted this position because he believed Hitler would win the war. Hitler turned to the Ustašas, a radical revolutionary group, after the most popular Croat leader, Vladko Maček,

refused the Nazi invitation to lead a Croatian puppet regime because he thought Hitler would lose the war.

[55] Fischer 511. A different account is presented by János Gyurgyák, who maintains that the deportation of the Hungarian Jewish population was physically carried out virtually unassisted by the Hungarian state. The Germans simply passed this work on to the Hungarians, placing their trust in the anti-Semitism and greed of a significant minority of the population, the cowardice of the majority and the racism of their servile government. For an elaboration of Gyurgyák's argument, see János Gyurgyák, *A Zsidókérdés Magyarszágon* (Budapest: Osiris, 2001).

[56] Fischer 511.

[57] Jan F. Triska, "'Work Redeems': Concentration Camp Labor and Nazi German Economy," *Journal of Central European Affairs* 19 (April 1959): 17.

[58] George Kren and Leon Rappoport, *The Holocaust and the Crisis of Human Behavior* (New York: Holmes and Meier, 1994) 76.

[59] Fischer 511-512.

[60] Daniel Goldhagen, *Hitler's Willing Executioners: Ordinary Germans and the Holocaust* (London: Little, Brown, 1996).

[61] Norman G. Finkelstein and Ruth Bettina Birn, *A Nation on Trial: The Goldhagen Thesis and Historical Truth* (New York: Henry Holt and Company, 1998). Also, R.B. Birn, "Historiographical Review: Revising the Holocaust," *Historical Journal* 40:1 (1997): 195-215.

[62] Thomas Sandkühler, *"Endlösung" Galizien: Der Judenmord in Ostpolen und die Rettungsinitiativen von Berthold Beitz, 1941-1944* (Bonn: J.H.W. Dietz, 1996). That any analysis dealing with the destruction of European Jewry confine itself not only to Germans is also suggested by Modris Eksteins, *Walking Since Daybreak* (Toronto: Key Porter, 1999) 147-154.

[63] Raul Hilberg, *The Destruction of European Jews* (New York: Holmes and Meier, 1985).

[64] Nolte 516.

[65] Friedländer 324.

[66] Frei 86.

[67] Fischer 513.

[68] Fischer 513.

[69] Fischer 514-515.

[70] Friedlander 187-245.

[71] Friedlander 295-296.

[72] Nolte 500-501.

[73] Lal, "Genocide, Barbaric Others, and Violence Categories: A Response to Omer Bartov," *The American Historical Review* 103:4 (October 1998): 1188.

[74] Nolte 502-503.

[75] Alfred M. De Zayas, *Nemesis at Potsdam: The Anglo-Americans and the Expulsion of the Germans* (London: Routledge and Kagan Paul, 1977).

[76] Wendelin Gruber, *In the Claws of the Red Dragon: Ten Years under Tito's Heel*, trans. Frank Schmidt (Toronto: St Michaelswerk-Toronto, 1988) 19.

[77] Nolte 504-507.

[78] Friedländer 87.

[79] Friedländer 88-106.

Chapter 6

[1] Chalk and Jonassohn, *The History and Sociology of Genocide: Analyses and Case Studies* (New Haven, CT: Yale University Press, 1990) 420.

[2] Chalk and Jonassohn, *History and Sociology of Genocide* 400.

[3] Chandler, *The Tragedy of Cambodian History: Politics, War, and Revolution since 1945* (New Haven: CT: Yale University Press, 1991) 239.

[4] Chandler, *Tragedy of Cambodian History* 239.

[5] William J. Duiker, "Kampuchea," *The Encyclopedia Americana,* international ed., 16 (1987): 276.

[6] Chandler, *The Tragedy of Cambodian History* 249.

[7] François Ponchaud, *Cambodia Zero Hour,* trans. Nancy Amphoux (Harmondsworth: Penguin, 1978) 62-63.

[8] Ponchaud 69.

[9] Ponchaud 70.

[10] Jean-Louis Margolin, "Cambodge: au pays du crime déconcernant," in *Le livre noir du communisme: Crimes, terreur et répression* (Paris: Éditions Robert Laffort, 1997) 639.

[11] David P. Chandler, *Brother Number One: A Political Biography of Pol Pot* (Boulder: Westview Press, 1992) 191-193, 197-198.

[12] Elizabeth Becker, *When the War was Over: The Voices of Cambodia's Revolution and Its People* (New York: Simon and Schuster, 1986) 171-172. Also see Chandler, *Tragedy of Cambodian History* 238, 242.

[13] Chandler, *Tragedy of Cambodian History* 243-244.

[14] Chandler, *Tragedy of Cambodian History* 240-241.

[15] Chandler, "A Revolution in full spate" 169, 175.

[16] Chandler, "A Revolution in full spate" 167.

[17] Chandler, *Tragedy of Cambodian History* 293.

[18] Chandler, *Tragedy of Cambodian History* 254.

[19] Pin Yathay and John Man, *Stay Alive My Son* (London: Bloomsbury, 1987) 384.

[20] Ponchaud 84; Chandler, *Tragedy of Cambodian History* 260.

[21] Ponchaud 82.

[22] Chandler, *Tragedy of Cambodian History* 269.

[23] Ponchaud 92.

[24] Ponchaud 52.

[25] Henri Locard, *Le goulag Khmer rouge* (University of Lyon II, Department of Languages, 1995) 6.

[26] Molyda Szymusiak, *The Stones Cry Out: A Cambodian Childhood, 1975 -1980,* trans. Linda Coverdale (New York: Hill and Wang, 1986) 64, 75. See also Ponchaud 80-81.

[27] Marek Sliwinski, *Le génocide Khmer Rouge: Une analyse démographique* (Paris: L'Harmattan, 1995) 76, 77.

[28] Margolin, "Cambodge" 648.

[29] Ben Kiernan, *The Pol Pot Regime: Race, Power, and Genocide in Cambodia under the Khmer Rouge, 1975-1979* (New Haven: Yale University Press, 1996) 297.

[30] Sliwinski 76.

[31] Sliwinski arrives at these figures by using demographic techniques, in which he takes cognizance of deaths through old age, disease or other natural causes. See Sliwinski 76. Kiernan, who concentrated on the different reports detailing Khmer Rouge attacks, concludes that the Cham population was reduced by 50 per cent under the Khmer Rouge. See Kiernan, 428-431.

[32] Kimmo Kiljunen et al., " "The People's Republic of Kampuchea," *Kampuchea: Decade of theGenocide*, ed. Kimmo Kiljunen (London: Zed Books, 1984) 25.

[33] ____, "Democratic Kampuchea," *Kampuchea: Decade of theGenocide*, ed. Kimmo Kiljunen (London: Zed Books, 1984) 18-19.

[34] Chandler, *The Tragedy of Cambodian History* 296-297; Kiernan 392-411.

[35] For an examination of the Chinese prison system, see Hondra Harry Wu, *Laogai–The Chinese Gulag*, trans. Ted Slingerland (Boulder: Westview Press, 1992).

[36] Margolin, "Cambodge" 670.

[37] Anthony Barnett and John Pilger, *Aftermath: The Struggle of Cambodia and Vietnam*, New Statesman Report no. 5 (London: New Statesman, 1982) 115.

[38] Kiernan 456-460.

[39] Sliwinski 49-67.

[40] Margolin, "Cambodge" 645.

[41] ____, "Cambodge" 638.

[42] Ponchaud 62-63.

[43] Sliwinski 76, 77.

[44] Margolin, "Cambodge" 651.

[45] Ponchaud 214.

Chapter 7

[1] Alan Bullock, *Hitler and Stalin: Parallel Lives* (Toronto: McClelland and Stewart, 1993) 970.

[2] Alain Besançon, *Le malheur du siècle: sur le communisme, le nazisme et l'unicité de la shoa* (Paris: Librairie Arthème Fayard, 1998) 149-152.

[3] Besançon 130.

[4] Ward Churchill, *A little matter of genocide: holocaust and denial in the Americas, 1492 to the present*, (San Francisco, CA: City Lights, 1997) 31-43.

[5] Bullock 970.

[6] Stéphane Courtois, "Pourquoi," *Le livre noir du communisme: Crimes, terreur et répression* (Paris: Éditions Robert Laffont, S.A., 1997) 810-814.

[7] N. Berdyaev, *The Origin of Russian Communism* (Ann Arbor: University of Michigan Press, 1962) 147.

[8] Erich Neumann, *Depth Psychology and a New Ethic*, trans. Eugene Rolfe (New York: G.P. Putnam's Sons, 1969) 44-45.

[9] Bertrand Russell, *A History of Western Philosophy* (New York: Simon and

Schuster, 1945) 308.

[10] Russell 477.

[11] K.D. Bracher, *The German Dictatorship* (New York: Praeger, 1971) 24.

[12] Bracher 7-34.

[13] K.R. Popper, *The Open Society and Its Enemies*, 3rd ed. (London: Routledge and Kegan Paul, 1957) 157-168.

[14] George Lichtheim, *Marxism* (London: Routledge and Kegan Paul) 350.

[15] Norman Rufus Colin Cohn, *The Pursuit of the Millennium: Revolutionary Millenarians and Mystical Anarchists of the Middle-Ages*, revised and expanded ed. (London: Maurice Temple Smith, 1970) 285-286.

[16] John Toland, *Adolf Hitler* (New York, Ballantine Books, 1976) 422. Grunberger defines *Gleichschaltung* as "co-ordination," which served to reduce different social organizations as well as society in general to a common denominator under the control of the Nazi hierarchy. See Richard Grunberger, *The 12-Year Reich: A Social History of Nazi Germany 1933-1945* (New York: Ballantine Books, 1971) 336-359, 441, 462-468.

[17] Toland 682.

[18] E. Cassirer, *The Myth of the State* (Garden City, NY: Doubleday Anchor Books, 1955) 358.

[19] Crane Brinton, *The Shaping of the Modern Mind* (New York: Mentor Books, 1953) 197.

[20] Robert Melson, *Revolution and Genocide: On the Origins of the Armenian Genocide and the Holocaust* (Chicago: University of Chicago Press, 1992) 250-251.

[21] Russell, *A History of Western Philosophy* 477.

[22] Russell 477.

[23] Russell 476.

[24] Bracher, *The German Dictatorship* 36-37.

[25] For Jung's view of the shadow, see Carl G. Jung, *The Collected Works of C.G. Jung*, vol. 9, *Aion*, 5th printing, trans. R.F.C. Hull (New Jersey: Princeton University Press, 1978) 266. Also see M-L. Von Franz, "The Process of Individuation," *Man and His Symbols*, ed. Carl G. Jung (New York: Dell Publishing, 1964) 171-185.

[26] For a discussion of the influence of this model on social theorizing, see, for example, T.S. Szasz, *The Manufacture of Madness: A Comparable Study of the Inquisition and the Mental Health Movement* (New York: Dell Publishing, 1970), and also, by the same author, *The Myth of Mental Illness* (New York: Harper and Row, 1974).

[27] The case described in the Bible was not only similar to the other holocaust-type genocides in that it targeted a group for total destruction; it was also similar in that the dynamics leading to the destruction, the ideological framework within which the destruction was carried out, were essentially the same. How is one to explain this? One possible explanation is that the Christians who drew on earlier Jewish traditions assumed the Book of Joshua to be true and then carried out in practice what may only have been mythological in the Book of Joshua. However, that does not explain how and why this particular mythology arose. After all, the genocide described in the Book of Joshua is quite different from genocides carried out by other ancient peoples. It is especially hard to explain how this mythology could have been developed by a people who had infiltrated the land peacefully, as some scholars assume. Everything considered, one can well argue that there is a

historical base for the conquests described in the Book of Joshua, and that war and the ban, or a holocaust-type genocide, had a role in the establishment of biblical Israel.

Part II

[1] Russell Thornton, *American Indian Holocaust and Survival: A Population History since 1492* (Norman: University of Oklahoma Press, 1987) 42-53.

[2] Thornton 44. Also, William H. McNeil, *Plagues and Peoples* (Garden City, NY: Doubleday, 1976) 211-213.

[3] Nathan Wachtel, *The Vision of the Vanquished: The Spanish Conquest of Peru through Indian Eyes, 1530-1570*, trans. Ben Reynolds and Siân Reynolds (New York: Barnes and Noble, 1977) 94-95.

[4] Thornton 73-74.

[5] McNeil 251.

[6] William T. Hagan, *American Indians* (Chicago: University of Chicago Press, 1961) 25.

[7] Thornton 78-79.

[8] Thornton 79.

[9] Ward Churchill, *A little matter of genocide: holocaust and denial in the Americas, 1492 to the present*, (San Francisco, CA: City Lights, 1997) 151-156.

[10] David E. Stannard, *American Holocaust: The Conquest of the New World* (New York: Oxford University Press, 1993) xiv.

[11] Stannard xii.

Chapter 8

[1] David E. Stannard, *American Holocaust: the Conquest of the New World* (New York: Oxford University Press) 221.

[2] Stannard 184.

[3] Stannard 165-167, 172-173.

[4] Stannard 71-72.

[5] Stannard 72.

[6] Stannard 74.

[7] Stannard 75.

[8] Stannard 76-77.

[9] Stannard 77-80.

[10] Stannard 81.

[11] Stannard 86.

[12] Stannard 85-91

[13] Stannard 82.

[14] Stannard 65-66.

[15] Stannard 89.

[16] Stannard 95.

[17] Stannard 221.

[18] Chalk and Jonassohn, *The History and Sociology of Genocide: Analyses and Case*

Studies (New Haven, CT: Yale University Press, 1990) 178.

[19] S.F. Cook and W.W. Borah, *Essays in Population History: Mexico and the Caribbean* (Berkeley: University of California Press, 1971) 1: 397, 401.

[20] Irving Rouse, "The Arawak," *Handbook of South American Indians* 4, ed. Julian H. Steward (New York: Cooper Square Publishers, 1963): 517-518.

[21] Churchill, *A little matter of genocide: holocaust and denial in the Americas, 1492 to the present* (San Francisco, CA: City Lights, 1997) 405-430.

[22] Chalk and Jonassohn, *History and Sociology of Genocide* 26.

[23] Chalk and Jonassohn, *History and Sociology of Genocide* 177.

[24] Churchill 140-143.

[25] Charles Gibson, *Spain in America* (New York: Harper and Row, 1966) 76-77.

[26] Ben Whitaker, *Revised and Updated Report on the Questions of Prevention and Punishment of the Crime of Genocide* (New York: UN Economic and Social Council, Commission on Human Rights, 1985).

[27] Churchill 431-437.

Chapter 9

[1] Churchill, *A little matter of genocide: holocaust and denial in the Americas, 1492 to the present* (San Francisco, CA: City Lights, 1997) 129, 133-136, 199.

[2] Churchill 137-141, 152- 196.

[3] Churchill 143-146, 211-244.

[4] David E. Stannard, *American Holocaust: the Conquest of the New World* (New York: Oxford University Press, 1993) 222-223. Although he uses the term "British America," Stannard essentially confines his discussion to the Thirteen Colonies and the United States. While concentrating on the United States, this study will also deal with Canada to determine to what extent the destruction of Natives in the northern half of British America was similar to the destruction of Native peoples in what was to become the United States.

[5] Chalk and Jonassohn, *The History and Sociology of Genocide: Analyses and Case Studies* (New Haven: CT: Yale University Press) 180.

[6] Russell Thornton, *American Indian Holocaust and Survival: A Population History since 1492* (Norman: University of Oklahoma Press, 1987) 69.

[7] Douglas E. Leach, *Flintlock and Tomahawk: New England in King Phillip's War* (New York: W. W. Norton, 1966) 192.

[8] Thornton 71.

[9] Thornton 75.

[10] Churchill 172-173.

[11] John Mason, "A Brief History of the Pequot War," *Massachusetts Historical Society Collections,* 2nd ser, 8 (1826): 140.

[12] Cotton Mather, *Magnalia Christi Americana: or, The Ecclesiastical History of New England from its planting in the year 1620, unto the year of Our Lord, 1698.* Originally published in 1702. (New York: Russell and Russell, 1967) 558.

[13] Gary B. Nash, *Red, White and Black: The Peoples of Early America,* 2nd ed. (Englewood Cliffs, NJ: Prentice-Hall, 1982) 85.

[14] William T. Hagan, *American Indians* (Chicago: University of Chicago Press, 1961) 44.

[15] Hagan 44.

[16] Arthur K. Moore, *The Frontier Mind* (Lexington: University of Kentucky Press, 1957), chap. 7.

[17] Chalk and Jonassohn, *History and Sociology of Genocide* 195.

[18] Jerald J. Johnson, "Yana," *Handbook of North American Indians: California* 8, ed. Robert R. Heizer (Washington: Smithsonian Institution, 1978): 362-363.

[19] Robert Heizer and Theodora Kroeber, eds. *Ishi the Last Yahi: A Documentary History* (Berkeley: University of California Press, 1979).

[20] Theodora Kroeber, *Ishi in Two Worlds: A Biography of the Last Wild Indian in North America* (Berkeley: University of California Press, 1961).

[21] Theodora Kroeber, *Ishi: Last of His Tribe* (Toronto: Bantam Books, 1973) 41-43, 70-72.

[22] Virginia P. Miller, "Yuki, Huchnom, and Coast Yuki," *Handbook of North American Indians: California* 8, ed. Robert R. Heizer (Washington: Smithsonian Institution, 1978): 249-250. Also, Chalk and Jonassohn, *History and Sociology of Genocide* 199.

[23] Lynwood Carranco and Estle Beard, *Genocide and Vendetta: The Round Valley Wars of Northern California* (Norman: University of Oklahoma Press, 1981) 14.

[24] Conner Gorry, "Wailaki;" "Yuki," *The Gale Encyclopedia of Native American Tribes* 4, ed. Sharon Malinowski and Anna Sheets (New York: Gale, 1998): 239-40.

[25] Carranco and Beard 55.

[26] Carranco and Beard chap. 4.

[27] Gorry, "Yuki" 240.

[28] Carranco and Beard chaps. 4, 5.

[29] S.F. Cook, *The Conflict between the California Indians and White Civilization* (Berkeley: University of California Press, 1976) 105.

[30] Quoted in E.D. Castillo, "The Impact of Euro-American Exploration and Settlement," *Handbook of North American Indians: California* 8, ed. Robert R. Heizer, 111.

[31] Thornton 206 - 207.

[32] Amanda B. McCarthy, "Synkyone," *The Gale Encyclopedia of Native American Tribes* 4, ed. Sharon Malinowski and Anna Sheets (New York: Gale, 1998): 173.

[33] Castillo 107.

[34] William R. Benson, "The Stone and Kelsey Massacre on the Shores of Clear Lake in 1849," *Quarterly of the California Historical Society* 11:3 (1932): 271-272.

[35] Ross J. Browne, *The Indians of California* (San Francisco: Colt Press, 1944) 62.

[36] Gorry, "Wailaki" 192-193.

[37] Castillo 108.

[38] Hubert Howe Bancroft, *History of California* (San Francisco: The History Company, 1884-90) 7: 477.

[39] Churchill 187.

[40] Miller, "Yuki, Huchnom, and Coast Yuki" 253.

[41] From James Mooney, *Myth of the Cherokee*, 130-133. The work was published in 1900 by the USA Government Printing Office. It was one of several papers ac-

companying the Nineteenth Annual Report of the U.S. Bureau of American Ethnology to the Secretary of the Smithsonian Institution, 1897-1898.

[42] Chalk and Jonassohn, *History and Sociology of Genocide* 197.

[43] United States Congress, Senate, Special Committee Appointed under Joint Resolution of March 3, 1865, *Condition of the Indian Tribes* (Senate Report 156, 39th Congress 2nd. sess., 1867) 416-417.

[44] David R. Wrone and Russel S. Nelson Jr. eds., *Who's the Savage?* Revised and enlarged edition (Malabar, FL: Robert E. Krieger Publishing, 1982) 112.

[45] Chalk and Jonassohn, *History and Sociology of Genocide* 199-200.

[46] Churchill 232.

[47] United States Congress, Senate, *Condition of the Indian Tribes* 95-96.

[48] United States, *Cases decided in the Court of Claims of the United States, at the term of 1897 - 98* (Washington: Government Printing Office, 1898) 320-323.

[49] United States Commissioner of Indian Affairs, *Annual Report of 1891* (Washington: Government Printing Office, 1891) 179-181.

[50] Stannard 222.

[51] Stannard 236-237.

[52] Stannard 230.

[53] Stannard 234-235.

[54] Stannard 232.

[55] Stannard 236.

[56] Stannard 236-246.

[57] Stannard 240. Commenting on the same subject, Wallace states that Jefferson's drive to push Native Americans from the western hinterland was part of a drive, both of encouraging the ascendancy of a culturally superior over a culturally inferior civilization and of ensuring that the United States would be governed by Anglo-Saxon yeomen. In Jefferson's view, Native Americans had either to become civilized, republican Americans or face extermination. Resistance was not a possibility. "In war, they will kill some of us," he wrote, but "we shall destroy all of them." See Anthony F.C. Wallace, *Jefferson and the Indians: The Tragic Fate of the First Americans* (Cambridge: Belknap Press of Harvard University Press, 1999) 14-20, 313.

[58] Stannard 240.

[59] Stannard 240-241.

[60] Quoted and discussed in Thomas G. Dyer, *Theodore Roosevelt and the Idea of Race* (Baton Rouge: Louisiana State University Press, 1980) 78, 86, 159-164.

[61] For a discussion of certain elements of this belief, see Clifford Longley, *Chosen People: the big idea that shapes England and America* (London: Hodder and Stoughton,2002) 180-181. Commenting on the same subject, Ruether and Ruether state that English colonists to America brought with them "an identification between England and Israel as God's elect people," a belief that was reinforced by Puritan settlers who saw their exodus from England as mirroring the Exodus of the Jews from Egypt. "The Native Americans were seen as Canaanites whose idolatry merited their displacement from the land in favour of God's elect. As relations between the colonists and Indians worsened, the Indians were even dubbed the Amalekites who deserved to be utterly exterminated." Rosemary Radford Ruether and Herman J. Ruether, *The Wrath of Jonah: The Crisis of Religious Nationalism in the*

Israeli-Palestinian Conflict, second edition (Minneapolis: Fortress Press, 2002) 80-81. Also see Conrad Cherry, *God's New Israel: Religious Interpretations of America's Destiny* (Englewood Cliffs, N.J.: Prentice-Hall, 1971).

[62] Longley 233.

[63] Longley 231.

[64] Longley 232.

[65] Longley 232.

[66] Longley 233-235.

[67] Longley 232.

[68] Longley 232.

[69] Chalk and Jonassohn, *History and Sociology of Genocide* 203.

Chapter 10

[1] F.W. Rowe, *Extinction: The Beothuks of Newfoundland* (Toronto: McGraw-Hill Ryerson, 1977) 146.

[2] Rowe 146.

[3] Barry Reynolds, "Beothuk," *Handbook of North American Indians* 15, ed. Bruce G. Trigger (Washington: Smithsonian Institution, 1978): 106-108.

[4] James P. Howley, *The Beothuks or Red Indians: the original inhabitants of Newfoundland,* facsimile edition (Toronto: Coles Pub. Co., 1980) 48.

[5] Howley 48.

[6] Howley 50.

[7] Howley 50.

[8] Howley 54-55.

[9] Peter Such, *Vanishing Peoples: The Archaic Dorset and Beothuk People of Newfoundland* (Toronto: NC Press, 1978) 65.

[10] Cited in Such 67.

[11] Such 67.

[12] Such 67.

[13] Ingeborg Marshall, *A History and Ethnography of the Beothuk* (Montreal: McGill-Queen's University Press, 1996) 68-225.

[14] Marshall 227.

[15] Gary Nash, *Red, White and Black: The Peoples of Early America,* 2nd. ed. (Englewood Cliffs, N.J.: Prentice Hall, 1982) 104-108.

[16] Nash 109-110.

[17] Ward Churchill, *A little matter of genocide: holocaust and holocaust denial in the Americas* (San Francisco, CA: City Lights) 194-195. Also Russell David Edmunds and Joseph L. Peyser, *The Fox Wars: The Mesquakie Challenge to New France* (Norman: University of Oklahoma Press, 1993) 136-201.

[18] Churchill 194-195.

[19] David R. Wrone and Russel S. Nelson, Jr, eds., *Who's the Savage?* (Malabar, FL: Robert E. Krieger Publishing, 1982) 16.

[20] W. L. Morton, *The Kingdom of Canada: A General History from Earliest Times* (Toronto: McClelland and Stewart, 1963) 150.

[21] Olive P. Dickason, *Canada's First Nations: A History of Founding Peoples from Earliest Times*, 2nd edition (Toronto: Oxford University Press) 153.

[22] Canada. Office of the Treaty Commissioner, "The Five Treaties of Saskatchewan: A Historical Overview." From "Statement of Treaty Issues: Treaties as a Bridge to the Future, 1998," published in *Expressions in Canadian Native Studies*, ed. Ron F. Laliberte et al. (Saskatoon, Sask.: University of Saskatchewan Extension Press, 2000) 242.

[23] Robert S. Allen, *His Majesty's Indian Allies: British Indian Policy in the Defence of Canada, 1774-1815* (Toronto: Dundurn Press, 1992) 193.

[24] John L. Tobias, "Protection, Civilization, Assimilation: An Outline History of Canada's Indian Policy," *The Western Canadian Journal of Anthropology* 6:2 (1976): 14.

[25] Canada. Office of the Treaty Commissioner 242.

[26] Dickason, *Canada's First Nations* 158.

[27] Bruce Wilson, *As She Began: An Illustrated Introduction to Loyalist Ontario* (Toronto: Dundurn Press, 1981) 66, 91.

[28] Canada. Office of the Treaty Commissioner 245.

[29] John L. Tobias, "Canada's Subjugation of the Plains Cree, 1879-1885," *Canadian Historical Review*, 64:4 (1983): 520.

[30] Dickason, *Canada's First Nations* 248.

[31] David Long and Olive P. Dickason, *Visions of the Heart: Canadian Aboriginal Issues*, 2nd ed. (Toronto: Harcourt Canada, 2000) 23-24.

[32] George F. G. Stanley, *The Birth of Western Canada: A History of the Riel Rebellions* (1936; Toronto: University of Toronto Press, 1992) 198.

[33] Tobias, "Canada's Subjugation of the Plains Cree" 545-546.

[34] Stanley 378-79.

[35] Dickason, *Canada's First Nations* 284.

Chapter 11

[1] John Molony, *The Penguin Bicentennial History of Australia* (Ringwood, Victoria: Viking Penguin Books, 1988) 143.

[2] Lloyd Robson, *A History of Tasmania*, vol. 1, *Van Diemen's Land from the Earliest Times to 1855* (Melbourne: Oxford University Press, 1983) 211.

[3] Robson 213.

[4] Robson 216-217.

[5] Robson 224-226.

[6] Robson 226.

[7] Robson 229.

[8] Robson 253.

[9] Lyndal Ryan, *The Aboriginal Tasmanians* (St. Lucia: University of Queensland Press, 1981) 209.

[10] Molony 82.

[11] Raymond Evans, Kay Saunders and Kathryn Cronin, *Exclusion, Exploitation and Extermination: Race Relations in Colonial Queensland* (Brookvale, NSW: Australia

and New Zealand Books, 1975) 67.

[12] Molony 191.

[13] Henry Reynolds, *Frontier: Aborigines, Settlers and Land* (North Sydney: Allan and Unwin, 1987) 133-157.

[14] Reynolds 36, 37.

[15] Reynolds 41-43.

[16] M.F. Christie, *Aborigines in Colonial Victoria 1835-36* (Sydney: Sydney University Press, 1979) 206-207.

[17] Michael Cannon, *Who Killed the Koories?* (Port Melbourne, Victoria: William Heinemann, 1990) 265.

[18] Cannon 265.

[19] Evans, Saunders and Cronin, *Exclusion, Exploitation and Extermination* 38.

[20] Reynolds, *Frontier* 180.

[21] Ward Churchill, *A little matter of genocide: holocaust and denial in the Americas, 1492 to the present* (San Francisco, CA.: City Lights, 1997) 133-136.

[22] Churchill 129.

[23] Olive P. Dickason, *Canada's First Nations: A History of Founding Peoples from Earliest Times*, 2nd edition (Toronto: Oxford University Press) 63.

[24] Quoted and discussed in Thomas G. Dyer, *Theodore Roosevelt and the Idea of Race* (Baton Rouge: Louisiana State University Press, 1980) 78, 86, 159-164.

Chapter 12

[1] Charles Gibson, *Spain in America*. New American Nations Series (New York: Harper and Row, 1966) 68-69.

[2] David E. Stannard, *American Holocaust: The Conquest of the New World* (New York: Oxford University Press, 1993) 204-206, 209-211.

[3] Stannard, 177-178, 183-188.

[4] Reynolds, *Frontier: Aborigines, Settlers and Land* (North Sydney: Allan and Unwin, 1987) 190.

[5] Reynolds 190.

[6] Reynolds 190-191.

[7] Reynolds 193-194.

[8] Robert Wiebe, *The Opening of American Society: From the Adoption of the Constitution to the Eve of Disunion* (New York: Vintage Books, 1985) 344.

Chapter 13

[1] In all instances where I use the term holocaust genocide or holocaust-type genocide, I am referring to ideological genocides that I have identified as expressing the characteristics of a holocaust. I do so essentially so that I don't have to repeat "ideological genocides identified as holocausts or expressing the characteristics of a holocaust." Should my conclusion lead to my including other genocides in this category, I will indicate this at that time.

[2] In fact, if one looks at all the cases scholars identified as holocausts, the attempt to bring about a radical transformation of the social environment is a prime motivator for all these societies. At the same time, the mass destruction comes about through the manner in which the group carrying out a social transformation links other groups to this process. In some instances, this link is established through identifying certain groups as dark forces whose very existence impedes the social transformation. In other instances, groups are identified in some other way that results in their destruction becoming part of the process of social transformation. As social transformation is so integral to all mass destructions scholars identified as holocausts, my next study on this subject will explore the holocaust with social transformation as the focus to determine what light this might shed on the holocaust-type genocide and the dynamics leading to it.

[3] A. B. Schmookler, *The Parable of the Tribes: The Problem of Power in Social Evolution* (Boston: Houghton Mifflin, 1984) 327.

[4] Steven Katz, *The Holocaust in Historical Context*, vol.1 *The Holocaust and Mass Death Before the Modern Age* (New York: Oxford University Press, 1994).

[5] Malcolm Bull, "One and Only," rev. of *The Holocaust in Historical Context*, vol. 1, by Steven Katz, *London Review of Books* 23 February 1995: 11-12. Also, David Stannard, *American Holocaust: The Conquest of the New World* (New York: Oxford University Press), 318.

[6] Martin Gilbert, "Final Solution," *The Oxford Companion to World War II*, ed. T.C.B. Dear (Oxford: Oxford University Press): 366-371. While Gilbert argues that an increasing radicalization of Nazi policy led to the final solution, Klein suggests that the destruction of European Jewry wasn't so much a policy as the result of Nazi reaction to circumstances. Peter Klein, "Die Rolle der Vernichtungslager Kulmhof (Chełmno), Belzec (Bełżec) und Auschwitz-Birkenau in den frühen Deportationsvorbreitungen," *Lager, Zwangsarbeit, Vertreibung und Deportation: Dimensionenen der Massenverbrechen in der Sowjetunion und in Deutschland 1933 bis 1945,* ed. Dattmar Dahlmann and Gerhard Hirschfeld (Essen: Klartext Verlag, 1999) 459-481.

[7] Arno J. Mayer, *Why Did the Heavens not Darken? The "Final Solution" in History,* expanded ed. (New York: Pantheon Books, 1990) 459, 461. This is also suggested by Naimark as he examines how the Nazi use of the term *Endlösung*, "final solution," changed from being used to describe their endeavours to expel Jews from Germany to being used to describe their attempt to destroy them. Norman M. Naimark, *Fires of Hatred: Ethnic Cleansing in Twentieth-Century Europe* (Cambridge, Massachusetts: Harvard University Press, 2001) 63-81.

[8] Suggested by Yehuda Bauer, *A History of the Holocaust* (New York: Franklin Watts, 1982) 13. Also see Naimark 73-74, and Klein 459-481. Before the war, the Nazis concentrated on forcing the Jews out of Germany. After the outbreak of war, the idea of expulsion, insofar as it arose, concentrated on sending the Jews either to Madagascar or Siberia. As neither solution was ever acted upon, it is difficult to determine just how destructive expulsion to either locale would have been to Jewish life. Naimark quotes Nazi leaders to suggest that such expulsion would have been extremely destructive (73-74). That expulsion, or using force to expel people from a territory, is not necessarily benign may be also observed when looking at the statistics in this chapter giving the percentage of people destroyed among the minorities expelled under Stalin, or even when looking at the percentage of Na-

tive peoples destroyed as they were being cleansed from their land in the United States.

[9] Klaus P. Fischer, *Nazi Germany: A New History* (New York: The Continuum Publishing, 1995) 499.

[10] Wolfgang Benz, ed., *Dimension des Völkermordes: Die Zahl der jüdischen Opfer des Nationalsozialismus* (Munich: R. Oldenburg Verlag, 1991) 9-10, 17.

[11] Robert Conquest, *Reflections on a Ravaged Century* (London: John Murray Publishers, 1999) 98.

[12] Michael Zimmermann, *Rassenutopie und Genozid: Die nationalsozialistische "Lösung der Zigeunerfrage"* (Hamburg: Hans Christians Verlag, 1996) 381-382.

[13] Robert Conquest, *The Harvest of Sorrow* (Edmonton: University of Alberta Press, 1987) 249. These figures are not very exact. There are several reasons for this. To an extent it resulted from the chaos in the country as a result of Stalin's programs of collectivization and food requisitioning. Another is that the Soviet Union suppressed the 1937 census results for a long time. These are now available but still present problems. For a brief discussion of these problems, see A. Perkovsky and S. Pirozhkov, "Population of Ukraine," *Encyclopedia of Ukraine* 4 (Toronto: University of Toronto Press, 1993): 148-152. Despite this, census statistics that are available suggest that Conquest's estimates are fairly accurate. Thus, census statistics state that 37.7 million was the total population of Ukraine in 1926. Of this 19 percent was urban and 81 percent rural. Census data for 1937 give a total population of 28.4 million, with no breakdown for urban and rural. This is a reduction of almost 10 million. Conquest's figures regarding Ukraine's total rural population are estimates based on the information available to him. If one looks at the figures for 1937 and estimates that the Ukrainian population was 80 per cent rural, the numbers Conquest arrives at regarding Ukraine's rural population are within a plausible range. Therefore one can assume that his estimate of a 20 to 25 per cent population loss as a result of the famine is also reasonable.

[14] Jean-Louis Margolin, "Cambodge: au pays du crime déconcernant," *Le livre noir du communisme: Crimes, terreur et répression* (Paris: Éditions Robert Laffont, 1997) 644-652. Also see Ben Kiernan, *The Pol Pot Regime: Race, Power, and Genocide in Cambodia under the Khmer Rouge, 1975-1979* (New Haven, CT: Yale University Press) 428-431; Marek Sliwinski, *Le génocide Khmer Rouge: Une analyse démographique* (Paris: L'Harmattan, 1995) 76-77.

[15] J. Otto Pohl, *The Stalinist Penal System: A Statistical History of Soviet Repression and Terror, 1930-53* (Jefferson, NC: McFarland and Company, 1997) 76-79, 81-83. Also see Robert Conquest, *The Nation Killers: The Soviet Deportation of Nationalities* (London: MacMillan, 1970) 160-162.

[16] Wendelin Gruber, *In the Claws of the Red Dragon: Ten Years Under Tito's Heel*, trans. Frank Schmidt (Toronto: St. Michaelswerk-Toronto, 1988) 19.

[17] For the different figures see Arnold J. Toynbee, "A Summary of Armenian History up to and including 1915," *The Treatment of Armenians in the Ottoman Empire: Documents presented to Viscount Grey of Fallodon, Secretary of State for Foreign Affairs* (London: HMSO, 1916) 648-650; Robert Melson, "Provocation or Nationalism: A Critical Inquiry into the Armenian Genocide of 1915," *The Armenian Genocide in Perspective*, ed. Richard G. Hovannisian (New Brunswick, NJ: Transaction Books, 1986) 66, 83; R. Hrair Dekmajian, "Determinants of Genocide: Armenians and Jews

as Case Studies," *The Armenian Genocide in Perspective,* ed. Richard G. Hovannisian (New Brunswick, NJ: Transaction Books, 1986) 87; Dickran Boyajian, *Armenia: The Case for a Forgotten Genocide* (Westwood, NJ: Educational Book Crafters, 1972) 287.

[18] Leo Kuper, "The Turkish Genocide of Armenians, 1915-1917, "*The Armenian Genocide in Perspective,* ed. Richard G. Hovannisian (New Brunswick, NJ: Transaction Books, 1986) 52.

[19] David E. Stannard, *American Holocaust: the Conquest of the New World* (New York: Oxford University Press, 1993) X, 11, 95.

[20] These figures are based on Ward Churchill's lower estimate of 9 to 12 million Amerindians at the time of first contact. Ward Churchill, *A little matter of genocide: holocaust and denial in the Americas, 1492 to the present* (San Francisco, CA: City Lights, 1997) 129, 199.

[21] Katz 28; Stannard 318; Bull 11-12.

[22] Robert Melson, *Revolution and Genocide: On the Origins of the Armenian Genocide and the Holocaust* (Chicago: University of Chicago Press) 250-253.

[23] Here I might emphasize that this conclusion was arrived at through a reductionist approach. This involved eliminating examples of the holocaust that did not meet the conditions established by the major definitions put forward to support the argument that the destruction of European Jewry by the Nazis was unique.

Chapter 14

[1] Roger W. Smith, "Human Destructiveness and Politics: the Twentieth Century as an Age of Genocide," *Genocide and the Modern Age: Etiology and Case Studies of Mass Death,* ed. Wallimann and Dobrowski (Westport, CT: Greenwood Press, 1987) 24-29; Frank Chalk and Kurt Jonassohn, *The History and Sociology of Genocide: Analyses and Case Studies* (New Haven, CT: Yale University Press) 129.

[2] Robert Melson, *Revolution and Genocide: On the Origins of the Armenian Genocide and the Holocaust* (Chicago: The University of Chicago Press, 1992) 250-253.

[3] Norman Rufus Colin Cohn, *Warrant for Genocide: The Myth of the Jewish World-Conspiracy and the Protocols of the elders of Zion* (London: Eyre and Spottiswoode, 1967).

[4] Lucy S. Dawidowicz, *The War Against the Jews: 1933-1945* (New York: Holt Rinehart and Winston, 1975).

[5] Raul Hilberg, *The destruction of the European Jews* (New York: Holmes and Meier, 1985); Hannah Arendt, *Eichmann in Jerusalem: A report on the Banality of Evil,* revised and enlarged ed. (New York: Penguin, 1977).

[6] I. L. Horowitz, *Genocide, State Power and Mass Murder* (New Brunswick, NJ: Transaction Books, 1976).

[7] Robert Melson, *Revolution and Genocide: On the Origins of the Armenian Genocide and the Holocaust* (Chicago: The University of Chicago Press, 1992).

[8] Ernst Nolte, *Der Europäische Bürgerkrieg 1917-1945: Nationalismus und Bolschewismus* (Berlin: Propyläen Verlag, 1987) 498-517.

[9] Alan Bullock, *Hitler and Stalin: Parallel Lives.* (Toronto: McClelland & Stewart Inc., 1993) 973-980.

[10] Brian P. Levack, *The Witch-Hunt in Early Modern Europe*, 2nd edition (New York: Longman, 1995) 106.

[11] Jean Delumeau, *Catholicism between Luther and Voltaire: A New View of the Counter-Reformation* (London: Burns and Oats, 1977) 155-172.

Chapter 15

[1] Discussed in Leo Kuper, *The Prevention of Genocide* (New Haven: Yale University Press, 1985) 148-170.

[2] See Vahakn N. Dadrian, "A Typology of Genocide," *International Review of Modern Sociology* 5:2(1975): 201-212; Roger W. Smith, "Human Destructiveness and Politics: The Twentieth Century as an Age of Genocide," *Genocide and the Modern Age: Etiology and Case Studies of Mass Death*, ed. Isidor Wallimann and Michael Dobrowski (Westport, Conn.: Greenwood Press, 1987) 24-29.

[3] Helen Fein, "Scenarios of Genocide: Models of Genocide and Critical Responses," *Toward the Understanding and Prevention of Genocide*, ed. Israel W. Charney (London: Westview Press, 1984) 3-31.

[4] Frank Chalk and Kurt Jonassohn, *The History and Sociology of Genocide: Analyses and Case Studies* (New Haven: Yale University Press, 1990) 29.

[5] Johannes Lehmann, *The Hittites: People of a Thousand Gods*, trans. J. Maxwell Brownjohn (New York: The Viking Press, 1977) 266-267.

[6] Georges Roux, *Ancient Iraq*, second edition (Harmondsworth, Middlesex: Penguin Books, 1980) 284.

[7] Henry Reynolds, *Frontier: Aborigines, Settlers and Land* (North Sydney: Allan and Unwin, 1987) 190.

[8] Chalk and Jonassohn, *History and Sociology of Genocide* 412-414.

Conclusion

[1] For an idea as to the creation and purpose of the shadow, see M-L. Von Franz, "The Process of Individuation," *Man and His Symbols*, ed. Carl G. Jung (New York: Dell Publishing, 1964) 171-184.

[2] Vinay Lal, "Genocide, Barbaric Others, and Violence Categories: A Response to Omer Bartov," *The American Historical Review* 103: 4 (October 1998): 1188.

[3] Lal 1187-1190.

[4] George Kren and Leon Rappoport, *The Holocaust and the Crisis of Human Behavior* (New York: Holmes and Meier Publishers, 1994) 5.

[5] Robert Conquest, *Stalin: Breaker of Nations* (New York: Viking Penguin, 1991) 322.

[6] Stéphane Courtois,"Pourquoi,"*Le livre noir du communisme: Crimes, terreur et répression* (Paris: Éditions Robert Laffont, 1997) 820-821.

[7] Ward Churchill, *A Little Matter of Genocide: Holocaust and Denial in the Americas, 1492 to the Present* (San Francisco, CA: City Lights, 1997) 48-75.

[8] Churchill 63-70, 117-119. That Churchill isn't expressing a strictly Native

American point of view may be observed from comments by others. See Norman Finkelstein, *The Holocaust Industry: Reflection on the Exploitation of Jewish Suffering* (New York: Verso, 2000); Anne Applebaum, "The battle for the Holocaust legacy," *Sunday Telegraph*, 16 July 2000: 3. The same is also suggested by Peter Novick, *The Holocaust in American Life* (New York: Houghton Mifflin, 1999) 279.

[9] The relationship between Herder's appreciation of German culture and his appreciation of other cultures may be observed in the following: Günther Mieth and Ingeborg Schmidt, comp., *Herder: Ein Lesebuch* (Berlin: Aufbau-Verlag, 1978); F.M. Barnard, ed. and trans, *J.G. Herder on Social and Political Culture* (Cambridge: Cambridge University Press, 1969).

Bibliography

Abrahamson, Irving, ed. *Against Silence: The Voice and Vision of Elie Wiesel*, vols. 1, 3. New York: Holocaust Library, 1985.

Albright, William F. *The Archaeology of Palestine*, revised ed. Harmondsworth, Middlesex: Penguin Books, 1956.

Allen, Glen. "The Harvest of Sorrow: Soviet Collectivization and the Terror-Famine," *Maclean's* (15 December, 1986), 56.

Allen, Robert S. *His Majesty's Indian Allies: British Indian Policy in the Defence of Canada, 1774-1815*. Toronto: Dundurn Press, 1992.

Allworth, Edward, ed.. *Tartars of the Crimea: Their Struggle for Survival*. London: Duke University Press, 1988.

Anderson, Bernard W. *Understanding the Old Testament*. Englewood Cliffs, NJ: Prentice Hall, 1957.

Andonian, Aram. *The Memoirs of Naim Bey*. Newton Square, PA: Armenian Historical Research Association, 1965.

Ankarloo, Bengt. "Sweden: The Mass Burnings 1668-1676." *Early Modern Witchcraft: Centres and Peripheries*. Ed. Bengt Ankarloo and Gustav Henningsen. Oxford: Clarendon Press, 1990. 285-317.

Applebaum, Anne. *Gulag: A History*. London: Doubleday, 2003.

Arendt, Hannah. *Eichmann in Jerusalem: A Report on the Banality of Evil*. Original ed., 1964. Revised and enlarged ed. New York: Penguin, 1977.

Bacon, Edwin. *The Gulag at War: Stalin's Forced Labour System in the Light of the Archives*. London: Macmillan Press Limited in association with the Centre for Russian and East European Studies, University of Birmingham, 1994.

Bacon, Elizabeth E. "Witchcraft," *The Encyclopedia Americana*. International Edition. Vol 29, 1994. 83-84.

Baez-Camargo, Gonzalo. *Archaelogical Commentary on the Bible*. New York: Doubleday, 1984.

Barnett, Anthony and John Pilger. *Aftermath: the Struggle of Cambodia and Vietnam*. New Statesman Report number 5. London: New Statesman, 1982.

Bartov, Omer. "Defining Enemies, making Victims: Germans, Jews, and the Holocaust." *The American Historical Review* 103:3 (June 1998): 771-816.

_____. "Forum Essay: Response Reply." *The American Historical Review* 103:4 (October 1998): 1191-1194.

Bauer, Yehuda A. *The Holocaust in Historical Perspective*. Seattle: University of

Washington Press, 1978.

_____. *A History of the Holocaust.* New York: Franklin Watts, 1982.

Becker, Elizabeth. *When the War was Over: The Voices of Cambodia's Revolution and Its People.* New York: Simon and Schuster, 1986.

Beckett, Francis. "Rosa Thornton: Daughter of British Communist stumbled on to one of Stalin's great crimes." *Globe and Mail* 19April 2000: R6.

Belich, James. *The Victorian Interpretation of Racial Conflict:The Maori, the British, and the New Zealand Wars.* Montreal: McGill-Queen's University Press, 1986.

Bennett, Christopher. *Yugoslavia's Bloody Collapse: Causes, Course and Consequences.* New York: New York University Press, 1995.

Benson, William R. "The Stone and Kelsey Massacre on the Shores of Clear Lake in 1849," *Quarterly of the California Historical Society,"* 11:3 (1932): 266-273.

Benz, Wolfgang, ed. *Dimension des Völkermordes: Die Zahl der jüdischen Opfer des Nationalsozialismus.* München: R. Oldenburg Verlag,1991.

Berdyaev, N. *The Origin of Russian Communism.* Ann Arbor: The University of Michigan Press, 1962.

Besançon, Alain. *Le malheur du siècle: sur le communisme, le nazisme et l'unicité de la shoa.* Paris: Librairie Arthème Fayard, 1998.

Birn, R.B. "Historiographical Review: Revising the Holocaust," *The Historical Journal.* 40:1 (1997): 195-215.

Boling, Robert G. et al. *Joshua: A New Translation with Notes and Commentary.* New York: Douleday, 1982.

Botting, Douglas. *In the Ruins of the Reich.* London: Grafton Books, 1986.

Bossy, J. "Moral Arithmetic: Seven Sins into Ten Commandments." *Conscience and Casuistry in early Modern Europe.* Ed. E. Leites. Cambridge: Cambridge University Press, 1988. 214-234.

Boyajian, Dickran. *Armenia: The Case for a Forgotten Genocide.* Westwood, N.J.: Educational Book Crafters, 1972.

Bracher, K.D. *The German Dictatorship.* New York: Praeger Publishers, 1971.

Briggs, Robin. *Witches and Neighbours: The Social and Cultural Context of European Witchcraft.* London: Harper Collins Publishers, 1996.

Brinton, Crane. *The Shaping of the Modern Mind.* New York: Mentor Books, 1953.

Browne, J. Ross. *The Indians of California.* San Francisco: Colt Press, 1944.

Browning, Christopher. "The Euphoria of Victory and the Final Solution: Summer-Fall 1941." *German Studies Review* 17:3 (1994): 473-481.

Bull, Malcolm. "One and Only," rev. of *The Holocaust in Historical Context,* vol. 1, by Steven Katz, in *London Review of Books* 23 February 1995: 11-12.

Bullock, Alan. *Hitler and Stalin: Parallel Lives.* Toronto: McClelland & Stewart Inc., 1993.

Burns, Sir Alan. *History of the British West Indies.* New York: Barnes and Noble, 1965.

Canada. Office of the Treaty Commissioner. "The Five Treaties of Saskatchewan: A Historical Overview." From "Statement of Treaty Issues: Treaties as a Bridge to the Future, 1998." Published in *Expressions in Canadian Native Studies,* ed. Ron F. Laliberte et al. Saskatoon, Sask.: University of Saskatchewan Extension Press, 2000. 232-264.

Cannon, Michael. *Who Killed the Koories?* Port Melbourne, Victoria: William Heinemann

Australia, 1990.

Carranco, Lynwood and Estle Beard. *Genocide and Vendetta: The Round Valley Wars of Northern California*. Norman: University of Oklahoma Press, 1981.

Carynnyk, Marco. "Blind Eye to Murder: Britain, the United States and the Ukrainian famine of 1933." *Famine in the Ukraine 1932-1933*. Ed. Roman Serbyn and Bohdan Krawchenko. Edmonton: Canadian Institute of Ukrainian Studies, 1986. 109-138.

_____. "Making the News fit to Print: Walter Duranty, the *New York Times* and the Ukrainian famine of 1933." *Famine in Ukraine 1932-1933*. Ed. Roman Serbyn and Bohdan Krawchenko. Edmonton: Canadian Institute of Ukrainian Studies, 1986. 67-95.

_____, Lubomyr Y. Luciuk and Bohdan S. Kordan, eds., *The Foreign Office and the Famine: British Documents on Ukraine and the Great Famine of 1932-1933* (Kingston: Limestone Press, 1988).

Cassirer, E. *The Myth of the State*. Garden City, N.Y.: Doubleday Anchor Book, 1955.

Casas, Bartolomé de las. *Tears of the Indians*. Williamstown, Mass. J. Lilburne, 1970.

Castillo, E.D. "The Impact of Euro-American Exploration and Settlement." *Handbook of North American Indians: California*. 8. Ed. Robert R. Heizer. Washington: Smithonian, 1978. 99-127.

Chalk, Frank and Kurt Jonassohn. *The History and Sociology of Genocide: Analyses and Case Studies*. New Haven: Yale University Press,1990.

_____. "Cambodia." *The History and Sociology of Genocide: Analyses and Case Studies*. New Haven: Yale University Press, 1990. 398-407.

Chamberlin, William Henry. *The Russian Revolution*. Vols. 1 and 2. New York: Grosset & Dunlap, 1965.

Chamoux, Francois. *The Civilization of Greece*. Trans. W.S. Maguinnes. New York: Simon & Schuster, 1965.

Chandler, David P. *The Tragedy of Cambodian History: Politics, War, and Revolution since 1945*. New Haven: Yale University Press, 1991.

_____. "A Revolution in Full Spate: Communist Party policy in Democratic Kampuchea, December 1976." *The Cambodian Agony*. Ed. David P. Ablin and Marlowe Hood. Armonk, New York: M.E. Sharpe, 1990. 165-179.

Charney, Israel W. and C. Rapaport, ed. *Toward the Understanding and Prevention of Genocide*. London: Westview Press, 1984.

Charney, Israel W. *How Can We Commit the Unthinkable? Genocide: the Human cancer*. Boulder,Colorado: Westview Press, 1982.

_____. *Genocide: A Critical Biographic Review*. London: Mansell, 1988.

Christie, M.F. *Aborigines in Colonial Victoria 1835-36*. Sydney, Australia: Sydney University Press, 1979.

Churchill, Ward. *A little matter of genocide: holocaust and denial in the Americas, 1492 to the present*. San Francisco, CA: City Lights, 1997.

Cohn, Norman Rufus Colin. *The Pursuit of the Millennium: Revolutionary Millenarians and Mystical Anarchists of the Middle-Ages*. Revised and expanded ed. London: Maurice Temple Smith 1970.

_____. *Warrant for Genocide: The Myth of the Jewish World-Conspiracy and the Protocols of the elders of Zion*. London: Eyre & Spottiswoode, 1967.

_____. *Europe's Inner Demons: An Enquiry Inspired by the Great-Witch-Hunt*. London: Sussex University Press, 1975.

Cole, Tim. *Images of the Holocaust: The Myth of the "Shoah Business"*. London: Duckworth, 1999.

Conquest, Robert, D. Dalrymple, J. Mace and M. Novak. *The Man-Made Famine in Ukraine*. Washington: American Enterprise Institute or Public Policy Research, 1984.

Conquest, Robert. *The Great Terror: Stalin's Purge of the Thirties*. London: Macmillan, 1968.

_____. *The Nation Killers: The Soviet Deportation of Nationalities*. London: MacMillan, 1970.

_____. *Kolyma: The Arctic Death Camps*. New York: Viking Press, 1978.

_____. *The Harvest of Sorrow*. Edmonton: University of Alberta Press,1987.

_____. *The Great Terror: A Reassessment*. Edmonton: University of Alberta Press, 1990.

_____. "Excess Deaths and Camp Numbers: Some Comment." *Soviet Studies* 43:5 (1991): 949-952.

_____. *Stalin: Breaker of Nations*. New York: Viking Penguin, 1991.

_____. *Reflections on a Ravaged Century*. London: John Murray, 1999.

Cook, S.F., and W.W. Borah. *Essays in Population History: Mexico and the Caribbean*, 2 vols. Berkeley and Los Angeles: University of California Press, 1971.

Cook, S.F. *The Conflict between the California Indians and White Civilization*. Berkeley: University of California Press, 1976.

Cotterell, Arthur, ed. *The Encyclopedia of Ancient Civilizations*. London: PAPERMAC, 1983.

Courtois, Stéphane. "Les crimes du communisme." *Le livre noir du communisme: Crimes, terreur, répression*. Paris: Éditions Robert Laffont, 1997. 11-41.

_____. "Pourquoi." *Le livre noir du communisme: Crimes, terreur, répression*. Paris: Éditions Robert Laffont, 1997. 795-826.

Craigie, Peter C. *The New International Commentary on the Old Testament: The Book of Deuteronomy*. Grand Rapids, Mich.: William B. Eerdmans Publishing, 1976.

_____. *The Old Testament:Its Background, Growth and Content*. Burlington, Ont.: Welch Publishing, 1986.

Dadrian, Vakhan N. "A Typology of Genocide." *International Review of Modern Sociology* 5:2 (1975): 201-212.

_____. *Warrant for Genocide: Key Elements of Turko-Armenian Conflict*. New Brunswick: NJ: Transaction Publishers, 1999.

Dark, Ken R. *Theoretical Archaeology*. Ithaca, N.Y.: Cornell University Press, 1995.

Davies, David. *The Last of the Tasmanians*. London: Frederick Muller, 1973.

Davies, Philip. "What separates a Minimalist from a Maximalist? Not much." *Biblical Archaeology Review* 26:2 (March/April 2000): 27-27, 72-73.

Davidowicz, Lucy S. *The War Against the Jews: 1933-1945*. New York: Holt Rinehart and Winston, 1975.

De Coulanges, Fustel. *The Ancient City: A Study on Religion, Laws, and Institutions of Greece and Rome*. Garden City, New York: Doubleday, 1956.

Dekmajian, R. Hrair. "Determinants of Genocide: Armenians and Jews as Case

Studies." *The Armenian Genocide in Perspective*. Ed. Richard G. Hovannisian. New Brunswick, N.J.: Transaction Books, 1986. 85-96.

Delumeau, Jean. *Catholicism between Luther and Voltaire: A New View of the Counter-Reformation*. London: Burns and Oats, 1977.

Dever, William G. "Archaeology and the Emergence of early Israel."*Archaeology and Biblical Interpretation*. Ed. John R. Bartlett. London and New York: Routledge, 1997. 20-50.

_____. "Archaeology, Syro-Palistinian and Biblical."*The Anchor Bible Dictionary*.Vol. 1. Ed. David Noel Freedman et al. New York: Doubleday, 1992. 354-367.

_____. "Archaeology and the Israelite 'Conquest.'" *The Anchor Bible Dictionary*. Vol. 3. Ed. David Noel Freedman et al. New York: Doubleday, 1992. 545-558.

DeZayas, Alfred M. *Nemesis at Potsdam: the Anglo-Americans and the expulsion of the Germans: background, execution, consequences*. London: Routledge and K. Paul, 1977.

Dickason, Olive P. *Canada's First Nations: A History of Founding Peoples from Earliest Times*, 2nd ed. Toronto: Oxford University Press, 1997.

Dolot, Miron. *Execution by Hunger: The Hidden Holocaust*. New York: W.W. Norton, 1985.

_____. *Who Killed Them and Why?* Cambridge, MA: Harvard University Press, 1984.

Duiker, William J. "Kampuchea." *Encyclopedia Americana*, international edition. Vol. 16. 1987. 273-283.

Dyer, Thomas G. *Theodore Roosevelt and the Idea of Race*. Baton Rouge: Louisiana State University Press, 1980.

Eccles, W.J. *France in America*. New York: Harper and Row, 1972.

Eksteins, Modris. *Walking Since Daybreak*. Toronto: Key Porter Books, 1999.

Edmunds, Russell David; Joseph L. Peyser. *The Fox Wars: The Mesquakie Challenge to New France*. Norman: University of Oklahoma Press, 1993.

Evans, Raymond; Kay Saunders and Kathryn Cronin. *Exclusion, Exploitation and Extermination: Race Relations in Colonial Queensland*. Brookvale, NSW: Australia and New Zealand Book Pty Ltd., 1975.

Ewen, C. L'Estrange. *Witchcraft and Demonianism*. London: Heath Cranton, 1933. Reprint. New York: AMS Press, 1984.

Fein, Helen. "Scenarios of Genocide: Models of Genocide and Critical Responses." *Toward the Understanding and Prevention of Genocide*. Ed. Israel W. Charney. London: Westview Press, 1984. 3-31.

_____. "Towards a Sociological Definition of Genocide," unpublished paper presented at the International Studies Association annual conference, St. Louis, April 2, 1988.

Finkelstein, Norman G; Ruth Bettina Birn. *A Nation on Trial: The Goldhagen Thesis and Historical Truth*. New York: Henry Holt, 1998.

Finkelstein, Israel and Nadav Na'aman, eds. *From Nomadism to Monarchy: Archaeological and Historical Aspects of Early Israel*. Jerusalem: Yad Izhak Ben-Zvi and the Israel Exploration Society, 1994.

Finkelstein, Israel and Neil A. Silberman. *The Bible Unearthed*. New York, NY: Free Press, 2001.

Finkelstein, Norman. *The Holocaust Industry: Reflection on the Exploitation of Jewish*

Suffering. New York: Verso, 2000.

Freedman, Michael. *Genocide in World-Historical Perspective.* Colchester, Essex: University of Essex. Essex Papers in Politics and Government, No. 8, 1984.

Fischer, Klaus P. *Nazi Germany: A New History.* New York: Continuum Publishing, 1995.

Frei, Norbert. *National Socialist Rule in Germany: The Führer State.* Trans. Simon B. Steyne. Oxford: Blackwell Publishers, 1993.

Friedländer, Saul. *Nazi Germany and the Jews,* vol. I: *The Years of Persecution, 1933-1939.* New York, NY: HarperCollins, 1997.

Friedlander, Henry; Sybil Milton, eds. *The Holocaust: Ideology, Bureaucracy and Genocide. The San Jose Papers.* Millwood, NY: Kraus International Publications, 1980.

Friedlander, Henry. *The Origins of Nazi Genocide: From Euthanasia to the Final Solution.* Chapel Hill & London: University of North Carolina Press, 1997.

Garlan, Yvon. *War in the Ancient World: A Social History.* Trans. Janet Lloyd. New York: WW Norton, 1975.

Gerlach, Christian. "Die Wannsee-Konferenz, das Schicksal der deutschen Juden und Hitlers politische Grundsatzenscheidigung, alle Juden Europas zu ermorden." *Werkstatt Geschichte* 18 (1997): 7-44.

Getty J. Arch, Gábor T. Rittersporn and Victor N. Zemskov. "Victims of the Soviet Penal System in the Pre-War Years: A First Approach on the Basis of Archival Evidence." *The American Historical Review* 98:4 (October 1993): 1017-1049.

Gibson, Charles. *Spain in America.* The New American Nations Series. New York: Harper and Row, 1966.

Gielis, M. "The Netherlandic Theologians' Views of Witchcraft and the Devil's Pact." *Witchcraft in the Netherlands: from the Fourteenth to the Twentieth Century.* Ed. Marijke Gijswijt-Hofstra and Willem Frijhoff. Rotterdam: Universitaire Pers., 1991. 37-52.

Gilbert, Martin. "Final Solution." *The Oxford Companion to World War II,* ed. I.C.B. Dear, Oxford: Oxford University Press, 1995. 364-371.

Giżejewska, Małgorzata. "Die Einzigartigkeit und der besondere Charakter der Konzentrationslager in Kolyma und die Möglichkeit des Überlebens." *Lager, Zwangsarbeit, Vertreibung und Deportation: Dimensionenen der Massenverbrechen in der Sowjetunion und in Deutschland 1933 bis 1945.* Ed. Dattmar Dahlmann and Gerhard Hirschfeld. Essen: Klartext Verlag, 1999. 245-260.

Goldhagen, Daniel J. *Hitler's willing executioners: Ordinary Germans and the Holocaust.* London: Little Brown and Company, 1996.

Good, E.M. "Joshua, Book of." *The Interpreter's Dictionary of the Bible: An Illustrated Encyclopedia.* Ed. G.A. Buttrick. New York: Abingdon Press, 1962. 988-996.

Gorry, Connor. "Wailaki;" "Yuki." *The Gale Encyclopedia of Native American Tribes.* Vol. 4. Ed. Sharon Malinowski and Anna Sheets. New York: Gale, 1998. 192-196, 239-243.

Grayson, A.K. "Assyria," *The Encyclopedia of Ancient Civilizations.* Ed. Arthur Cotterell. London: Macmillan, 1980. 101-109.

Grossman, Vasilii. *Forever Flowing.* Trans. T. Whitney. New York: Harper & Row, 1972.

Gruber, Wendelin. *In the Claws of the Red Dragon: Ten Years Under Tito's Heel.* Trans.

Frank Schmidt. Toronto: St. Michaelswerk, 1988.

Grunberger, R. *The 12 - Year Reich: A Social History of Nazi Germany 1933 - 1949.* New York: Ballantine Books, 1971.

Gurney, O.R. "The Hittites," *The Encyclopedia of Ancient Civilizations.* Ed. Arthur Cotterell. London: Macmillan, 1980. 111-115.

Hagan, William T. *American Indians.* The Chicago History of American Civilization. Chicago: University of Chicago Press, 1961.

Heyd, U. *Foundations of Turkish Nationalism: The Life and Teachings of Ziya Gölkap.* London: Luzac, 1950.

Heikkinen, Antero and Timo Kervinen. "Finland: The Male Domination." *Early Modern European Witchcraft: Centres and Peripheries.*" Ed. B. Ankarloo and G. Henningsen. Oxford: Clarendon Press, 1990. 319-338.

Heizer, Robert F. and Theodora Kroeber, eds. *Ishi the Last Yahi: A Documentary History.* Berkely and Los Angeles: University of California Press, 1979.

Hiden, John and Patrick Salmon. *The Baltic Nations and Europe: Estonia, Latvia and Lithuania in the Twentieth Century.* New York: Longman, 1991.

Hilberg, Raul. "The Anatomy of the Holocaust." *Holocaust: Ideology, Bureaucracy, and Genocide. The San José Papers.* Ed. Henry Friedlander and Sybil Milton. Millwood, NY: Kraus International Publications, 1980. 85-94.

_____. *The destruction of the European Jews.* New York: Holmes and Meier, 1985.

Himka, John-Paul. "Ukrainian Collaboration in the Extermination of the Jews During the Second World War: Sorting out the Long-Term and Conjunctural Factors. "*The Fate of European Jews, 1939-1945: Continuity or Contingency.* Ed. Jonathan Frenkel. New York: Oxford University Press, 1997. 170-189.

Hochschild, Adam. *King Leopold's Ghost.* New York: Houghton Mifflin Company, 1998.

Hofmann, Tessa. "German Eyewitness Reports of the Genocide of the Armenians, 1915-16." *A Crime of Silence: The Armenian Genocide, The Permanent People's Tribunal.* Ed. Gerald G. Libaridian. London: Zed Books, 1985. 61-92.

Horowitz, I.L. *Genocide, State Power and Mass Murder.* New Brunswick, NJ: Transaction Books, 1976.

Hovannisian, Richard G. *The Armenian Holocaust: A Bibliography Relating to the Deportations, Massacres, and Dispersion of the Armenian People, 1915-1923.* Cambridge, MA: Armenian Heritage Press, 1980.

Hovannisian, Richard G., ed. *The Armenian Genocide in Perspective.* New Brunswick, NJ: Transaction Books, 1986.

Howley, James P. *The Beothuks or Red Indians: the aboriginal inhabitants of Newfoundland.* Cambridge: Cambridge University Press, 1915. Toronto: Coles Pub. Co., 1980.

Hryshko, Wasyl. *The Ukrainian Holocaust of 1933.* Ed. and trans. Marco Carynnyk. Toronto: Bahriany Foundation, 1983.

Hughes, Pennethorne. *Witchcraft.* Harmondsworth, Middlesex, Penguin, 1965.

Jacobs, Wilbur R. *Dispossessing the American Indian: Indians and Whites on the Colonial Frontier.* New York: Charles Scribner's Sons, 1972.

Jacobsen, T. "Sumer." *The Encyclopedia of Ancient Civilizations.* Ed. Arthur Cotterell. London:Macmillan Publishers, 1980. 72-89.

Johansen, Jens Christian V. "Denmark: The Sociology of Accusations." *Early Mod-*

ern Witchcraft: Centres and Peripheries. Ed. Bengt Ankarloo and Gustav Henning-sen. Oxford: Clarendon Press, 1990. 339-365.

Johnson, Jerald J. "Yana." *Handbook of North American Indians: California.* 8. Ed. Robert R. Heizer. Washington: Smithonian, 1978. 361-369.

Jung, Carl G., ed. *Man and his Symbols.* New York: Dell Publishing, 1964.

_____. *The Collected Works of C.G. Jung,* vol. 9, *Aion,* 5th printing. Trans. R.F.C. Hull. New Jersey: Princeton University Press, 1978.

Kalman, Matthew. "Archaeologist tries to rip out Jewish history's biblical roots." *USA Today* 3 November 1999: 11D.

Karasek-Strzygowski, H. *Wolhynisches Tagebuch.* Marburg: N.G. Edwert Verlag, 1979.

Katz, Steven. *The Holocaust in Historical Context.* Vol. I: *The Holocaust and Mass Death before the Modern Age.* New York: Oxford University Press, 1994.

Kenyon, Kathleen M. *Archaeology in the Holy Land.* London: Ernest Benn, 1960.

Kenrick, Donald and Gratton Puxon. *The Destiny of Europe's Gypsies.* New York: Basic Books, 1972.

Kieckhefer, Richard. *European Witch Trials: Their Foundation in Popular and Learned Culture, 1300-1500.* Berkeley: University of California Press, 1976.

Kiljunen, Kimmo et al. "Democratic Kampuchea." *Kampuchea: Decade of the Geno-cide.* Ed. Kimmo Kiljunen. London: Zed Books, 1984. 10-21.

_____. "The People's Republic of Kampuchea." *Kampuchea: Decade of the Genocide.* Ed. Kimmo Kiljunen. London: Zed Books, 1984. 22-45.

Kiernan, Ben. *The Pol Pot Regime: Race, Power, and Genocide in Cambodia under the Khmer Rouge, 1975-1979.* New Haven: Yale University Press, 1996.

Kivelson, Valerie A. "Through the Prism of Witchcraft: Gender and Social Change in Seventeeth-Century Muscovy." *Russia's Women: Accomodation, Resistance, Transformation.* Ed. B.E. Clements, B.A. Engel and C.D. Worobec. Berkeley: University of California Press, 1991. 74-94.

Klein, Peter. "Die Rolle der Vernichtungslager Kulmhof (Chełmno), Belzec (Bełżec) und Auschwitz-Birkenau in den frühen Deportationsvorbreitungen." *Lager, Zwangsarbeit, Vertreibung und Deportation: Dimensionenen der Massenverbre-chen in der Sowjetunion und in Deutschland 1933 bis 1945.* Ed. Dattmar Dahlmann and Gerhard Hirschfeld. Essen: Klartext Verlag, 1999. 459-481.

Kluger, H.V. *Satan in the Old Testament.* Evanston, USA: Northwestern University Press, 1967.

Kopelev, Lev. *To be Preserved Forever.* Trans. Anthony Austin. New York and Phila-delphia: J.B. Lippincott, 1977.

_____. *The Education of a True Believer.* Trans. Gary Kern. New York: Harper & Row, 1980.

Kort, Micheal. *The Soviet Colossus: History and Aftermath.* 4th ed. New York: M.E. Sharpe, 1996.

Kren, George; Leon Rappoport. *The Holocaust and the Crisis of Human Behavior.* New York: Holmes and Meier Publishers, 1994.

Kroeber, Theodora. *Ishi: Last of his Tribe.* Toronto: Bantam Books, 1973.

_____. *Ishi in Two Worlds: A Biography of the Last Wild Indian in North America.* Ber-kely and Los Angeles: University of California Press, 1961.

Kuper, Leo. *Genocide: Its Political Use in the Twentieth Century.* London: Yale University Press, 1981.

_____. *The Prevention of Genocide*. New Haven: Yale University Press, 1985.

_____. "The Turkish Genocide of Armenians, 1915-1917." *The Armenian Genocide in Perspective*. Ed. Richard G. Hovannisian. New Brunswick, NJ: Transaction Books, 1986. 43-59.

Lal, Vinay. "Genocide, Barbaric Others, and Violence Categories: A Response to Omer Bartov," *The American Historical Review* 103:4 (October 1998): 1187-1190.

Laliberte, Ron F. et al., eds. *Expressions in Canadian Native Studies*. Saskatoon, Sask.: University of Saskatchewan Extension Press, 2000.

Larner, Christina. *Witchcraft and Religion: The Politics of Popular Belief.* Oxford: Basil Blackwell, 1984.

_____. "Crimen Exceptum? The Crime of Witchcraft in Europe." *Witch-Hunting in Early Modern Europe*. Vol. 3. Ed. Brian P. Levack. New York: Garland Publishing, 1992. 79-105.

Leach, Douglas E. *Flintlock and Tomahawk: New England in King Phillip's War*. New York: W. W. Norton, 1966.

Lehmann, Johannes. *The Hittites: People of a Thousand Gods*. Trans. J. Maxwell Brownjohn. New York: The Viking Press, 1977.

Lemkin, Raphael. *Axis Rule in Occupied Europe*. Washington, DC: University Press of America, 1944.

Leschnitzer, Adolf. *The Magic Background of Modern Anti-Semitism: An Analysis of the German-Jewish Relationship*. New York: International Universities Press, 1956.

Levack, Brian P. *The Witch-Hunt in Early Modern Europe,* second edition. New York: Longman, 1995.

Lewis, Bernard. *The Emergence of Modern Turkey*. Oxford: Oxford University Press, 1961.

Lichtheim, George. *Marxism*. London: Routledge and Kegan Paul, 1964.

Liddell, Henry George; Robert Scott, comp. *A Greek-English Lexicon*, 9th ed. Oxford: Clarendon Press, 1961.

Lifton, Robert. *The Broken Connection: On Death and the Continuity of Life*. New York: Simon and Schuster, 1979.

Lipstadt, Deborah. *Denying the Holocaust: The Growing Assault on Truth and Memory*. New York: The Free Press, 1993.

Long, David and Olive P. Dickason. *Visions of the Heart: Canadian Aboriginal Issues*. 2nd ed. Toronto: Harcourt Canada, 2000.

Longley, Clifford: *Chosen People: the big idea that shapes England and America*. London: Hodder and Stoughton, 2002.

Lovejoy, Arthur Oncken. *The great chain of being: a study of the history of an idea/ The William James lectures delivered at Harvard University, 1933*. Cambridge, Mass: Harvard University Press, 1936.

Lüdemann, Gerd. *The Unholy in Holy Scripture: The Dark Side of the Bible*. Trans. John Bowden. Louisville, KY: Westminster John Knox Press, 1997.

McCarthy, Amanda B. "Synkyone." *The Gale Encyclopedia of Native American Tribes*. Vol. iv. Ed. Sharon Malinowski and Anna Sheets. New York: Gale, 1998. 173-176.

Maccoby, Hyam. "Theologian of the Holocaust." *Commentary*. 19 December, 1982. 33-37.

Macfarlane, Alan. "Murray's Theory: Exposition and Comment." *Witchcraft and Sorcery*, 2nd edition, enlarged and revised. Ed. Max Marwick. New York: Penguin Books, 1982. 233-234.

McNeil, William H. *Plagues and Peoples*. Garden City, N.Y.: Doubleday, 1976.

Manser, Martin H.; Nigel D. Turton. *The Penguin Wordmaster Dictionary*. Harmondsworth, Middlesex: Penguin Books, 1987.

Margolin, Jean-Louis. "Cambodge: au pays du crime déconcertant." *Le livre noir du communisme*: *Crimes, terreur et répression*. Paris: Éditions Robert Laffont, S.A., 1997. 630-695.

Marrus, Michael R. *The Holocaust in History*. Hanover, N.H.: University Press of New England, 1987.

Marshall, Ingeborg. *A History and Ethnography of the Beothuk*. Montreal: McGill-Queen's University Press, 1996.

Marwick, Max, ed. *Witchcraft and Sorcery*, 2nd edition, enlarged and revised. New York: Penguin Books, 1982.

Mason, John. "A Brief History of the Pequot War," Massachusetts Historical Society *Collections*. 2nd Ser, 8 (Boston, 1826): 140-141.

Mather, Cotton. *Magnalia Christi Americana: or, The Ecclesiastical History of New England from its planting in the year 1620, unto the year of Our Lord, 1698*. Originally published in 1702. New York: Russell and Russell, 1967.

Mayer, Arno J. *Why did the Heavens not Darken? The "Final Solution" in History*. Expanded Edition. New York: Pantheon Books, 1990.

Melson, Robert *Revolution and Genocide: On the Origins of the Armenian Genocide and the Holocaust*. Chicago: The University of Chicago Press, 1992.

_____. "Provocation or Nationalism: A Critical Inquiry into the Armenian Genocide of 1915." *The Armenian Genocide in Perspective*. Ed. Richard G. Hovannisian. New Brunswick, N.J. and Oxford: Transaction Books, 1986. 61-84.

Midelfort, H.C. *Witch Hunting in Southwestern Germany, 1562-1684: The Social and Intellectual Foundations*. Stanford: Stanford University Press, 1972.

Mieth, Günther and Ingeborg Schmidt, comp. *Herder: Ein Lesebuch*. Berlin: Afbauverlag Berlin und Weimar, 1978.

Miller, Harold. *Race Conflict in New Zealand, 1814-1865*. Aukland: Blackwood and Janet Paul, 1966.

Miller, Virginia P. "Yuki, Huchnom, and Coast Yuki." *Handbook of North American Indians: California*. 8. Ed. Robert R. Heizer. Washington: Smithonian Institution, 1978. 249-255.

Misunas, R. J. and R. Taagepera. *The Baltic States: Years of Dependence, 1940-1990*. Expanded and updated edition. Berkely and Los Angeles: University of California Press, 1993.

Molony, John. *The Penguin Bicentennial History of Australia*. Ringwood, Victoria: Viking Penguin Books Australia, 1988.

Mooney, James. *Myth of the Cherokee*. Published in 1900 by the USA Government Printing Office. It was one of several papers accompanying the Nineteenth Annual Report of the USA Bureau of American Ethnology to the Secretary of the Smithsonian Institution, 1897-98.

Moore, Arthur K. *The Frontier Mind*. Lexington: University of Kentucky Press, 1957.

Moore, Barrington, Jr. *Social Origins of Dictatorship and Democracy: lord and peasant in the making of the modern world.* Boston: Beacon Press, 1967.

_____. *Moral Purity and Persecution in History.* Princeton, New Jersey: Princeton University Press, 2000.

Morgenthau, Henry. *Ambassador Morgenthau's Story.* Garden City, NY: Doubleday & Page, 1918.

Morton, W.L. *The Kingdom of Canada: A General History from Earliest Times.* Toronto: McClelland and Stewart, 1963.

Mosse, George L. *Nazi Culture.* Trans. S. Ottanasio et al. New York: Grosset & Dunlop, 1966.

_____. *Toward the Final Solution: A History of European Racism.* Madison: University of Wisconsin Press, 1987.

Munro, Dana Carleton, ed. *Translations and Reprints from the Original Sources of European History,* vol. 3. Philadelphia: Department of History of the University of Pennsylvania, 1896.

Naimark, M. Norman. *Fires of Hatred: Ethnic Cleansing in Twentieth-Century Europe.* Cambridge, MA: Harvard University Press, 2001.

Nash, Gary. *Red, White and Black: The Peoples of Early America,* 2nd. ed. Englewood Cliffs, N.J.: Prentice Hall, 1982.

Neumann, Erich. *Depth Psychology and a New Ethic.* Trans. Eugene Rolfe. New York: G.P. Putnam's Sons, 1969.

Nicholson, E.W. *Deuteronomy and Tradition.* Oxford: Basil Blackwell, 1967.

Niditch, Susan. *War in the Hebrew Bible: A Study in the Ethics of Violence.* New York: Oxford University Press, 1993.

Nolte, Ernst. *Der Europäische Bürgerkrieg 1917-1945: Nationalismus und Bolschewismus.* Berlin: Propyläen Verlag, 1987.

Novick, Peter. *The Holocaust in American Life.* New York: Houghton Mifflin Company, 1999.

Oliver, W.H. *The Story of New Zealand.* London: Faber and Faber, 1960.

Olmstead, A. *History of Assyria.* Chicago: the University of Chicago Press, 1951.

Plyuskch, Vasyl. *Genocide of the Ukrainian People.* Muenchen: Ukrainisches Institut fuer Bildungspolitik, 1973.

Pohl, J. Otto. *The Stalinist Penal System: a statistical history of Soviet repression and terror, 1930-53.* Jefferson, NC: McFarland, 1997.

Ponchaud, François. *Cambodia Zero Hour.* Trans. Nancy Amphoux. Harmondsworth: Penguin, 1978.

Ponton, Geoffrey. *The Soviet Era: Soviet Politics from Lenin to Yeltsin.* Oxford: Blackwell Publishers, 1994.

Popper, K.R. *The Open Society and its Enemies,* 3rd. ed. London: Routledge & Kegan Paul, 1957.

Prager, D. et al. *Why the Jews: The Reason for Antisemitism.* New York: Simon & Schuster, 1983.

Rector, Frank. *The Nazi Extermination of Homosexuals.* New York: Stein and Day, 1981.

Reynolds, Barry. "Beothuk." *Handbook of North American Indians.* 15. Ed. Bruce G. Trigger. Washington: Smithsonian, 1978. 106-108

Reynolds, Henry. *Frontier: Aborigines, Settlers and Land.* North Sydney: Allan &

Unwin Australia, 1987.

Rigg, Brian Mark. *Hitler's Jewish Soldiers: The Untold Story of Nazi Racial Laws and Men of Jewish Descent in the German Military.* Lawrence, KS: University Press of Kansas, 2002.

Robbins, Rossell Hope. *The Encyclopedia of Witchcraft and Demonology.* New York: Crown Publishers, 1959.

Robson, Lloyd. *A History of Tasmania,* vol. 1: *Van Diemen's Land from the Earliest Times to 1855.* Melbourne: Oxford University Press, 1983.

Rouse, Irving. "The Arawak." *Handbook of South American Indians.* 4. Ed. Julian H. Steward. New York: Cooper Square Publishers, 1963. 507-539.

Rowe, F.W. *Extinction: The Beothuks of Newfoundland.* Toronto: McGraw-Hill Ryerson, 1977.

Russel,B. *A History of Western Philosophy.* New York: Simon & Schuster, 1945.

Ryan, Lyndal. *The Aboriginal Tasmanians.* St. Lucia, Queensland: University of Queensland Press, 1981.

Sandkühler, Thomas. *"Endlösung" in Galizien: Der Judenmord in Ostpolen und die Rettungsinitiativen von Berthold Beitz 1941-1944.* Bonn: J.H.W. Dietz, 1996.

_____. "Die Ingangsetzung der "Endlösung" im Generalgouvernement am Beispiel des Distrikts Galizien, 1941/42." *Lager, Zwangsarbeit, Vertreibung und Deportation: Dimensionenen der Massenverbrechen in der Sowjetunion und in Deutschland 1933 bis 1945.* Ed. Dattmar Dahlmann and Gerhard Hirschfeld. Essen: Klartext Verlag 1999. 435-458.

Schawcross, William. *The Quality of Mercy: Cambodia, Holocaust and Modern Conscience.* New York:Simon & Schuster, 1984.

Schmookler, A.B. *The Parable of the Tribes: The Problem of Power in Social Evolution.* Boston: Hougton Mifflin Company, 1984.

Serbyn, Roman; Bohdan Krawchenko, eds. *Famine in Ukraine 1932 - 1933.* Edmonton: Canadian Institute of Ukrainian Studies, 1986.

Serbyn, Roman. "The famine of 1921-1932: A Model for 1932-1933?" *Famine in Ukraine 1932 - 1933.* Ed. R. Serbyn and B. Krawchenko. Edmonton: Canadian Institute of Ukrainian Studies, 1986. 147-178.

Shipler, David K. *Russia: Broken Idols, Solemn Dreams.* New York: Penguin Books, 1984.

Shuttle, Penelope and Peter Redgrove. *The Wise Wound: Menstruation and Everywoman.* London: Paladin Grafton Books, 1986.

Sliwinski, Marek. *Le génocide Khmer Rouge: Une analyse démographique.* Paris: L'Harmattan, 1995.

Smith, Roger. "Human Destructiveness and Politics: The Twentieth Century as an Age of Genocide." *Genocide and the Modern Age: Etiology and Case Studies of Mass Death.* Ed. Isidor Wallimann and Michael Dobrowski. Westport, Conn.: Greenwood Press 1987. 21-39.

Stanley, George F. G. *The Birth of Western Canada: A History of the Riel Rebellions.* London: Longmans, Green, 1936. Republished with new Introduction, by Thomas F. Flanagan. Toronto: University of Toronto Press, 1992.

Stannard, David E. *American Holocaust: the Conquest of the New World.* New York: Oxford University Press, 1993.

Starkey, Marion L. "Witchcraft." *Collier's Encyclopedia.* 23. Toronto: Maxwell Macmillan

Canada, 1992.

Stettner, Ralf. *"Archipel GULag": Stalins Zwangslager-Terrorinstrument und Wirtschaftsgigant: Entstehung, Organisation und Funktion des sowjetischen Lagersystems 1928-1956.* Paderborn: Verlag Ferdinand Schöningh, 1996.

Subtelney, Orest. *Ukraine: A History.* 3rd ed. Toronto: University of Toronto Press, 2000.

Such, Peter. *Vanishing Peoples: The Archaic Dorset and Beothuk People of Newfoundland.* Toronto: NC Press, 1978.

Szasz, Thomas. *The Manufacture of Madness: A Comparable Study of the Inquisition and the Mental Health Movement.* New York: Dell Publishing, 1970.

_____. *The Myth of Mental Illness.* New York: Harper & Row, 1974.

Szymusiak, Molyda. *The Stones Cry Out: A Cambodian Childhood, 1975-1980.* Trans. Linda Coverdale. New York: Hill and Wang, 1986.

Talmon, I.L. *The Origins of Totalitarian Democracy.* Harmondsworth, Middlesex: Penguin Books, 1986.

Thompson, Thomas L. *Biblical Archaeology and the Myth of Israel.* New York: Basic Books, 1999.

Thornton, Russell. *American Indian Holocaust and Survival: A Population History since 1492.* Norman and London: University of Oklahoma Press, 1987.

Thucydides. *The Peloponnesian War.* Trans. Rex Warner. London: Cassell, 1962.

Tobias, John L. "Protection, Civilization, Assimilation: An Outline History of Canada's Indian Policy." *The Western Canadian Journal of Anthropology.* 6:2 (1976): 14-30.

Tobias, John L. "Canada's Subjugation of the Plains Cree, 1879-1885." *Canadian Historical Review.* 64:4 (1983): 519-548.

Toland, John. *Adolf Hitler.* New York, Ballantine Books, 1976.

Toynbee, Arnold J. "A Summary of Armenian History up to and including 1915." *The Treatment of Armenians in the Ottoman Empire: Documents presented to Viscount Grey of Fallodon, Secretary of State for Foreign Affairs.* London: H.M.S.O., 1916.

Trevor-Roper, H.R. *Religion, the Reformation and Social Change.* London: Macmillan, 1967.

Triska, Jan F. "'Work Redeems': Concentration Camp Labor and Nazi German Economy," *Journal of Central European Affairs.* 19 (April 1959): 3-22.

United States. Cong. Senate. Special Committee Appointed under Joint Resolution of March 3, 1865. *Condition of the Indian Tribes.* Senate Report 156, 39th Congress 2nd. sess., 1867.

United States. *Cases decided in the Court of Claims of the United States, at the term of 1897-98* Washington: Government Printing Office, 1898.

United States. Commissioner of Indian Affairs. *Annual Report of 1891.* Washington: Government Printing Office, 1891.

Upton, L.F.S. "The Extermination of the Beothucks of Newfoundland." *The Canadian Historical Review.* 58:2 (1977): 135-153.

Vogelfanger Isaac J. *Red Tempest: The Life of a Surgeon in the Gulag.* Montreal: McGill-Queen's University Press, 1996.

Volkogonov, Dmitrii A. *Stalin: triumph and tragedy.* Ed. and trans. Harold Shukman. New York: Grove Weidenfeld, 1991.

Von Franz, M-L. "The Process of Individuation," *Man and His Symbols.* Ed. Carl G. Jung.

New York: Dell Publishing, 1964. 171-184.

Wallace, Anthony F.C. *Jefferson and the Indians: The Tragic Fate of the First Americans.* Cambridge, MA: Belknap Press of Harvard University Press, 1999.

Walter, James, ed. *Australian Studies: A Survey.* Melbourne: Oxford University Press, 1989.

Warmington, B.H. *Carthage.* London: Robert Hale, 1980.

Werth, Nicolas. "Un État contre son peuple: Violence, répressions, terreurs en Union soviétique." *Le livre noir du communisme: Crimes, terreur et répression.* Paris: Éditions Robert Lafont, S.A., 1997. 42-295.

Westwood, J. N. *Endurance and Endeavour: Russian History, 1812-1992.* 4th ed. Oxford: Oxford University Press, 1993.

Whitaker, Ben. *Revised and Updated Report on the Question of the Prevention and Punishment of the Crime of Genocide.* United Nations Economic and Social Council, Commission on Human Rights, 1985.

Wiebe, Robert. *The Opening of American Society: From the Adoption of the Constitution to the Eve of Disunion.* New York: Vintage Books, 1985.

Wilson, Bruce. *As She Began: An Illustrated Introduction to Loyalist Ontario.* Toronto: Dundurn Press, 1981.

Wood, Bryant. "Did the Israelites conquer Jericho? A new look at the archaeological evidence." *Biblical Archaeology Review.* 16:2 (1992): 44-58.

Woropay, Olexa. *The Ninth Circle.* Cambridge, Massachusetts: Harvard University, 1983.

Wrone, David R. and Russel S. Nelson, Jr., eds. *Who's the Savage?* 1973. Revised and enlarged edition. Malabar, FL: Robert E. Krieger Publishing, 1982.

Yin, Robert K. *Case Study Research: Design and Methods.* Beverly Hills, CA.: Sage Publications, 1984.

Zguta, Russell "Was there a Witch-Craze in Muscovite Russia?" *Southern Folklore Quarterly,* 40 (1977): 119-127.

Zevit, Ziony. *The Religions of Ancient Israel: a synthethis of parallactic approaches.* New York: Continuum, 2000.

Zimmermann, Michael *Rassenutopie und Genozid: Die nationalsozialistische "Lösung der Zigeunerfrage."* Hamburg: Hans Christians Verlag, 1996.

Index

www.ingramcontent.com/pod-product-compliance
Lightning Source LLC
Chambersburg PA
CBHW020604270326
41927CB00005B/169